Forum Shopping in International Adjudication

Forum shopping, which consists of strategic forum selection, parallel litigation, and serial litigation, is a phenomenon of growing importance in international adjudication. Preliminary objections (or a party's placement of conditions on the existence and development of the adjudicatory process) have been traditionally conceived as barriers to adjudication before single forums. This book discusses how adjudicators and parties may refer to questions of jurisdiction and admissibility in order to avoid conflicting decisions on overlapping cases, excessive exercises of jurisdiction, and the proliferation of litigation. It highlights an emerging, overlooked function of preliminary objections: transmission belts of procedure-regulating rules across the "international judiciary." Activating this often dormant, managerial function of preliminary objections would nurture coordination of otherwise independent and autonomous tribunals.

LUIZ EDUARDO SALLES is a partner at Barretto Ferreira e Brancher (BKBG) in São Paulo, where he practices international trade and competition law. He holds a PhD (summa cum laude) in International Law from the Graduate Institute of International and Development Studies, Geneva, and he has taught international law at several Brazilian universities.

CAMBRIDGE STUDIES IN INTERNATIONAL AND COMPARATIVE LAW

Established in 1946, this series produces high quality scholarship in the fields of public and private international law and comparative law. Although these are distinct legal sub-disciplines, developments since 1946 confirm their interrelations.

Comparative law is increasingly used as a tool in the making of law at national, regional, and international levels. Private international law is now often affected by international conventions, and the issues faced by classical conflicts rules are frequently dealt with by substantive harmonization of law under international auspices. Mixed international arbitrations, especially those involving state economic activity, raise mixed questions of public and private international law, while in many fields (such as the protection of human rights and democratic standards, investment guarantees, and international criminal law) international and national systems interact. National constitutional arrangements relating to "foreign affairs," and to the implementation of international norms, are a focus of attention.

The series welcomes works of a theoretical or interdisciplinary character, and those focusing on the new approaches to international or comparative law or conflicts of law. Studies of particular institutions or problems are equally welcome, as are translations of the best work published in other languages.

A list of books in the series can be found at the end of this volume.

Forum Shopping in International Adjudication

The Role of Preliminary Objections

Luiz Eduardo Salles

CAMBRIDGE
UNIVERSITY PRESS

CAMBRIDGE
UNIVERSITY PRESS

University Printing House, Cambridge CB2 8BS, United Kingdom

Cambridge University Press is part of the University of Cambridge.

It furthers the University's mission by disseminating knowledge in the pursuit of education, learning and research at the highest international levels of excellence.

www.cambridge.org
Information on this title: www.cambridge.org/9781107035966

First published 2014

A catalogue record for this publication is available from the British Library

Library of Congress Cataloguing in Publication data
Salles, Luiz Eduardo, author.
Forum shopping in international adjudication : the role of preliminary objections / Luiz Eduardo Salles.
pages cm – (Cambridge studies in international and comparative law ; 105)
Based on author's dissertation (doctoral) – Graduate Institute of International and Development Studies (Geneva, Switzerland), 2011.
Includes bibliographical references and index.
ISBN 978-1-107-03596-6 (hardback)
1. International courts. 2. Commercial courts. 3. Forum shopping.
4. Jurisdiction (International law) I. Title.
KZ6250.S25 2014
347'.012–dc23
2013045308

ISBN 978-1-107-03596-6 Hardback

À minha "Grande Família"

Contents

Foreword

Watching a student brilliantly defend a doctoral thesis is a professor's delight. To witness the upgrading of that thesis to a sophisticated, practice-oriented monograph marketed by one of the world's most prestigious legal publishing houses truly marks an occasion. Dr Salles has achieved both.

Fragmentation of international law and forum shopping before a proliferating number of international tribunals are surely not novel topics. To write a book about them, after nearly twenty years of heated debate, is daring. What news can be added?

This book does break new ground and will, no doubt, become a reference work for both academics and practitioners. Rather than taking a normative stand on fragmentation and proliferation, Salles takes a pragmatic, procedural turn, looking for coordinated solutions under international law as it stands today.

This is the first major work that combines two traditional legal debates in international law: forum shopping and – a topic even older than forum shopping and too often neglected today – preliminary objections.

In a world of few international tribunals (think of the pre-1990s age), preliminary objections were the internationalist's nightmare: procedural shields invoked by sovereignty-conscious defendants aimed at blocking the legal adjudication of international disputes. Today, in a world of many tribunals, preliminary objections re-emerge as coordination tools or transmission belts to divide and coordinate the operation of an increasing diversity of tribunals. Offering procedural-technical tools such as inadmissibility of claims (notwithstanding jurisdiction of the tribunal) or stay of proceedings awaiting the outcome before another tribunal, preliminary questions offer a focal point for managing the international judiciary, case-by-case, "nurturing procedural cosmopolitanism in international adjudication." As Dr Salles puts it: "Procedure is the filter for forum shopping activity, and preliminary questions referring to jurisdiction, action and procedure in a narrow sense are the filtering elements." This is a world where the distinction between, for example, jurisdiction (tribunal-centered) and admissibility (claim-centered), "makes a difference."

The book's uniqueness further resides in its scope: drawing together experiences and insights from all relevant branches of international law, including the ICJ, WTO law, investor-state arbitration, and the law of the sea.

Starting with the original concerns of forum shopping (some party-driven, others system-wide) and ending with the coordination tools it proposes (abstention, aggregation, and preclusion norms), the book takes a hands-on, solutions-oriented approach. Construing international law as ultimately a single, albeit extremely diverse, "system" of law, the book rightly highlights the inherent jurisdiction or power of international tribunals to sort out overlaps, dismiss, or stay a proceeding, even though the tribunal may be operating to enforce a limited set of treaty rules, such as WTO-covered agreements only.

Salles forces us to shift our attention from substantive, often value-driven debates on fragmentation, conflict of norms, and forum shopping, to a procedural, pragmatic approach, to be decided case-by-case but following general rules of thumb. As he puts it, "admissibility shifts the focus of analysis from the architecture of the international judiciary or overt clashes of legal regimes to the preclusive effects of procedural norms on litigation strategies."

This book brings us considerably closer to implementing the idea of an international judiciary at the service of both the disputing parties and the overall system of international law.

Joost Pauwelyn

Acknowledgments

This book is a revised and updated version of the PhD dissertation that I began in 2007 and presented at the Graduate Institute of International and Development Studies (HEID, Geneva) in 2011. It is the result of a jammed, long and winding road along which I have accumulated incredible indebtedness in Switzerland, Brazil, the United States, and the United Kingdom.

At the HEID, I am mostly indebted to Joost Pauwelyn. I owe him my gratitude for his sharpness and most generous guidance and encouragement; and for his supervision and friendship during and after my PhD. Marcelo Kohen and Laurence Boisson de Chazournes were always extremely supportive and enlightening during the almost four years that I spent in Geneva for the DEA and the PhD. Professor Kohen's 2006 class on *règlement pacifique des différends* actually offered me the first opportunity to pursue the topic that I would embrace here. He and Professor Boisson de Chazournes were wonderful PhD examiners too. I would also like to thank the participants of the doctoral seminar at HEID in which I presented an earlier paper on the subject; in addition to Beatriz Garcia, Isabelle Van Damme, Vera Thorstensen, Mary Picard, Lauro Locks and Miguel Burnier for discussions and help reflected here.

In the United States, I am especially grateful to Virginia Gordan and Steven Ratner, who offered me a cozy temporary home at the University of Michigan Law School. Without my research stay in Ann Arbor, neither the thesis nor this book would ever have seen the light of day. Thanks also to the 2010 cohort of Research Scholars there; and to Dave Peris for correcting my English at an earlier stage.

While I was in the United States, my colleagues at BKBG (especially Carla Junqueira and Marina Carvalho) had to endure an extra amount of work in São Paulo. They too are sincerely recognized, as well as the other partners of the firm for their support. Wagner Menezes (USP) underwent a true marathon from Mexico City to São Paulo and Geneva to take part at my PhD defense, and was a highly kind and clever examiner. And I cannot neglect to mention Roberto Luiz Silva (UFMG) and Taiane Las Casas (PUC/MG), as they personify the institutions at which my personal itinerary in law and international relations started. My road begins in Belo Horizonte and will hopefully swing by it ever more.

At Cambridge University Press, I benefitted greatly from comments by Professor James Crawford and two anonymous readers for the Press. From the CUP team, Finola O'Sullivan, Richard Woodham, Nienke van Schaverbeke, and Elizabeth Spicer were all instrumental for this work coming into being. Thanks to Emma Wildsmith and Deborah Renshaw too.

I also especially thank, for the financial contributions that I was awarded during my studies in Switzerland and in the United States, the Swiss Federal Commission of Scholarships for Foreign Students (special thanks to Olivier Lombard), the HEID, and the Feris Foundation of America (through the Gallatin Fellowship Program, with special thanks to Professor Allen Lynch).

Finally, I am so obliged to my family, to whom I dedicate this work, for their constant love and encouragement which I will never be able to repay. I am the luckiest son and brother. Mariana's incredible patience, and unconditional understanding and support were also essential: you are so wonderful. And my friends have always been there when I needed them. I name, on their behalf, Vinicius for the logistics operations in Geneva, and Rafael for reading parts of the manuscript at a critical stage, Nhien, Tarcísio and Robson for their patience, Familóide and Riencontro for their companionship.

Acronyms and abbreviations

ACHR	American Convention on Human Rights
ACtHPR	African Court on Human and Peoples' Rights
Afr YBIL	*African Yearbook of International Law*
AJCL	*American Journal of Comparative Law*
AJIL	*American Journal of International Law*
Arb Int'l	*Arbitration International*
Arch Phil D	*Archives de philosophie du droit*
Australian YBIL	*Australian Yearbook of International Law*
Berkeley JIL	*Berkeley Journal of International Law*
BIT	Bilateral Investment Treaty
BYBIL	*British Yearbook of International Law*
CCJ	Caribbean Court of Justice
CCSBT	Convention for the Conservation of Southern Bluefin Tuna
CERD	Convention on the Elimination of All Forms of Racial Discrimination
CETS	*Council of Europe Treaty Series*
Chi J Int'l L	*Chicago Journal of International Law*
CJAC	Court of Justice of the Andean Community
Colum J Transnat'l L	*Columbia Journal of Transnational Law*
Cornell ILJ	*Cornell International Law Journal*
CTEI	Center for Trade and Economic Integration
Curr Leg Probs	*Current Legal Problems*
DSB	Dispute Settlement Body
DSU	Understanding on Rules and Procedures Governing the Settlement of Disputes/Dispute Settlement Understanding (WTO)
Duke J Comp&Int'l L	*Duke Journal of Comparative and International Law*

Duke LJ	*Duke Law Journal*
EC	European Community/European Communities
ECHR	European Convention on Human Rights (Convention for the Protection of Human Rights and Fundamental Freedoms)
ECtHR	European Court of Human Rights
ECJ	European Court of Justice/Court of Justice of the European Union
ECOWAS	Economic Community of West African States
ed./eds.	editor/editors
edn	edition
EEC	European Economic Community
EFTA	European Free Trade Association
EJIL	*European Journal of International Law*
Emory LJ	*Emory Law Journal*
EU	European Union
EURATOM	European Atomic Energy Community
FTA	Free Trade Agreement
GATS	General Agreement on Trade in Services
GATT	General Agreement on Tariffs and Trade
Geo Wash ILR	*George Washington International Law Review*
German L J	*German Law Journal*
GTCJ	*Global Trade and Customs Journal*
Harv L Rev	*Harvard Law Review*
Hastings Int'l Comp LR	*Hastings International and Comparative Law Review*
HILJ	*Harvard International Law Journal*
HRC	Human Rights Committee
IACtHR	Inter American Court of Human Rights
ICC	International Criminal Court
ICCPR	International Covenant on Civil and Political Rights
ICJ	International Court of Justice
ICLQ	*International and Comparative Law Quarterly*
ICSID	International Centre for the Settlement of Investment Disputes
ICSID Convention	Convention on the Settlement of Investment Disputes between States and Nationals of Other States
ICSID Rev	*ICSID Review*

ICTR	International Criminal Tribunal for Rwanda
ICTY	International Criminal Tribunal for the Former Yugoslavia
ILM	*International Legal Materials*
ILR	*International Law Reports*
Int'l Lawyer	*International Lawyer*
IO	*International Organization*
ITLOS	International Tribunal on the Law of the Sea
IUHEI	Institut universitaire de hautes études internationales
JI Crim Just	*Journal of International Criminal Justice*
JIDS	*Journal of International Dispute Settlement*
JIEL	*Journal of International Economic Law*
JWIT	*Journal of World Investment and Trade*
JWT	*Journal of World Trade*
LGDJ	Librairie générale de droit et jurisprudence
LJIL	*Leiden Journal of International Law*
LPICT	*Law and Practice of International Courts and Tribunals*
L Policy Int'l Bus	*Law and Policy in International Business*
Max Planck YBIL	*Max Planck Yearbook of International Law*
Max Planck YB UN L	*Max Planck Yearbook of United Nations' Law*
McGill LJ	*McGill Law Journal*
Mel JIL	*Melbourne Journal of International Law*
MERCOSUR	Southern Common Market
MFN	Most Favored Nation
Minn JGT	*Minnesota Journal of Global Trade*
Minn L Rev	*Minnesota Law Review*
MJIL	*Michigan Journal of International Law*
NAFTA	North American Free Trade Agreement
NILR	*Netherlands International Law Review*
Nw J Int'l L Bus	*Northwestern Journal of International Law & Business*
Nw ULR	*Northwestern University Law Review*
NYUJILP	*New York University Journal of International Law and Politics*
NYULR	*New York University Law Review*
OSCE	Organization for Security and Co-operation in Europe
OSPAR Convention	Convention for the Protection of the Marine Environment of the North-East Atlantic
PCA	Permanent Court of Arbitration

PCIJ	Permanent Court of International Justice
PRT	Permanent Review Tribunal (MERCOSUR)
RBDI	*Revue belge de droit international*
RGDIP	*Revue générale de droit international public*
RHDI	*Revue hellenique de droit international*
RTA	Regional Trade Agreement
S Cal L R	*Southern California Law Review*
SCM Agreement	Agreement on Subsidies and Countervailing Measures (WTO)
SFDI	Société française pour le droit international
SPS Agreement	Agreement on Sanitary and Phytosanitary Measures (WTO)
Stanf L Rev	*Stanford Law Review*
Syracuse LR	*Syracuse Law Review*
TBT Agreement	Agreement on Technical Barriers to Trade (WTO)
Texas ILJ	*Texas International Law Journal*
Trade L&Dev	*Trade Law and Development*
TRIPS (Agreement)	(Agreement on) Trade-Related Aspects of Intellectual Property Rights
U Cal L Rev	*University of California Law Review*
U Chi L Rev	*University of Chicago Law Review*
UN	United Nations
UNCITRAL	United Nations Commission on International Trade Law
UNCLOS	United Nations Convention on the Law of the Sea
UNRIAA	*United Nations Reports of International Arbitral Awards*
UNTS	*United Nations Treaty Series*
U Penn L Rev	*University of Pennsylvania Law Review*
US	United States of America
U Wash L Rev	*University of Washington Law Review*
Va JIL	*Virginia Journal of International Law*
Vand JIL	*Vanderbilt Journal of International Law*
VCLT	Vienna Convention on the Law of Treaties
W&M L Rev	*William and Mary Law Review*
WTO	World Trade Organization
WTR	*World Trade Review*
Yale L J	*Yale Law Journal*
YB Comm Arb	*Yearbook of Commercial Arbitration*

Table of cases

Arbitration

Arbitration (investor-state)

Note: Unless stated otherwise, investor-state arbitration documents were extracted from the University of Victoria's electronic database available at http://ita.law.uvic.ca, last accessed 10 June 2013.

Noble Energy Inc and Machala Power Cia Ltda v. *Ecuador and Consejo Nacional de Electricidad*, ICSID Case No ARB/05/12, Decision on Jurisdiction, 5 March 2008. 94

Pan American Energy LLC, and BP Argentina Exploration Company v. *Argentina*, ICSID Case No ARB/03/13, Decision on Preliminary Objections, 27 July 2006. 162–3

Pantechniki S.A. Contractors & Engineers (Greece) v. *Albania*, ICSID Case No ARB/07/21, Award of 28 July 2009. 2, 248–50

Petrobart Ltd v. *The Kyrgyz Republic*, Arbitral Award of 29 March 2005. 267

Philip Morris Asia Limited v. *Australia*, Arbitration under UNCITRAL rules, Notice of Arbitration of 21 November 2011; Australia's Response to the Notice of Arbitration of 21 December 2011, pending as of 10 June 2013. 2

Rachel S. Grynberg, Stephen M. Grynberg, Myriam Z. Grynberg, and RSM Production Corporation v. *Grenada*, ICSID Case No ARB/10/6, Award of 30 November 2010. 104, 272–3, 276

The Rompetrol Group NV v. *Romania*, Decision on Preliminary Objections, ICSID Case No ARB/06/13, 18 April 2008. 91, 99

RSM Production Corporation v. *Grenada*, ICSID Case No ARB/05/14, Award of 13 March 2009. 273

RSM Corporation v. *Grenada*, ICSID Case No ARB/05/14, Annulment Proceeding, RSM Production Corporation's Application for a Preliminary Ruling of 29 October 2009, Decision of 7 December 2009, available at http://icsid.worldbank.org/ICSID/FrontServlet?requestType=CasesRH&actionVal=showDoc&docId=DC1350_En&caseId=C58, last accessed 10 June 2013. 122

Salini Costruttori S.p.A. and Italstrade S.p.A. v. *Jordan*, ICSID Case No ARB/02/13, Decision on Jurisdiction, 9 November 2004. 94

Salini Construttori S.p.A. and Italstrade S.p.A. v. *Kingdom of Morocco*, ICSID Case No ARB/00/4, Decision on Jurisdiction, 16 July 2001. 102

SGS Société Générale de Surveillance S.A. v. *Pakistan*, ICSID Case No ARB/01/13, Decision on Jurisdiction, 6 August 2003. 156–7

SGS Société Générale de Surveillance S.A. v. *Republic of the Philippines*, ICSID Case No ARB/02/6, Decision of the Tribunal on Objections to Jurisdiction, 29 January 2004. 157, 177, 212, 214–6, 224

Southern Pacific Properties (Middle East) Limited v. *Egypt*, ICSID Case No ARB/84/3, Decision on Jurisdiction, 27 November 1985, 3 *ICSID Rep* (1995) 101. 212

Southern Pacific Properties (Middle East) Limited v. *Egypt*, ICSID Case No ARB/84/3, Decision on Jurisdiction, 14 April 1988, 3 *ICSID Rep* (1995) 131. 213

Tokios Tekelès v. *Ukraine*, ICSID Case No ARB/02/18, Decision on Jurisdiction, 29 April 2004. 2, 26

Trans-Global Petroleum Inc. v. *Jordan*, ICSID Case No ARB/07/25, Decision on the Respondent's Objection under Rule 41(5) of the ICSID Arbitration Rules, 12 May 2008. 102, 106

ECJ

ECtHR

Note: ECtHR's documents were extracted from the Hudoc database available at www.echr.coe.int/ECHR/EN/Header/Case-Law/Decisions+and+judgments/HUDOC+database/, last accessed 10 June 2013.

IACtHR

ICJ/PCIJ

Note: ICJ and PCIJ documents were extracted from www.icj-cij.org, last accessed 10 June 2013.

Advisory opinions

Contentious cases

ICTY

Note: ICTY documents were extracted from www.icty.org, last accessed 10 June 2013.

ITLOS

Note: ITLOS documents were extracted from www.itlos.org/start2_en.html, last accessed 10 June 2013.

The M/V Saiga (No 2) Case (Saint Vincent and the Grenadines v. *Guinea)*, ITLOS Case No 2, Judgment of 1 July 1999. 87–8, 171–2
Southern Bluefin Tuna Case (Australia and New Zealand v. *Japan)*, ITLOS Cases No 3 & 4, Order on Provisional Measures, 27 August 1999. 72–3, 261

MERCOSUR

Aplicação de Medidas Antidumping contra a exportação de frangos inteiros, Arbitral Award of 21 May 2001, available at www.sice.oas.org/dispute/mercosur/laudo4_p.asp, last accessed 10 June 2013. 1

NAFTA

Canfor Co. v. *United States, and Tembec et al.* v. *United States, and Terminal Forest Products* v. *United States*, Order of the Consolidation Tribunal, 7 September 2005, available at www.naftalaw.org, last accessed 10 June 2013. 285–7
Corn Products International, Inc. v. *Mexico*, ICSID case No ABR(AF)/04/1, and *Archer Daniels Midland Company and Tate & Lyle Ingredients Americas, Inc.* v. *Mexico*, ICSID case No ARB(AF)/04/5, Order of the Consolidation Tribunal, 20 May 2005, available at www.naftalaw.org, last accessed 10 June 2013. 285–7
Review of the Final Determination of the Antidumping Investigation on Imports of High Fructose Corn Syrup Originating from the United States of America, NAFTA Case Mex-USA-98-1904-01, 3 August 2001, Courtesy Translation, Public Version, available at http://registry.nafta-sec-alena.org/cmdocuments/2b2b0d9a-570f-4f8c-bd47-a66bf4553ba2.pdf, last accessed 3 May 2011. 218

UN HRC

Note: United Nations' Human Rights Committee documents were extracted from http://tb.ohchr.org/default.aspx, last visited 10 June 2013.
Béatrice Marin v. *France*, Communication No 1793/2008, UN doc. CCPR/C/99/D/1793/2008, 14 September 2010. 2, 255–7
Edith Loth – and her heirs v. *Germany*, Communication No 1754/2008, UN doc. CCPR/C/98/D/1755/2008, 21 May 2010. 2, 255–7
Frantisek Brychta v. *Czech Republic*, Communication No 1618/2007, UN doc. CCPR/C/91/D/1618/2007, 26 November 2009. 252
Panagiotis A. Sechremelis, Loukas G. Sechremelis and Angeliki widow of Ioannis Balagouras v. *Greece*, Communication No 1507/2006, UN doc. CCPR/C/100/D/1507/2006/Rev.1, 7 January 2011. 252–3
Ruppert Althamer v. *Austria*, Communication No 998/2001, UN doc. CCPR/C/78/D/998/2001, 22 September 2003. 254

WTO/GATT

Chile – Swordfish
Chile – Measures Affecting the Importation and Transit of Swordfish, WT/DS193 [last joint communication by the parties to the DSB dated 3 June 2010]. 1, 283
China – Publications and Audiovisual Products
Appellate Body Report, *China – Measures Affecting Trading Rights and Distribution Services for Certain Publications and Audiovisual Entertainment Products*, WT/DS363/AB/R, adopted 19 January 2010; Panel Report, WT/DS363/R and Corr.1, adopted 19 January 2010, as modified by Appellate Body Report WT/DS363/AB/R. 81
China – Raw Materials
Panel Report, *China – Measures Related to the Exportation of Various Raw Materials*, WT/DS394/R, WT/DS395/R, WT/DS398/R, as modified by Appellate Body Report WT/DS394/AB/R, WT/DS395/AB/R, WT/DS398/AB/R, adopted 22 February 2012. 86
Colombia – Ports of Entry
Panel Report, *Colombia – Indicative Prices and Restrictions on Ports of Entry*, WT/DS366/R and Corr.1, adopted 20 May 2009. 85, 144
EC – Approval and Marketing of Biotech Products
Panel Report, *European Communities – Measures Affecting the Approval and Marketing of Biotech Products*, WT/DS291/R, WT/DS292/R, WT/DS293/R, Add.1 to Add.9, and Corr.1, adopted 21 November 2006. 130
EC – Asbestos
Appellate Body Report, *European Communities – Measures Affecting Asbestos and Asbestos-Containing Products*, WT/DS135/AB/R, adopted 5 April 2001. 210
EC – Bananas III
Appellate Body Report, *European Communities – Regime for the Importation, Sale and Distribution of Bananas*, WT/DS27/AB/R, adopted 25 September 1997. 144, 152
EC – Bananas III (Article 21.5 – Ecuador II) / EC – Bananas III (Article 21.5 – US)
Appellate Body Reports, *European Communities – Regime for the Importation, Sale and Distribution of Bananas – Second Recourse to Article 21.5 of the DSU by Ecuador*, WT/DS27/AB/RW2/ECU, adopted 11 December 2008, and Corr.1 / *European Communities – Regime for the Importation, Sale and Distribution of Bananas – Recourse to Article 21.5 of the DSU by the United States*, WT/DS27/AB/RW/USA and Corr.1, adopted 22 December 2008. 198, 200
EC and certain member States – Large Civil Aircraft
Appellate Body Report, *European Communities and Certain Member States – Measures Affecting Trade in Large Civil Aircraft*, WT/DS316/AB/R, Panel Report, WT/DS316/R, adopted 1 June 2011, as modified by Appellate Body Report. 86, 130–2, 209–10, 258

US - Upland Cotton (Article 21.5 - Brazil)
Appellate Body Report, *United States - Subsidies on Upland Cotton - Recourse to Article 21.5 of the DSU by Brazil*, WT/DS267/AB/RW, adopted 20 June 2008. 210
US - Wool Shirts and Blouses
Appellate Body Report, *United States - Measure Affecting Imports of Woven Wool Shirts and Blouses from India*, WT/DS33/AB/R, adopted 23 May 1997, and Corr.1. 131, 202
US - Zeroing (Japan)
Appellate Body Report, *United States - Measures Relating to Zeroing and Sunset Reviews*, WT/DS322/AB/R, adopted 23 January 2007; Panel Report, WT/DS322/R, adopted 23 January 2007, as modified by Appellate Body Report WT/DS322/AB/R. 40

Domestic jurisdictions

The Atlantic Star v. *Bona Spes*, House of Lords, 10 April 1973, AC (1974) 436 (1973, United Kingdom). 29
Czech Republic v. *CME*, Challenge of Arbitration Award, Judgment of the Court of Appeal, Case No T 8735-01, 42 *ILM* (2003) 919 (2003, Sweden). 274
Egypt v. *Southern Pacific Properties Limited and Southern Pacific Properties (Middle East) Limited*, Cour d'appel, Paris (First Additional Chamber), 12 July 1984, 3 *ICSID Rep* (1995) 79 (1984, France). 212
Egypt v. *Southern Pacific Properties Limited and Southern Pacific Properties (Middle East) Limited*, Cour de cassation, Paris (First Civil Chamber), 6 January 1987, 3 *ICSID Rep* (1995) 96 (1987, France). 212
Gulf Oil Corporation v. *Gilbert*, 330 US 501, (1947, United States). 219, 221
Hilton v. *Guyot*, 159 US 113 (1895, United States). 217
Oceanic Sun Line Special Shipping Co. Inc. v. *Fay*, 165 CLR 197 (1988, Australia). 219
Spiliada Maritime Corp. v. *Cansulex Ltd.*, AC 460 (1987, United Kingdom). 219, 224

Table of treaties

Table of documents

Rules of procedure

Minutes of meetings, reports, draft articles, declarations

Model bilateral investment treaties (BITs)

Note: Model BITs were extracted from the University of Victoria's electronic database available at http://ita.law.uvic.ca, last accessed 10 June 2013.

Domestic statutes and model laws

Introduction

The research question and this book's perspective

How can and how should respondents and judges react to unilateral forum shopping before international tribunals? This is the question that gives rise to this book. It is a very practical question facing litigants and adjudicators in increasingly numerous cases and forums across the spectrum of international adjudication. At the World Trade Organization (WTO), cases involving Argentina and Brazil,[1] and Mexico and the United States[2] have spurred discussion about the use of multilateral dispute settlement to circumvent regional dispute settlement. Chile and the European Union (EU) have struggled with an overlap in related disputes before the WTO and a chamber of the International Tribunal on the Law of the Sea (ITLOS).[3] The European Commission, Ireland, and the United Kingdom grappled with multiple proceedings before four different adjudicative bodies in connection with the

[1] Panel Report, *Argentina – Definitive Anti-Dumping Duties on Poultry from Brazil*, WT/DS241/R, adopted 19 May 2003 (deciding that anti-dumping duties imposed by Argentina on certain poultry from Brazil were WTO-inconsistent); *Aplicação de Medidas Antidumping contra a exportação de frangos inteiros*, Award by MERCOSUR Arbitral Tribunal, 21 May 2001 (previously deciding that the same anti-dumping duties imposed by Argentina on certain poultry from Brazil were MERCOSUR-consistent).

[2] Appellate Body Report, *Mexico – Tax Measures on Soft Drinks and Other Beverages*, WT/DS308/AB/R, adopted 24 March 2006; Panel Report, WT/DS308/R, adopted 24 March 2006, as modified by Appellate Body Report WT/DS308/AB/R.

[3] *Case Concerning the Conservation and Sustainable Exploitation of Swordfish Stocks in the South-Eastern Pacific Ocean (Chile/European Community)*, ITLOS Case No 7, discontinued 16 December 2009; *Chile – Measures Affecting the Importation and Transit of Swordfish*, WT/DS193, last joint communication by the parties to the DSB dated 3 June 2010, WTO doc. WT/DS193/4.

construction and operation of a nuclear plant.[4] A distinguished arbitral tribunal has been at pains to justify a jurisdictional option by Belgium and the Netherlands in the face of the likely exclusive jurisdiction of the European Court of Justice (ECJ).[5] Japan has successfully argued that an outside treaty – to which itself, Australia, and New Zealand were parties – divested an arbitral tribunal established under the United Nations Convention on the Law of the Sea (UNCLOS) of its jurisdiction.[6] A company that was 99 percent owned by Ukrainian nationals has been authorized to proceed with claims against Ukraine as a Lithuanian investor under an investment treaty between Ukraine and Lithuania,[7] and a private investor from Greece has been prohibited from pursuing alleged investment-treaty rights after litigating an investment dispute before Albanian domestic courts.[8] Philip Morris Asia Limited has sought arbitration against Australia under a bilateral investment treaty (BIT) between Australia and Hong Kong, where the company alleges that Australia's plain-packaging tobacco campaign violates, among others, WTO obligations that would have been incorporated into the bilateral treaty by virtue of an "umbrella clause."[9] Individuals have had their communications before the Human Rights Committee (HRC) blocked because they had brought cases before the European Court of Human Rights (ECtHR) previously.[10]

The term *unilateral forum shopping* depicts the idea that rational litigants exploit existing avenues for litigating cases to their own advantage. In domestic and private international law procedures, forum shopping is often used to refer to the selection of one among multiple

[4] *Access to Information under Article 9 of the OSPAR Convention (Ireland* v. *United Kingdom)*, Arbitral Award, 2 July 2003; *The MOX Plant Case (Ireland* v. *United Kingdom)*, ITLOS Case No 10, Order on Provisional Measures, 3 December 2001; *MOX Plant Case (Ireland* v. *United Kingdom)*, Arbitral Tribunal under ITLOS Annex VII, terminated 6 June 2008; *Commission* v. *Ireland*, C-459/2003, Judgment of the Court, 30 May 2006.

[5] *Iron Rhine Railway (Belgium* v. *The Netherlands)*, Arbitral Award, 24 May 2005.

[6] *Southern Bluefin Tuna Case (Australia and New Zealand* v. *Japan)*, Award on Jurisdiction and Admissibility, 4 August 2000.

[7] *Tokios Tekelès* v. *Ukraine*, ICSID Case No ARB/02/18, Decision on Jurisdiction, 29 April 2004.

[8] *Pantechniki S.A. Contractors & Engineers (Greece)* v. *Albania*, ICSID Case No ARB/07/21, Award of 28 July 2009.

[9] *Philip Morris Asia Limited* v. *Australia*, Arbitration under UNCITRAL Rules, Notice of Arbitration of 21 November 2011; Australia's Response to the Notice of Arbitration of 21 December 2011.

[10] *Béatrice Marin* v. *France*, Communication No 1793/2008, UN doc. CCPR/C/99/D/1793/2008, 14 September 2010; *Edith Loth – and her heirs* v. *Germany*, Communication No 1754/2008, UN doc. CCPR/C/98/D/1755/2008, 21 May 2010.

alternatively available forums.[11] Throughout this book, the term *forum shopping* includes, in addition to choosing between alternative avenues for litigation, other options prompted by the overlapping jurisdictions of international tribunals. Specifically, forum shopping consists of (i) *strategic forum selection*; (ii) attempts to litigate identical or related actions or claims in more than one forum at the same time – or *parallel litigation*; and (iii) attempts to litigate claims sequentially – or *serial litigation*.[12]

In answering the question of the manner in which aggrieved respondents and adjudicators can cope with unilateral forum shopping, this book adopts a procedural standpoint. From this perspective, forum shopping raises issues about the existence and reach of adjudicators' jurisdiction, the propriety of its exercise, and the admissibility of claims and submissions before an international tribunal. In a nutshell, forum shopping gives rise to *preliminary questions* and *preliminary objections*. Preliminary questions, which refer to requirements for the existence and development of an adjudicatory process as such, and preliminary objections, by which parties raise these requirements, are old widgets in the international lawyer's toolbox. Unwilling litigants have challenged the jurisdiction of tribunals or the admissibility of the claims brought against them since the dawn of modern international adjudication.[13] In doing so, reluctant litigants essentially try to avoid a ruling based on factors extrinsic to the ultimate merits

11 *See* Note, 'Forum Shopping Reconsidered,' 103 *Harv L Rev* (1990) 1677, using Black's Law Dictionary definition of forum shopping as "a litigant's attempt to have his action tried in a court or jurisdiction where he feels he will receive the most favourable judgment or verdict."

12 *See* Laurence Helfer, 'Forum Shopping for Human Rights,' 148 *U Penn L Rev* (1999) 285, at 290. See also Robert Cover, 'The Uses of Jurisdictional Redundancy: Interest, Ideology, and Innovation', 22 *W&M L Rev* (1981) 639, at 646–8, calling the three possibilities described here "strategic choice," "synchronic redundancy," and "sequential redundancy."

13 For instance, in one of the first arbitrations under the Jay Treaty, a jurisdictional question was raised. See *Cunningham's Case*, Mixed Commission under Article VI of the Treaty between Great Britain and the United States of 19 November 1774, as described in John Bassett Moore, *International Adjudications: Ancient and Modern, History and Documents*, vol. II (Oxford University Press, 1929) 47–52. Already in its second case, the Permanent Court of International Justice (PCIJ) had to deal with an objection related "not merely [to] whether the nature and subject of the dispute before the Court are such that the Court derives from them jurisdiction to entertain it, but also [to] whether the conditions upon which the exercise of this jurisdiction is dependent are all fulfilled in the present case." *See Mavrommatis Palestine Concessions*, Judgment of 30 August 1924, PCIJ Ser A No 2 (1924), at 10.

of a given case. This unveils the essence of preliminary objections: they are *procedural shields.*

As procedural shields, preliminary objections have often been portrayed as hurdles to the judicial settlement of disputes. In fact, from a consent-oriented perspective, preliminary objections reflect a sovereign right to curtail even discussion of a matter before an impartial adjudicator unless the disputing states jointly agree to do so.[14] As it happens, however, the objective of preliminary objectors may be achieved, contrary to their opponents' (and most international lawyers') desire for international justice.[15] This mismatch may offer an almost psychological explanation for the international legal scholarship's oversight of preliminary objections during the last five decades.[16] It is as

[14] See, for example, *Barcelona Traction Light and Power Company, Limited (New Application) (Belgium* v. *Spain)*, Preliminary Objections, Judgment of 24 July 1964, at 44: "the object of a preliminary objection is to avoid not merely a decision on, but even any discussion of the merits."

[15] *See* Mohieddine Mabrouk, *Les exceptions de procédure devant les juridictions internationales* (Paris: LGDJ, 1966), at 2: "Il est, certes, à déplorer que l'État qui a souscrit à l'obligation arbitrale ou judiciaire ne se considère pas pour autant avoir accepté la justice internationale. D'une main il essaie de retirer ce qu'il a donné de l'autre … Est-il cité en justice, le premier réflexe de l'État devenu défendeur consiste, le plus souvent, à soulever nombre d'exceptions de procédure. En conséquence, la marche de l'instance, vers le déroulement final, est entravée …"; see also Hugh Thirlway, 'Preliminary Objections,' in *Max Planck Encyclopedia of Public International Law* (Oxford University Press, 2007, electronic version), at 28: "Since 1987, preliminary objections have been brought in the majority of cases before the [International] [C]ourt [of Justice]. This is perhaps in itself hardly a development to be welcomed"; Alexander Orakhelashvili, 'The Concept of International Judicial Jurisdiction: A Reappraisal' 3 *LPICT* (2003) 501, at 501: "[I]nternational tribunals are often expected to contribute to international justice and maintenance of the basic values of the international community, and the jurisdictional objections may indeed operate as a factor preventing them from accomplishing this task, thereby causing serious concerns for those safeguarded and protected by international law."

[16] For a review of the extensive literature on preliminary objections until the late 1960s, see J. Witenberg, 'La recevabilité des réclamations devant les juridictions internationales,' 41 *Recueil des Cours* III (1932) 1; J. Witenberg, *L'organisation judiciaire, la procédure et la sentence internationales: Traité pratique* (Paris: Pedone, 1937); Maarten Bos, *Les conditions du procès en droit international public* (Leiden: Brill, 1957); Ibrahim Shihata, *The Power of the International Court to Determine Its Own Jurisdiction* (The Hague: Martinus Nijhoff, 1965); Mabrouk, *Les exceptions de procédure*; Georges Abi-Saab, *Les exceptions préliminaires dans la procédure de la Cour Internationale* (Paris: Pedone, 1967). Academic development of the topic slowed down after the *South West Africa* and *Barcelona Traction* judgments by the ICJ (see *Barcelona Traction Light and Power Company, Limited (New Application) (Belgium* v. *Spain)*, Second Phase, Judgment of 5 February 1970; and *South West Africa Cases (Ethiopia* v. *South Africa) (Liberia* v. *South Africa)*, Second Phase, Judgment of 18 July 1966). These judgments have been lamented as unhappy decisions on preliminary issues or "technicalities." See, for

if preliminary objections, enmeshed in international law's primitive structure and sheltering potential wrongdoers from international justice,[17] were an obstacle to the international lawyer's dream of compulsory jurisdiction.[18] Perhaps it is then understandable that, in the field of international adjudication - long troubled by claims of its irrelevance - preliminary objections have not attracted major academic interest lately.

While preliminary objections may prevent adjudication of claims, the dearth of recent studies focusing on them should be seriously lamented. Preliminary objections have always been a technique whose primary aim is to control the existence and exercise of jurisdiction and the respect for other procedural requirements. In a terrain where jurisdiction is invariably granted by delegation - normally directly by the very states that will later be subject to adjudication - this makes for an object worthy of study in its own right. But even if these reasons were not enough, certain structural changes in international adjudication have elicited an expansion in the use and function of preliminary objections, making their study all the more important. First, the multiplication of international tribunals increases the number of venues where preliminary objections come to the fore. This speaks to the use of preliminary objections, and detailed accounts of this use in the new landscape of international adjudication have yet to be given. Regarding the function of preliminary objections, many of the newly established forums have automatic and overlapping jurisdictions. This

example, 'Apartheid Foes Lose Suit in World Court over South-West Africa; an 8–7 Verdict; South Africa is Victor on a Technicality in UN Mandate Case,' *New York Times*, 19 July 1966. See also Shabtai Rosenne, *Procedure in the International Court: A Commentary of the 1978 Rules of the International Court of Justice* (The Hague: Martinus Nijhoff, 1983), at 160: "It is probably true to say that of all factors that have harmed the Court as an institution in recent years (and in an inhospitable political climate), the handling of preliminary objections … has been the most powerful and in some respects the most politically oriented of the Court's actions."

17 See references in n. 15 above.

18 See, for example, Heinhard Steiger, 'Plaidoyer pour une Juridiction Internationale Obligatoire,' in Jerzy Makarczyk (ed.), *Theory of International Law at the Threshold of the 21st Century: Essays In Honour of Krzystof Skubiszweski* (The Hague: Kluwer, 1996) 817; Wilfred Jenks, *The Prospects of International Adjudication* (London: Stevens & Sons, 1964); Hans Kelsen, 'Compulsory Adjudication of International Disputes,' 37 *AJIL* (1943) 397. See also Marcelo Kohen, 'Manifeste pour le droit international du XXIe siècle,' in Laurence Boisson de Chazournes and Vera Gowlland (eds.), *The International Legal System in Quest of Equity and Universality: Liber Amicorum Georges Abi-Saab* (The Hague: Kluwer, 2001) 123; Antonio Cançado Trindade, *International Law for Humankind: Towards a New* Jus Gentium (Leiden: Martinus Nijhoff, 2010), at 567–591.

enhances complainants' ability to initiate litigation unilaterally and enlarges their spectrum of choice of adjudicatory venues. Moreover, the emergence of private parties as litigants or as the true force underlying litigation has undermined the capacity of sovereign states to control recourse to and use of international tribunals. In short, the doors are opening to forum shopping in international law. This development upsets the usual perception that preliminary objections are exclusively *obstacles* to promoting the judicial settlement of disputes. It emphasizes that preliminary objections also *protect* and may actually *promote* judicial settlement – for instance, by preventing litigation before an inappropriate forum.

This book stresses that preliminary questions and the technique of preliminary objections ensure procedural due process and may foster jurisdictional and procedural coordination. A defendant who invokes a preliminary objection brings to the attention of the adjudicator procedure-regulating norms that may govern the parties' resort to adjudication. These norms may address forum selection, as well as parallel or serial litigation across international tribunals. In applying these norms, the international judge decides on the legality and appropriateness of a party's use of a particular adjudicatory mechanism and possibly on the relationship between tribunals and proceedings. In this sense, preliminary objections can be seen as devices to guarantee the integration of procedural norms. They are transmission belts of procedural rules that bind the parties beyond the directly governing instruments of a tribunal seized of a case. In a world of multiple international tribunals with overlapping jurisdictions, preliminary objections can thus help enforce predictability for litigants and guarantee a more orderly flow of complaints to the various tribunals. They may also allow tribunals to avoid conflicting decisions, notwithstanding the facts that the institutional context of international law is noncentralized and horizontal and that international tribunals are autonomous in relation to each other.

Preliminary objections, therefore, can be a technique for the governance of the new "international judiciary." Although their managerial function was practically dormant throughout most of the nineteenth and twentieth centuries, preliminary objections have served a managerial role for a long time in domestic legal systems and in private international litigation. Notions such as *conflits de compétence*, *res judicata*, *lis pendens*, or *forum non conveniens* and other "abstention doctrines," while representing obstacles to adjudication, also act as mechanisms for coordinating between various actors in a common judicial enterprise.[19] Formerly superfluous tools in a landscape where one might not find a single tribunal to turn to – let alone two whose jurisdiction overlapped – preliminary objections can now be studied as a means of supervising forum selection, coordinating the exercise of jurisdiction in overlapping cases across tribunals, and avoiding conflicting decisions. They can promote the judicial settlement of disputes by enabling a cosmopolitan application of procedure-regulating norms that permits the management of forum shopping.

The importance of the framework suggested in this book

The present book combines two superimposed stories that have so far been told disjunctively. By bringing the stories of preliminary objections and forum shopping together, it suggests that a new age may be forthcoming with regard to preliminary objections, one in which they are properly seen as devices to ensure the just resolution of disputes and to permit coordination between international tribunals. Under this perspective, the activation of preliminary objections' managerial function is a reflex of international law's becoming more complex and sophisticated.

The focus on procedure adopted here is also important because forum shopping raises intertwined substantive and procedural questions. However, there has been a disproportionate focus on the substantive law issues raised by the use of different tribunals to adjudicate similar questions of law. Indeed, the boom in international tribunals in the 1980s and 1990s motivated a flurry of scholarship about the question of whether specialized tribunals linked to specific regimes might lead to incoherence and the fragmentation of international law.[20] The attitude of the International Law Commission (ILC) Study

[19] See, for example, Arthur von Mehren, 'Theory and Practice of Adjudicatory Authority in Private International Law: A Comparative Study of the Doctrine, Policies and Practices of Common and Civil-Law Systems,' 295 *Recueil des cours* (2002), at 306 ff., discussing *forum non conveniens* and *lis pendens* as means to fine-tune exercises of adjudicatory authority. See also Stephen Burbank, 'Jurisdictional Equilibration, the Proposed Hague Convention and Progress in National Law,' 49 *AJCL* (2001) 203.

[20] See, for example, Jonathan Charney, 'Is International Law Threatened by Multiple International Tribunals?' 271 *Recueil des cours* (1998) 101; Cesare Romano, 'The Proliferation of International Judicial Bodies: the Pieces of the Puzzle,' 31 *NYUJILP* (1999) 709; Georges Abi-Saab, 'Fragmentation or Unification: Some Concluding Remarks,' 31 *NYUJILP* (1999) 919; Pierre-Marie Dupuy, 'L'unité de l'ordre juridique

Group on the "fragmentation of international law" was emblematic of these concerns. The Commission decided to focus on "substantive problems" and to leave the issue of institutional competencies aside, since those issues could, according to the Commission, better be dealt with by the institutions themselves. Hence, whereas the ILC implicitly recognized the potential of jurisdictional and procedural coordination in the course of specific proceedings, it refused to study the matter further.[21]

But substantive law considerations do not provide a complete response to the concerns arising from forum shopping. To put it simply, even if one accepts the view that "international law is a system" and that international tribunals, absent an explicit rule to the contrary, are entitled to apply all international law – which is the view to which this study subscribes – forum shopping will still happen. Tribunals may apply the law differently in concrete cases. More importantly, the authority of international tribunals to address claims of violation with finality is established on treaty lines and is therefore limited and asymmetrical. The procedure and remedies tribunals offer also vary, and complainants will find incentives to frame their cases to maximize their litigation outcomes. Hence, while forum shopping relates to the broader issue of fragmentation of international law, it is necessary to go beyond substantive law and analyze existing procedural mechanisms that can promote links between the various international tribunals and proceedings before them. This study draws on scholarship focused on the applicability of norms to coordinate the exercise of jurisdiction by international tribunals,[22] while taking a step back to look

international: cours générale de droit international public,' 297 *Recueil des cours* (2000) 1; Thomas Buergenthal, 'Proliferation of International Courts and Tribunals: Is It Good or Bad?' 14 *LJIL* (2001) 267; Shane Spelliscy, 'The Proliferation of International Tribunals: A Chink in the Armor,' 40 *Colum J Transnat'l L* (2001) 143; SFDI, *La juridictionnalisation du droit international* (Paris: Pedone, 2003); Gilbert Guillaume, 'Proliferation of International Courts: A Blueprint for Action,' 2 *JI Crim Just* (2004) 300; Pemmaraju Rao, 'Multiple International Judicial Forums: a Reflection of the Growing Strength of International Law or its Fragmentation?' 25 *MJIL* (2004) 929; Rosa Riquelme Cortado, *Derecho Internacional: Entre un Orden Global y Fragmentado* (Madrid: Ortega y Gasset, 2005).

21 International Law Commission, 'Fragmentation of International Law: Difficulties Arising from the Diversification and Expansion of International Law' (2006), Report of the Study Group, UN doc. A/CN.4/L.682.

22 See, for example, Yuval Shany, *The Competing Jurisdictions of International Courts and Tribunals* (Oxford University Press, 2003); Andrea Gattini, 'Un regard procédural sur la fragmentation du droit international,' 110 *RGDIP* (2006) 303; Vaughan Lowe, 'Overlapping Jurisdictions in International Courts and Tribunals,' 20 *Australian*

at the procedural techniques through which defendants and adjudicators generally utilize those norms in the context of proceedings to foster coordination.

The procedural angle adopted here also supplements an emerging scholarly call for international adjudicators to consider themselves as part of a "global community"[23] guided by a cosmopolitan conception of the rule of law.[24] Legal scholars from different perspectives have agreed that the fate of the international judiciary lies ultimately in the hands of the adjudicators.[25] If adjudicators perceive their function through a perspective of identity, that is, as judges rather than through allegiances to specific substantive agendas,[26] then the task of jurisdictional and procedural coordination may come within reach. International adjudicators, just as domestic judges, fulfill a common

YBIL (1999) 191; Joost Pauwelyn and Luiz Eduardo Salles: 'Forum Shopping Before International Tribunals: (Real) Concerns, (Im)Possible Solutions,' 42 *Cornell ILJ* (2009) 77; August Reinisch, 'The Use and Limits of *Res Judicata* and *Lis Pendens* as Procedural Tools to Avoid Conflicting Dispute Settlement Outcomes,' 3 *LPICT* (2004) 37. See also, focusing on specific regimes, Helfer, 'Forum Shopping for Human Rights'; Joost Pauwelyn, 'How to a Win World Trade Organization Dispute Based on Non-World Trade Organization Law? Questions of Jurisdiction and Merits,' 37 *JWT* (2003) 997; Kyung Kwak and Gabrielle Marceau, 'Overlaps and Conflicts of Jurisdiction between the World Trade Organization and Regional Trade Agreements,' in Lorand Bartels and Federico Ortino (eds.), *Regional Trade Agreements and the WTO Legal System* (Oxford University Press, 2006) 465; Giles Cuniberti, 'Parallel Litigation and Foreign Investment Dispute Settlement,' 21 *ICSID Rev* (2006) 381.

23 Anne-Marie Slaughter, 'A Global Community of Courts,' 44 *HILJ* (2003) 191.

24 Campbell McLachlan, Lis Pendens *in International Litigation* (Leiden: Martinus Nijhoff, 2009).

25 See Georges Abi-Saab, 'Whither the Judicial Function? Concluding Remarks,' in Laurence Boisson de Chazournes, Cesare Romano and Ruth Mackenzie (eds.), *International Organizations and International Dispute Settlement: Trends and Prospects*, (New York: Transnational Publishers, 2002) 241, at 247: "In sum, it all depends on the epistemic community of those who act as judges, in affirming what the judicial function is, what its limits are, and what are its incompressible minimum requirements." See also Gilbert Guillaume, 'Préface,' in Olivier Delas *et al.* (eds.), *Les juridictions internationales: complémentarité ou concurrence?* (Brussels: Bruylant, 2005) vii; Charles Koch Jr, 'Judicial Dialogue for Legal Multiculturalism,' 25 *MJIL* (2004) 879; Jenny Martinez, 'Towards an International Judicial System,' 56 *Stanf L Rev* (2004) 429.

26 See the cautionary notes of Martti Koskenniemi and Paivi Leïno, 'Fragmentation of International Law? Postmodern Anxieties,' 15 *LJIL* (2002) 553 and Andreas Fischer-Lescano and Gunther Teubner, 'Regime Collisions: The Vain Search for Legal Unity in the Fragmentation of Global Law,' 25 *MJIL* (2004) 999, which underscore the limits to the compatibilization of different rationalities or policies inbuilt and advanced by different regimes, including through the work of adjudicators.

function – to decide legal disputes – through the use of a common code, the binary code of legality/illegality.[27] It may be circular, but the essential thing about judges is that they are judges.[28] And, as Anne-Marie Slaughter puts it, if international courts and tribunals look at each other from that "perspective of identity" rather than from a "perspective of difference," then "the power shifts from the dispute resolvers to the disputes themselves, and to the common values that all judges share in guaranteeing litigant rights and safeguarding an efficient and effective system."[29] If this mindset prevails, it may play a fundamental guiding role. Yet, it is necessary to take it beyond the realm of "judicial sisterhood," to jump from broad notions of a common judicial enterprise, which reflect at best a loose inclination for systematization, to coordination in practice.[30] This simply cannot be done without an understanding of how the existing procedural techniques for coordination play out in international adjudication.

More specifically, certain international trade scholars have pointed to a technical deadlock preventing procedural coordination between WTO and preferential trade agreement dispute settlement. On the practical front, North American Free Trade Agreement (NAFTA) members have shied away from challenging each other's selection of the WTO, when an argument could be made that the NAFTA agreement itself determined that certain disputes be brought before NAFTA, not the WTO. This book takes issue with the apparent limitation of WTO dispute settlement to recognize forum selection clauses in preferential trade agreements allegedly because the WTO's "limited jurisdiction" or "exclusive jurisdiction" deters a solution to jurisdictional overlaps. It

27 See generally Niklas Luhmann, *Law as a Social System* (Cambridge University Press, 2004).

28 See generally Daniel Terris, Cesare Romano and Leigh Swigart, *The International Judge: An Introduction to the Men and Women Who Decide the World's Cases* (Oxford University Press, 2007).

29 Slaughter, 'Global Community of Courts,' at 217.

30 Abi-Saab notices that "[u]ntil recently, there was a dearth of international judicial bodies with very little probability of their collision. There was no need for a system relating them into a constellation in a coherent manner. Now, we do need such a judicial system, but we do not dispose of the necessary institutional arrangements." See Abi-Saab, 'Whither the Judicial Function?' at 247. This study illustrates that some coordination is already possible even without major institutional reform. The framework developed here explains coordination without centralization of international tribunals. To some extent, it enables what Abi-Saab has called, in a previous piece, a "cumulative process" that may "condense and crystallize the different particles of consensual or authoritative jurisdictional empowerment into a certain structure." Abi-Saab, 'Fragmentation or Unification,' at 927.

offers a different perspective, and argues that coordination is both possible and appropriate between the WTO and preferential trade forums, given the dozens of procedure-regulating clauses seriously negotiated by a large number of WTO members between themselves.

To return to the broader realm of international adjudication, it is also hoped that the general framework on preliminary objections sketched here will be capable of application beyond the specific problem of forum shopping. From this perspective, this book may be also read as an initial account of the operation of preliminary objections in the new landscape of international adjudication. This account is arguably missing in the international law's scholarship.

The thrust of the argument

The driving claim here is that preliminary objections are central tools for dealing with unilateral forum shopping and nurturing procedural cosmopolitanism in international adjudication. Rather than a revolution, this is an incremental step in the evolution of preliminary objections. To be sure, preliminary objections remain procedural shields. On the other hand, they become central tools to address forum shopping because international adjudication normally lacks the institutionalized means whereby tribunals may transfer or refer cases among themselves, or give effect to events from one proceeding to another in their own motion. Where a party seeks to tame forum shopping, it will normally raise a preliminary objection to the *jurisdiction* of the tribunal (its existence or the propriety of its exercise) or the *admissibility* of a claim before the tribunal that should not have been examining or should not decide the case. Upon such an objection, the tribunal receiving the objection may either terminate the proceedings or stay them until the underlying concerns are resolved.

One might argue that staying or terminating proceedings is not really tantamount to jurisdictional or procedural coordination; the tribunal that gives up a case is, in effect, subordinating itself to the other tribunal that will continue or begin the assessment. But that is not the point. First, a stay is not the equivalent of throwing up one's hands. It is an attempt to entice the other tribunal to do its job. If that strategy is successful, then the staying tribunal can take the case back and do its own part of the job, should there be a job for it at all. Second, a tribunal that admits that a given case before it should not have been brought for a legal reason and therefore closes the file is actually safeguarding the integrity of its *own* proceedings and the rule of law. It is living up to a tribunal's essence as a court of law which must police its own procedures and proceedings. Such recognition, if successful, may resolve concerns arising from the lack of coordination that would otherwise exist. Coordination thus lies in the recognition of another tribunal or proceeding, resulting in a change in what would have been the behavior of the coordinating tribunals or the outcome of the proceedings.

The present focus on preliminary objections, a procedural technique, naturally places the spotlight on the law as it is. Importantly, then, while a few modest suggestions regarding the future of procedural coordination are made, this book remains committed essentially to a "law-taker's" – as opposed to a "law-maker's" – perspective. This is not to say that the law discussed here is clear and not subject to discussion; we are actually extremely far from clarity and unanimity. It is hoped, however, that the argument that follows will contribute to a better understanding of preliminary objections and help to address some concerns arising from forum shopping in future cases.

The structure of this book

This book offers a conceptual framework that explains and enables the interplay of procedural principles and norms across international tribunals in order to tackle concerns arising from forum shopping strategies. After this introduction, it is structured in seven chapters and one conclusion. Chapter 1 presents the specific phenomenon to which the study of preliminary objections will apply: forum shopping in international adjudication. It provides context for the development of a "market" of international adjudication and the potential concerns that may arise from forum shopping in international law. To put the identified concerns in context, Chapter 1 points to the functions of procedural norms: their *delegation*, *enabling*, *protective*, and *allocative* functions. The articulation of those functions and of their underlying principles in concrete cases implicates one's overall conception of adjudication and the specific relationship between tribunals. This attests to the relativity and context-specific nature of the assessment of forum shopping.

Chapter 2 contextualizes this book's discussion about the role of preliminary objections in addressing forum shopping as an exercise that focuses on procedure – an area of international law that has been relatively overlooked. Chapter 2 provides a concept of *procedure* built around the notions of jurisdiction, action, and procedure in a narrow sense. Forum shopping implicates the elements of that triad and raises squarely procedural questions. Approaching forum shopping from a procedural perspective sheds light on the ambivalent role of preliminary objections: their traditional role as guarantors of the regularity of adjudication, as procedural shields, and their emerging role as coordination tools, as transmission belts of procedure-regulating norms. Nonetheless, procedure as such does not address the ultimate concerns arising from forum shopping. To emphasize procedure is to modestly shed light on a filter for forum shopping activity, where different policies and preferences may influence the assessment. Whereas this book is not about the judicial politics, policies, or preferences in the light of forum shopping, in order to account for their importance in the assessment and remediation of forum shopping Chapter 2 presents three levels where broader considerations are likely to be influential, and roughly relates each of these levels to functions of procedural norms discussed in Chapter 1.

Chapter 3 turns to the concept of *preliminary questions* and the technique of *preliminary objections*. The working concept of preliminary questions is based on a contextual distinction between the requirements for the existence and development of the adjudicatory process (i.e., preliminary questions, which refer to jurisdiction, action, and procedure in a narrow sense) on the one hand; and the ultimate object of the process (i.e., questions of merits) on the other hand. The contextual factor in the preliminary-versus-merits questions distinction is the object of the request. The concept of preliminary questions and objections adopted, it is submitted, is both broad enough for the subsequent analysis to cut across international tribunals and narrow enough to delimit the scope of the research.

Chapter 4 argues that the power to dismiss claims without deciding on them is an inherent power of international tribunals. To this effect, it disentangles the concept of international judicial jurisdiction into three components: *adjudicatory* jurisdiction, *principal* jurisdiction, and *incidental* jurisdiction. It posits that principal jurisdiction provides the justification for the power to rule on preliminary questions, and that the possession of adjudicatory jurisdiction is the source of this power. The authority to rule on preliminary questions is therefore a form of incidental jurisdiction that flows from the possession of a judicial character. The distinction between principal and incidental jurisdiction also contributes to an understanding of why the applicable law before international tribunals potentially entails any existing, valid norm that regulates the relationship between two disputing parties, and justifies the application of existing rules on procedural coordination across the international judiciary. Finally, the distinction between principal and incidental jurisdiction gives rise to a further difference between the definitive effect of decisions made in the exercise of principal jurisdiction, which are upheld across international tribunals and proceedings, and the relative, specific effect of decisions made under incidental jurisdiction, which is restricted to the proceedings at stake.

Chapter 5 then discusses the dual categorization of preliminary objections into objections to *jurisdiction* and *admissibility*. It discusses the significance of this twofold categorization and examines its contours in the case law of international tribunals. It presents three typical approaches to the categorization in the case law, namely: (i) not to recognize a distinction between jurisdiction and admissibility (the *indifference* approach); (ii) to adopt an objective approach to the distinction based on the target of the objection (the *objectivist* approach); and (iii) to adopt a conventionalist perspective with regard to jurisdiction and a residualist perspective concerning admissibility (the *conventionalist–residualist* approach). Chapter 5 then provides an analytical basis on which to frame the question of overlapping jurisdictions of international tribunals from a cosmopolitan procedural perspective, based on conventionalism–residualism: direct mediation of jurisdictional overlaps as jurisdictional questions, and indirect mediation of overlaps as questions of admissibility. Particularly, admissibility shifts the focus of analysis from the architecture of the international judiciary or overt clashes of legal regimes to the preclusive effects of procedural norms on litigation strategies.

Chapter 6 focuses, from an empirical perspective, on the nature of tribunals' power to decline from ruling on the merits of claims because of a procedural obstacle. In particular, do tribunals have *discretion* not to decide a case under their jurisdiction? That chapter surveys the case law of selected international tribunals and argues that such authority in international law is currently very limited, at best. On the other hand, international tribunals do have the power to control the pace of proceedings before them. This power, Chapter 6 argues, may operate as a functional equivalent to discretion in some cases of forum shopping, since it fosters adjudicators' ability to resort to comity- and *forum non conveniens*-based considerations in a temporary manner. Doctrines that tackle forum shopping based on discretionary means are grouped as *abstention* doctrines. These can be contrasted with nondiscretionary rules and principles permitting procedural coordination through the prism of preliminary questions, dealt with in Chapter 7 as *preclusion* doctrines.

Chapter 7, based on a number of existing procedure-regulating rules, presents specific uses of preliminary questions and objections in reaction to forum shopping under the current state of play in international law. Specifically, it discusses how preclusion techniques and *aggregation* techniques may be used to address forum shopping strategies. To this effect, the chapter maps and discusses the application of preclusion doctrines stemming from treaty disciplines on forum selection, claim preclusion, and relatively less importantly, of general principles such as *res judicata* or *lis pendens* through the prism of preliminary objections, with a view to maximizing procedural coordination. It also briefly discusses aggregation doctrines, based on provisions that allow joinder of proceedings.

The conclusion summarizes the main arguments of the book

1 The rise of forum shopping

1.1 Introduction

This chapter contextualizes the rise of forum shopping before international tribunals and discusses the main concerns originating from this phenomenon. The rise of forum shopping is a corollary to a combination of developments on both the supply side and demand side of international adjudication. On the supply side, there has been a noteworthy increase in international tribunals with automatic jurisdiction. On the demand side, parties have been increasingly active in pushing for international adjudication.

Forum shopping strategies raise questions of legitimacy, fairness, systemic integrity, and cost. They may attempt to force litigation or relitigation which would not otherwise be open to a complainant, or to skew results. These attempts may lead to questions regarding the consensual basis of the authority of international tribunals and fairness towards the defendants. Forum shopping strategies may also disturb the balance in place between two given tribunals, depending on the level of systematization between these tribunals (a systemic question). In addition, serial litigation risks upsetting previous decisions with the force of law (a systemic question that directly affects also the parties). Finally, the multiplicity of litigation that forum shopping engenders is costly for the forum-shopped parties and the judiciary.

However, forum shopping is not necessarily problematic, and the assessment of concerns potentially arising from it requires consideration of a number of factors. As a threshold matter, forum shopping first calls for a determination of the extent to which the tribunal has been granted authority to adjudicate, and to which the complainant has been entitled to sue. Second, forum shopping may require balancing between complainants' autonomy and fairness to defendants with regard to the specific proceedings at play. Third, forum shopping may entail an examination of allocative concerns related to the division of labor, if any, between the relevant international tribunals. Because determining the existence and scope of consent to adjudicate is not always easy, and because the degree of a party's ability to employ a forum shopping strategy and the degree of international tribunals' systematization are significantly contingent upon the applicable normative context, this chapter's basic message is that the assessment of forum shopping strategies in public international law is a relative and complex exercise.

This chapter's discussion of the rise in forum shopping and resulting concerns is structured as follows. Section 1.2 explains that the multiplication of international tribunals, the move to automatic jurisdiction, and the "privatization" of adjudication set the stage for increased forum shopping in international law, through the emergence of a "market" for international adjudication. Section 1.3 identifies the concerns arising from forum shopping before international tribunals in light of (i) the persistence of consent as a basic principle of international adjudication, (ii) a focus on complainants' autonomy versus a focus on fairness to the defendant, (iii) a system-based versus regime-based approach to international tribunals, and (iv) a risk of mutually contradictory decisions. These emphasize the desirability of tools to curb concerns that may stem from forum shopping strategies. Section 1.4 presents concluding remarks.

1.2 The transformation of international adjudication

Underlying the present book is the view that judicial settlement of international disputes can no longer be appropriately described as the result of mutual choice by two sovereign parties which must agree – for each and every case – upon whether judicial settlement is the proper means to address their dispute and on the forum to be used (as exemplified in the traditional and solemn *compromis* and in arbitration based on ad hoc consent). By contrast to the situation throughout most of international law's history, potential complainants are now more likely to find a judicial body (and sometimes judicial bodies) which they can use to remedy an alleged international wrong. The possibility that a complainant could unilaterally bring an opponent to the courtroom and choose the mechanism(s) to be seized has thus become part of the calculus in international dispute resolution. This state of affairs can be described with reference to three major developments in the international adjudication's landscape. Two developments change the "supply side" of international adjudication: first, we now have more courts and tribunals; second, "automatic" jurisdiction is becoming a significant pattern in international law. A third development, which affects the "demand side" of adjudication, is that resorting to international tribunals is becoming an extension of private, transnational action, less amenable to control by a single state. Together, these developments lead to a revolutionary, albeit uneven "market" of international litigation that elicits a rise in forum shopping.

1.2.1 The multiplication of international tribunals

In one of the first pieces addressing the multiplication of international courts and tribunals at the end of the twentieth century, Cesare Romano hailed the phenomenon as the single most important development of the post-Cold War age in international law.[1] The eruption of new bodies in the past twenty years has been as impressive as their accompanying acronyms can be discouraging. In a more recent article, Romano proposes a taxonomy of international bodies that lists, among others, the following active international courts and tribunals – that is, (i) permanent bodies (ii) established by an international legal instrument, which (iii) rely on international law as the applicable law, (iv) decide cases based on predetermined rules of procedure, (v) are composed of independent adjudicators, and to which (vi) at least one of the parties is a state or intergovernmental organization:[2]

- State-only courts: International Court of Justice (ICJ, operating since 1946),[3] International Tribunal on the Law of the Sea (ITLOS, operating since 1996), WTO Appellate Body (operating since 1995);
- Human rights courts: ECtHR (operating since 1959), Inter-American Court of Human Rights (IACtHR, operating since

[1] Cesare Romano, 'The Proliferation of International Judicial Bodies: The Pieces of the Puzzle,' 31 *NYUJILP* (1999) 709, at 709.

[2] Cesare Romano, 'A Taxonomy of International Rule of Law Institutions,' 2 *JIDS* (2011) 241. The present list is partial, based on Romano's taxonomy. It does not include, in particular, international administrative tribunals, which essentially adjudicate cases between international civil servants and international organizations, or hybrid criminal tribunals.

[3] The ICJ is the successor to the PCIJ, which became operational in 1922.

1979), African Court on Human and Peoples' Rights (ACtHPR, operating since 2006);

- Courts of regional economic or political integration agreements: Court of Justice of the European Union (operating since 2010),[4] Benelux Court of Justice (operating since 1974), European Free Trade Association (EFTA) Court (operating since 1994), Common Court of Justice and Arbitration of the Organization for the Harmonization of Corporate Law in Africa (operating since 1997), East African Court of Justice (operating since 2001), Court of Justice of the Economic Community of West African States (ECOWAS Court of Justice, operating since 2001), Court of Justice of the Andean Community (CJAC, operating since 1984), Caribbean Court of Justice (CCJ, operating since 2001), Permanent Review Tribunal of the Southern Common Market (MERCOSUR PRT, operating since 2004);
- International criminal courts: International Criminal Court (ICC, operating since 2004), International Criminal Tribunal for the Former Yugoslavia (ICTY, operating since 1993), International Criminal Tribunal for Rwanda (ICTR, 1995).

The listing could include many other bodies which are an integral part of the recent expansion of international adjudication, such as a series of important automatic arbitration mechanisms between different states and between investors and states. In fact, as this book will illustrate, such mechanisms are sometimes the center of gravity of forum shopping action.

The recent explosion becomes even more evident with a glance at the panorama of international adjudication from a chronological perspective. Listing standing bodies prior to the 1990s was rather easy: the ICJ, the ECtHR, the European Courts, the IACtHR, the Benelux Court, and the CJAC.[5] But these courts were themselves part of a slow landscape

[4] The Court of Justice of the European Union is the judicial body of the EU. It consists of three international courts: the ECJ (originally established in 1952 as the Court of Justice of the European Coal and Steel Communities, and after 1958 the Court of Justice of the European Communities), and two courts partially subordinated to it: the General Court (created in 1988; formerly the Court of First Instance) and the Civil Service Tribunal (created in 2004). See Romano, 'Taxonomy of International Institutions.'

[5] Charter of the United Nations and Statute of the International Court of Justice, 1 *UNTS* 16 (UN Charter, ICJ Statute); Convention for the Protection of Human Rights and Fundamental Freedoms as amended by Protocols No 11 and No 14, 194 *CETS*

change beginning after World War II. Throughout its history, the PCIJ, and for some time its successor, the ICJ, were one of a kind. And before the twentieth century, while international law could be called law, it was definitely law without a judge.[6]

Multiple adjudicative bodies are certainly a fortunate development in international law.[7] On the positive side, to have several forums available is a boon for aggrieved parties. It may also guarantee that all elements of a multifaceted dispute are actually resolved; for example, consider a dispute over territorial delimitation at the ICJ, with a related trade restriction at the WTO.[8] A healthy level of competition between tribunals may also improve the quality of rulings and the expediency of proceedings. One tribunal keeping a critical eye over another can, finally, offer a welcome level of control over international tribunals and indirectly enhance their legitimacy.[9] But, especially when combined

(European Convention on Human Rights or ECHR); Treaty Establishing the European Coal and Steel Community, 261 *UNTS* 143 (In 1957, the EEC and the EURATOM were established and the ECJ competence was enlarged to include: Treaty Establishing the European Economic Community (EEC Treaty), 298 *UNTS* 11; Treaty Establishing the European Atomic Energy Community (EURATOM Treaty), 298 *UNTS* 167. See also Treaty on the Functioning of the European Union (Treaty on the Functioning of the EU), Official Journal of the European Union C83/210, 30 March 2010); American Convention on Human Rights, 1144 *UNTS* 123 (ACHR); Treaty Concerning the Establishment and the Statute of the Benelux Court of Justice, 924 *UNTS* 3; Treaty Creating the Court of Justice of the Cartagena Agreement, 18 *ILM* 1203. One could also add the Iran–US Claims Tribunal, functioning on a semi-permanent basis since 1981. See Algiers Accord, 20 *ILM* 223.

6 See John Austin, *The Province of Jurisprudence Determined* (London: John Murray, Prometheus Books, 1832, 2000), conceptualizing law as orders backed by threats and categorizing international law as “positive morality” for the lack of sanctions.

7 See also Rosalyn Higgins, ‘A Babel of Judicial Voices? Ruminations from the Bench,’ 55 *ICLQ* (2006) 804; Syméon Karagiannis, ‘La multiplication des juridictions internationales: un système anarchique?’ in SFDI, *La juridictionnalisation du droit international* (Paris: Pedone, 2003) 7; Pemmaraju Rao, ‘Multiple International Judicial Forums: A Reflection of the Growing Strength of International Law or its Fragmentation?’ 25 *MJIL* (2004) 929.

8 See Minutes of the DSB Meeting of 7 April 2000, WT/DSB/M/78, referring to Nicaragua’s taxes on imports from Honduras and Colombia (see *Nicaragua – Measures Affecting Imports from Honduras and Colombia*, WT/DS188, WT/DS201), allegedly imposed as a response to an agreement on maritime delimitation between Honduras and Colombia which would have violated Nicaragua’s rights. Honduras highlighted that “the subject of maritime delimitation did not fall within the WTO mandate, and should be dealt with by the competent forum such as the International Court of Justice.” The ICJ eventually ruled on the maritime boundary between Nicaragua and Honduras. See *Case Concerning Territorial and Maritime Dispute between Nicaragua and Honduras in the Caribbean Sea (Nicaragua* v. *Honduras)*, Judgment of 8 October 2007.

9 See Jacob Cogan, ‘Competition and Control in International Adjudication,’ 48 *Vand JIL* (2008) 411.

with the emergence of automatic jurisdiction, diverse tribunals can and do raise the problem of how to coordinate jurisdictional overlaps and tackle forum shopping.

Looking ahead, one might argue that the number of international tribunals tends to stabilize rather than maintain the rapid pace of previous expansion, since most areas amenable to adjudication in the current context have apparently experienced their momentum with the creation of an adjudicative or regulatory body.[10] For instance, it does not seem conceivable in the short-to-medium term that a tribunal would be created to deal with financial or exchange matters, even though that area has been regulated by different instruments and certain corners have called for action on "currency manipulation." In Africa, members of the African Union decided to merge the Court of Justice of African Union and the ACtHPR, even before the former started operating and before the ACtHPR had its first case.[11] Indeed, the expansion of international monitoring and adjudication in the past years has generated an increasing cost concern, all the more so in the current times of serious financial distress.

1.2.2 *From ad hoc consent to inbuilt consent to jurisdiction*

Another key dimension of recent judicialization is the establishment of inbuilt consent to the jurisdiction of dispute-settlement mechanisms[12] (or "automatic jurisdiction"). This opens the possibility for one party to unilaterally resort to adjudication – such as in most international trade and regional integration dispute-settlement regimes, or in myriad bilateral investment arbitration treaties. In Romano's words, there has been:

> a fundamental shift in the concept and practice of international adjudication from a traditional consensual paradigm, in which express and specific consent is a prerequisite to jurisdiction and adjudication largely takes place with the assent and cooperation of both parties, to a compulsory paradigm, in which consent is largely formulaic either because it is implicit in the ratification of treaties creating certain international organizations endowed with adjudicative bodies or because it is jurisprudentially bypassed and litigation is often undertaken unilaterally.[13]

10 See also Romano, 'Taxonomy of International Institutions.'

11 Protocol on the Statute of the African Court of Justice and Human Rights.

12 See also Philippe Sands, Ruth Mackenzie, and Yuval Shany, *Manual on International Courts and Tribunals* (London: Butterworths, 1999) xvii–xviii.

13 Cesare Romano, 'The Shift From the Consensual to the Compulsory Paradigm in International Adjudication: Elements for a Theory of Consent,' 39 *NYUJILP* (2007) 791, at 794–5.

This claim, especially when it addresses consent being jurisprudentially bypassed, is likely to face resistance and might seem to be far-fetched in the current state of play in key areas of international law:[14] consent is still the fundamental pillar of international adjudication.[15] As we are always told, in international affairs "even compulsory jurisdiction is voluntary."[16] This is especially true for parties who come before the ICJ. That the mantra of state consent to jurisdiction is in substance as valid today as it was at the inception of the law of nations[17] hints at the remoteness of some international lawyers' endeavors to achieve general compulsory jurisdiction.[18] The question, to be clear, is not about the substance of the principle of consent. The basic change is of form. But form matters here. As Elihu Lauterpacht anticipated in 1991, "exact consent, closely linked in time and substance to the exercise of jurisdiction, may have become so worn away

[14] As the discussion in Sections 1.2.1 above and 1.2.4 below make clear, judicialization is not an all-embracing or uniform phenomenon. Still, the importance of the change in the form in which consent operates within a number of newly created bodies, as discussed herein, must not be neglected.

[15] Romano himself concedes that the principle of consent has not been extinguished. He submits "[t]he principle remains valid, but its significance has been gradually reduced, transforming it into a pale simulacrum of its old self." Romano, 'Shift to the Compulsory Paradigm,' at 795.

[16] John Merrils, *International Dispute Settlement*, 3rd edn (Cambridge University Press, 1999), 292.

[17] Compare *Status of Eastern Carelia*, Advisory Opinion of 23 July 1923, PCIJ Ser B No 5 (1923), 27 (" … no State can, without its consent, be compelled to submit its disputes … to arbitration, or any other kind of pacific settlement") with *Case Concerning Armed Activities on the Territory of Congo (New Application: 2002) (Democratic Republic of the Congo* v. *Rwanda)*, Jurisdiction and Admissibility, Judgment of 3 February 2006, para. 125 (recalling the principle that "its jurisdiction always depends on the consent of the parties" even when *erga omnes* obligations and *jus cogens* norms are at stake). But see the joint separate opinion of Judges Higgins, Kooijmans, Elaraby, Owada, and Simma in *Armed Activities, ibid.*, paras. 24–9 ("It must be regarded as a very grave matter that a State should be in a position to shield from international judicial scrutiny any claim that might be made against it concerning genocide," at para. 24). In substance, consent is essential even in the context of human rights. In case there is an invalid reservation of a specific jurisdictional provision, there is still the question of consent to be bound by the instrument as a whole. See *Case of Loizidou* v. *Turkey*, Application No 15318/89, Judgment on Preliminary Objections, 23 March 1985.

[18] See Antonio Cançado Trindade, *International Law for Humankind: Towards a New* Jus Gentium (Leiden: Martinus Nijhoff, 2010), at 567–591; Heinhard Steiger, 'Plaidoyer pour une Juridiction Internationale Obligatoire,' in Jerzy Makarczyk (ed.), *Theory of International Law at the Threshold of the 21st Century* (The Hague: Kluwer, 1996) 817; Wilfred Jenks, *The Prospects of International Adjudication* (London: Stevens & Sons, 1964).

as to require profound reconsideration of the fundamentals of the subject."[19] Inbuilt consent has eclipsed ad hoc consent, particularly with the expression of consent being linked to treaty-making exercises in many areas of international law.[20]

As a result of automatic jurisdiction, the operation and implementation of consent changes drastically. The anticipation of consent takes away from individual states the right to veto adjudication when disputes eventually arise. Parties no longer jointly act as gatekeepers of international adjudication. Each party has its own master key.[21] On its own, this development increases the likelihood that preliminary objections crop up. But over and above automatic jurisdiction, the availability of multiple forums compounds the problem. For under this scenario, both the method of settlement (adjudication) and the specific adjudicatory body are subject to strategic maneuvering by one party acting unilaterally.[22] Unwilling defendants are likely to resist those attempts.

1.2.3 The "privatization" of international litigation

A third dimension of the recent judicialization of international law consists of the emergence of non-state actors as participants in international adjudication, with an intensity that had not been seen before. This is manifest under three related trends. First, non-state actors have increasingly graduated to the rank of litigants. In short, they are granted

[19] Elihu Lauterpacht, *Aspects of the Administration of International Justice* (Cambridge: Grotius, 1991), at 25.

[20] See also speech by H. E. Rosalyn Higgins, President of the ICJ, to the Sixth Committee of the General Assembly, 31 October 2008: "Virtually all the great international institutions of the world have, as a concomitant of membership, the obligation to accept the compulsory jurisdiction of the Court of that institution … But membership in the United Nations does not carry this obligation … The United Nations stands almost alone in this state of affairs."

[21] See further discussion in Section 1.3.1 below.

[22] Contrast this scenario to Articles 33(1) and 95, UN Charter; and Declaration on Principles of International Law Concerning Friendly Relations and Cooperation among States in Accordance with the Charter of the United Nations, A/RES/2625, 24 October 1970. It is important to recognize that automatic jurisdiction overturns the freedom of means only relatively. As is well established, there is nothing wrong with the fact that states decide through an international agreement to restrict sovereign rights – in this case, the right to choose the method of settling its disputes. See *Case of the SS Wimbledon*, Judgment of 17 August 1923, PCIJ Ser A No 1 (1923) 14, at 25 (the possibility of restricting sovereign rights through international agreements is a corollary of sovereignty itself). This is why I prefer not to use the term "compulsory jurisdiction" and to use "automatic jurisdiction" instead, since the former may imply that consent has changed in substance, which is not the state of the law.

standing to participate in their own capacity as parties to international proceedings. Of course, this is not a complete novelty.[23] However, the establishment of new venues for litigation combined with an intensified emergence of non-state parties – most visible with the outburst of international human rights litigation in Europe[24] and of investment arbitration,[25] and the phenomenon of regional integration[26] – has changed the dynamics of adjudication in important ways. International tribunals more open to non-state actors abridge states' gatekeeping capacities. Furthermore, non-state actors with standing to litigate may face constraints different from those of governments.[27] In particular, private parties may worry less about tit-for-tat reciprocity in the form of counterlitigation[28] or precedent-creating constraints[29] than would governments. Consequently, private parties tend to generate more litigation than does classic interstate dispute resolution.[30]

[23] A measure of non-state direct participation has been accepted at least since the Central American Court of Justice's establishment in 1908. Throughout that court's existence, five claims by individuals were submitted. Four failed on admissibility grounds and one on the merits. The Peace Treaties after World War I allowed nationals of allied and associated powers to bring claims against the defeated states before mixed arbitral tribunals. See Marek Korowicz, 'The Problem of the International Personality of Individuals,' 50 *AJIL* (1956) 546.

[24] See Articles 32, 34, ECHR.

[25] See especially Article 25, Convention on the Settlement of Investment Disputes between States and Nationals of Other States, 575 *UNTS* 159 (ICSID Convention).

[26] See, for example, Articles 263, 265, Treaty on the Functioning of the EU, Articles 19, 37, Treaty Creating the Court of Justice of the Cartagena Agreement (access of individuals concerning the annulment of decisions and the claims against violation of the governing treaties by regional institutions); Articles 1904(1) and Chapter 11, Section B, North American Free Trade Agreement, 32 *ILM* 289 (NAFTA, private participation in bi-national review panels on final anti-dumping and subsidization determinations and in investment disputes).

[27] See also Robert Hudec, 'Transcending the Ostensible: Some Reflections on the Nature of Litigation between Governments,' 72 *Minn L Rev* (1988) 211.

[28] For instance, in investor-state arbitration, states appear as respondents. But see Gustavo Laborde, 'The Case for Host State Claims in Investment Arbitration,' 1 *JIDS* (2010) 97.

[29] For instance, in trade disputes, governments may discount their own policies and the potential to generate adverse precedents that might be used in the future against them, before deciding to move to litigation. See also Marc Busch, 'Overlapping Institutions, Forum Shopping, and Dispute Settlement in International Trade,' 61 *IO* (2007) 735. Although the logic potentially applies to private parties, states perform a broader range of activities, pursue a broader range of goals, and are repeated players in international adjudication. Thus, one given entity or individual would possess a narrower horizon of possible action to be concerned about when deciding on the potential adverse effects of a precedent.

[30] Robert Keohane, Andrew Moravcsik, and Anne-Marie Slaughter, 'Legalized Dispute Resolution: Interstate and Transnational,' 54 *IO* (2000) 457.

The second trend is that non-state actors have increasingly functioned as the true forces underlying many disputes addressed under otherwise purely interstate litigation. This is also not totally new: one need only remember that the second case before the PCIJ was essentially a matter of private rights taken up to the international level by Greece.[31] The ability of non-state actors to influence interstate litigation has nonetheless developed remarkably, to the extent that Christina Davis was able to show that pressure from domestic interest groups is the primary selection criterion among cases submitted for WTO adjudication, for instance.[32] Her claim confirms what Gregory Shaffer has called the "blurring of the public and the private in international trade law."[33]

Third, in addition to the blurring of the public and the private, economic globalization and the transnationalization of private interests also blur the domestic and the foreign in international law. The *Gambling* case brought by Antigua and Barbuda against the United States at the WTO comes to mind.[34] In 1998, US federal prosecutors brought criminal charges against twenty-one US citizens allegedly connected to offshore internet gambling. Jay Cohen, who had been operating an Antigua-based website, was one of the indicted. Mr Cohen did not enter a guilty plea and went back to the United States to contest his case in

[31] That case dealt with the recognition of the rights of Mr Mavrommatis under contracts executed by him with the Ottoman Empire concerning concessions for the construction of public works. See *Mavrommatis Palestine Concessions*, Judgment of 30 August 1924, PCIJ Ser A No 2 (1924) 1. Note, however, that the PCIJ affirmed that the case related to Greece's own right – "its right to ensure, in the person of its subjects, respect for the rules of international law" (at 12). Although this is still considered to be the state of customary international law, there has been a move toward broader recognition of the rights underlying diplomatic protection. See especially International Law Commission, Draft Articles on Diplomatic Protection with Commentaries (2006), UN doc. A/61/10, 16, Article 19 and accompanying commentary.

[32] Christina Davis, 'Forum Choice in Trade Disputes: WTO Adjudication, Negotiation, and US Trade Policy,' Paper prepared for presentation to the International Political Economy Society Annual Meeting 2007, 9–10 November 2007, Stanford University. On the influence of private actors on the initiation of WTO disputes by the United States and the European Community, see also Gregory Shaffer, *Defending Interests: Public-Private Partnerships in WTO Litigation* (Washington, D.C.: Brookings Institution, 2003).

[33] Shaffer, *Defending Interests*, at 1.

[34] See *United States – Measures Affecting the Cross-Border Supply of Gambling and Betting Services*, WT/DS285. The following account of the case relies on Isaac Wohl, 'The Antigua-United States Online Gambling Dispute,' Web version, July 2009. At the time of publication of his article, Wohl was an International Trade Analyst in the Office of Industries of the United States International Trade Commission. The author disclaimed that views in the article were his own.

court. He was eventually sentenced to twenty-one months in prison and fined, becoming the first US citizen convicted in that country for operating an offshore gambling website. This case was brought to the attention of Mark Mendel. In Mendel's view, the United States had violated WTO-based obligations under the General Agreement on Trade in Services (GATS) by restricting offshore gambling. Antigua hired Mendel and brought a complaint against the United States before the WTO. A panel and the Appellate Body found that certain restrictions on gambling violated United States' GATS-based commitments to liberalize trade in "other recreational services." Further rulings established that the United States remained noncompliant with the original decision several months later. Antigua was deemed entitled to retaliate in the amount of 21 million dollars per year against the United States and threatened to retaliate by resorting to suspensions of its own commitments related to intellectual property rights. Therefore, the dispute became an object of concern for other, intellectual property-intensive industries, including other multinational companies based in the United States that initially had no connection whatsoever to the *Gambling* affair. The United States, for its part, has engaged in renegotiations of its prior GATS-based commitment to the liberalization of recreational services with other interested WTO members.[35] The renegotiation implicated interests of service suppliers and industries from several countries. In December 2012, Antigua formally requested authorization to suspend obligations concerning Trade-Related Aspects of Intellectual Property Rights (TRIPS) vis-à-vis the United States, which has generated renewed attention concerning the case.[36] In summary: the indictment of a US citizen operating a gambling business from Antigua for online gamblers in the United States was the triggering event of a long-standing dispute between Antigua and that country before the WTO. This dispute ended up implicating other WTO members and a number of different industries from different countries.

Another interesting example of the blurring of the domestic and foreign frontier can be found in the *Tokios Tekelès* v. *Ukraine* investment arbitration under the Lithuania–Ukraine BIT.[37] Tokios Tekelès was

[35] Formal renegotiations have involved at least India, the EC, Japan, Costa Rica and Macao, China, in 2007, in addition to Antigua and Barbuda itself.

[36] *US – Gambling*, Recourse by Antigua and Barbuda to Article 22.7 of the DSU, WTO doc. WT/DS285/25, 13 December 2012.

[37] *Tokios Tekelès* v. *Ukraine*, ICSID Case No ARB/02/18, Decision on Jurisdiction, 29 April 2004.

a company established in Lithuania. However, 99 percent of Tokios Tekelès shares actually belonged to Ukrainian nationals. Despite its overwhelming Ukrainian ownership, Tokios Tekelès was able to sue Ukraine for damages as a "Lithuanian" investor for alleged violations of the BIT. In essence, the arbitral tribunal's majority (composed of the two party-appointed arbitrators) highlighted the fact that the claimant was "established under the laws of Lithuania" and that this was the "only relevant"[38] consideration under the terms of the BIT regarding the nationality of the investor. The tribunal thus asserted jurisdiction to decide the case on the merits. Put bluntly: a company 99 percent owned by Ukrainian nationals was able to sue Ukraine for an investment that the company had made in Ukraine – and all of this grounded in international law instruments and before an international tribunal.

The three aforementioned interrelated trends (i.e., non-state actors as (i) parties to proceedings in their own name, (ii) the force pushing litigation, and (iii) with transnational interests) converge, making it more difficult for states to handle through diplomacy questions of overlapping disputes and forum shopping. As Benedict Kingsbury has synthesized:

> [T]he range of problems is large, and the ability of states to manage them through foreign ministry diplomacy is limited by the increasing involvement not only of other parts of government but also of non-state actors either as litigants or as the truly interested forces behind litigation.[39]

To put it briefly, the "privatization" of litigation may drag states to adjudication.

1.2.4 *The new market of international adjudication: let's go shopping*

The boom in international tribunals and the rise of automatic jurisdiction thus change the supply side of the market of international adjudication, and the privatization of litigation brings the market's demand curve upwards. One result that we have seen in practice over the last years is a growth in the amount of litigation. Moreover, we have seen overlapping disputes and heard of forum shopping and clashes

[38] *Ibid.*, especially at para. 38. The dissenting arbitrator, unusually, was the non-party appointed arbitrator and president of the tribunal. The dissent vigorously argued that the dispute was outside the ICSID's jurisdiction.

[39] Benedict Kingsbury, 'Is the Proliferation of International Courts and Tribunals a Systemic Problem?' 31 *NYUJILP* (1999) 679, at 683–4.

of jurisdiction.[40] The problem is compounded by the lack of comprehensive division of labor among international tribunals and the asymmetrical configuration of the international judiciary. International tribunals are autonomous in the precise sense that each of them is the only one to decide for itself and that each decides exclusively for itself.[41] Normally, there is neither hierarchy nor centralization, as with most of international law.[42] As a matter of fact, the establishment of international tribunals is not part of any master plan to forge an integrated international judiciary. Quite the contrary, the specialized judicial dispute-settlement mechanisms linked to specific legal regimes reflect functional differentiation and are an inevitable consequence of deeper clashes of rationalities within a fragmented global society,[43] where compromise between functional requirements of social subsystems, political control objectives, and requirements internal to the legal system is considerably precarious.[44] In this context, new mechanisms are answers to localized demands, which may involve broad, universal ambitions by specific groups within the process of particular negotiations.[45] The creation of these new mechanisms is therefore not necessarily the result of pure economic or legal rationality.[46] Moreover,

[40] See, for example, the alerts by Gilbert Guillaume in his addresses to the UN General Assembly in 2000 and 2001: Speech by H. E. Gilbert Guillaume, President of the ICJ, to the Plenary Session of the United Nations General Assembly, 26 October 2001; Speech by H. E. Gilbert Guillaume, President of the ICJ, to the Plenary Session of the United Nations General Assembly, 26 October 2000.

[41] This follows from the principle of *la compétence de la compétence*. See also *Prosecutor v. Dusko Tadic a/k/a "Dule,"* Case IT-94-1, Defense Motion for Interlocutory Appeal on Jurisdiction, Decision of 2 October 1995, para. 11.

[42] See generally Jean Combacau, 'Le droit international: bric-à-brac ou système?' 31 *Arch Phil D* (1986) 85.

[43] See Andreas Fischer-Lescano and Gunther Teubner, 'Regime Collisions: the Vain Search for Legal Unity in the Fragmentation of Global Law,' 25 *MJIL* (2004) 999.

[44] See Gunther Teubner, '"And God Laughed ..." Indeterminacy, Self-Reference and Paradox in Law,' 12 *German L J* (2011) 376, at 400–1.

[45] See also Martti Koskenniemi and Paivi Leïno, 'Fragmentation of International Law? Postmodern Anxieties,' 15 *LJIL* (2002) 553.

[46] See, for example, Shigeru Oda's critique of unnecessary proliferation by the creation of the ITLOS in overlap with the ICJ (Shigeru Oda, 'Dispute Settlement Prospects in the Law of the Sea,' 44 *ICLQ* (1995) 863). Notwithstanding criticism, the ITLOS was the result of political considerations, as with other international courts and tribunals. In the case of the Law of the Sea Tribunal, compromise was reached between states not ready to grant automatic jurisdiction to the ICJ and those that distrusted arbitration. See Tullio Treves, 'Le Tribunal International du Droit de la Mer dans la Pléiade des Juridictions Internationales,' in Olivier Delas *et al.* (eds.), *Les Juridictions Internationales: Complémentarité ou Concurrence?* (Brussels: Bruylant, 2005)

jurisdictions frequently overlap,[47] and the degree of judicialization varies across areas and regimes. In practice, judicialization comes in pockets, and one finds different combinations of the three developments mentioned above (creation of new international tribunals, automatic jurisdiction, and emergence of non-state actors) across areas.[48] Asymmetrical judicialization leads in turn to asymmetrical enforcement: where certain norms and behaviors are directly backed up by strong adjudicatory mechanisms, others are less judicialized, and still others simply receive no third-party supervision at all. In short, the international judiciary is stratified. This provides incentives for tailor-making one's case according to the relative strength of dispute-settlement mechanisms.

Therefore, one key practical effect of asymmetrical judicialization is the opening of doors for complainants to shop around in a market of tribunals of diverse shapes and colors from which an aggressive complainant can draw.[49] Add to this the loosening of states' gate-keeping capacities, and the necessary conditions for forum shopping are met. Essentially, forum shopping can be explained in terms of rational litigating behavior and thus can be considered a natural occurrence, even if the phrase can be sometimes used pejoratively. In this sense, the famous remarks by Lord Simon in the House of Lords judgment in *The Atlantic Star* are apposite also to international adjudication:

> Forum Shopping is a dirty word; but it is only a pejorative way of saying that, if you offer a plaintiff a choice of jurisdictions, he will naturally choose the one in which he thinks his case can be most favourably presented: this should be a matter neither for surprise nor for indignation.[50]

However, just as "shopping" may flow from rational choice, it is reasonable to assume that defendants will respond by adducing

9, at 9–10. See generally David Caron, 'Towards a Political Theory of International Courts and Tribunals,' 24 *Berkeley JIL* (2006) 401.

47 See especially Yuval Shany, *The Competing Jurisdictions of International Courts and Tribunals* (Oxford University Press, 2003).

48 See Jose Alvarez, 'The New Dispute Settlers: (Half) Truths and Consequences,' 38 *Texas ILJ* (2003) 441.

49 See also Andrew Bell, *Forum Shopping and Venue in Transnational Litigation* (Oxford University Press, 2003), arguing that the existence of concurrent jurisdictions is the *sine qua non* of forum shopping (at 5), whereas lack of uniformity is critical to igniting strategic battles over venue (at 28).

50 *The Atlantic Star* v. *Bona Spes*, House of Lords, 10 April 1973, AC (1974) 436 (1973, United Kingdom), at 471.

as many defenses as possible against a forum shopping strategy. This increases the strategic and tactical importance of preliminary objections and the challenge for adjudicators to deal with them in the light of actual or potential idiosyncrasies in their own fields and tribunals.

1.3 Potential concerns arising from forum shopping

Forum shopping not only increases the tactical importance of preliminary objections, but it also arguably grants them novel normative connotations. Traditional concerns arising from forum shopping in domestic and private international law relate principally to the fairness and impartiality of adjudication and to the orderly functioning of the judiciary. The same concerns can be identified in international law. Moreover, forum shopping in international law is particularly problematic in light of the consensual bedrocks where lay international tribunals' jurisdiction and parties' entitlement to sue. Accordingly, in addition to fairness-driven and allocative concerns regarding exercises of jurisdiction that forum shopping engenders – or perhaps even before these concerns are even thought of – in international law there is a potential delegation or legitimacy-related concern regarding the existence of jurisdiction and the complainant's entitlement to sue the respondent in the particular circumstances.

One way to visualize the main concerns arising from forum shopping in international law is to refer to the scope and function of procedural norms understood in a broad sense. Regarding their scope, these norms regulate three interlinked sets of interactions, namely (i) the relationship between the parties, (ii) the relationship between each of the parties and a given tribunal or tribunals, and (iii) the relationship between different tribunals. Forum shopping has the potential to disturb each of these relationships. For instance, strategic forum selection by the complaining party may prove inconsistent where there is an agreement between the parties on the method to settle a given dispute, or it may benefit the party who chooses the battleground because the applicable law in that case favors the electing party. Parallel litigation can increase costs to the forum-shopped party and to the general contributors to a tribunal's budget, and may disturb the underlying division of labor between two or more given tribunals. The last issue also comes about when serial litigation takes place. Furthermore, serial litigation risks leading to two conflicting decisions which can, in turn, disrupt the relationship between the parties (i.e., which legal entitlement should prevail, the one in favor of A or the one which favors B?) and that between two tribunals (i.e., which tribunal's decision should prevail?).

Turning to function, in the context of public international law the primary function of procedural norms is to grant authority. This may be called a *delegation* function. Because international law normally recognizes no authority above states and recognizes states as equals, states are under no obligation of principle to give account of their reasons before any third parties, unless they agree to be so obligated. Therefore, adjudicatory jurisdiction in international law (i.e., the power to state the law with finality with regard to a legal dispute) is limited by the terms of the delegation (i.e., subject-matter jurisdiction and personal jurisdiction).[51] In addition to this delegation function that is particularly pronounced in international adjudication, procedural norms understood in a broad sense have among their main functions an enabling function, a protective function, and an allocative function.[52] Under their *enabling* function, procedural norms aim to guarantee parties' access to the judiciary. Under their *protective* function, they seek to maintain the equality of arms between the parties, thus guaranteeing fairness to them all. Under their *allocative* function, procedural norms establish a division of labor between different components of the judicial system, while attempting to channel jurisdiction to the most appropriate forum.[53] These last three functions will likely be found in most legal systems, even if they do not perfectly match across legal systems and their relative importance can vary with the situation and normative background considered. Each of them can be identified also in international law, and they thus provide useful criteria to explain the potential concerns arising from forum shopping.

[51] Temporal jurisdiction (jurisdiction *ratione temporis*), and geographic or territorial jurisdiction (jurisdiction *ratione loci*), which are usually also referred to as headings of jurisdiction even in international law, herein are considered to be included in subject-matter jurisdiction (jurisdiction *ratione materiae*) or personal jurisdiction (jurisdiction *ratione personae*). In short, they are specifications of these broader headings of jurisdiction. See also discussion in Chapter 4.

[52] This articulation of the enabling, protective, and allocative functions is based on part of a book project by Ralf Michaels that was presented at the Doctoral Research Seminar in International Law, Graduate Institute of International and Development Studies, Geneva, 20 March 2009. Ralf Michaels, 'US Courts as World Courts,' manuscript on file with the author.

[53] *Ibid.*

1.3.1 The delegation function of procedural norms in a dynamic context: the puzzle of inbuilt consent

Although the functions of procedural norms presented here are deeply interrelated and may overlap in practice, it is useful to keep them separate for the sake of discussion. Considering that the question of delegation is a threshold one (i.e., it defines whether jurisdiction exists in the first place), it is appropriate to highlight this function before discussing the enabling, protective, and allocative functions as they play out in international adjudication. Jurisdictional norms consist of grants of international adjudicatory authority to third parties. Consent is thus essential as a front-end matter in international adjudication: it determines and delimits international tribunals' jurisdiction. But who determines the existence and extent of consent? In the answer to this question lies a deep tension, for while adjudicators' authority is determined by the terms of the delegation, there is often a controversy between the parties in dispute regarding those very terms. Beyond doubt, this is not the end of the game: adjudicators become "judges in their own cause" and are themselves definitely empowered to interpret and implement the terms of the delegation. Thus, they determine the existence and extent of consent.[54] Yet, while the so-called principle of "competence-competence" squares the circle from a formal perspective, it does not do away with the difficulty of ensuring that adjudicators remain confined to the terms of the delegation. The risk remains that adjudicators are accused of trespassing the boundaries of the delegation. While this accusation may be just or unjust from a given viewpoint, it may have an impact on the legitimacy of international adjudication and adjudicators, given the inherent link between consent and authority to adjudicate.

In the context of a legal dispute where each party may be perceived either as a "winner" or a "loser," it is unlikely that the two opposing parties will agree on whether the "neutral" third party has gone beyond the limits of its mandate. And, to make matters more complicated, there is normally no third party with authority to determine that very question in the event that it becomes disputed. Of course, this fundamental riddle of consent to adjudication is no novelty in

[54] See, for example, Ibrahim Shihata, *The Power of the International Court to Determine its Own Jurisdiction* (The Hague: Martinus Nijhoff, 1965); Bin Cheng, *General Principles of Law as Applied by International Courts and Tribunals* (Cambridge University Press, 1953, 2006), at 275–78.

international law – let alone law. Under the traditional *compromis* and arbitration based on ad hoc consent, the exact same question arises about the limits of the jurisdictional grant. Nonetheless, in the context of ad hoc consent, the disputing parties' mutual choice to adjudicate a concrete matter is directly linked to the establishment of the terms of the delegation. In that context, the jurisdictional grant may be narrowly defined to cover a specific set of facts, limited obligations, and a strictly defined group of litigants. Precise, more determinate terms of delegation and direct agreement thereupon tend to reduce the odds of perceived "over-adjudication." Conversely, unanticipated developments are much more likely to take place under a less determinate jurisdictional grant that goes forward indefinitely, even if the subject matter covered by the grant is restricted to a certain category of claim. Since treaty negotiators and drafters cannot predict the future with perfect accuracy, concerns of over-adjudication tend to be more pronounced where inbuilt consent is the dominant expression of consent, as opposed to ad hoc consent. Inbuilt consent, therefore, further challenges adjudicators with regard to the interpretation of their mandate, as cases may come up that the grantors of jurisdiction had not possibly foreseen at the moment of the original grant.

This challenge arises acutely in the controversial *Abaclat* v. *Argentina* ICSID arbitration currently ongoing under the Argentina–Italy BIT.[55] In that case, a majority decision on jurisdiction and admissibility allowed claims by roughly 60,000 holders of security entitlements in Argentinean sovereign bonds to proceed to the merits stage. While that ongoing case features many unique and considerably complex features, it suffices for present purposes to consider the novelty of "collective claims" brought on behalf of many thousands of claimants under the ICSID jurisdictional scheme. Argentina argued that the tribunal had no jurisdiction under the ICSID Convention or the relevant BIT to address "mass-claims." As the tribunal's majority and the dissent agreed, the ICSID Convention and the relevant BIT were silent on the eventuality of mass proceedings such as the one they confronted. In that context, the majority and the dissent reached opposite conclusions. The majority held that it would be contrary to the "purpose of the BIT" and the "spirit of ICSID" to require, in addition to the consent to ICSID arbitration in general (which the majority had deemed to exist in the circumstances),

[55] *Abaclat and others* v. *Argentina*, ICSID Case No ARB/07/5, Decision on Jurisdiction and Admissibility, 4 August 2011, Dissenting Opinion, 28 October 2011.

a "supplementary express consent to the form of such arbitration" (given the number of claimants).[56] The majority noted that, at the time of conclusion of the ICSID Convention "collective proceedings were quasi inexistent, and although some discussions seem to have taken place with regard to multi-party arbitrations, these discussions were not conclusive on the intention to either accept or refuse multi-party arbitrations."[57] The majority drew support from this to conclude that collective proceedings should be accepted under the ICSID Convention and the BIT. It then considered that the arbitral tribunal had powers to envisage and adapt rules of procedure to address the collective aspect of the proceedings.[58] By contrast, the dissenting arbitrator argued that "[t]he requirement to ascertain the existence and scope of consent" in international law meant neither "the restrictive interpretation of the jurisdictional title (the old theory of interpretation in favour of sovereignty)" nor "its expansive interpretation beyond the 'horizon of foreseeability'; i.e. extending jurisdiction to what the party or parties could not have foreseen at the time the treaty was concluded or consent was given."[59] He then attributed this "expansive interpretation" to the majority. To the dissent, the majority's reference to "quasi-inexistent" collective proceedings at the time of conclusion of the ICSID Convention was "paradoxical" because it supported a conclusion that was opposite to the one that the majority had come to:

> The fact that class actions or representative proceedings were almost unknown in national jurisdictions, and more so on the international level, at the time of the conclusion of the ICSID Convention ... proves that these representative proceedings were way beyond the "horizon of foreseeability" of the drafters of the ICSID Convention. Those drafters could not have envisaged such proceedings; nor is there any basis to assume that they would have included them, had they envisaged them, given the fundamental differences between these proceedings and the arbitration model familiar to them (as discussed below). Those drafters were simply creating a framework for ad hoc international arbitration, within the parameters of ad hoc international arbitration as they knew them at that time, particularly its specific consensual basis for every case, as with all international adjudication. They were not establishing an open-ended standing court of general jurisdiction (*juridiction de droit commun*) covering all possible present and future disputes.[60]

[56] *Ibid.*, para. 517.

[57] *Ibid.*, para. 519. [58] *Ibid.*, paras. 520–47.

[59] *Ibid.*, Dissenting Opinion, para. 16.

[60] *Ibid.*, para. 165. The dissent further considered that consent specific to the collective aspect of the procedures should be found and that allowing the case to continue

Abaclat is not likely to end any time soon. Apart from the fact that the merits stage is likely to be extremely convoluted given the complexity of the proceedings, the ICSID Convention provides for the possibility of requests for the annulment of an award based on the grounds that a tribunal "has manifestly exceeded its powers" or departed from "a fundamental rule of procedure."[61] Contrasting the majority and the dissenting arbitrator's views shows that there may be further proceedings after the merits stage where the opposing views will be confronted. If one were to agree with the view expressed by the dissenting arbitrator, one would perceive *Abaclat* as an exercise of forum shopping (so far successful for the claimants) that led to adjudication notwithstanding the lack of consent by Argentina under the ICSID Convention and the BIT. Regardless of where one stands in the debate as to whether the *Abaclat* majority's decision to proceed to the merits stage was correct or the best one, it is important to note that the majority and the dissenter shared the conclusion that the relevant legal instruments under interpretation were silent regarding the possibility of mass claims, only to reach irreconcilable conclusions about the consequences of such silence. This result illustrates the difficulties of assessing the delegation function of jurisdictional norms in international adjudication, especially under inbuilt consent. It is impossible to fully predict what will arise in the future when drafting a jurisdictional clause and this may lead to claims of over- or under-adjudication, and therefore raise legitimacy concerns as unanticipated issues confront disputing parties and adjudicators.

1.3.2 *The enabling and protective functions of procedural norms in a dynamic context: a balance between complainant's autonomy and fairness-to-the-defendant considerations*

With regard to the enabling and protective functions of procedural norms, it is argued that they are common to and freely transposable between domestic and international law, and vice versa. In short, guaranteeing parties' access to the judiciary and the equality of arms between the parties would be necessary aims of any adjudicatory system, whether national or international, as these are normally understood in the present. Of course, jurisdiction in international law must

would require impermissible amendments to ICSID arbitration rules. See paras. 166–262.

[61] Article 52, (b) and (d), ICSID Convention.

be attributed to the tribunal by the very states that will be subject to it later. However, few people would disagree with the general proposition that international courts should protect their own jurisdiction, provided it exists – thus guaranteeing party access to the courts – and exercise that jurisdiction in a thoroughly impartial and fair manner towards the parties. Using this general proposition as a starting point, it follows that forum shopping may be an issue in international adjudication to the extent that it tips the balance between the enabling and the protective functions of international procedural norms.

From the standpoint of a typical proceeding where forum shopping is argued to have taken place, respondents will try to fight the forum selection, or the parallel or serial litigation strategy, employed by the complainant. To that effect, respondents will downplay the enabling function of procedural norms. In other words, respondents will try to convince the tribunal that the complainant should not have access to the courtroom. Secondly, respondents will emphasize the protective function to their own benefit, disqualifying the complainant's selection and strategy. Complainants, to the contrary, will focus their arguments on the need to be granted court access and on their own autonomy when it comes to forum selection and litigation strategy, thus emphasizing the enabling function. The specific procedural principles and rules at stake will be major factors to decide on that quarrel. Abstractly, however, the adjudicator's actual decision-making can be depicted through a scale which ranges from (*a*) maximum freedom of choice to the complainant and minimum concern over fairness to the defendant, to (*z*) minimum freedom of choice to the complainant and maximum concern over fairness to the defendant.[62] The more that judges emphasize freedom of choice, as in (*a*), the less they will perceive forum shopping as being problematic. Conversely, the more that judges lean toward point (*z*), the more that forum shopping will raise fairness-related issues to the judges. Therefore, while the final balance between the enabling function that the complainant will normally emphasize and the protective function that the respondent

[62] See also *Case Concerning Border and Transborder Armed Actions (Nicaragua* v. *Honduras)*, Jurisdiction and Admissibility, Judgment of 20 December 1988, Declaration of Judge Lachs: "In taking these decisions [on issues of procedure, i.e., jurisdiction and admissibility], this Court has to exercise the utmost care to discourage attempts to resort to it in any case lacking a proper jurisdictional foundation, but at the same time not to deny States their right to benefit from its decision where such a jurisdictional foundation does exist. Sometimes the mere opening of the door may bring about a solution to a dispute."

will normally emphasize is relative, forum shopping has a potential to upset the protective function of procedural norms in international adjudication.

Complainants may find a "friendly forum" to litigate the whole dispute or a forum that becomes just friendly enough if they slice a broad dispute into pieces and litigate only one parcel of the whole controversy there. In those cases, though the forum seized can be in principle unbiased and independent, and even discounting the possibility that findings of fact might vary depending on evidentiary issues specific to each court, the forum can still be "friendly" in the sense that the law primarily enforceable by it is biased toward the complainant. Moreover, the complainant was entitled to choose the battleground in the first place. This could lead to unreasonable outcomes, which in turn could undermine the authority of the decision maker and the effectiveness of adjudication.[63] Such possibility also calls for a balance between complainants' autonomy to select the forum and fairness considerations. Fairness implies that similar cases should have similar outcomes.[64] On the other hand, if shopping always works, it means that international law and adjudication is susceptible to potentially capricious manipulation by its subjects. That could impair the aura of impartiality on which rest to a great extent the legitimacy and authority of international adjudication.

Consider *Canada – Periodicals*,[65] a WTO dispute where the United States successfully challenged certain measures by Canada that were discriminatory toward foreign periodicals. For present purposes, it is important to mention one element that was never an issue before the WTO panel or the Appellate Body, namely, NAFTA Article 2106, which states:

> Notwithstanding any other provision of this Agreement, as between Canada and the United States, any measure adopted or maintained with respect to cultural industries … shall be governed under this Agreement exclusively.[66]

[63] See generally Mattias Kumm, 'The Legitimacy of International Law: A Framework of Analysis,' 15 *EJIL* (2004) 907 (at 927, arguing that outcome reasonableness is one factor affecting the legitimacy of international law).

[64] See generally John Rawls, *A Theory of Justice* (Cambridge, MA: Harvard University Press, 1971).

[65] Appellate Body Report, *Canada – Certain Measures Concerning Periodicals*, WT/DS31/AB/R, adopted 30 July 1997, DSR 1997:I, 449; Panel Report, WT/DS31/R and Corr.1, adopted 30 July 1997, as modified by Appellate Body Report WT/DS31/AB/R.

[66] Article 2106, NAFTA.

Article 2106 also incorporates the provisions of the Canada–United States Free Trade Agreement, Article 2005(1) of which reads: "Cultural industries are exempt from the provisions of this Agreement"[67] Thus, Article 2106 arguably carves cultural industries out of the disciplines on national treatment and quantitative restrictions under NAFTA[68] and provides that measures with respect to cultural industries shall be governed exclusively under NAFTA. One could also argue that Article 2106 exempts cultural industries from both the WTO and NAFTA dispute settlement, in light of the broad exclusionary language in it.[69] Pursuant to NAFTA Article 103(2), NAFTA prevails over the General Agreement on Tariffs and Trade (GATT) in cases of inconsistency between the two agreements. Consequently, it is reasonable to speculate that, had the United States brought the *Periodicals* dispute under NAFTA, the outcome of the case would have been the opposite of the WTO's decision.[70] Along these lines, the United States' securing of the

[67] Article 2107(a), NAFTA in turn defines cultural industries as persons engaged in "the publication, distribution, or sale of books, magazines, periodicals, or newspapers in print or machine readable form but not including the sole activity of printing or typesetting any of the foregoing." Article 2106 would be therefore applicable to the bilateral dispute on periodicals between Canada and the United States. The point of debate would be whether the NAFTA exception is restricted to NAFTA or whether it extends to United States–Canada relations as determined in other agreements. Note, in this respect, that Article 103(2), NAFTA, entitled "Relation to Other Agreements," establishes: "In the event of any inconsistency between this Agreement and such other Agreements [the GATT and other agreements to which such Parties are party], this Agreement shall prevail to the extent of the inconsistency..."

[68] Granted, at the same time, Canada's WTO commitments apply on a most-favored-nation (MFN) basis and do not include a similar carve-out.

[69] Note that Article 2106 speaks of "any other provision of this Agreement," which would cover all provisions. This reasoning finds support in the interpretation of the *Canfor* tribunal under Article 1901(3) of the NAFTA, which interpreted comparable exclusionary language therein as covering also dispute settlement. See *Canfor Corporation* v. *United States*, Decision on Preliminary Question, Ad hoc Arbitral Tribunal under UNCITRAL Rules, 6 June 2006, holding that Article 1901(3) of the NAFTA "in the absence of any express provision to the contrary, encompasses all obligations stemming from Chapter Eleven, including those related to dispute settlement (para. 273)."

[70] Critics of the decision in *Periodicals* have noted with dismay that the disparity of obligations on cultural industries in the multilateral and regional framework, in effect, renders the NAFTA exception void (see Aaron Scow, 'The Sports Illustrated Canada Controversy: Canada Strikes Out in its Bid to Protect its Periodical Industry from U.S. Split Run Periodicals,' 7 *Minn JGT* (1998) 245, at 284; Chi Carmody, 'When "Cultural Identity Was Not at Issue": Thinking About *Canada – Certain Measures Concerning Periodicals*' 30 *L Policy Int' Bus* (1999) 231. This position, however, assumes that the applicable law in WTO proceedings is limited to WTO law. This book

"friendlier" WTO forum may have determined its success and, conversely, Canada's defeat.

Now take *Mexico – Taxes on Soft Drinks*, a dispute that started with the squabble between Mexico and the United States concerning sugar quotas purportedly allocated to Mexico under NAFTA. When Mexico requested a NAFTA panel to enforce its alleged quota rights under that agreement, the procedure stalled in the panel selection stage. According to Mexico, the United States simply refused to appoint panelists in violation of NAFTA. To retaliate against this state of affairs, Mexico imposed a discriminatory tax on United States' soft drinks. Subsequently, the United States challenged the tax at the WTO, not NAFTA. At the WTO, Mexico tried to convince the panel and the Appellate Body that it would not be appropriate to decide the dispute there. Both the panel and the Appellate Body sided with the United States, while Mexico's claims under NAFTA remain undecided.[71]

Thus, in both *Canada – Periodicals* and *Mexico – Taxes on Soft Drinks*, the enabling function of WTO procedural rules clearly prevailed over NAFTA. So did the complainant. However, from a source-legitimacy or a process-legitimacy perspective, one could question whether Canada and Mexico should not have been able to avoid the "WTO-only" outcomes. These examples demonstrate that forum shopping may risk undermining the protective function of procedural norms. However, because from a procedural standpoint the respondent and the complainant are likely to battle over the protective and enabling aspects of procedural norms – the respondent underscoring the protective function, the complainant underscoring the enabling function – forum shopping can be pictured in a dynamic context through the complainant's autonomy scale suggested above: from (*a*) maximum freedom of choice to the complainant and minimum concern over fairness to the defendant, related to the enabling function of procedural norms; to (*z*) minimum freedom of choice to the complainant and maximum concern over fairness to the defendant, related to the protective function.

subscribes to the view that the applicable law in WTO dispute settlement is not restricted to WTO law (see discussion in Chapter 4). While the United States' strategy made it less straightforward for Canada to justify its measures, Canada still had a strong case that the NAFTA cultural exception prevailed over the GATT's obligations at play as *lex specialis* in bilateral disputes with the United States. Let it be clear that Canada did not construe its case this way.

71 See Joost Pauwelyn, 'Adding Sweeteners to Softwood Lumber: The WTO-NAFTA Spaghetti Bowl is Cooking,' 9 *JIEL* (2006) 197.

1.3.3 The allocative function of procedural norms in a dynamic context: a system-based versus a regime-based approach to international tribunals

In addition to impairing the delegation and protective function of procedural norms, forum shopping can upset such rules' allocative function. Put differently, shopping has the potential to disturb the judicial system. However, the allocative function is generally less developed in international than in domestic law. Therefore, while a more straightforward analogy can be made to domestic legal systems as to the enabling and protective functions of procedural norms, the analogy is more subtle when it comes to the allocative function. As has been mentioned before, and contrary to most domestic legal systems, international law usually lacks a top-down division of labor among tribunals. The international judiciary is such that the authority of each body is limited by its own governing instruments, and there is no general statute defining the authority of tribunals in relation to each other. Accordingly, if there is no system in the first place, forum shopping cannot threaten any "system."[72] The questions then arise, to name only a few: (i) do investor-state tribunals operating under different bilateral investment treaties belong to the same investment system?;[73] (ii) do MERCOSUR tribunals and WTO panels operate in the same system?;[74] (iii) do an arbitral tribunal and the ECJ operate in the same system?;[75] and (iv) do WTO panels disagreeing with an earlier WTO Appellate Body report operate in the same system?[76] Put broadly, when one assesses systemic

[72] See Kingsbury, 'Is Proliferation a Systemic Problem?' at 692.

[73] Compare *Lauder* v. *Czech Republic*, Arbitral Tribunal under UNCITRAL Rules, 3 September 2001 with *CME Czech Republic B.V. (The Netherlands)* v. *Czech Republic*, Arbitral Tribunal under UNCITRAL Rules, Partial Award, 13 September 2001 (reaching different conclusions on the merits of claims arising from the same measures).

[74] See Appellate Body Report, *Brazil – Measures Affecting Imports of Retreaded Tyres*, WT/DS332/AB/R, adopted 17 December 2007 (considering that exempting Uruguayan imports pursuant to a MERCOSUR ruling led to "arbitrary or unjustifiable" discrimination in the application of Brazil's import ban under GATT, Article XX); Panel Report, *Argentina – Definitive Anti-Dumping Duties on Poultry from Brazil*, WT/DS241/R, adopted 19 May 2003 (accepting that the same measure be challenged sequentially before a MERCOSUR arbitral tribunal under the Protocol of Brasilia, and WTO dispute settlement).

[75] Compare *Iron Rhine Railway (Belgium* v. *The Netherlands)*, Arbitral Award, 24 May 2005 (deciding a dispute between two European Union member states) with *MOX Plant Case (Ireland* v. *United Kingdom)*, terminated 6 June 2008, (declining to decide on a dispute between two European Union member states).

[76] Compare Panel Report, *United States – Final Ant-Dumping Measures on Stainless Steel from Mexico*, WT/DS344/R (deciding the panel had "no option but to respectfully

concerns originating in forum shopping, the question of whether international tribunals comprise a system plays a significant role.

Unsurprisingly, scholars, parties, and judges may have diverse and diverging views on this question. To put it into context, it is useful again to refer to a scale rather than to a fixed point. This time, the scale ranges from unity to diversity, or from a full-fledged judicial system to sealed-off individual tribunals. The more systemic and holistic one's approach to international tribunals, the more forum shopping will raise concerns and, in turn, call for systemic solutions.

International tribunals are obviously far from comprehensive systematization, but this precludes neither the emergence of systemic elements nor the presence of systemic considerations. Crucially, systematization is not only about looking for a pyramidal structure of institutions and rules. It can also happen through different configurations and progressive, bottom-up organization. In the words of Abi-Saab, a cumulative process may with time "condense and crystallize the different particles of consensual or authoritative jurisdictional empowerment into a certain structure."[77] Indeed, some notion of a system is considered to be endemic to the very idea of law, and international law is itself depicted as a system[78] – although that does not

disagree with the line of reasoning developed by the Appellate Body regarding the WTO-consistency of simple zeroing in periodic reviews"), with Panel Report, *United States – Measures Relating to Zeroing and Sunset Reviews*, WT/DS322/R, and Appellate Body Report, *United States – Measures Relating to Zeroing and Sunset Reviews*, WT/DS322/AB/R, adopted 23 January 2007 (the Panel considering that "simple zeroing" is permissible, the Appellate Body considering it is not). The Appellate Body reversed the Panel's findings in *US – Stainless Steel (Mexico)*, noting: "We are deeply concerned about the Panel's decision to depart from well-established Appellate Body jurisprudence clarifying the interpretation of the same legal issues. The Panel's approach has serious implications for the proper functioning of the WTO dispute settlement system." See Appellate Body Report, *US – Stainless Steel (Mexico)*, WT/DS344/AB/R, adopted 20 May 2008, para. 162. "Ensuring 'security and predictability' in the dispute settlement system, as contemplated in Article 3(2) of the DSU, implies that, absent cogent reasons, an adjudicatory body will resolve the same legal question in the same way in a subsequent case." *Ibid.*, at para. 160.

[77] Georges Abi-Saab, 'Fragmentation or Unification: Some Concluding Remarks,' 31 *NYUJILP* (1999) 919, at 927. Abi-Saab draws his argument from the fact that international law, in the absence of a unified "legislative power," was able to develop a "legislative process." See also Georges Abi-Saab, 'La coutume dans tous ses états, ou le dilemme du développement du droit international dans un monde éclaté,' in Ronald S. J. Macdonald (ed.), *International Law at the Time of its Codification: Essays in Honour of Roberto Ago*, (Milano: Giuffrè, 1987) 53.

[78] See International Law Commission, 'Fragmentation of International Law: Difficulties Arising from the Diversification and Expansion of International Law' (2006), Report of the Study Group, UN doc. A/CN.4/L.682.

mean everyone agrees on the exact contours of such system. At any rate, if international law is a system of norms, how could international courts and tribunals, which are set up and function pursuant to international law, be completely nonsystemic?

Even from a relatively weak systemic perspective, if international norms are systemically related, if and when those norms control forum shopping, they should apply across the international judiciary, regardless of the possible lack of a comprehensive system of jurisdiction. In this sense, an allocative function of procedural norms can also be found, albeit in various degrees, in international law. It is present, at a bare minimum, when specific norms that limit forum selection and parallel and serial litigation are applicable to the case at hand. As will be seen throughout the remainder of this book, in spite of the absence of a constitution or code of procedure defining the relationships between the whole set of international tribunals, certain constitutive instruments and other treaties do contain norms of those types. For instance, there are exclusive jurisdiction clauses, such as Article 344 of the Treaty on the Functioning of the European Union (formerly Article 292 of the Treaty Establishing the European Community), or clauses establishing default jurisdiction, which provide that a tribunal should not decide a dispute that could be submitted to another mechanism, such as Article 282 of the UNCLOS.[79] When in force, those clauses are part of the procedural framework setting the relationship among the parties, between the parties and the relevant tribunals, or among tribunals. Such norms have the ability to prevent a party from unilaterally forcing a ruling of merit upon another and may thus be conceived as a brake on forum shopping. Parties are entitled to invoke these norms, and adjudicators should apply them. To admit the contrary would be to say that a party may agree that it will not do something, while allowing that party to do that which it has already committed not to do. This would render that party's previous commitment meaningless and would contradict international law's most basic rule that *pacta sunt servanda*. In a nutshell, a call for a cosmopolitan

[79] See discussion in Chapter 7; Article 344, Treaty on the Functioning of the EU. Article 344 is the equivalent of Article 292, Treaty Establishing the European Community (EC Treaty). Throughout this study, reference is made primarily to Article 292 because this was the provision at stake in the cases discussed herein. Where discussed outside the context of specific past cases, Article 344 is referred to as Article 344 (formerly Article 292), and the reference points to the Treaty on the Functioning of the EU.

attitude toward procedural norms ultimately stems from the obligation to respect prior commitments in good faith as a mediating principle of the relationship between the parties to a dispute and, in turn, of their relationship before international tribunals.

Furthermore, the lack of comprehensive systematization in international law does not of necessity overshadow the appropriateness of at least some coordination. In this sense, the previously mentioned scale balancing freedom of choice of the complainant against fairness to the defendant is related to, but not dependent upon, the systemic question dealt with here. Moreover, the use of conflict-of-laws coordination techniques by different domestic legal systems in transnational litigation further indicates that a closely integrated system need not be the main condition, let alone a *sine qua non* for coping with forum shopping. In this sense, although the systemic question influences the concerns over forum shopping, it does not invariably void those concerns, the need for solutions to them, or the availability of some techniques to address them.[80]

1.3.4 *Systemic- and party-driven concerns arising from conflicting rulings: the question of mutually (in)consistent rulings*

Setting aside the systemic question discussed above, a key situation where coordination is clearly indicated takes place where there is a risk of conflicting decisions between any two tribunals in cases involving the same parties. There is a debate over whether inconsistent decisions risk impairing the functioning of the international judiciary[81] or lead to self-correction throughout the system and in turn to better decisions.[82] This debate demonstrates again that the risks of forum shopping, as with other legal phenomena, may largely depend on the eye of the beholder. And again, the adequacy of the system-versus-regime scale, as opposed to a fixed perspective, is on point. Nonetheless, even if no system is found to exist, and if the concern of systemic stability therefore does not arise, there is a concrete and immediate concern that the parties may be left with inconsistent rulings which do not

[80] See generally Ralf Michaels and Joost Pauwelyn, 'Conflicts of Norms or Conflicts of Law? Different Techniques in the Fragmentation of International Law,' 22 *Duke J Comp & Int'l L* (2012) 349; Campbell McLachlan, Lis Pendens *in International Litigation* (Leiden: Martinus Nijhoff, 2009).

[81] See Gilbert Guillaume, 'Proliferation of International Courts: a Blueprint for Action,' 2 *JI Crim Just* (2004) 300.

[82] See Cogan, 'Competition and Control.'

settle the dispute between them.[83] This problem is further amplified in international law, which lacks a supreme court to settle inconsistent decisions. At best, conflicting decisions mean that parties will face their original dispute once again, after having spent resources to settle it.[84] Or worse, conflicting decisions may drag the parties into new disputes. The party-centered concern over inconsistent rulings may, therefore, take precedence over the system-based concern.[85] It is submitted that such concerns provide another key reason for respondents to react to forum shopping, and for adjudicators to deal with it.

The situation Ireland and the United Kingdom faced with regard to the *Access to Information* arbitration and the *MOX Plant* case is illustrative. Ireland triggered the *Access to Information* proceedings first, and subsequently, the UNCLOS *MOX Plant* proceedings. When Ireland's request for provisional measures in *MOX Plant* reached the ITLOS, the proceedings under the Convention for the Protection of the Marine Environment of the North-East Atlantic (OSPAR Convention) were already under way. The ITLOS quickly prescribed provisional measures exhorting Ireland and the United Kingdom to "cooperate" and "enter into consultations forthwith," in order to, inter alia, "exchange further *information* with regard to possible consequences for the Irish Sea arising out of the commissioning of the MOX plant."[86] Nevertheless, the parallel OSPAR arbitral proceeding involved Ireland's alleged *right to information* under Article 9 of the OSPAR Convention. Granted, the OSPAR dispute did not refer to any information on the plant's impact on the Irish Sea. Rather, it referred to specific information contained in certain consultation reports, under the scope of Article 9(2) of the OSPAR Convention. Yet, the disputed right to information in the OSPAR

[83] As Giles Cuniberti puts it: "[T]he existence of conflicting decisions in different legal orders can cause harm… [T]he situation of the parties will be intolerable, with each of them in danger of being deprived in one place of what it has been awarded in another." Giles Cuniberti, 'Parallel Litigation and Foreign Investment Dispute Settlement,' 21 *ICSID Rev* (2006) 381, at 421.

[84] See generally Torbjörn Andersson, 'Parallel and Conflicting Enforcement of Law,' in Torbjörn Andersson (ed.), *Parallel and Conflicting Enforcement of Law* (The Hague: Martinus Nijhoff, 2005) 18.

[85] Cuniberti, 'Parallel Litigation,' at 395–6 (arguing that inconsistencies and the absence of settlement can be more fundamental a problem than the concern with intra-systemic coherence, and therefore submitting that mechanisms should be available to avoid inconsistent decisions even across different systems).

[86] *The MOX Plant Case (Ireland v. United Kingdom)*, ITLOS Case No 10, Order on Provisional Measures, 3 December 2001, para. 89 (emphasis added).

Convention, established in Article 9(2), refers to "*any information* ... on the state of the maritime area, *on activities or measures adversely affecting or likely to affect it*."[87] The overlap between the ITLOS order and the text of the provision at stake in the OSPAR arbitration is thus clear.

One might wonder about the effect of the ITLOS order on provisional measures – asking the parties to cooperate by exchanging information about the plant's impact on the Irish Sea – on related proceedings where the obligation to make available information of allegedly the same character was the core of the dispute. The ITLOS based its order on the fact that "prudence and caution" required the parties to "cooperate in exchanging information concerning risks or effects of the operation of the MOX plant."[88] For its part, the OSPAR tribunal considered in its final decision that the specific information Ireland sought in the OSPAR dispute did not fall under the scope of Article 9(2) of the OSPAR Convention. The two orders could then be made mutually coherent: on the one hand, the parties were required to exchange information on the plant's impact on the Irish Sea pursuant to the ITLOS order; on the other hand, the United Kingdom was not required to provide the specific information to which the OSPAR dispute refers. However, at least from 3 December 2001 (when the ITLOS issued its order) to 2 July 2003 (the date of the OSPAR tribunal's final award) the situation was completely unclear. During this lapse, Ireland could use the ITLOS order to insist on the United Kingdom's cooperation with respect to matters that were under analysis before a different forum.

In conclusion, in addition to the legitimacy questions related to delegation, forum shopping may raise concerns depending on a specific balance that involves (i) the level of freedom of choice of the complainant versus fairness to the defendant, (ii) systemic versus regime-based considerations, and (iii) the risk of conflicting decisions. Where the risk of conflicting rulings is present, in particular, inter-systemic solutions should be explored. Generally, the more one emphasizes freedom of choice and adopts a regime-based approach, the fewer concerns forum shopping will raise. Conversely, the more one underscores fairness-to-the-defendant concerns and a systemic approach to international tribunals, the more forum shopping will be considered to be problematic.

[87] Article 9(2), OSPAR Convention (emphasis added). See *Access to Information under Article 9 of the OSPAR Convention (Ireland v. United Kingdom)*, Arbitral Award, 2 July 2003.

[88] *The MOX Plant Case*, Order on Provisional Measures, para. 84.

1.4 Concluding remarks

Forum shopping is a corollary to multiple jurisdictional or venue options and the rational behavior of international law's subjects. It is likely to remain a phenomenon of concern for international lawyers in the medium-to-long term given the spread of international tribunals with specific and automatic jurisdiction and the rise of private parties as forces capable of reaching the litigation arenas on their own or through their influence upon states, while the consensual substratum of international law remains. These developments are themselves part of a broader phenomenon of the fragmentation of law, stemming from functional differentiation of society and the law.

Forum shopping remains relatively unregulated, and comes about in many different shapes. It need not necessarily be considered a problem for adjudicators every time respondents try to characterize it as such. The assessment of forum shopping is relatively indeterminate, and this implies that it will normally take place by reference to the use of broad principles. The scales referred to above suffice to make clear that all-encompassing formulas to understand and cope with forum shopping are hardly available. On the other hand, forum shopping does raise legitimacy concerns when the delegation function of procedural norms is undermined; fairness concerns when the delicate equilibrium between the complainant's freedom of choice (enabling function of procedural norms) and protection to the defendant (protective function of procedural norms) is upset; and systemic concerns when the balance between the autonomy and integration of international tribunals (allocative function of procedural norms) is disrupted. Another chief, party-driven concern independent from one's systemic inclinations is the risk of conflicting decisions, since it threatens not only the legal system as such, but also the concrete situation of the parties in dispute.

In conclusion, forum shopping strategies pose challenges for international adjudicators and this may, in turn, call for means to resolve such challenges. The stage is thus set for the next chapter to suggest procedure as the arena where adjudicators and parties grapple with the challenges of forum shopping; and for the remainder of the book to look into the technique of preliminary objections as a focal tool for coordinating the overlapping work of different international tribunals.

2 Forum shopping and procedure

2.1 Introduction

Chapter 1 presented the conditions for a rise of forum shopping in international adjudication: the multiplication of international tribunals with automatic jurisdiction and an increasing propensity to litigate in the context of an emergence of non-state actors. It also pointed to concerns that surface with the rise in forum shopping, by focusing on the functions of procedural norms. It argued that, in addition to tactical concerns for respondents, forum shopping raises questions of delegation, fairness, allocation, systemic-integrity, and consistency. Against that background, the bulk of this study outlines a procedural framework for parties and adjudicators to tackle forum shopping strategies and to implement procedural coordination – with reference to preliminary objections.

A procedural approach to the question of how forum shopping is assessed and addressed in international adjudication can be justified by a two-step exercise of progressive approximation. First, and more generally, a procedural perspective such as the one adopted here is relatively uncommon in the scholarship. Given that this is the case, it is particularly important to provide a concept of procedure and to discuss the promise and limits of this book's approach. Second, and more specifically, there has been no articulation of the coordinative role of preliminary objections in the present context of multiple international tribunals with overlapping jurisdictions. Consequently, joining a discussion of forum shopping and an account of preliminary objections in the current landscape of international adjudication provides an opportunity to offer fresh insights on both the phenomenon under study (forum shopping) and this major technique of international litigation (preliminary objections).

This chapter contextualizes the framework enunciated in this book by delineating a notion of procedure, and explains the relevance and limitations of this book's option to approach forum shopping from a procedural perspective centered on preliminary objections. It includes four sections after this introduction. Section 2.2 presents the concept of procedure that will be used as a basis to conceptualize preliminary questions and objections in Chapter 3. The concept of procedure is grounded in the notions of jurisdiction, action, and procedure in a narrow sense. Section 2.3 posits that the connection of forum shopping and procedure sheds light on the so far dormant role of preliminary objections as transmission belts of procedure-regulating norms. Yet, a focus on procedure has limited reach and does not as such determine one's approach to forum shopping and specific preliminary objections. As a result, whereas this book is not about the role of judicial politics, policies, and preferences in the assessment of forum shopping and quest for solutions to it, it is necessary to recognize that such elements play a role. To that effect, Section 2.4 acknowledges some limitations of the current focus and restates this book's ambitions. The Section then briefly describes three levels at which policy perspectives (that this book does not fully articulate) can be relevant. Section 2.5 offers concluding remarks.

2.2 Procedure

Generations of scholars have painted procedure as a *vieux parent pauvre* in international law's family. In 1935, Abraham Feller described international procedure as the "Antarctica of international law."[1] Forty-five years later, V. S. Mani concurred that "few attempts have been made in the past to study international procedure as such,"[2] and in 1996, Hugh Thirlway asserted that "[t]he law governing international judicial procedure has not been a subject of wide general interest."[3] Cesare Romano reiterated in 2007 that "the law

[1] Abraham Feller, *The Mexican Claims Commissions, 1923–1934: A Study in the Law and Procedure of International Tribunals* (New York: Macmillan, 1935), vii.

[2] V. S. Mani, *International Adjudication: Procedural Aspects* (Leiden: Martinus Nijhoff, 1980), xv.

[3] Hugh Thirlway, 'Procedural Law and the International Court of Justice,' in Vaughan Lowe and M. Fitzmaurice (eds.), *Fifty Years of the International Court of Justice: Essays in Honour of Robert Jennings* (Cambridge University Press, 1996) 394, at 394.

and procedure of international dispute settlement has long been the Cinderella of international law, neglected both by mainstream international legal scholarship and diplomats," opining that the mechanics of procedure "have understandably less appeal to scholars than does research into substantive international law."[4] In a 2012 paper, Andre Nollkaemper argues that "the distinction between the procedure and substance of international law is under-studied and under-theorized ... the question of where the dividing line lies, and how they are connected, is usually neglected."[5] To return to Feller's allegory in the light of the subsequent quotes above, then, it would not seem a great exaggeration to say that international procedure is still our Antarctica – no longer uncharted territory by any means, but still relatively unexplored when compared to other objects of study in international law. The present option to address forum shopping with reference to preliminary objections is motivated by the relative lack of exploration of procedures in international law's scholarship.

This approach calls for at least a rough concept of procedure in the context of international adjudication to frame the study. Crucially, the concept of procedure adopted here offers a base for conceptualizing preliminary questions and objections in a manner that covers the myriad international tribunals from a general standpoint. In the context of adjudication, procedure in its broad sense (*la procédure*) can be conceptualized as the set of principles and rules that govern the adjudicatory process.[6] Procedure is a method that comprises three basic and interrelated juridical notions that a procedural relationship entails:

[4] Cesare Romano, 'The Shift from the Consensual to the Compulsory Paradigm in International Adjudication: Elements for a Theory of Consent,' 39 *NYUJILP* (2007) 791, at 868.

[5] Andre Nollkaemper, 'International Adjudication of Global Public Goods: The Intersection of Substance and Procedure,' 9 Shares Research Paper (2012), ACIL 2012–08, at 4.

[6] See also Robert Kolb, 'General Principles of Procedural Law,' in Andreas Zimmermann *et al.*, *The Statute of the International Court of Justice: A Commentary* (Oxford University Press, 2009) 793, conceptualizing procedure as the "rules related to international judicial action" (at 795); and Chester Brown, *A Common Law of International Adjudication* (Oxford University Press, 2007), conceptualizing procedure as including "all elements of the adjudicatory process other than the application of primary rules of international law which determine the rights and obligations in dispute, and the application of secondary rules of international law which determines the consequences of breaches of primary rules" (at 8).

jurisdiction (*juridiction*), action or suit (*l'action*), and procedure in a narrow sense[7] (*l'instance*).[8]

Adjudicatory jurisdiction consists of the authority of third-party adjudicators to state the law with the objective of settling disputes by resolving claims submitted to them.[9] It is a delegated, inert and substitutive power. It is delegated, since it is based on consent. It is inert, for one of the parties must push for or provoke its exercise by requesting a solution to a grievance. It is substitutive in the sense that adjudication is conducted with a view to settling a dispute in lieu of the (frustrated) efforts by the parties in dispute toward directly agreeing upon a solution to their grievance. Adjudicatory jurisdiction is thus exercised to the extent that it has been granted and put in motion, and so long as there is a dispute.

Action, in turn, refers to the entitlement to bring a claim, counterclaim, objection, or defense before the adjudicator. The action is correlative with adjudicators' duty to exercise jurisdiction, provided that the conditions for acting have been met. Proper action – and fulfilling requirements related to jurisdiction and procedure in a narrow sense – implies an entitlement to a response in the form of a decision, judgment, or award. However, being entitled to a response has no bearing on the content of the decision. As a result, the requirements of the action have a different function than, and are analytically separable from, the conditions that one must fulfill for one's claim to be positively or negatively answered by an adjudicator.[10] In other words, the entitlement to act is autonomous from the (potential) determination that a claim or submission is well- or ill-founded.[11]

[7] Procedure in a narrow sense should be distinguished from procedure understood in a broad sense. One's definition of "procedure" has many practical implications. For instance, it influences the determination of tribunals' delegated powers to frame procedural rules or adopt procedural decisions: Article 30, ICJ Statute states that the Court "shall lay down rules of procedure"; Article 17(9), DSU states that "working procedures shall be drawn up by the Appellate Body"; and Article 44, ICSID Convention states that "if any question of procedure arises which is not covered by this Section or the Arbitration Rules or any rules agreed by the parties, the Tribunal shall decide the question." The definition of procedure is directly relevant for the interpretation of such provisions.

[8] See also Georges Abi-Saab, *Les exceptions préliminaires dans la procédure de la Cour Internationale* (Paris: Pedone, 1967), who adopted a tridimensional view of procedure substantially similar to the one espoused here.

[9] See discussion in Chapter 4.

[10] See also Gaetano Morelli, 'La théorie générale du procès international,' 61 *Recueil des Cours* III (1937) 253–373, at 363 (emphasizing the autonomy of the action from the rights claimed).

[11] See, for example, *South West Africa Cases (Ethiopia* v. *South Africa) (Liberia* v. *South Africa)*, Second Phase, Judgment of 18 July 1966, para. 64: "It is a universal and

Finally, procedure in a narrow sense covers the acts and stages connected to the evolution of the procedural relationship, which includes the series of concatenated acts and phases normally beginning with the *seisin* of the tribunal (*la saisine*) and terminating with the final decision by the adjudicator (a definitive judgment or award).[12] Procedure in a narrow sense links the action and the exercise of jurisdiction on the one hand, and the adjudicators and parties on the other hand. Procedural requirements play out in the context of procedure in a narrow sense, which is the main *locus* of the procedural relationship. In short, if a matter relates to jurisdiction, action, or procedure in a narrow sense, it is a procedural matter. This book focuses on such matters, in particular, on preliminary objections – which target those matters – in the context of forum shopping.

European and Latin-American lawyers trained in civil procedural law are familiar with tridimensional conceptions of procedure that are grounded in the notions of jurisdiction, action, and procedure in a narrow sense along the lines of the concept sketched above.[13] During the nineteenth and into the early twentieth century, procedure gradually emerged as an autonomous concept and object of study in many continental European countries.[14] For a long time, the entitlement to an action in law was still drawn in the rightfulness of one's claim.[15] Around the middle of the nineteenth century, a number of scholars began to argue for a conceptual separation between the right to an action in law and the right to have one's claimed right recognized or remedied.[16] With this separation, and once the use of the notions of jurisdiction, action, and procedure in a narrow sense as elements of

necessary, but yet almost elementary principle of procedural law that a distinction has to be made between, on the one hand, *the right to activate a court* and the right of the court to examine the merits of the claim, and, on the other, the plaintiff party's legal right in respect of the subject-matter of that which it claims, which would have to be established to the satisfaction of the Court" (emphasis added).

12 See also Kolb, 'General Principles,' at 796.

13 See, for example, Antonio Carlos Cintra *et al.*, *Teoria Geral do Processo*, 28th edn (São Paulo: Malheiros, 2012); Serge Guinchard *et al.*, *Procédure Civile: Droit interne et droit communautaire*, 29th edn (Paris: Dalloz, 2008); José Ramiro Podetti, *Teoría y Técnica del Proceso Civil y Trilogía Estructural de la Ciencia del Proceso Civil* (Buenos Aires: Ediar, 1963).

14 The turning point would have been the separation between the concept of action from the substantive right, claimed by German scholars. Such separation is often attributed to Bernhard Windscheid and Theodor Muther (1856) and Oskar Von Bülow (1868). For nomination of the main scholars and works, see, for example, Cândido Rangel Dinamarco, *Instituições de Direito Processual Civil*, 4th edn (São Paulo: Malheiros, 2004), at 257–271.

15 See, for example, Guinchard *et al.*, *Procédure Civile*, at 126, for a short discussion.

16 See n. 14 above.

the concept of procedure or as entailed in a procedural relationship was progressively adopted into the mainstream, the notion of procedure gained density. That analytical armor gradually liberated domestic law proceduralists to study procedure as an object, and enabled the development of procedure-focused scholarship and doctrine in many civil law countries.

The notion of procedure suggested above will be used to anchor the concept of preliminary questions as "questions of procedure" or questions that refer to the requirements for the existence and development of an adjudicatory process, as discussed in Chapter 3. A concept of procedure along the lines above would arguably retain explanatory value for procedure in common law countries as well, due to the presence across legal systems of adjudication of the three basic legal notions that ground the concept. For the same reason, it is a valuable concept also for international law.[17] Yet, a tridimensional notion of procedure along the lines above does not seem to be typical in English-speaking scholarship and doctrine. Rather, there seems to be a prevailing tendency to discuss the notion of procedure, taken as *procedural law*, directly in contradistinction with the notion of substance, taken as *substantive law*.[18] But, because a dichotomy between procedural law and substantive law is very hard to sustain,[19] this approach arguably makes it difficult for studies devoted to international procedure as such to develop.

Writings of international law scholars sometimes incorporate this deadlock. For instance, Shabtai Rosenne affirms in his treatise that international law recognizes no sharp distinction between procedural law and substantive law. The reason for this, according to Rosenne, is that "[i]n so far as regular legal procedures exist for the judicial settlement of international disputes, their norms are indistinguishable, in their creation as to their effect, from those substantive norms through

[17] Granted, the notions of jurisdiction, action, and procedure in a narrow sense must take into account the structure of international adjudication where they operate. For instance, jurisdiction in domestic law does not rest on consensual elements in the same way that it does in international law. For a similar concept of procedure in a broad sense, see Kolb, 'General Principles,' at 795.

[18] See Thomas Main, 'The Procedural Foundation of Substantive Law,' 87 *U Wash L R* (2010) 801; see also Walter Cook, '"Substance" and "Procedure" in the Conflict of Laws,' 42 *Yale L J* (1932) 333. In international law, see, for example, Shabtai Rosenne, *The Law and Practice of the International Court, 1920–2005*, vol. III, 4th edn (Leiden: Martinus Nijhoff, 2006), at 1021–8; see generally, the references in nn. 2–5 above.

[19] See Main, 'The Procedural Foundation'; and the discussion in Chapter 3 for specific examples of the crisscross between procedural law and substantive law, substance and procedure.

the application of which that dispute will be settled."[20] One could add that this is the case not only in international law. In fact, the difficulty of separating procedural and substantive law is an issue in law and adjudication more generally, since both impact outcomes and may derive from the same ultimate sources.[21]

Nonetheless, recognition that procedural and substantive law intersect need not hinder the relevance, let alone the possibility of approaching legal phenomenon from a procedural perspective. While Rosenne is right that there may be common ground between substantive and procedural law in terms of sources and impact, his remarks raise a prior question of whether one needs to look for an overarching dichotomy between procedural law and substantive law as a threshold matter. For present purposes, the pedagogical value of the substance–procedure distinction as a contrast of ideal types is well recognized, and the intuitive element in the distinction roughly delineates the outer limits of the study. But the distinction between procedure and substance is conceived as being context dependent. While the hurdle to draw an ultimate line between procedure and substance even in concrete cases is acknowledged, a concept of procedure based on the notions of jurisdiction, action, and procedure in a narrow sense does not necessarily beg a black-and-white approach to "substantive law" versus "procedural law." Given that the concept of procedure is filled with content (e.g., jurisdiction, action, and procedure in a narrow sense) without begging a procedural–substantive law dichotomy in the first place, the line between procedure and substance can be drawn later – not abstractly but in concrete cases. When it comes to adjudication, as Chapter 3 argues, the distinction between procedure and substance (and thus of preliminary questions and questions of merit) is drawn contextually (and therefore relatively) based on the object of the request. The distinction does not stem from an absolute dichotomy based on the "essence of the norms."

[20] Rosenne, *The Law and Practice*, at 1024 (emphasis added); see also Mani, *International Adjudication*, at xv.

[21] See also Mauro Cappelletti and Briant Garth, 'Introduction: Policies, Trends and Ideas in Civil Procedure, in Mauro Cappelletti (ed.), *International Encyclopaedia of Comparative Law: Civil Procedure* (Leiden: Mohr Siebeck/Martinus Nijhoff, 1988, inst. 24), at 14: "If one tries to argue that procedure becomes substance when it determines the 'outcome' of a legal dispute, then it appears necessary to concede that almost everything is substance. On the other hand, if procedure is confined to the legal methods by which legal claims are initiated and proved, there is little doubt that much of the substantive law governs procedure."

Moreover, while Rosenne is also right that both procedure and substance certainly impact outcomes, these do not impact outcomes in concrete cases in the same way. To touch upon another discussion that Chapter 3 develops, a decision on the merits of the request (e.g., substance) is the ultimate object of the adjudicatory process and the outcome of full-fledged adjudication – where the dispute is settled. As to the requirements under each element in the jurisdiction-action-procedure triad, they can be seen as prerequisites to that ultimate outcome. These requirements are separable from the object of the process and a decision on them does not settle the dispute. To be sure, a tribunal's decision that full-fledged adjudication is not warranted for some reason (e.g., a terminative decision on procedural grounds) is an outcome in itself. But it is an outcome that curtails the adjudicatory process and refers to that process, not to the request. In conclusion, while there might be no abstract, essential dichotomy between procedural and substantive law hanging out there to be discovered, it is possible to fill the notion of procedure with content by referring to the notions of jurisdiction, action, and procedure in a narrow sense. Once the notion of procedure is delineated, the question of separating procedure from substance becomes a case-specific question; that of separating preliminary questions from questions of merit.

2.3 Procedure in the context of forum shopping: a new, emerging role for preliminary objections

The multiplication of international tribunals and the potential concerns this engenders have caught the attention of a number of international lawyers. Different authors have drawn attention to the existence and extent of the phenomenon,[22] and looked at norms to tackle the emerging "conflicts of jurisdiction" associated with jurisdictional overlaps.[23] This book builds on that effort. But, amid the discussion about procedure-regulating norms that may address forum

[22] See especially Cesare Romano, 'The Proliferation of International Judicial Bodies: The Pieces of the Puzzle,' 31 *NYUJILP* (1999) 709. Some scholars adopt a negative tone and refer to the phenomenon as "proliferation" of international tribunals. See, for example, Shane Spelliscy, 'The Proliferation of International Tribunals: A Chink in the Armor,' 40 *Colum J Transnat'l L* (2001) 143; Gilbert Guillaume, 'Proliferation of International Courts: a Blueprint for Action,' 2 *JI Crim Just* (2004) 300.

[23] See especially Yuval Shany, *The Competing Jurisdictions of International Courts and Tribunals* (Oxford University Press, 2003). See also Nicolaos Lavranos, *Jurisdictional Competition: Selected Cases in International and European Law* (Groningen: Europa

shopping, which this book complements and updates, the means and techniques whereby these norms of coordination come into play have been overlooked. As Section 2.2 above pointed out, the relative underdevelopment of a procedural tack in international law is a broader tendency. More specifically with regard to scholarship focused on procedure and on preliminary objections, the predominance of works in the French language, dated more than forty years ago and centering on the International Court of Justice is noticeable.[24] While procedure-focused studies,[25] and more recent studies on preliminary objections before other specific institutions can surely be found,[26] there has been no account of preliminary objections from a generalist standpoint in the current scenario of multiple international tribunals.

Given the practical importance of preliminary objections in international litigation, an overview of this technique would be justifiable in itself. But the phenomenon of forum shopping further justifies a closer look at the role and operation of procedures in this context.

Law, 2009); Andrea Gattini, 'Un regard procédural sur la fragmentation du droit international,' 110 *RGDIP* (2006) 303; Vaughan Lowe, 'Overlapping Jurisdictions in International Courts and Tribunals,' 20 *Australian YBIL* (1999) 191; Joost Pauwelyn and Luiz Eduardo Salles: 'Forum Shopping Before International Tribunals: (Real) Concerns, (Im)Possible Solutions,' 42 *Cornell ILJ* (2009) 77; August Reinisch, 'The Use and Limits of *Res Judicata* and *Lis Pendens* as Procedural Tools to Avoid Conflicting Dispute Settlement Outcomes,' 3 *LPICT* (2004) 37; and, focusing on specific regimes, Laurence Helfer, 'Forum Shopping for Human Rights,' 148 *U Penn L Rev* (1999) 285; Joost Pauwelyn, 'How to a Win World Trade Organization Dispute Based on Non-World Trade Organization Law? Questions of Jurisdiction and Merits,' 37 *JWT* (2003) 997; Kyung Kwak and Gabrielle Marceau, 'Overlaps and Conflicts of Jurisdiction between the World Trade Organization and Regional Trade Agreements,' in Lorand Bartels and Federico Ortino (eds.), *Regional Trade Agreements and the WTO Legal System* (Oxford University Press, 2006) 465; Giles Cuniberti, 'Parallel Litigation and Foreign Investment Dispute Settlement,' 21 *ICSID Rev* (2006) 381.

[24] See, for example, J. Witenberg, 'La Recevabilité des réclamations devant les juridictions internationales,' 41 *Recueil des Cours* III (1932) 1; J. Witenberg, *L'organisation judiciaire, la procédure et la sentence internationales: Traité pratique* (Paris: Pedone, 1937); Morelli, 'La théorie générale du procès international;' Maarten Bos, *Les conditions du procès en droit international public* (Leiden: Brill, 1957); Mohieddine Mabrouk, *Les exceptions de procédure devant les juridictions internationales* (Paris: LGDJ, 1966); and Abi-Saab, *Les exceptions préliminaires*.

[25] See, for example, Kenneth Carlston, *The Process of International Arbitration* (Westport: Greenwood Press, 1946); Mani, *International Adjudication*; and, more recently, Brown, *A Common Law of International Adjudication*.

[26] See, for example, Scott Little, 'Preliminary Objections to Panel Requests and Terms of Reference: Panel and Appellate Body Rulings on the First Line of Defence in WTO Dispute Settlement,' 35 *JWT* (2001) 517; and Jo Pasqualucci, 'Preliminary Objections Before the Inter-American Court of Human Rights: Legitimate Issues and Illegitimate Tactics,' 40 *Va JIL* (1999) 2.

Forum shopping raises procedural issues and is challenged in the context of adjudication, normally through recourse to preliminary objections. Procedure is a filter for forum shopping activity; and jurisdiction, action, and procedure in a narrow sense, around which preliminary questions gravitate, are the elements of this filter. Moreover, forum shopping normally implicates plural institutional settings. Accordingly, a study of forum shopping and the role of preliminary objections can unfold at a broader level of generality. In sum, the fact that forum shopping strategies implicate different tribunals offers an opportunity to take a step back and look at a traditional technique through which parties and adjudicators grapple with it from a broader perspective. Meanwhile, it is possible to draw on, complement, and update the discussion on jurisdictional overlaps with reference to procedure-regulating norms.

2.3.1 Preliminary objections as procedural shields

The discussion of forum shopping anchored on the concept of procedure adopted here brings to light a complementary, emerging role for preliminary objections as transmission belts of procedure-regulating norms across international tribunals with overlapping jurisdictions. The change in context from that of a single tribunal and a single proceeding to that of multiple tribunals and multiple proceedings elicits this development; and stressing this latent role might contribute to dissipating at least some of the embedded antipathy toward the technique of preliminary objections[27] within the "invisible college of international lawyers."[28]

The antipathy is related to the principal, traditional role of preliminary objections as procedural shields in international adjudication, particularly where the conditions for forum shopping described in Chapter 1 do not operate. Throughout the history of international law, in most cases, there was simply no international court to turn to, let alone two with overlapping jurisdictions. In a single tribunal, single proceeding context, preliminary objections prevent or postpone adjudication of a

[27] See, for example, Mabrouk, *Les exceptions de procédure*, at 2; Hugh Thirlway, 'Preliminary Objections' in *Max Planck Encyclopedia of Public International Law* (Oxford University Press, 2007, electronic version), at 28; Pasqualucci, 'Preliminary Objections Before the IACtHR'; Alexander Orakhelashvili, 'The Concept of International Judicial Jurisdiction: A Reappraisal' 3 *LPICT* (2003) 501, at 501.

[28] Oscar Schachter, 'The Invisible College of International Lawyers,' 72 *Nw ULR* (1977) 217.

dispute. This reveals how far international law was and in many cases still is from the desire of a good part of the invisible college to make adjudication before a world court compulsory.[29] On the other hand, the tactical benefit that preliminary objections offer to respondents – delay or termination of the proceedings – is an incentive for their abuse. And this abuse underlies familiar critiques of the technique as a means to obstruct substantive justice and as belittling the role of adjudication in international relations.[30] As Alexander Orakhelashvili synthesizes, these objections may operate as a factor preventing international tribunals from accomplishing the task of providing international justice and maintaining the basic values of the international community, "thereby causing serious concerns for those safeguarded and protected by international law."[31]

This is a valid cautionary note: the abuse of preliminary objections is to be taken seriously. The present study does not challenge qualified statements that procedural requirements may be used in attempts to obstruct substantive justice. However, acknowledging the role of preliminary objections as procedural shields is neither to endorse formalism ineludibly nor to adopt an anti-adjudication bias. Indeed, form is a means, not the objective, of procedure, and therefore proceduralism should not be confused with formalism, in a pejorative sense.[32] Moreover, if procedural and substantive norms, in their creation and

[29] See, for example, Heinhard Steiger, 'Plaidoyer pour une Juridiction Internationale Obligatoire,' in Jerzy Makarczyk (ed.), *Theory of International Law at the Threshold of the 21st Century: Essays In Honour of Krzystof Skubiszweski* (The Hague: Kluwer, 1996) 817; Wilfred Jenks, *The Prospects of International Adjudication* (London: Stevens & Sons, 1964); Hans Kelsen, 'Compulsory Adjudication of International Disputes,' 37 *AJIL* (1943) 397. See also Marcelo Kohen, 'Manifeste pour le droit international du XXIe siècle', in Laurence Boisson de Chazournes and Vera Gowlland (eds.), *The International Legal System in Quest of Equity and Universality:* Liber Amicorum *Georges Abi-Saab* (The Hague: Kluwer, 2001) 123; Antonio Cançado Trindade, *International Law for Humankind: Towards a New* Jus Gentium (Leiden: Martinus Nijhoff, 2010), at 567–591.

[30] See references in n. 27 above.

[31] Orakhelashvili, 'The Concept of International Judicial Jurisdiction,' at 501.

[32] Neither should the present argument about the importance of procedure be construed as an apology of form. International adjudication has arguably an anti-formalist tradition. See, for example, *The Mavrommatis Palestine Concessions*, PCIJ Ser A No 2, Judgment of 30 August 1924, at 34: "The Court, whose jurisdiction is international, is not bound to attach to matters of form the same degree of importance which they might possess in municipal law." See also *Velásquez Rodríguez Case*, Preliminary Objections, Judgment of 26 June 1987, IACtHR Ser C No 1, para. 33; and contrast the above cases to the more recent *ICS Inspection and Control Services Limited v. Argentina*, PCA Case No 2010–09, Award on Jurisdiction under UNCITRAL Rules, 10 February 2010, para. 250.

in their effect are similar, as discussed above, there is aprioristic reason neither to interpret these two sets of norms differently nor to lean toward a restrictive interpretation of jurisdictional requirements in favor of sovereignty.[33]

But, setting aside potential excesses, procedures and procedural requirements are first and foremost guarantors of the regularity and the legitimacy of international adjudication. From a general standpoint, there is broad normative justification for the fact that procedural requirements can obstruct a decision on the merits of a dispute. First, procedures tend to be correlative with, underdetermined by, and calibrated to a (desired) level of substantive protections and guarantees in a given area. This remark by Representative John Dingell in a Congressional hearing in the United States, albeit in a different context, drives the point home for its sharpness: "I'll let you write the substance ... you let me write the procedure, and I'll screw you every time."[34] Therefore, one should be wary of arguments that matters are "merely procedural" and, for that reason, less important than "substantive" matters or solely "adjectival." More likely, those who diminish the force of procedure as "innocent formality or technicality" and undermine its relevance are being naïve or deceptive, or simply wrong. Thus, if procedures are not a mere technicality, and if they incorporate a balance between the formal, institutional structure of the legal system and its substantive, normative structure, then recognizing that a preliminary objection may prevent full-fledged adjudication is not invariably a cause of "serious concern for those safeguarded by international law." Instead, the role of preliminary objections as procedural shields arguably correlates to the level of safeguard actually offered by international law when it comes to options for adjudication.

More broadly, the role of preliminary objections as shields is a matter of procedural justice.[35] A minimalist view of procedural justice would posit that the function of procedure is solely to guarantee a perfect application of law to the facts that triggered the dispute at reasonable

[33] There is no justification for an automatically restrictive interpretation of procedural requirements as a matter of principle, just as there is no such justification for that interpretation on questions of "substantive law." See, for example, Orakhelashvili, 'The Concept of International Judicial Jurisdiction.'

[34] Regulatory Reform Act: Hearing on H.R. 2327. Before the Subcommittee on Administrative Law and Governmental Regulations of the House Committee on the Judiciary, 98th Cong. 312 (1983) (statement of Rep. John Dingell), quoted in Main, 'The Procedural Foundation,' at 821.

[35] See generally Lawrence Solum, 'Procedural Justice,' 78 *S Cal L R* (2004) 181.

cost, thus enabling a just and efficient resolution of disputes. From this perspective, the value of procedure would lie in its ability to strike a balance between maximum accuracy of outcomes and minimum cost of the means to achieve that, or to guarantee access to justice while keeping the social cost of doing justice at acceptable levels. In this sense, the ability of procedures to postpone or even prevent a judgment on questions of merit can be considered to hamper justice, particularly if the technique set to protect dispute resolution is turned on its head in order to prevent dispute resolution.[36]

However, notwithstanding the validity of this minimalist view as a warning that procedure is but an instrument of justice, its downgrading of procedures cannot be pushed to an extreme. As a matter of fact, adjudicators may and do err - even if it may be challenging to independently verify that they have erred in any given case. In light of the inescapable possibility of adjudicatory error, the minimalist view of procedural justice begs a hard question: how can one regard oneself as obligated by legitimate authority to comply with a judgment that one believes (or even knows) to be in error with respect to the questions of merit?[37] Considering that adjudicators may err and that judgment can only be given after the adjudicatory process unfolds, just procedures are a necessary safety-net to confer legitimate authority on outcomes.[38] Assuming that the requirements of the adjudicatory process in place reflect common ground about what just procedures consist of, and a prevailing balance between substantive protections and guarantees and the disposition to enforce these underlying a legal system; then it is possible to conclude that observing procedural requirements is essential to keep the legitimacy of the enterprise of adjudication. In sum, the fact that procedure is potentially outcome determinative is justifiable, and adherence to procedural requirements ensures the regularity of adjudication as a particular method of dispute resolution. Preliminary objections as procedural shields are instrumental to that objective.

The quest for procedural regularity is especially ingrained in international adjudication involving states. In domestic law, given the link between the making of justice and state power, the top-down nature of adjudicatory jurisdiction, and the entrenchment of adjudication as

[36] See generally José Roberto Bedaque, *Efetividade do Processo e Técnica Processual* (São Paulo: Malheiros, 2006).

[37] Solum, 'Procedural Justice,' at 190.

[38] *Ibid.*

an institution in many societies, the discussion about procedural legitimacy tends to be closely connected to the rights of participation of litigants.[39] In international law, by contrast, the discussion is pushed in multiple directions in light of the absence of a monopoly to do justice, the less than fully integrated nature of the societal system at stake, and the bottom-up nature of adjudication. In this context, the hard question of procedural justice posed above begs a prior question that further challenges adjudicators: how can one state regard itself as obligated by legitimate authority to comply with a "procedural" decision to decide a dispute on its questions of merit, if it believes (or even knows) the "procedural" decision be in error? As discussed in Chapter 1, formally, the principle of competence-competence turns adjudicators into judges in their own cause and squares this circle. But the practical challenge remains.

The challenge is acuter from a state-centered perspective; and because adjudication by public international law tribunals has been created by states, this perspective cannot be dismissed out of hand too readily. In domestic law, adjudicators in their public function will normally replace direct settlement by the parties in dispute regardless of whether a resistant party consented to adjudication. In international law, adjudicators can only substitute the will of each party for the "will of the law" by exercising jurisdiction when a resistant state has assented to adjudication, and pursuant to the conditions of adjudication that state has agreed to. From the perspective of states, this agreement on the possibility of adjudication (the delegation function of procedural norms) is a self-standing requirement that emphasizes the relevance of procedural decisions for the legitimacy of international adjudication. Actually, the delegation requirement stresses the mutually contingent relationship between procedure and substance in law making. Thus, states may agree on stricter substantive regulations on currency exchange so long as the procedural hurdles for adjudicating claims of violation of those obligations are set especially high; or they may refrain from establishing further environmental regulations or investment protection obligations in the event that the existing procedural thresholds for corresponding claims are deemed low. Each procedural decision by an international adjudicator, in practice, assesses and re-strikes that kind of balance between procedure and substance.

[39] *Ibid.*

A major consequence of the centrality of decisions on procedural requirements is the fact that they call for thorough justification as a legitimating factor. Legitimacy, broadly understood as a justification for authority,[40] is also a justification for the authority of international adjudication.[41] The notion of fairness may be taken as the metrics for the right allocation of authority, and the notion of procedural due process may be taken as the metrics for the right procedures for enforcing the rules and regulations applicable to a case.[42] These two dimensions roughly correspond to what is sometimes referred to as source legitimacy (fairness) and process legitimacy (procedural due process) in international law and adjudication. In a legal system such as international law, where those dimensions score highly,[43] adjudicators have to be attentive to the established channels for the delegation of jurisdiction, the exercise of one's entitlement to sue, and the organization of adjudication as criteria to confer legitimate authority on both the exercise of adjudication and its end results. Sidestepping those dimensions may lead to backlashes with lingering consequences for the enterprise of international adjudication – both for the adjudicators who so behave or for their institutional frameworks, and for international adjudication as a whole.[44]

It is as if international adjudication unfolded in two successive logical steps:[45] first, an assessment of procedural compliance; and second, so

[40] See, for example, Rüdiger Wolfrum, 'Legitimacy of International Law from a Legal Perspective: Some Introductory Considerations,' in Rüdiger Wolfrum and Volker Röben (eds.), *Legitimacy in International Law* (Berlin: Springer, 2008) 1, at 6–7; Allen Buchanan and Robert Keohane, 'The Legitimacy of Global Governance Institutions,' in Wolfrum and Röben, *Legitimacy in International Law*, at 25; Daniel Bodansky, 'The Legitimacy of International Governance: A Coming Challenge for International Environmental Law?' 93 *AJIL* (1999) 596. See generally Thomas Franck, *The Power of Legitimacy Among Nations* (Oxford University Press, 1990).

[41] See, for example, Nienke Grossman, 'Legitimacy and International Adjudicative Bodies,' 41 *Geo Wash ILR* (2010) 107.

[42] See generally Ronald Dworkin, *Law's Empire* (Cambridge, MA: Harvard University Press, 1986), at 404–5, mentioning fairness and procedural due process along these lines in the context of a political system (in addition to justice, as a matter of outcomes).

[43] See generally Matthew Lister, 'The Legitimating Role of Consent in International Law,' 11 *Chi J Int'l L* (2011) 1.

[44] See generally Grossman, 'Legitimacy and International Adjudicative Bodies,' at 143–52, arguing that international tribunals' reiterated decisions that do not coincide with international actors' interests and values may detract from tribunals' legitimacy and their use by states.

[45] These two steps are logically successive but not necessarily diachronic, for the "preliminary" and "merits" stages may not be separate stages from a timeline-based perspective. The analytical separation remains possible. See discussion in Chapter 3.

long as the conditions for moving forward are present for the given claims, an assessment of the disputed rights and obligations of the parties vis-à-vis one another to answer the particular claims. Therein rests the obvious, but often controversial characteristic of preliminary objections as procedural shields. They are checkpoints of compliance with procedural requirements, and therefore, guarantors of procedural regularity and of the legitimacy of international adjudication.

2.3.2 Preliminary objections as transmission belts of procedure-regulating rules

Preliminary objections have thus, traditionally and controversially, functioned as procedural shields. The rise of forum shopping activates a less obvious role of theirs as transmission belts of procedure-regulating norms across international tribunals. This role can be controversial as well in any given case, but for reasons different from those which worry international lawyers in a single tribunal, single-proceeding context. Crucially, where alternative forums or multiplicative litigation are at stake, the ability of preliminary objections to operate so as to prevent adjudication is considerably softened – or is at least made more complex. Return to the examples discussed in Chapter 1 about the propriety of adjudicating the *Periodicals* and the *Taxes on Soft Drinks* disputes at either the NAFTA or the WTO. Against the backdrop of jurisdictional overlaps, a given preliminary issue becomes chiefly one about *which adjudicator* should decide rather than *whether adjudication* should take place. Preliminary objections are means to raise both the former and the latter question. In the latter case, they operate as procedural shields; and, while they certainly also operate as procedural shields in the former case, there they further permit the integration, before a tribunal, of the procedure-regulating norms that regulate resort to adjudication in any given case. Emphasizing this ability of preliminary objections as transmitters of procedure coordination norms is to stress their role as instruments to balance the enabling and protective functions of procedural norms or to uphold those norms' allocative function. Preliminary objections thus become means to manage the administration of international justice in a plural court setting, analogous to the role played by defenses such as *exceptions de compétence*, litispendence, connectivity, and abstention doctrines available in various domestic legal systems and in transnational litigation.[46]

[46] See generally Arthur von Mehren, 'Theory and Practice of Adjudicatory Authority in Private International Law: A Comparative Study of the Doctrine, Policies and Practices

This study's option to focus on forum shopping in international adjudication from a procedural perspective permits it to unearth this up-to-now dormant dimension of preliminary objections. From this perspective, they become means to coordinate, in the context of specific proceedings, the exercise of overlapping jurisdiction by international tribunals, possibly under a cosmopolitan conception of the rule of law applied to procedural norms.[47] Approached this way, preliminary objections may turn a loose inclination for the coordination and systematization of the work of international tribunals into a practical, technical ability to coordinate exercises of jurisdiction, through recourse to existing rules and principles that call for and legitimize such coordination.

In general international law, the foundation for the claim that preliminary objections permit the integration of procedural principles across different international tribunals is embedded in the cosmopolitanism of general principles of law such as *res judicata*. More importantly, the notion of party autonomy is a strong foundation for the claim that preliminary objections permit the integration of conventional international procedural rules across different normative spaces, nurturing these rules' cosmopolitanism, absent express provision to the contrary. Party autonomy (or "private autonomy") is an expression of "contractual freedom" that, applied to dispute resolution, means that disputing states (or, generally, "parties") are entitled to jointly decide on the means to settle their grievances. And once a joint decision is made, *pacta sunt servanda*. While party autonomy in international law derives from the broader principles of consent and sovereign equality, it is also specifically formulated in Article 33(1) of the UN Charter,[48] and generally recognized as a self-standing principle under the notion of "freedom of means" to settle disputes.[49]

Importantly, two given states are normally entitled to jointly decide on a specific forum to adjudicate a bilateral dispute between them,

of Common and Civil-Law Systems,' 295 *Recueil des cours* (2002), at 306 ff; Campbell McLachlan, Lis Pendens *in International Litigation* (Leiden: Martinus Nijhoff, 2009).

47 McLachlan, Lis Pendens *in International Litigation*.

48 Article 33(1), UN Charter: "The parties to any dispute, the continuance of which is likely to endanger the maintenance of international peace and security, shall, first of all, seek a solution by negotiation, enquiry, mediation, conciliation, arbitration, judicial settlement, resort to regional agencies or arrangements, or other peaceful means of their own choice."

49 See Declaration on Principles of International Law Concerning Friendly Relations and Cooperation among States in Accordance with the Charter of the United Nations, A/RES/2625, 24 October 1970.

notwithstanding the fact that there may be a previous grant of jurisdiction to another forum. Even if such a previous grant of jurisdiction and the conditions for the action are established in a multilateral treaty, Article 41(1) of the Vienna Convention on the Law of Treaties (VCLT) allows states to bilaterally contract out of those provisions (as between themselves) and opt for another means of settlement for a given dispute or category thereof. Article 41(1)(b) authorizes modifications to multilateral treaties by subsets of parties to such treaties, as long as the multilateral treaty at stake does not prohibit the modification, and the modification in question "does not affect the enjoyment by the other parties of their rights under the treaty or the performance of their obligations," and "does not relate to a provision, derogation from which is incompatible with the effective execution of the object and purpose of the treaty as a whole."[50]

Now, if it is true as matter of principle (i) that two parties to a dispute are free to settle that dispute in a manner that suits them;[51] (ii) that the adjudicatory function is substitutive of direct settlement by the parties-in-dispute; and (iii) that no party to a dispute is obliged to file suit with regard to that given dispute; then why would it not also be true as a matter of principle that (iv) both parties to a dispute may jointly agree not to use any forum at all (i.e., agree not to file suit); and that (v) both parties to a dispute may jointly agree to use a forum that is different from the one established under the multilateral treaty (i.e., agree to file suit somewhere else)?[52] In this sense, Article 41(1)(b) can be considered as a pro-party autonomy provision that permits modifications to multilateral grants of jurisdiction or jointly agreed-upon conditions for the action before a given jurisdiction by the parties to the controversy. In summary, two states actually implicated in a dispute may consensually

[50] Article 41(1)(b)(i),(ii), Vienna Convention on the Law of Treaties, 1155 *UNTS* 331.

[51] Provided that the settlement does not affect other parties to the multilateral treaty that are not parties to the dispute.

[52] This would be acceptable unless the very act of resorting to a different forum were considered to "affect the enjoyment by the other parties of their rights under the treaty" or to be "incompatible with the effective execution of the object and purpose of the treaty as a whole." Yet, since two disputing parties may well abstain from resorting to adjudication in a given case (i.e., there is no obligation to file suit, parties may settle directly), it is hard to see how resorting to adjudication before another forum could itself be tantamount to affecting other parties. Naturally, if the *result* of adjudication affects other parties, then it would violate the multilateral treaty (direct settlement to the detriment of other parties would just as well amount to a violation). But this does not mean that the very possibility to resort to a forum of choice by the parties to the dispute is precluded.

establish a new forum or procedural requirements for resorting to a forum – even when there is another (including multilateral) treaty governing dispute settlement among the parties to that treaty.

The possibility to raise objections grounded in procedure-regulating norms across international tribunals implies the possibility of "systematizing" the international judiciary through the rearview mirror. Tomer Broude has argued that the fact that normative integration would require complex authority-integrating solutions would be one of the main reasons that deter normative integration, despite the values of coherence and consistency the latter would promote.[53] Conversely, if preliminary objections may enhance authority-integrating ability, they may also facilitate normative integration. It follows from the notion of party autonomy that, as a matter of principle, adjudicators are bound to respect and enforce two parties' mutual choice when it comes to forum selection and parallel and serial litigation, regardless of the origin of the procedure-regulating rule. This principle permits a procedural rule agreed to in one context, say MERCOSUR or bilaterally, to apply in another context, say the WTO, so as to prevent or postpone adjudication by the latter institution. Preliminary objections permit carrying a procedure-regulating rule from one normative or institutional space into another. This may facilitate authority integration under the umbrella of the notion of party autonomy, which is to say that procedure-regulating rules have the ability to operate in cosmopolitan fashion.

2.4 Some limitations of the present approach

Having provided a concept of procedure to frame the study and further justified the procedural angle adopted here by pointing to the emerging role of preliminary objections as transmission belts of procedural norms, two cautionary notes are on point as a restatement of this book's ambitions. First, the present procedural perspective does not (and cannot) provide a complete account of international adjudication. Clearly, procedure does not exist in a vacuum, let alone applies for its own sake. Procedure remains a means, an instrument for the (potential) resolution of disputed claims. It exists as an organized way of processing disputes. By focusing on procedure as an object, the present

[53] Tomer Broude, 'Fragmentation(s) of International Law: On Normative Integration as Authority Allocation,' in Tomer Broude and Yuval Shany (eds.), *The Shifting Allocation of Authority in International Law: Considering Sovereignty, Supremacy and Subsidiarity* (Oxford: Hart Publishing, 2008) 99, at 114.

discussion leaves certain key elements implicated in international adjudication relatively obscure – such as the examination of questions of merit and the determination of remedies.[54]

With regard to questions of merit in particular, the framework articulated here does not discuss in depth the potential use of "anti-suit injunctions" by public international law tribunals. In transnational litigation, anti-suit injunctions are orders directed to one or several of the parties in dispute not to pursue adjudication in a foreign court.[55] Anti-suit injunctions are a technique of private international law in which a procedure-regulating norm is actually the basis for the request to that court order. Hence, in the anti-suit injunction context, the dispute itself revolves around the violation of the procedure-regulating norm. In other words, therein the alleged violation of the procedure-regulating norm is a question of merit, whereas under the framework suggested here the same procedure-regulating norm offers a ground to a preliminary objection. Procedure-regulating norms in public international law can afford a basis for actions akin to the anti-suit actions in private international law. As Campbell McLachlan points out with regard to the private international law experience, there may be a need for one court to control to some extent the conduct of the parties regarding identical litigation before other forums, in particular to uphold party autonomy. On the other hand, as the same author observes, the experience with anti-suit injunctions in transnational cases suggests that they may "aggravate conflicts between courts, rather than resolve them… It is generally preferable to allow the other court to make its own decision as to jurisdiction."[56] At any rate, contrary to the abundant experience regarding preliminary objections, including against forum shopping strategies, the use of procedure-regulating norms as direct causes of action before public international law tribunals is extremely rare.[57] Therefore, the possibility of anti-suit injunctions in international adjudication will not be discussed in detail here.

Second, approaching forum shopping from a procedural perspective cannot in itself provide a pointer to decisions on actual forum

[54] The same occurs when adjudicators decide cases on procedural grounds and do not determine questions of merit or remedies.

[55] See generally Emmanuel Gaillard, *Anti-suit Injunctions in International Arbitration* (Huntington, NY: Juris Publishing, 2005).

[56] McLachlan, Lis Pendens *in International Litigation*, at 157 and 188.

[57] But see the discussions in Chapters 3 and 7 regarding *Commission* v. *Ireland*, C-459/2003, Judgment of the Court, 30 May 2006. That case and its outcome have similarities to a request for an anti-suit injunction.

shopping strategies. It merely puts the filter of forum shopping activity (i.e., procedure) on the spot. What will eventually be filtered depends on filtering elements (i.e., procedural requirements); and on the specific facts, norms, and broader conceptions of procedure applicable and applied to the situation at hand. Procedure can be apprehended in general fashion to cover tribunals broadly, but forum shopping strategies, their regulation, and approaches to such regulation may differ. The present study focuses primarily on general aspects, and emphasizes commonalities across international tribunals. However, it is also necessary to articulate particular interpretations of procedural principles and rules and their interrelationship. These will depend on the specific tribunals, norms, and cases at stake. In sum, lower levels of abstraction, required to provide a satisfactory response to the question of how parties and adjudicators may address forum shopping strategies in specific cases, must be adopted in the context of discussions about specific instances of jurisdictional overlaps.

Nevertheless, the law on procedural coordination is far from settled, and forum shopping cases tend to be difficult ones. This, after all, is one of the things that makes the present topic worth the ink. The relative abstract character of principles, the open texture of procedure-regulating rules and the margin for qualifying the actual circumstances make general conclusions tentative at best. Resorting to principles and balancing in concrete cases will be unavoidable. In this context, judicial politics, policies, and preferences that are indissociable from technical and doctrinal considerations in practice are relevant explanatory factors. In spite of this recognition, this study does not articulate determinants of judicial politics as descriptors of outcomes. Neither does it deeply investigate social, attitudinal, strategic, or institutional constraints that might incline adjudicators to decide procedural issues in a given way.[58] While factors internal to adjudicators (e.g., psychological conditions, social background, nationality, pure self-interest) and external to adjudicators (e.g., collegial decision-making, political pressure, and peer pressure) may shape the law-in-action, it is beyond the scope

[58] See David Schneiderman, 'Judicial Politics and International Investment Arbitration: Seeking an Explanation for Conflicting Outcomes,' 30 *Nw J Int'l L Bus* (2010) 383, for this terminology, a review of typical political science approaches to explain outcomes in the US constitutional context, and an attempt to explain conflicting outcomes in three investor-state arbitration awards based on an adaptation of those approaches.

of this project to discuss those motivations in themselves.[59] Based on the author's considered judgments, this book attempts to explicate and synthesize arguably "canonical" principles, materials, decisions, and opinions to construe an argument about the law and the direction it points to when it comes to addressing forum shopping strategies from a general procedural perspective. This is, again, a limited effort.

Indeed, when this chapter delineates the realm of procedure and justifies the present study, it implies a view that some argument about a "legal object" is possible. Accordingly, this book does not adhere to a view that "anything goes." Principles and rules and a shared understanding of what they mean, and the obligation that adjudicators decide based on them and justify their decisions accordingly underdetermine adjudicatory reasoning and decision-making.[60] Bearing in mind that this study seeks to answer a question about how respondents and adjudicators may address forum shopping strategies, it seems appropriate to conduct the present discussion from this doctrine-driven standpoint – even if the potential for judicial politics and preferences is well recognized.

2.4.1 Three levels at which politics, policies, and preferences influence the assessment of forum shopping

Whereas the focus here is not on the determinants of judicial politics, policies, and preferences, the very recognition of their role in the assessment and remediation of forum shopping warrants an outline of key competing perspectives potentially at stake. When it comes to

[59] See *ibid.* for a work that focuses on such motivations. See also Jared Wessel, 'Judicial Policy-Making at the International Criminal Court: An Institutional Guide to Analyzing International Adjudication,' 44 *Colum J Transnat'l L* (2005) 377, discussing what he terms creational, external, and internal factors as influencing judicial policy-making at the ICC; Eric Posner and Miguel de Figueiredo, 'Is the International Court of Justice Biased?' University of Chicago Law & Economics, Olin Working Paper 234 (2004), discussing nationality bias and its relation to economic wealth, political organization, and culture (language and religion) at the ICJ; and Rosalyn Higgins, 'Policy Considerations and the International Judicial Process,' 17 *ICLQ* (1968) 58, contrasting US and British international lawyers' views on the nature of international law and the role of courts. See generally Daniel Terris *et al.*, *The International Judge: An Introduction to the Men and Women Who Decide the World's Cases* (Oxford University Press, 2007).

[60] See generally Laurence Solum, 'On the Indeterminacy Crisis: Critiquing the Critical Dogma,' 54 *U Chi L Rev* (1987) 462 and Ken Kress, 'Legal Indeterminacy,' 77 *U Cal L Rev* (1989) 283. This book does not delve into the debate concerning the (in)determinacy of law. It does not accept the extreme version of the "no right answer" (indeterminacy) thesis and accepts that law is not only a system of rules (i.e., it consists of both

forum shopping, these competing perspectives influence both the perception of this phenomenon as a problem and the quest for solutions to it. Such factors operate on three related levels in adjudication, which may be separated for the sake of explanation, since each of these levels roughly dovetails with one or more of the functions of procedural norms described in Chapter 1.

A first level of adjudication where judicial politics, policies, and preferences are significant refers to the assertion and exercise of jurisdiction by tribunals. At that level, two ideal types of approach may be construed. From one typical approach, adjudicators decide from a consent-based perspective. From an opposite typical approach, they reason from a compulsion-based perspective. The contrast between these two ideal types is reminiscent of the opposing scales that refer to the delegation function of procedural norms discussed in Chapter 1. Applied to forum shopping strategies, a compulsion-based perspective to adjudication would limit consideration of forum shopping as a problem to be remedied and the reach of procedural coordination, if each adjudicator implicated deems its own regime to be compulsory. Conversely, a consent-based perspective would more easily depict a choice of jurisdiction as a forum shopping strategy and lead a tribunal to be deferential toward other tribunals implicated, thus potentially expanding the likely reach of procedural coordination.

At a second level, judicial policies are relevant with regard to the definition of the claims brought by the complainant or the actual dispute between the parties as the object of adjudication. The discussion in this regard is suggestive of the balance between the enabling and protective functions of procedural rules. A complainant's lawyerly task when submitting claims to adjudication is to construe the case under the normally specific jurisdictional clauses of international tribunals. By contrast, a respondent can try to show that the real dispute between the parties is not exactly mirrored by the complainant's claims. The respondent, by dislocating the focus proposed by the complainant, can question the latter's right to a judgment or the jurisdiction of the tribunal to deal with the real dispute – as opposed to any individual claims brought by the complaining party. Faced with such opposing constructions, the judge may either decide on the claims as

principles and rules). See Ronald Dworkin, 'Is Law a System of Rules?' in Ronald Dworkin (ed.), *The Philosophy of Law* (Oxford University Press, 1977) 38, for an account of law as a system of both principles and rules.

elements of a defined dispute properly brought, or stop without doing so – for instance, because the claims do not reflect the underlying dispute between the parties and would thus not warrant a judgment on the merits of the claims, or because the claims are similar to claims pending elsewhere. The tension between these two options was aptly described by Yuval Shany, who explained the methodological choice to address jurisdictional relations across treaty regimes in terms of a "disintegrationism versus integrationism" dichotomy. At that level, adjudicators can either (i) disintegrate a broad dispute into specific claims under different legal instruments, and deal only with those aspects of the dispute which directly arise under the treaty in question (disintegrationism); or (ii) integrate the related claims into one dispute and take into account the potential influence of other regimes and mechanisms (integrationism).[61] The way adjudicators configure the real dispute at play will influence their emphasis on forum shopping as a problem.[62] In general, disintegrationism minimizes forum shopping as a phenomenon of concern while more easily dispensing with the possibility of procedural coordination. Integrationism, in turn, contemplates a larger space for overlaps and more likely exacerbates the need for procedural coordination.

Finally, a third level where judicial policies play out relates to the definition and interpretation of the applicable law, evocative of the allocative function of procedural norms. This level becomes relevant, from an analytical viewpoint, once adjudicators perceive forum shopping as at least potentially problematic, according to their definition of the actual dispute under their jurisdiction. There is widespread preference for coherence, consistency, and order over randomness,

[61] Yuval Shany, *Regulating Jurisdictional Relations Between National and International Courts* (Oxford University Press, 2007) at 107–121. See also M. E. Tardu, 'Protocol to the UN Covenant on Civil and Political Rights and the Inter-American System: A Study of Coexisting Procedures,' 70 *AJIL* (1976) 778, contrasting a "procedural *laissez-faire*" and a "unification" doctrine for assessing dispute identity.

[62] The literature on "overlapping jurisdictions" highlights the question of defining the dispute, since the problem would only come into play if a "single dispute" could be or were submitted before different tribunals. See, for example, Lowe, 'Overlapping Jurisdictions,' at 191; Shany, *The Competing Jurisdictions*, at 21–3. However, as McLachlan points out, one should not confuse the criteria for defining identical disputes with the criteria for the application of traditional procedure-regulating rules such as *lis pendens* and *res judicata*. See McLachlan, Lis Pendens *in International Litigation*; see also Luiz Eduardo Salles, '"Conflitos de Competência" entre Tribunais Internacionais,' in Barbara Oliveira and Roberto Luiz Silva, *Manual de Direito Processual Internacional* (São Paulo: Saraiva, 2012) 75.

inconsistency, and disorder. Accordingly, if complete disintegrationism is perceived as an inadequate judicial policy option to address a procedural overlap, the following step is to look inside the legal toolkit for norms that remedy the situation. In fact, the view that permeates this research is premised on the fact that complete disintegrationism may, in some cases, be inappropriate. In addressing preliminary objections as a means to contain forum shopping, the present study assumes that forum shopping can be problematic in some concrete cases,[63] and that there are certain norms allowing parties and adjudicators to hold it back. Those norms recognize party autonomy and are not only general principles of law but also conventional norms agreed upon by the disputing parties, whether in a single governing instrument or in several of them.

At the third level under discussion, it is possible to adopt a broader or narrower approach to the applicable procedure-regulating rules and their interpretation. That level thus refers to the readiness of a judge to consider multiple sources of law in tackling forum shopping and broadly or narrowly interpreting them.[64] In this regard, the international judge has three initial options. First, the judge may follow only the explicit rules agreed to by the parties within the forum law. Unless the *lex fori* itself invokes explicit procedural regulating norms that resolve the problem, this option will mean the judge simply proceeds and decides the case. Second, the judge can rely on general principles of law or domestic law analogies. This would, for instance, open the way for considering principles such as *res judicata* and *lis pendens* to address serial and parallel litigation. Third, the judge could insist on relying only upon party-agreed solutions, as in the first option, but be willing to look for those solutions outside the forum law, as in the second option. For example, the judge could examine whether the parties in a WTO dispute have agreed to forum selection or preclusion clauses in the outside treaty which created the forum shopping problem in the first place, such as a fork-in-the-road clause in NAFTA or another trade agreement. A judge who is more open to considering different sources of the law to help limit forum shopping (from an expansive rather than a restrictive perspective) is more likely to find a principle or rule to address these concerns. Moreover, a judge ready to apply a procedural principle or rule to tackle forum shopping must

[63] See discussion in Chapter 1.

[64] See Pauwelyn and Salles, 'Forum Shopping Before International Tribunals.'

interpret it. Depending on how open-textured the norm is, the interpreter may opt for a broader, or narrower, construction of the rule to address forum shopping. To return to the previous examples, a judge who applies *res judicata* or *lis pendens* to a given action could either relax or strictly formulate the criteria of identity of action embedded in those rules. Similarly, a judge who assesses a fork-in-the-road clause in NAFTA or an investment treaty could adopt a restrictive or an expansive interpretive approach in applying the clause. Ultimately, the possibility of stopping a given proceeding on a preliminary basis may well rest on how the criteria for the application of those principles are formulated by the international judge.

The three different levels pointed to above combine in practice to influence the fate of a preliminary objection targeting a particular forum shopping strategy. Take the ITLOS orders on provisional measures in *Southern Bluefin Tuna* and *MOX Plant*, and compare such orders to the arbitral tribunals' approach in each of those cases.[65] The ITLOS emphasized, in both cases, the compulsory character of its jurisdiction to rule on provisional measures and the less stringent, *prima facie* standard that must be met to assert jurisdiction in that regard. It also highlighted the UNCLOS-based aspects of the disputes. Basically, a less stringent standard for asserting jurisdiction and a disintegrationist approach led the ITLOS to issue interim measures despite the potential impact of other treaties on the proceedings before it.[66] As a further consequence of choosing disintegrationism, the ITLOS downplayed the third level of policy options (sources available and interpretation of procedure-regulating rules). Coherent with its own methodological choice, the ITLOS avoided wandering outside the four corners of the UNCLOS

[65] *Southern Bluefin Tuna Case (Australia and New Zealand* v. *Japan)*, ITLOS Cases Nos 3 & 4, Order on Provisional Measures, 27 August 1999; *The MOX Plant Case (Ireland* v. *United Kingdom)*, ITLOS Case No 10, Order on Provisional Measures, 3 December 2001; *Southern Bluefin Tuna Case (Australia and New Zealand* v. *Japan)*, Award on Jurisdiction and Admissibility, 4 August 2000; *MOX Plant Case (Ireland* v. *United Kingdom)*, terminated 6 June 2008. Note, however, the different scope of the respective exercises of jurisdiction of ITLOS and the arbitral tribunals: provisional measures pending the constitution of the arbitral tribunal (Article 290(5), UNCLOS) versus integral assessment of jurisdiction and admissibility by the arbitral tribunal.

[66] *Southern Bluefin Tuna*, Order on Provisional Measures, and *MOX Plant*, Order on Provisional Measures. Note, however, the special considerations related to provisional measures (urgency and reversibility) and the fact that the standard therein is *prima facie* jurisdiction as opposed to definitive jurisdiction. These factors arguably push adjudicators toward a "compulsion-based" perspective of jurisdiction (first level discussed here) and toward "disintegrationism" (second level discussed here).

jurisdictional framework in both cases. In *MOX Plant*, for instance, the ITLOS considered that clauses in outside treaties do not play out in the *prima facie* jurisdictional test employed at the provisional measures stage.[67] In *Southern Bluefin Tuna*, although the ITLOS considered Article 16 of the Convention for the Conservation of Southern Bluefin Tuna (CCSBT) tangentially, it adopted a compulsion-based approach to its jurisdiction and interpreted the CCSBT strictly in the sense that it did not "exclude" the applicants' right to invoke an UNCLOS dispute settlement with regard to the conservation and management of tuna.[68]

The assessment of the arbitral tribunals after the provisional measures stage in *Southern Bluefin Tuna* and *MOX Plant* differed remarkably from the ITLOS's approach. Unlike the ITLOS, the arbitral tribunals emphasized the existence of other treaties and mechanisms bearing on the disputes before them and, as a consequence, did not rule on the merits of the cases. To begin with the *Southern Bluefin Tuna* arbitral tribunal underscored that the dispute, while centered in the CCSBT, also arose under the UNCLOS.[69] Specifically, according to the tribunal:

> [T]he parties to this dispute ... are the same parties grappling not with two separate disputes but with what in fact is a single dispute arising under both conventions. To find that, in this case, there is a dispute actually arising under UNCLOS which is distinct from the dispute that arose under the CCSBT would be artificial.[70]

Following its integration of the disputes under UNCLOS and the CCSBT, the arbitral tribunal examined Article 16 of the CCSBT and interpreted it broadly in combination with Article 281(1) of the UNCLOS,[71] to the effect that the former "excludes any further procedure within the

[67] *MOX Plant*, Order on Provisional Measures, paras. 52–3.

[68] *Southern Bluefin Tuna*, Order on Provisional Measures, paras. 51–3. Article 16, Convention for the Conservation of Southern Bluefin Tuna, 1819 *UNTS* 360 reads in the relevant part: "1. If any dispute arises between two or more of the Parties concerning the interpretation or implementation of this Convention, those Parties shall consult among themselves with a view to having the dispute resolved by negotiation, inquiry, mediation, conciliation, arbitration, judicial settlement or other peaceful means of their own choice. 2. Any dispute of this character not so resolved shall, with the consent in each case of all parties to the dispute, be referred for settlement to the International Court of Justice or to arbitration."

[69] *Southern Bluefin Tuna*, Award on Jurisdiction and Admissibility, para. 52.

[70] *Ibid.*, para. 54.

[71] *Ibid.*, paras. 56–7: "[T]he terms of Article 16 of the 1993 Convention do not expressly and in so many words exclude the applicability of any procedure, including the procedures of Section 2 of Part XV of UNCLOS" (at 56), and: "[T]he absence of an express exclusion of any procedure in Article 16 is not decisive" (at 57).

contemplation of Article 281(1) of UNCLOS."[72] As a result, the tribunal decided it lacked jurisdiction to decide the dispute.[73] The *MOX Plant* arbitral tribunal also started with integrationism and emphasized that the dispute before it involved intricate issues of "international law" and "European Community law." Next, it took into account a provision in an outside treaty, namely, Article 292 of the EC Treaty. The tribunal emphasized the influence of European Community (EC) law on the proceeding before it, and on that ground stayed the proceeding.[74] *Southern Bluefin Tuna* and *MOX Plant* therefore stand for the proposition that, where a tribunal adopts a disintegrationist approach, it will most likely proceed and decide on the claims before it. In contrast, where a tribunal adopts an integrationist approach, it may tend to stop the proceedings on a preliminary basis.[75]

In conclusion, an adjudicator's approach to the definition of her own jurisdiction will enhance or diminish the possibility of strategic forum selection and of measures to cope with such strategy. Moreover, an adjudicator with pronounced systemic orientation, and who is concerned about the restrictions to the complainant's freedom of choice when it comes to forum shopping strategies would be inclined to opt for a more integrationist perspective in defining the dispute, to look for solutions beyond the *lex fori*, and to interpret jurisdictional and procedural regulating rules more broadly, so as to address the corresponding concerns. On the other hand, a judge preoccupied with guarding the peculiarities of a regime, and who is deferential toward complainants' autonomy on forum selection and litigation strategy would be inclined to follow a more disintegrationist track in defining the dispute, to remain

[72] *Ibid.*, para. 59. Article 281(1) UNCLOS establishes that "1. If the States Parties which are parties to a dispute concerning the interpretation or application of this Convention have agreed to seek settlement of the dispute by *a peaceful means* of their own choice, the procedures provided for in this Part apply only where no settlement has been reached by recourse to *such means* and the agreement between the parties does not exclude any further procedure" (emphasis added). The arbitral tribunal itself conceded that Article 16 CCSBT is not "a peaceful means" in the sense of Article 281(1) UNCLOS. But since in the tribunal's view there was an inseparable dispute under the two conventions, it considered that Article 16 fell "within the terms and intent" of Article 281(1). *Southern Bluefin Tuna*, Award on Jurisdiction and Admissibility, para. 55. See also Bernard Oxman, 'Complementary Agreements and Compulsory Jurisdiction,' 95 *AJIL* (2001) 277.

[73] *Southern Bluefin Tuna*, Award on Jurisdiction and Admissibility, para. 72.

[74] *MOX Plant*, Order 3 of the Arbitral Tribunal, paras. 25–30.

[75] See also Shany, *Regulating Jurisdictional Relations*, at 107–21.

exclusively within the jurisdictional and procedural corners of its own statutes, and to interpret coordinating rules restrictively.

Although this outline is not exhaustive, it serves to point out, again, that both the identification of forum shopping and the reactions to it are susceptible to politics, policies, and preferences. This recognition makes clear that procedures do not exist nor apply in a vacuum. However, this does not undermine the importance of a procedural perspective itself, modest as this perspective may be. Adjudicatory decision-making as well as academic writing remains contingent on a number of internal and external factors. In this work, attempt has been made to highlight specificities and policy elements in the discussions that follow, but those factors will not be highlighted with equal emphasis in the present analysis.

2.5 Concluding remarks

Forum shopping strategies, in particular when alternative forums and multiplicative litigation are at stake, underscore the question about *which* adjudicator should decide a given claim or dispute relative to the otherwise dominant question of *whether* adjudication is possible. This change of tone sheds novel light on procedural requirements and preliminary objections as instruments to manage the interrelationship between international tribunals and proceedings in situations of jurisdictional overlap. In a plural court setting, approaching forum shopping strategies from a procedural perspective can thus offer new insights into the role of preliminary objections.

However, a turn to procedure does not, itself, determine the approaches and decisions that will ensue from specific forum shopping strategies. Judicial politics and preferences, and competing approaches to the concrete circumstances under the law and to the law itself continue in operation. In this sense, a shift to procedure is not automatically a turn to a "neutral" or "innocent" terrain where the puzzles of forum shopping strategies are discussed. In any event, the present shift in focus captures an overlooked dimension of international law and highlights the arena where forum shopping comes into play. The discussion that follows can now turn specifically to preliminary objections as a technique to address forum shopping, and to the procedure-regulating principles and rules that equip this technique with the ability to function as a tool to manage jurisdictional overlaps in international adjudication.

3 Preliminary questions and preliminary objections

3.1 Introduction

Chapter 2 argued that procedure is a significant dimension in assessing and addressing forum shopping. From a practical perspective, adjudicators or parties who object to a specific instance of forum shopping will normally point to some restriction imposed upon the adjudicatory process that interrupts the proceedings – or leads to their termination – before a resolution on the merits can be reached. This is where preliminary questions enter the forum shopping picture and can fulfill a procedural coordination role by mitigating concerns originating from multiplicative litigation or strategic forum selection. It is in this sense that preliminary questions become transmission belts of other norms permitting international tribunals to coordinate their activities and decisions. In a nutshell, preliminary questions provide a procedural mechanism to address forum shopping.

An essential step for this book is to conceptualize preliminary questions and objections in international adjudication. To accomplish this, this chapter unfolds as follows. Section 3.2 presents in more detail the concept of preliminary *questions* adopted throughout this book; it then derives from that concept a working definition of preliminary *objections*. This definition is based on the autonomy of procedural requirements (which give rise to preliminary *questions* and, consequently, preliminary *objections*) from the *merits* of claims (which give rise to questions of merit). Section 3.3 presents a functional, contextual demarcation method to draw the line between preliminary questions and questions of merit. Yet, separating these two categories may be a tough call in practice, since facts related to preliminary and merits questions may be entangled. In light of this practical limitation, Section 3.4 presents three basic practical alternatives that adjudicators have employed to attempt to maintain the integrity of procedure when separation is hard to achieve. Section 3.5 offers concluding remarks.

3.2 The concept of preliminary questions and objections in international adjudication

This book is grounded in the conceptual autonomy of preliminary questions in international adjudication. Such autonomy stems from a distinction between (i) the adjudicatory *process* as such, or *procedure*; and (ii) the object of the adjudicatory process or *substance*, which comprises the *merits* of the controverted claims underlying a process. The conceptual autonomy of preliminary questions can be described by reference to a contextual separation between the *procedural requirements for a judgment on the merits* and the *merits* proper of a claim. Procedural requirements, as Chapter 2 suggested, refer to one of the three essential and interrelated institutions of jurisdiction, action, and procedure in a narrow sense. Requirements under each element of that triad can be seen as prerequisites to the adjudicatory process that are independent of the object of that process. The object of the process is the resolution of controverted claims submitted to judicial settlement. In theory, each requirement related to jurisdiction, action, and procedure in a narrow sense must be fulfilled for the proceeding to move forward and a judgment on the merits of the request to be rendered.[1] Because in the context of international adjudication the requirements related to jurisdiction, action, and procedure in a narrow sense all come into play within concrete proceedings, this book refers to them broadly as procedural requirements. They give rise to preliminary questions, as further explained below. It is important, however, to keep the distinction between jurisdiction, action, and procedure in a narrow sense in the background.[2] To avoid confusion between procedural requirements that cover procedure in a broad sense (i.e., jurisdiction, action,

[1] A procedural requirement may or may not have a peremptory (as opposed to a merely dilatory) effect on the adjudicatory process. Moreover, an unmet requirement can be deemed not so critical that it would prevent a decision of merit. For instance, a minor defect of form may not be so critical that it would lead to a dismissal of the case based on non-compliance with a formal procedural requirement.

[2] This distinction may be useful for other purposes. For instance, the distinction between jurisdiction, action, and procedure in a narrow sense may help in the construction or application of the distinction between objections to jurisdiction and objections to admissibility, discussed in Chapter 5.

and procedure in a narrow sense) and "procedural requirements" specifically related to procedure in a narrow sense, when speaking of requirements related exclusively to procedure in a narrow sense, this book refers to procedural requirements *stricto sensu*.

The separation between prerequisites to a decision of merit and the merits themselves is familiar to lawyers of both civil law and common law systems. Think only of the French law institutions of *exceptions d'incompétence*, *exceptions de procédure*, and *fins-de-non-recevoir*; the common law notions of pleas in bar, pleas in abatement, and demurrers; or of certain American federal law abstention doctrines, lack of jurisdiction, improper venue, or insufficiency of service of process, which essentially act as obstacles to reaching a decision on the merits of claims. These doctrines govern the expected course of the adjudicatory process without normally impinging on the merits of the claims. While a general "procedural versus substantive law" dichotomy seems harder to find, international adjudication clearly recognizes a distinction between procedural requirements and questions of merit.[3]

As pointed out above, the concept of preliminary questions stems from the distinction between the requirements for reaching a judgment on the merits of claims, and the merits of the claims themselves.[4] Thus described, preliminary questions relate to the adjudicatory process. They are linked to jurisdiction, action, and procedure in a narrow sense, as opposed to those questions underlying the request that is the object of the process (that is, questions of merit). Consequently, *preliminary questions* consist of those issues which refer to the prerequisites to the existence and development of the adjudicatory process as such.[5] Under this meaning, it is possible to speak of preliminary questions whenever the adjudicatory process is approached independently from its irreducible object – even if the specific requirements for a preliminary question to be raised and to succeed may change depending on the proceeding at stake. Since procedure is a *sine qua non* of judicial dispute

[3] See, for example, *Jurisdictional Immunities of the State (Germany* v. *Italy: Greece Intervening)*, Judgment of 3 February 2012, paras. 82, 95, and 100.

[4] As the ICJ puts it, "a matter which is essentially one of the merits ... is not a matter that may be the proper subject of a preliminary objection." *Case Concerning Application of the Convention on the Prevention and Punishment of the Crime of Genocide (Croatia* v. *Serbia)*, Preliminary Objections, Judgment of 18 November 2008, para. 139.

[5] See J. Witenberg, *L'organisation judiciaire, la procédure et la sentence internationales: Traité pratique* (Paris: Pedone, 1937), at 110; Mohieddine Mabrouk, *Les exceptions de procédure devant les juridictions internationales* (Paris: LGDJ, 1966), at 4–13; and, generally, Maarten Bos, *Les conditions du procès en droit international public*, (Leiden: Brill, 1957).

settlement, the concept described here has the necessary breadth to assess the requirements governing adjudication across the range of international tribunals. The concept is general and embraces preliminary questions as a uniform analytical category.[6]

Preliminary objections can be conceptualized with reference to preliminary questions: preliminary objections are the means by which a party, normally the respondent,[7] raises a preliminary question. In short, a preliminary objection is a preliminary question brought up by a party. Or, put differently, preliminary objections occur when a party raises an allegedly unmet requirement for the existence or development of the adjudicatory process so as to impede or postpone a decision of merit. In the practice of international adjudication, most preliminary questions become concrete by means of preliminary objections. In fact, this book explains that from a litigant's perspective, it is important that interested parties resort to preliminary objections explicitly and promptly, lest they risk failing to discharge their burden to raise a given objection. However, for present purposes, it is important to make the distinction between preliminary questions and objections: by acknowledging the more specific scope of preliminary objections (party action referring to prerequisites to the adjudicatory process) as opposed to preliminary questions (any questions referring to the prerequisites themselves), one respects an antecedent distinction between the abstract entitlement to raise a procedural issue (which may be available to both the adjudicators and the parties), and the actual raising of an issue (which is often the responsibility of the party that intends to avail itself of that issue, but sometimes can also be a matter for the judge).[8]

[6] See Georges Abi-Saab, *Les exceptions préliminaires dans la procédure de la Cour Internationale* (Paris: Pedone, 1967), at 27–33. The concept of preliminary objections proposed here is inspired by Abi-Saab's remarks that the preliminary character and effect of preliminary objections are, from a material standpoint, inherent to their legal technique, whereas their procedural character and effect are related to the rules governing the procedure of given tribunals.

[7] The standard "preliminary objector" is the responding party, and this study follows this perspective. There has been one case before the ICJ where the applicant state raised a preliminary question to the Court's jurisdiction, but this is clearly not the normal course of events. See *Case of the Monetary Gold Removed from Rome in 1943 (Italy v. France, United Kingdom and United States of America)*, Preliminary Question, Judgment of 15 June 1954, at 28–9.

[8] The distinction between preliminary questions and objections is sometimes unnoticed in the English language. See, for example, Shabtai Rosenne, *Procedure in the International Court: A Commentary of the 1978 Rules of the International Court of Justice*

It is established that tribunals are entitled to raise preliminary questions on their own motion at least in some cases, despite the lack of party action in that regard. One can envision three scenarios when an interested party misses the chance to raise a preliminary objection:

(i) The tribunal cannot entertain the preliminary question if such question was not explicitly and timely raised by a party or, put differently, a party's failure to make a preliminarily objection is a sufficient condition to enable the proceeding to move forward. In those cases, preclusion operates against the party that is missing in action. Inaction brings a change in the relative positions of the parties, and what could have represented a procedural obstacle had the objector raised it can no longer affect the decision-making process.[9] Put differently, in certain cases a party that does not raise an objection in a timely manner may be understood to have waived its right to do so. This is the case, for example, where a respondent does not explicitly advance a preliminary objection unrelated to the question of a WTO panel's jurisdiction. Thus, the Appellate Body has drawn a distinction between questions going to the roots of their jurisdiction, which are so fundamental that WTO panels must examine them, and other procedural questions, which a party must raise in order to have them analyzed.[10]

(ii) Despite a party's inaction, the tribunal *must entertain the preliminary question*, since it is so fundamental that the tribunal cannot proceed without disposing of it. This is normally the case with questions affecting the jurisdiction of international tribunals, as mentioned above in the case of the WTO[11] and as further developed in Chapter 5.

(iii) Notwithstanding a party's inaction, the preliminary question *may still be taken up by the tribunal*. The possibility that such a scenario actually takes place depends on whether tribunals

(The Hague, Martinus Nijhoff, 1983), at 159: "It is to be regretted that the English language has to use the word 'objection' and not 'question'..." In French, Spanish, and Portuguese, for instance, the distinction is widespread. See, for example, Abi-Saab, *Les exceptions préliminaires*.

9 See *Temple of Preah Vihear (Cambodia v. Thailand)*, Judgment of 15 June 1962, Separate Opinion of Judge Fitzmaurice, at 62–63.

10 See Appellate Body Report, *Mexico – Anti-Dumping Investigation of High Fructose Corn Syrup (HFCS) from the United States – Recourse to Article 21.5 of the DSU by the United States*, WT/DS132/AB/RW, adopted 21 November 2001, paras. 36–53.

11 *Ibid.*, para. 36.

have a discretionary power to raise and entertain a given preliminary question. Normally, an international tribunal does not have such discretionary power in the context of dismissals, but it does have a margin of discretion to raise and entertain preliminary objections as a matter of case management, as discussed in Chapter 6.

In order to encompass the above scenarios (ii) and (iii) and to provide a more complete discussion of the possibilities of procedural coordination across international tribunals, this book covers both the broader concept of preliminary questions, which can be raised by parties and adjudicators, and the narrower concept of preliminary objections, which are those preliminary questions actually raised by a party. However, it is important to keep in mind that in the practice of international adjudication, most preliminary questions which come into being are explicitly raised by the party interested in avoiding a decision of merit and therefore actually qualify as preliminary objections. In this regard, preliminary questions of admissibility should normally be explicitly raised in order to be entertained, as Chapter 5 further discusses.

3.2.1 *Material character and effect of preliminary questions*

The notion of preliminary questions discussed here comprises two material aspects, the first of which relates to their character and the second to their effect.[12] Regarding their character, preliminary questions invariably limit the possibility of an analysis of merit and, as a matter of logic, must be assessed and decided before the merits are decided.[13] Chapter 2 implied such logically preliminary character by

[12] See Abi-Saab, *Les exceptions préliminaires*, for an elegant articulation of the material and procedural aspects of preliminary objections, in terms of character and effect, focusing on the ICJ context.

[13] See, for example, Panel Report, *China – Measures Affecting Trading Rights and Distribution Services for Certain Publications and Audiovisual Entertainment Products*, WT/DS363/R, adopted 19 January 2010, as modified by Appellate Body Report WT/DS363/AB/R, at para. 7.12, in relation to certain preliminary objections by China: "China did not request that the Panel make a preliminary ruling on these matters. Nevertheless, the resolution of these objections is a prerequisite for the Panel moving forward with a substantive analysis of the US claims. Therefore, we will address these issues first, before moving on to the substance of the US claims." The IACtHR has, in its own words, "sustained that preliminary objections are acts that seek to prevent the examination of the merits of the aspect in question." *Case of Cabrera Garcia and Montiel Flores*, Preliminary Objections, Merits, Reparation and Legal Costs, Judgment of 26 November 2010, IACtHR Ser C No 220, at para. 17.

discussing that international adjudication unfolds in two successive logical steps, the first related to procedural compliance and the second regarding substance.[14] Concerning their effect, preliminary questions potentially stall or terminate proceedings before a decision of merit is reached. But whether this effect is actually achieved depends upon the scope of the preliminary question (i.e., whether it affects the whole action or only certain claims),[15] and the ability of this question to effectively curtail the adjudicatory process (which depends on the tribunal's assessment).[16]

Importantly, from a material viewpoint, the successful use of preliminary objections to impede or postpone a decision of merit does not necessarily require that they be raised at the first opportunity to do so or that they lead to a specific preliminary stage in the proceeding, or that an independent "preliminary ruling" deal exclusively with procedural questions in advance of substantive issues from a strictly *chronological* perspective. Since this book defines preliminary questions based on a distinction between the prerequisites for the existence and development of the adjudicatory process and the merits, a question related to a requirement of the adjudicatory process is no less preliminary just because it may be argued and decided in a stage in the proceeding

[14] See also *Jurisdictional Immunities (Germany* v. *Italy: Greece Intervening)*, para. 82 (stating that there would be a "logical problem" in striking down immunity from jurisdiction for the reason that the substantive violation alleged is serious).

[15] It is well established that a preliminary objection may refer to the absence of prerequisites to proceed to a judgment on the merits as a whole or only with regard to given claims. See, for example, *Case Concerning Territorial and Maritime Dispute (Nicaragua* v. *Colombia)*, Preliminary Objections, Judgment of 13 December 2007, para. 85.

[16] As a potential effect, it cannot be considered a constitutive element of preliminary questions. But see Abi-Saab, *Les exceptions préliminaires*. Abi-Saab characterizes both elements – preliminary character and effect of ending proceedings before the merits – as essential elements related to the technique of preliminary objections (at 32). Note that Abi-Saab qualifies the proposition that the latter element is essential by the hypothesis that the objection is upheld (at 30). The potential effect of curtailing the adjudicatory process unveils the purpose of a genuine preliminary objection. But it should not be forgotten that preliminary objections, as a matter of litigation strategy, may be used to achieve other objectives. For instance, a party may raise preliminary questions in an attempt to merely delay an outcome that it expects to be negative. See generally Jo Pasqualucci, 'Preliminary Objections before the Inter-American Court of Human Rights: Legitimate Issues and Illegitimate Tactics', 40 *Va JIL* (1999) 2. At any rate, a balance should be found between the need to take into account preliminary objections and to avoid unnecessarily disturbing the normal development of the adjudicatory process. The striking of that balance can be different across individual adjudicatory regimes.

which also involves arguments on the merits.[17] Preliminary questions' material character and effect are stressed for present purposes, not their exclusively "procedural (in a narrow sense)," "chronological," or "timeline-related" character and effect, which are important, but not essential elements of preliminary objections.

3.2.2 "Timeline-related" character and effect of preliminary questions

To be sure, preliminary questions may have a preliminary character also from a strictly chronological perspective. This is when parties (tribunal) raise a preliminary objection (question) *in limine litis*, at the first opportunity that they have in the proceedings. From the same perspective, preliminary objections (questions) may also have a preliminary effect, which is to interrupt argument and proceedings on the merits and to begin a separate stage in the proceedings – a separate round of arguments and decisions normally called "preliminary."[18] The idea, in short, is that preliminary objections' procedural character (i.e., the fact that they are raised *in limine litis*) results in their procedural effect (i.e., a separate stage in the proceedings). This is the case in ICJ procedure, for instance. According to the proceeding established by Article 79 of the ICJ Rules of Court, an objection by the respondent shall be made in writing as soon as possible, and not later than three months after the delivery of the memorial.[19] The Court then opens an independent

[17] As stated in *Canfor Corporation* v. *United States*, Decision on Preliminary Question, Arbitral Tribunal under UNCITRAL Rules, 6 June 2006, regarding jurisdictional issues: "it is not required that these jurisdictional issues must be addressed by a tribunal in a separate, preliminary phase prior to consideration of the merits" (para. 173).

[18] Certain scholars adopt a chronologically oriented concept of preliminary objections and emphasize their timeline-related character and effect. For Rosenne, "[t]he main feature of a preliminary objection is that the decision on the objection is requested before any further proceedings on the merits take place and raises issues that can be dealt with in a formal decision at the relevant preliminary stage in the proceedings." Shabtai Rosenne, 'International Courts and Tribunals, Jurisdiction and Admissibility of Inter-State Applications,' in *Max Planck Encyclopedia of Public International Law* (Oxford University Press, 2008, electronic version). Rosenne distinguishes between preliminary objections and pleas in bar, which "can be made in a regular pleading at any time in the course of the proceedings provided that it is made as soon as possible after the pleading giving rise to the plea, and the court or tribunal will decide on the disposal together with the decision on the merits." Therefore, Rosenne's distinction between preliminary objections and pleas in bar is based on the timeline-based character and effect of the former. The present book, by contrast, defines preliminary objections based on their common aspects across the international judiciary and thus cannot be based on their strictly timeline-based character and effect, which may vary.

[19] ICJ Rules of Court (1978, as amended), Article 79(1).

round of arguments and pleadings,[20] and thereupon gives a decision in the form of an actual judgment. In its judgment, the Court may uphold or reject the objection, or yet declare that the objection does not, in the circumstances of the case, possess a preliminary character.[21] The declaration that the objection does not possess a preliminary character, in effect, results in the joining of the objection to the merits. Other international tribunals adopt a similar structure. For instance, Article 97 of the ITLOS Rules of Procedure was modeled after Article 79 of the ICJ Rules. Before the International Center for the Settlement of Investment Disputes (ICSID) arbitral tribunals, it is also standard practice to have a separate proceeding on preliminary questions and, if the objection is upheld, to have a specific award to that effect.[22]

By contrast, some tribunals' rules of procedure do not foresee a timeline-related distinction between proceedings on preliminary issues and proceedings on the merits.[23] Contrast the provisions in the ICJ, ITLOS, or ICSID contexts, briefly described above, with the law at the WTO. Neither the Dispute Settlement Understanding (DSU) nor the standard

[20] *Ibid.*, Article 79(5). [21] *Ibid.*, Article 79(9).

[22] ICSID Rules of Procedure for Arbitration Proceedings (Arbitration Rules, April 2006), Rule 41(4), ICSID/15, 99 (ICSID Arbitration Rules). See also ICSID Convention, Article 41(2).

[23] The IACtHR Rules of Procedure, for instance, provide that "The presentation of preliminary objections shall not suspend the proceedings on the merits, nor their respective deadlines." Article 42(3), Rules of Procedure of the Inter-American Court of Human Rights, Approved by the Court during its LXXXV Regular Period of Sessions, held from 16 to 28 November 2009. The rule may be justified by the special concern that objections delay remedying human rights violations or their condemnation. It has also been argued that it is important in light of the rare success rate of preliminary objectors at the Inter-American Court. See Jo Pasqualucci, 'Preliminary Objections before the Inter-American Court', at 103. But the Rules are also flexible, in that they permit the court to "convene a special hearing on the preliminary objections presented, after which it shall rule thereon" and provide that the court "may decide upon the preliminary objections, the merits, and the reparations and costs of the case in a single judgment." In practice, the court tends to separate the stages. The ECtHR's rules are also flexible, in that a chronological effect to preliminary objections may or may not be recognized. According to Rule 54A of the ECtHR Rules of Court: "When giving notice of the application to the responding Contracting Party ... the Chamber may also decide to examine the admissibility and merits at the same time... The Court may, however, decide at any stage, if necessary, to take a separate decision on admissibility." See also ECHR, Article 29(1). In another context, Article 21(4) of the United Nations Commission on International Trade Law (UNCITRAL) Arbitration Rules leaves it up to the tribunal to rule on jurisdictional questions as "preliminary questions" (from a timeline-based standpoint) or to rule on them only in the final award (UNCITRAL Arbitration Rules, as revised in 2010).

working procedures provide explicit guidance on the eventuality of anticipated rulings involving preliminary issues. As the panel observed in *Mexico – Taxes on Soft Drinks*, where a preliminary objection was at stake, nothing in the DSU or the working procedures obliged the panel to issue a preliminary ruling.[24] Accordingly, panels have used discretion in issuing "preliminary rulings"[25] prior to hearings on the merits or before issuing final reports. For instance, in *United States – Softwood Lumber IV (Article 21.5 – Canada)*, the United States explicitly asked for a preliminary ruling on a jurisdictional issue by the panel. The panel's reaction was to simply ask the parties to continue their arguments and pleadings, on the assumption that the panel would reject the preliminary objection.[26] The panel emphasized that its instruction to the parties was without prejudice to the panel's actual decision.[27] As a result, the parties had to develop and discuss all their arguments on the merits despite the possibility that a procedural obstacle might ultimately preclude a decision on those arguments by the panel. One could question whether the *Softwood Lumber IV* approach should be followed in cases where the preliminary question is ripe for decision and is raised at the respondent's first opportunity. From a procedural economy perspective, it seems inappropriate to ask the respondent to develop arguments and pleadings on the merits, while the case might end because of an issue that is separate from and antecedent to the subject matter of the substantive dispute.[28] In other cases such as in *Soft Drinks*,

24 Panel Report, *Mexico – Tax Measures on Soft Drinks and Other Beverages*, WT/DS308/R, adopted 24 March 2006, as modified by Appellate Body Report WT/DS308/AB/R, para. 7.2. See also Panel Report, *Canada – Measures Affecting the Export of Civilian Aircraft*, WT/DS70/R, adopted 20 August 1999, upheld by Appellate Body Report WT/DS70/AB/R, para. 9.15.

25 The term is a misnomer. Under the DSU, panels make *findings* and issue *recommendations* that "assist" the DSB in making *rulings* under the reverse-consensus rule.

26 Panel Report, *United States – Final Countervailing Duty Determination with Respect to Certain Softwood Lumber from Canada – Recourse by Canada to Article 21.5 [of the DSU]*, WT/DS257/RW, adopted 20 December 2005, as upheld by Appellate Body Report WT/DS257/AB/RW, para. 5.1. See also Panel Report, *Argentina – Measures Affecting Imports of Footwear, Textiles, Apparel and Other Items*, WT/DS56/R, adopted 22 April 1998, as modified by Appellate Body Report WT/DS56/AB/R, para. 6.7; Panel Report, *Colombia – Indicative Prices and Restrictions on Ports of Entry*, WT/DS366/R and Corr.1, adopted 20 May 2009, para. 7.14.

27 Panel Report, *US – Softwood Lumber IV (Article 21.5 – Canada)*, para. 5.1.

28 It may be necessary for complaining parties to outline their case on the merits, nonetheless, in order to allow the respondent and the tribunal to deal with issues related to jurisdiction *ratione temporis* or *materiae*. To that effect, rules of procedure may have complainants submit memorials on the merits before the respondent even raises a preliminary objection.

while taking into account the fact that they were not obligated to issue a preliminary ruling, panels have decided on preliminary issues and communicated them to the parties before the report was made available.[29] This approach mitigates the risk that arguments and pleadings on the subject matter of the substantive dispute develop that might be doomed never to be assessed by the panel.[30]

Concern for isolating and overcoming pressing preliminary issues at an earlier stage of the proceedings is one of the reasons for a recent development to issue findings on preliminary questions at an early stage in the proceedings also at the WTO.[31] Thus, in the recent *China – Raw Materials* case,[32] a panel organized preliminary hearings even before the complainants had submitted their first written submissions. The panel decided to issue a two-staged preliminary ruling to "ensure that China is able to defend itself appropriately and that this panel process is not unduly delayed."[33] First, the panel ruled on certain issues that could not be clarified at any other stage in the proceedings. In this regard, the panel considered that the broad language used in the panel requests was not sufficient to comply with the requirements of Article 6(2) of the DSU.[34] However, second, the panel considered that it would be better to decide on the preliminary issue of whether the panel requests sufficiently identified the product coverage of each of

[29] See Panel Report, *Australia – Subsidies Provided to Producers and Exporters of Automotive Leather – Recourse to Article 21.5 of the DSU by the United States*, WT/DS126/RW and Corr.1, adopted 11 February 2000, at para. 9.9; Panel Report, *Mexico – Taxes on Soft Drinks*, at paras. 7.1–7.2. Even in those cases the complete content of the decision was made available together with the report. See also Panel Report, *European Communities and Certain Member States – Measures Affecting Trade in Large Civil Aircraft*, WT/DS316/R, adopted 1 June 2011, as modified by Appellate Body Report.

[30] As a side note, in order to guarantee the losing party's right to appeal, it is important that the preliminary findings be incorporated in the final report of the panel.

[31] See *China – Measures Related to the Exportation of Various Raw Materials*, WTO docs. WT/DS394/9, WT/DS395/9, WT/DS398/9, para. 3 (reproduced in Annex F to the Panel Report). See also Fernando Piérola, 'The Issuance of Preliminary Rulings before the Issuance of the Panel Report: A Development in the Management of Panel Proceedings?' 6 *GTCJ* (2011) 35.

[32] *China – Raw Materials*, WTO docs. WT/DS394/9, WT/DS395/9, WT/DS398/9, para. 3.

[33] *Ibid.*, para. 46.

[34] DSU, Article 6(2), establishes that Panel requests shall indicate the measures at issue and provide a brief summary of the legal basis of the complaint sufficient to present the problem clearly. It is often a ground for preliminary objections by WTO respondents and is perhaps the most litigated of all WTO provisions. See Scott Little, 'Preliminary Objections to Panel Requests and Terms of Reference: Panel and Appellate Body Rulings on the First Line of Defence in WTO Dispute Settlement,' 35 *JWT* (2001) 517.

the listed measures after the written submissions were before it.[35] In sum, the preliminary ruling that the panel organized served to exclude some, but not all, matters from the scope of future proceedings.

Certainly, the fact that a preliminary question does or does not stop the proceeding may also impact the ability of tribunals to coordinate proceedings and decisions where overlapping disputes are at stake. The earlier a potential overlap is identified and the tribunal interrupts proceedings to assess an alleged forum shopping strategy, the more room there will be for implementing procedural coordination. This was the case, for example, in the UNCLOS *MOX Plant* arbitration, where the proceedings were interrupted and the question of whether Ireland's action breached the exclusive jurisdiction of the ECJ was settled by the ECJ, bringing the arbitral proceedings to an end.[36] In the event that the preliminary objection is successful, an advance notice to that effect, furthermore, relieves the respondent from the burden of pushing its case forward (and, incidentally, also alleviates the tribunal's docket). In turn, where the preliminary objection is not upheld and the proceeding continues normally, an early answer may help the parties concentrate on the substantive aspects of the dispute and possibly define their litigation strategy before the other forum, dealing with overlapping issues while taking into account the decision on the preliminary objection. On the other hand, moving forward with the proceeding despite the raising of a preliminary objection may foster other policy goals, such as accelerating the decision-making process. In cases where forum shopping is at stake and the procedural rules do not specifically determine which one of those two alternative tracks (to stay or not to stay arguments on the merits) the adjudicator must elect, it will fall to the judge to strike the balance between the potentially conflicting goals of either accelerating decision-making or enhancing the prospects for coordination across different forums. Such policy decisions and the way they specifically affect the timeline of the proceedings, however, are not decisive for purposes of defining a preliminary objection, according to the concept adopted here.

In fact, even before those tribunals where an independent proceeding for dealing with preliminary questions does exist, from a

35 *China – Raw Materials*, WTO docs. WT/DS394/9, WT/DS395/9, WT/DS398/9, para. 46.

36 See *MOX Plant (United Kingdom v. Ireland)*, Suspension of Proceedings on Jurisdiction and Merits and Request for Further Provisional Measures, Order No 3, 24 June 2003; Termination of Proceedings, Order No 6, 6 June 2008.

material viewpoint a question does not lose its preliminary character just because it does not result in the interruption of proceedings on the merits and the opening of a separate preliminary stage. Consider *Saiga*, where Saint Vincent and Grenadines challenged Guinea's preliminary objections, among other factors, on the ground that they were submitted after the expiration of the ninety-day time limit for their presentation established in Article 97(1) of the ITLOS rules. Interpreting Article 97(1), the ITLOS explained that

> Article 97 deals with objections to jurisdiction or admissibility that are raised as preliminary questions to be dealt with in incidental proceedings. As stated therein, the article applies to an objection "the decision upon which is requested before any further proceedings on the merits". Accordingly, the time-limit in the article does not apply to objections to jurisdiction or admissibility which are not requested to be considered before any further proceedings on the merits.[37]

In the ICJ context, from which the ITLOS rules were inspired, where the Court does not consider a preliminary objection to be ripe for decision during the preliminary stage of the proceedings[38] or where a party does not raise a preliminary objection from a strictly procedural viewpoint (that is, under the proceeding established in Article 79 of the Rules of Court),[39] such objections may still be argued and decided together with the merits stage.[40] In the event that the objections refer to a prerequisite to the existence or development of the adjudicatory process, they are presented in the judgment separately before the Court proceeds to its considerations on the merits.[41] The recent

[37] *The M/V Saiga (No 2) Case (Saint Vincent and the Grenadines* v. *Guinea)*, ITLOS Case No 2, Judgment of 1 July 1999, para. 53.

[38] See *Case Concerning the Right of Passage over Indian Territory (Portugal* v. *India)*, Preliminary Objections, Judgment of 26 November 1957, 32–6.

[39] See *Case Concerning Avena and Other Mexican Nationals (Mexico* v. *United States)*, Judgment of 31 March 2004, para. 24.

[40] See also *Fisheries Jurisdiction (United Kingdom* v. *Iceland)*, Judgment of 25 July 1974, para. 42; *Fisheries Jurisdiction (Federal Republic of Germany* v. *Iceland)*, Judgment of 25 July 1974, para. 74, which dealt with issues of jurisdiction which had not yet been decided despite an express finding of jurisdiction in the previous judgments; *Fisheries Jurisdiction (United Kingdom* v. *Iceland)*, Preliminary Objections, Judgment of 2 February 1973, para. 46; *Fisheries Jurisdiction (Federal Republic of Germany* v. *Iceland)*, Preliminary Objections, Judgment of 2 February 1973, para. 46.

[41] See also Shabtai Rosenne, *The Law and Practice of the International Court: 1920–2005*, vol. II, 4th edn (Leiden: Martinus Nijhoff, 2006), at 876–81. At 807: "The preliminary objection procedure … applies when the decision is requested 'before any proceedings on the merits.' This does not prevent objections to the jurisdiction of the Court

ICJ decision at the merits stage of the *Territorial and Maritime Dispute* between Nicaragua and Colombia provides an illustration.[42] Colombia argued that Nicaragua had made a new claim after the preliminary question stage of the case had closed. In the view of Colombia, the new claim was inadmissible. The Court rejected the preliminary objection, holding that the claim fell within and arose directly out of the dispute. In siding with Nicaragua on the admissibility issue, the Court reminded the parties, however, that it was not addressing the issue of the validity of the legal grounds on which the claim was based.[43] In other words, this objection, decided at the preliminary stage, retained its materially preliminary character notwithstanding the fact that it was argued at the merits stage. An analogous approach has been followed by ICSID tribunals.[44]

In contrast to their contingent timeline-related effect of preventing further proceedings on the merits, preliminary questions' material effect on the analysis of merit and on the final outcome of the litigation is readily apparent and well accepted across international tribunals. It follows from the material character and effect of preliminary questions that these questions do not prejudice the merits of a case. The rule has been long established: a tribunal that rules on a preliminary question does not, in so doing, in any way prejudice the final outcome of the argument on the merits of the case.[45] In sum, the foremost consequence of upholding a preliminary question is that the outcome of the litigation or proceeding is affected without thereby the merits of the case being affected.[46]

or the admissibility of submissions from being raised in the course of the later written and oral proceedings, but they … do not have the effect of suspending proceedings on the merits."

42 *Territorial and Maritime Dispute (Nicaragua* v. *Colombia)*, 19 November 2012, paras. 108–12.

43 *Ibid.*, para. 112. On the merits of that claim, the Court sided with Colombia (at para. 131).

44 See *Bureau Veritas, Inspection, Valuation, Assessment and Control, BIVAC BV* v. *Paraguay*, ICSID Case No ARB/07/9, Decision of the Tribunal on Objections to Jurisdiction, 29 May 2009, paras. 50–3 (where the tribunal did not decide at the preliminary stage a new – and late – argument related to the standing of the claimant, but joined the argument to the merits stage under Article 41(2) of the ICSID Convention, to the extent that the respondent would maintain the argument).

45 See *Mavrommatis Palestine Concessions*, Judgment of 30 August 1924, PCIJ Ser A No 2 (1924), 10. This characteristic allows one to draw a method of demarcation between preliminary questions and questions of merit. See discussion in Section 3.3 below.

46 This is not to say that it is always simple to decide a preliminary question without touching at all on any aspect which may also be related to the merits. There

3.3 Procedure versus substance, back again

The distinction between preliminary questions (which refer to the development of the adjudicatory process: can or will the request be decided?) and questions of merit (which refer to the request before the tribunal: if and when procedural requirements are fulfilled, how is the request to be decided?) is based on a contextual distinction between procedure and substance for the purposes of adjudication. In this context, substantive issues relate to the subject matter of the dispute and arise from the request and the controverted claims surrounding the request. In turn, procedural issues are related to jurisdiction, action, and procedure in a narrow sense and arise from the requirements for the development of the adjudicatory process as such. As clear as this distinction may seem to be in theory, though, it is often blurred in practice. The difficulty in drawing an abstract line between the two notions implicates a difficulty also in identifying preliminary issues and issues of merit in borderline cases.

3.3.1 Procedure mutates into substance, and vice versa: a contextual distinction

Some illustrations help to visualize the potential crossover between preliminary questions (procedure) and questions of merit (substance). If a tribunal or a party raises a preliminary question, a "mini dispute" opens on that preliminary question. The procedural requirements that triggered the discussion (the preliminary questions) become, in a way, the "mini merits" of the dispute on preliminary objections, which normally reverses the roles of the applicant (who faces the objection) and the respondent (the objector). Hence, in a proceeding where a preliminary question arises and is positively argued, procedure and substance become, in effect, juxtaposed.[47] This occurs routinely in cases

may be, first, a difficulty in establishing the distinction between procedure and substance and, second, a difficulty in deciding preliminary issues which involve complex factual questions or questions of fact that are also to be answered as part of the merits. See discussion in Section 3.3 below.

[47] This problem puzzled J. H. W. Verzijl, who, in discussing the *Ambatielos* case, said that there were "two kinds of merits involved in this case, which is very confusing, I intend to distinguish them by writing 'merits' where Great Britain's obligation to arbitrate is at stake and merits where allusion is made to the validity of the claim of Mr. Ambatielos." See J. H. W. Verzijl, 'Problems of Jurisdiction in the Ambatielos Case,' 1 *NILR* (1953) 58, at 60; and *Ambatielos Case (Greece* v. *United Kingdom)*, Merits, Judgment of 19 May 1953. From an analytical viewpoint, the juxtaposition between procedure and substance is only apparent, for the procedure on preliminary

of double-decked jurisdiction such as that of the WTO, if the panel and the appellate stage are analyzed independently. A decision by a panel on a preliminary question – if and when appealed – becomes part of the "merits" of the appeal.[48] By contrast, the appeal stage has its own procedural requirements, which target the requirements for the development of the appellate phase in and of itself.[49]

Similarly, a norm generally seen as a substantive rule can operate as a procedural requirement. For instance, when the principle of the nationality of claims is at stake, the rules on the attribution of nationality under international law may turn into prerequisites to the development of the adjudicatory process.[50] Take the second phase of *Nottebohm*,[51] where the issue before the ICJ was the admissibility of the application of Liechtenstein. In holding the application to be inadmissible, the Court had to "ascertain whether the nationality conferred on Nottebohm ... can be validly invoked as against Guatemala"[52] on the basis of international law. Hence, the "substantive" rules on nationality actually entailed a "procedural" hurdle – a hurdle Liechtenstein would not overcome.

questions will have its own jurisdictional and procedural requirements which can be, in turn, separated from the merits of the issue.

48 The Appellate Body, nonetheless, still often analyzes these questions as preliminary questions. And indeed, as defined above, they remain preliminary, for they target the requirements for the development of the adjudicatory process and they limit the possibility of a panel's findings of merit. See Appellate Body Report, *India – Patent Protection for Pharmaceutical and Agricultural Chemical Products*, WT/DS50/AB/R, adopted 16 January 1998, paras. 85–96, where the Appellate Body reverses the panel's finding on the United States' claims under Article 63, TRIPS because they were not within the panel's terms of reference. As a consequence, the panel's findings on that claim have no legal effect, and it was not necessary for the Appellate Body to consider the correctness of the panel's recommendations under the said Article.

49 For instance, it is not possible to appeal or conditionally appeal panels' findings through an appellee's submission (Rule 22, Working Procedures for Appellate Review, WTO doc WT/AB/WP/6 – Appellate Body Working Procedures); an appeal or conditional appeal must be made through an appellant's submission (Rule 23, Appellate Body Working Procedures). See Appellate Body Report, *United States – Standards for Reformulated and Conventional Gasoline*, WT/DS2/AB/R, adopted 20 May 1996, at 11–12.

50 This situation is not uncommon in investment arbitration. See, for example, *Rompetrol Group NV* v. *Romania*, ICSID Case No ARB/06/13, Decision on Preliminary Objections, 18 April 2008, where the "substantive" rules on the attribution of nationality to the claimants under general international law and the Netherlands-Romania BIT are discussed in the context of an objection to the jurisdiction *ratione personae* of the tribunal.

51 *Nottebohm Case (Liechtenstein* v. *Guatemala)*, Second Phase, Judgment of 6 April 1955, at 16.

52 *Ibid.*, at 16–17.

Moreover, a procedural requirement in one proceeding may well turn out to be part of another dispute's merits. This converts what one could characterize as "procedure" in one case into "substance" in another.[53] Witness the imbroglio that arose from the construction of the MOX Plant and involved Ireland, the United Kingdom, and the European Commission. In one proceeding, Ireland brought claims against the United Kingdom before an arbitral tribunal under the UNCLOS.[54] At the core of the United Kingdom's preliminary objections in that case was Article 292 of the EC Treaty, a norm which granted exclusive jurisdiction to the ECJ for disputes under the EC Treaty. Subsequently, the European Commission brought a case before the ECJ, in which it claimed that Ireland had violated the ECJ's exclusive jurisdiction under Article 292 by instituting the UNCLOS arbitral proceedings against the United Kingdom.[55] Here, the arguments brought by the Commission were not very different from those that the United Kingdom had articulated before the arbitral tribunal. Indeed, they could well have been identical. However, unlike the parallel arbitral proceedings in which Article 292 was part of a jurisdictional (procedural) issue, the same Article 292 was now at the center of the merits question of whether Ireland had violated the exclusive jurisdiction of the ECJ.

As a result of the fluidity between procedure and substance, the distinction between preliminary questions and questions of merit functions contextually. The lesson of the foregoing examples is that the actual lines between preliminary questions and questions of merit

[53] As Gerald Fitzmaurice noted on successive questions of jurisdiction, analyzing the *Ambatielos* case: "Where one jurisdictional issue leads to another, and the first jurisdictional issue is whether the tribunal has jurisdiction to determine the second, then the second issue might, in relation to the first, be said to constitute the merits of the case." Gerald Fitzmaurice, *The Law and Procedure of the International Court of Justice*, vol. II (Cambridge: Grotius, 1986) 449. Compare *Ambatielos Case (Greece* v. *United Kingdom)*, Preliminary Objection, Judgment of 1 July 1952 (concerning the jurisdiction of the ICJ to decide on the issue of the United Kingdom's obligation to arbitrate the dispute) and *Ambatielos Case (Greece* v. *United Kingdom)*, Merits, Judgment of 19 May 1953 (now concerning the United Kingdom's obligation to arbitrate). For a recent example of this conversion, see *Jurisdictional Immunities of the State (Germany* v. *Italy: Greece Intervening)*, where the rules on jurisdictional immunities which the ICJ characterized as "procedural in nature" (at para. 58) were at the heart of Germany's claim and were therefore part of the merits of the case.

[54] *MOX Plant Case (Ireland* v. *United Kingdom)*, Arbitral Tribunal, Order No 3, 24 June 2003.

[55] *Commission* v. *Ireland*, C-459/2003, Judgment of the Court, 30 May 2006.

depend on the object of the request[56] and the controverted claims and defenses around it. Because the distinction between the process and the object of process is case sensitive, instead of a permanent frontier one should seek elements for a method of demarcation which, while taking into account the fact that the line is context dependent, would guarantee a degree of coherence in classification and predictability for litigants. Under this contextual approach, it is possible to say without blowing hot and cold that preliminary objections target questions of procedure, whereas defenses of merit target "substantive" questions.

3.3.2 *A functional and contextual demarcation method based on the object of the request and the controverted claims*

Procedure and substance in the context of adjudication, or preliminary questions and questions of merit, may first be distinguished from a functional perspective. Procedure and substance have different impacts on the outcomes of litigation. The controverted claims by the parties on their merits, built around or in opposition to the request, are the ultimate (or principal) object of an adjudicatory process. The base-line for defining those controverted claims is the request. A decision about those claims (i.e., the substance of the dispute, or the dispute's requirements of merit) is different from a decision that does not touch upon them (i.e., which is limited to preliminary requirements). Whereas a decision on a preliminary question may bring litigation and adjudication to an end just like a decision on a question of merit, the former decision refers directly to the *process* and does not prejudice the *object of the process.* Quite differently, a decision on the merits refers to and resolves the controversy around the *object of the process*, and normally explicitly or implicitly incorporates a previous decision that procedural requirements have been complied with. In sum, the outcomes embedded in procedural and substantive decisions are outcomes of *purposefully distinct exercises* applicable to different objects – on the one hand, the adjudicatory process itself; on the other hand, the object of that adjudicatory process.

In addition, using the object of the request as a starting point, the separation between preliminary and merits questions can draw on the identification of the requirements linked to the institutions entailed in the procedural relationship (jurisdiction, action, and

[56] See also Abi-Saab, *Les exceptions préliminaires*, at 179–81; Fitzmaurice, *Law and Procedure*, at 448–9.

procedure in a narrow sense) discussed in Chapter 2. Under this perspective, a question would be preliminary if it relates either to the authority of the tribunal to decide the case (jurisdiction), to the existence and exercise of the action by a party (action), or to a procedural requirement *stricto sensu* (procedure in a narrow sense). It is possible to treat all requirements linked to each of the institutions referred to above as procedural requirements in a broad sense. However, the consensual substratum of international law has led adjudicators to broadly separate "jurisdictional requirements," which refer to jurisdiction and tend to be given primary relevance, and other procedural requirements that refer to the action and procedure. This separation roughly underlies the distinction between preliminary questions of jurisdiction and preliminary questions of admissibility, as Chapter 5 further discusses.

The separation between procedural questions and questions of merit can also be described in schematic terms. From this perspective, in assessing preliminary objections by Arcadia against Randomnia, the international judge proceeds under two provisional assumptions.[57] The judge can assume, first, that Randomnia is correct with regard to the facts it alleges. Based on that assumption, the judge verifies if the facts are capable of raising a matter within jurisdiction. This verification is meant to resolve the question of whether the facts as claimed raise an issue or issues under provisions upon which the adjudicator is entitled to pronounce. The test is often expressed as an examination of whether the facts as claimed are capable of constituting breaches of provisions that fall under the judge's jurisdiction.[58] International

[57] This schema assumes that there is no question of justiciability at stake.

[58] See J. Witenberg, 'La Recevabilité des réclamations devant les juridictions internationales,' 41 *Recueil des Cours* III (1932), at 18. See also the jurisdictional test articulated by Judge Higgins in *Case Concerning Oil Platforms (Iran* v. *United States of America)*, Preliminary Objections, Judgment of 12 December 1996, Separate Opinion of Judge Higgins, para. 32, to accept *pro tem* the facts as alleged by the applicant to be true and to see on the basis of the claims of fact whether there *could* occur a violation of the clauses of the treaty on which jurisdiction is being established. This test has been taken up by several ICSID arbitral tribunals. See, for example, *Noble Energy Inc and Machala Power Cia Ltda* v. *Ecuador and Consejo Nacional de Electricidad*, ICSID Case No ARB/05/12, Decision on Jurisdiction, 5 March 2008, paras. 151–2 (at para. 152: "the Tribunal will assess for each claim if the facts alleged may be capable, *if proved*, of constituting breaches of the BIT"); *BP American Production Company & Ors* v. *Argentina*, ICSID Case No ARB/04/8, Decision on Preliminary Objections, 27 July 2006, paras. 47–51; *Salini Costruttori S.p.A. and Italstrade S.p.A.* v. *Jordan*, ICSID Case No ARB/02/13, Decision on Jurisdiction, 9 November 2004, para. 151. The present

judges routinely ask this question since their jurisdiction is not general – although sometimes this step is implicit, such as in cases where no objection to jurisdiction is raised.[59] This guarantees that the judge has authority to proceed under the delegation of the parties. Once the jurisdictional hurdle is overcome, the judge can then further assume that Randomnia is right both as a matter of fact and law on the merits of its case. The judge then assesses the objections raised without affecting this successive assumption of the claimants' success. If the judge can assess the objections raised by Arcadia without touching upon the assumptions over the facts and the law described above, the objections are indeed preliminary. If, on the contrary, Arcadia's objections require the judge to upset the aforementioned assumptions about the facts and law underlying the request, then the judge will be providing a response that involves a question of merit. The schema underscores the notion that preliminary objections are not prejudicial to the merits of the claim.[60]

author's preferred formulation would be slightly different: whether an issue is raised that the corresponding provision *covers* rather than whether an issue is raised that could violate the corresponding provision. This formulation would avoid a common confusion: sometimes, tribunals step beyond the test and require some evidence that suggests "culpability," "lack of frivolousness," or "lack of abuse," requiring a *prima facie* case on the facts over the merits – as opposed to a case for jurisdictional and admissibility purposes strictly. It is argued that this approach confuses preliminary questions and questions of merit. See, for example, *BP & Ors* v. *Argentina*, para. 52 (admitting of this theoretical possibility); *Wena Hotels Limited* v. *Egypt*, ICSID Case No ARB/98/4, 25 May 1999, 41 *LLM* (2002) 881, at 891 (hinting at evidence as to "culpability" for jurisdictional purposes).

59 See *Genocide (Croatia* v. *Serbia)*, para. 68: "the Court is [not] under an obligation to treat this question [of whether a state may properly appear before it] expressly in the reasoning in any judgment in which it rules on a preliminary objection to jurisdiction… [I]t may well choose to omit from the reasoning in the judgment any specific discussion of the point and confine itself to responding to the arguments raised by the parties. It may also choose, if it finds appropriate, to deal with the point expressly in its reasoning."

60 This is what distinguishes preliminary objections themselves from other issues that, while being part of the merits (in the sense of subject matter of the dispute), are antecedent to the "ultimate merits" of the claims. The term "ultimate merits" was used in *Case Concerning the Northern Cameroons (Cameroon* v. *United Kingdom)*, Preliminary Objections, Judgment of 2 December 1963, Separate Opinion of Judge Fitzmaurice, 103, and integrated into the vocabulary of the Court in *Appeal Relating to the Jurisdiction of the ICAO Council (India* v. *Pakistan)*, Judgment of 18 August 1972, para. 18. I understand this expression to refer to the irreducible legal value of the claim and to normally comprise the opposing requests in the final submissions of the parties with regard to the request. To avoid confusing such "preliminary questions of merit" – which give rise to defenses of merit (see *South West Africa (Ethiopia* v. *South Africa; Liberia* v. *South Africa)*, Second Phase, Judgment of 18 July

A difficult example of the demarcation between preliminary questions and questions of merit is found in *Brazil – Desiccated Coconut*, where the WTO panel regretted that "the substantive questions raised by the parties" to the dispute were of major concern, but decided "not to reach any conclusion with respect to those substantive questions" because the "issue of applicable law" was "dispositive" in that dispute.[61] In essence, the panel reasoned that the General Agreement on Tariffs and Trade (GATT) could not apply to countervailing duty investigations independent of the WTO Agreement on Subsidies and Countervailing Measures (SCM Agreement). As a result, the panel held that the Philippines' claims under the GATT (brought in isolation from the SCM agreement) "were not properly before it" and that they could not be "considered."[62] The report's wording in relation to the Philippines' claims could be interpreted to the effect that the panel issued a preliminary decision. However, under the framework suggested here, the panel decided the dispute in substance.[63] The panel, reasoning that the Philippines' claims were not properly before it because the GATT could not apply independently of the SCM Agreement, actually rejected the Philippines' claims that Brazil had acted inconsistently under the GATT. Granted, the answer was not as complete as the Philippines might have expected. It came through the answer to an antecedent question: whether there would be a violation of the GATT without a violation of the SCM Agreement. This question was part of the subject matter of the dispute, not part of the procedural requirements for a judgment on the merits of the Philippines' claims. Because the panel held that there could not be a violation of the

1966 Declaration of President Spender, at para. 26, calling a preliminary question of merit a question which renders "further examination of the merits superogatory") – with preliminary questions themselves, which do not prejudge the merits of a case, I will use the term "antecedent question" to describe a question that is prior to another, but which does not necessarily fall under the concept of preliminary objections described here. The ICJ itself used the expression "antecedent question" in *South West Africa*, Second Phase (*ibid.*), for instance, at para. 4.

[61] Panel Report, *Brazil – Measures Affecting Desiccated Coconut*, WT/DS22/R, adopted 20 March 1997, as upheld by Appellate Body Report WT/DS22/AB/R.

[62] *Ibid.*

[63] Or, more precisely, the panel decided the case on an antecedent question of merit. On the distinction between antecedent questions (of merit) and preliminary questions, see n. 60 above. Similar to the upholding of a preliminary objection, the panel's decision brought the adjudicatory process to a halt before the opposing final submissions of the parties had been addressed. Nevertheless, the decision on "applicable law" in *Brazil – Desiccated Coconut*, unlike a decision on a preliminary question, prejudged the merits of the claim.

GATT independent of the SCM Agreement, the panel in effect decided that there was no violation of the GATT. Seen from the standpoint of the dichotomy between the requirements of process and the merits of claims, this is not a preliminary question. The Philippines requested a finding on Brazil's alleged violation of the GATT. But the question of whether the GATT applied independently could not be answered by the panel without upsetting the assumption that there was a GATT violation. Indeed, in answering that question, the panel's decision changed that assumption. It was a decision on a question of merit.

A further example can be taken from *Certain Phosphate Lands in Nauru*. In that case, Australia alleged that Nauru had waived its claims related to the rehabilitation of certain phosphate lands and therefore could not bring the case to the ICJ. [64] One could be inclined to consider this objection a defense on the merits. After all, a waiver concerning Nauru's claims on their very merits was at stake. But the ICJ assessed the objection as preliminary. The Court declined to hold that the Nauruan authorities had at any time clearly and unequivocally waived the claims. Under the framework proposed here, this objection would also qualify as preliminary. In spite of the merits of Nauru's claims (i.e., whether Nauru had a right to the rehabilitation), a waiver by Nauru of its claims would have precluded the possibility that Nauru could go back and make those claims in the first place (i.e., whether Nauru had a right to raise the question of rehabilitation at all). In short, there would be a block to the very submission of those claims to adjudication – a preliminary matter. In deciding that issue, the Court could well assume that Nauru possessed the substantive rights it claimed and did not need to change that assumption.

3.4 Preliminary questions and facts entangled with the merits: practical alternatives

The method described above arguably makes it easy in many cases to distinguish between preliminary requirements and matters related to substance; and should make this easier in most cases. Yet, it is not uncommon for the resolution of a preliminary question to require extensive assessment of facts. In those cases the exercise becomes

[64] *Case Concerning Certain Phosphate Lands in Nauru (Nauru* v. *Australia)*, Preliminary Objections, Judgment of 26 June 1992, paras. 12–21.

complex even if one may still be able to distinguish procedural and substantive matters from the functional perspective laid out above (i.e., whether the purpose of the assessment is to resolve a question about the object of the adjudicatory process or about the process itself). In particular, where the factual context to decide on a preliminary requirement is entangled with the factual context of the substance of the dispute there is a practical problem of distinguishing preliminary questions and questions of merit from a chronological perspective, because the parties will need to develop arguments that may refer both to procedure and to substance for the preliminary question to be resolved. For example, in the *Tuna and Tuna Products* WTO dispute between Mexico and the United States,[65] the analysis of a potential preliminary objection based on Article 2005(4) of the NAFTA would likely have required detailed assessment of the facts in dispute, which would also refer to the merits. After all, for NAFTA Article 2005(4) to apply and preclude WTO litigation, the WTO panel would need to decide (i) whether the dispute involved a sanitary, phytosanitary, or standards-related measure, (ii) whether that measure was adopted or maintained by the United States to protect its environment or its human, animal, or plant life, and (iii) whether the dispute would raise factual issues concerning the environment, health, safety, or conservation, including directly related scientific matters. A decision on those matters would be unlikely to be reached without an examination of issues entangled with the substance of the dispute. Still, the assessment would be conducted in connection with a prerequisite to the development of the WTO process (i.e., the question of whether Article 2005(4) of the NAFTA precluded Mexico's WTO claims) rather than the substantive questions at issue (i.e., whether Mexico's WTO claims were well founded under the Agreement on Technical Barriers to Trade (TBT), for instance).

In order to respect the notion that preliminary issues should not prejudice the merits of claims, tribunals have developed alternatives that seek, first, to weigh the importance of disposing of preliminary issues at an early stage, thus deciding on the continuity of the proceedings or at least narrowing down the scope of the proceeding on the merits to the extent that this is possible; and second, to avoid precipitating decisions on issues where further clarification by the parties may be

[65] *United States – Measures Concerning the Importation, Marketing and Sale of Tuna and Tuna Products*, WT/DS/381.

important and even necessary.[66] The following discussion refers to the three basic alternatives that have been employed in this regard.

3.4.1 *Alternative 1: postponing the decision on the preliminary question until the merits stage*

One alternative that tribunals employ is to postpone the decision on the preliminary question until reaching the merits stage. This option nullifies the intended chronological effect of a preliminary question from the respondents' perspective (i.e., termination of the proceedings before the merits stage). However, it guarantees that the tribunal does not resolve questions that are not ripe for a decision, that is, before the disputing parties exhaustively make their case on such questions. This is the approach, in effect, adopted by the ICJ when it declares that a preliminary objection "does not possess, in the circumstances of the case, an exclusively preliminary character."[67] For instance, in *Activities in and Against Nicaragua*, the Court had to determine whether any third state would be "affected" by its ruling before it could decide whether it had jurisdiction under the United States' declaration of acceptance.[68] However, the Court could not determine whether there were "affected" states – and therefore could not determine its jurisdiction based on the United States' declaration of acceptance – without a better sense of what would be the general lines of its judgment on the merits. This question, according to the Court, concerned matters of substance related to the merits.[69] Accordingly, the Court joined the issue to the merits stage. Subsequently, at the merits stage, the Court found that it did not have jurisdiction to entertain the claims by Nicaragua based on multilateral treaties, as a result of the conclusion that El Salvador would be affected by the Court's decision.[70]

66 *Territorial and Maritime Dispute (Nicaragua* v. *Colombia)*, 13 December 2007, at para. 51: "In principle, a party raising preliminary objections is entitled to have these objections answered at the preliminary stage of the proceedings unless the Court does not have before it all facts necessary to decide the questions raised or if answering the preliminary objection would determine the dispute, or some elements thereof, on the merits." See also *Empresas Luchetti, S.A. and Luchetti Peru S.A.* v. *Peru*, ICSID Case No ARB/03/4, Decision on Annulment, 13 August 2007, Dissenting Opinion of Sir Franklin Berman.

67 Article 79(9), ICJ Rules of Court.

68 *Case Concerning Military and Paramilitary Activities in and against Nicaragua (Nicaragua* v. *United States of America)*, Jurisdiction and Admissibility, Judgment of 26 November 1984, paras. 75–6.

69 *Ibid.*

70 *Case Concerning Military and Paramilitary Activities in and against Nicaragua (Nicaragua* v. *United States of America)*, Merits, Judgment of 27 June 1986, paras. 42–56.

The option to postpone a decision on a preliminary question until the merits stage is also expressly foreseen and frequently employed in the context of ICSID arbitration.[71] Indeed, investor-state arbitral tribunals have often joined to the merits stage situations concerning determinations of complex factual questions – for example, the critical date of an alleged expropriation for the assessment of jurisdiction *ratione temporis*,[72] or whether investments were made "in accordance with the law" – as prerequisites to a ruling of merit.[73] Joining a decision to the merits stage guarantees that the parties fully develop their arguments within the context of the dispute as a whole. This option may be called for to ensure procedural fairness and the rights of both parties to be heard. On the other hand, where the objection is eventually upheld in the subsequent stage of the proceedings, joining it to the merits stage will have prolonged the proceedings. This raises issues of costs and legal certainty for the parties and for the dispute-settlement machinery involved.[74]

[71] Article 32(2), ICSID Convention. See, for example, *Rompetrol* v. *Romania*, paras. 111–15; *Ioannis Kardassopoulus* v. *Georgia*, ICSID Case No ARB/05/18, Decision on Jurisdiction, 6 July 2007, paras. 257–61; *World Duty Free Company Limited* v. *Kenya*, ICSID Case No Arb/00/7, Award of 4 October 2006, para. 102; *Generation Ukraine, Inc.* v. *Ukraine*, ICSID Case No ARB/00/9, Award of 16 September 2003, paras. 6.1–6.4.

[72] See *Ioannis Kardassopoulus* v. *Georgia*, paras. 257–61. Note that, in other cases, tribunals may consider the question to be ripe for decision, based on the arguments of the parties. See *African Holding Company of America Inc. (AHL) and the Society of Construction in Congo (SARL)* v. *The Democratic Republic of Congo*, ICSID Case No ARB/05/21, Decision on Jurisdiction and Admissibility, 23 July 2008 and *Empresas Luchetti, S.A. and Luchetti Peru S.A.* v. *Peru*, ICSID Case No ARB/03/4, 7 February 2005, paras. 48–62. See also *Luchetti and Luchetti Peru* v. *Peru*, Decision on Annulment. Note that the Annulment Committee upheld the tribunal's decision, but not without criticism.

[73] See *Hulley Enterprises Limited (Cyprus) v. Russia*, PCA Case No AA 226, Interim Award on Jurisdiction and Admissibility under UNCITRAL Rules, 30 November 2009, para. 435; *Veteran Petroleum Limited (Cyprus)* v. *Russia*, PCA Case No AA 228, Interim Award on Jurisdiction and Admissibility under UNCITRAL Rules, 30 November 2009, para. 492; and *Yukos Universal Limited (Isle of Man)* v. *Russia*, PCA Case No AA 227, Interim Award on Jurisdiction and Admissibility under UNCITRAL Rules, 30 November 2009, para. 436.

[74] Thus, as a reaction to the ICJ decisions in *South West Africa (Second Phase)* and *Barcelona Traction Light and Power Company, Limited (New Application) (Belgium* v. *Spain)*, Second Phase Judgment of 5 February 1970, there was a call from United Nations members and academics to encourage decisions on preliminary objections to be made at the earliest possible stage. See discussion in Rosenne, *Law and Practice*, at 810–11. The issue is also relevant in the ICSID context, especially in the light of the cost of ICSID proceedings.

3.4.2 *Alternative 2: provisionally concluding on facts related to the merits at the preliminary stage*

Another alternative to avoid precipitating decisions related to the merits is to limit the decision on the preliminary question involving facts bound with the merits solely to the preliminary context.[75] In this option, the tribunal decides the preliminary question by means of a "provisional conclusion" which does not prejudice a conclusion related to the same facts as a question of merit.[76] This option enables an early decision on the preliminary question to be made, while the tribunal remains at liberty to address it again as a question of merit. For example, in *German Interests in Upper Silesia*, the PCIJ was faced with a preliminary objection by Poland. But in presenting the objection, Poland did not refrain from making some arguments related to the merits in support of its preliminary objection. The Court held that it had to proceed to the inquiry, even if this would involve touching upon subjects belonging to the merits of the case. The Court cautioned, however, that it was "to be clearly understood that nothing which the Court says in the present judgment can be regarded as restricting its freedom to estimate the value of any arguments advanced by either side on the same subjects during the proceedings on the merits."[77] This approach raised the possibility of contradictions between provisional conclusions on the facts for the sole purpose of continuing the proceedings, and a potential definitive conclusion on the facts. Although the object and purpose of assessing a preliminary question and of assessing the merits are different, potential internal contradictions within the same proceedings should clearly be avoided. In order to minimize that risk, it is important to limit the assessment on the preliminary stage to

[75] See Abi-Saab, *Les exceptions préliminaires*, at 189–94.

[76] See *Interhandel Case (Switzerland* v. *United States of America)*, Preliminary Objections, Judgment of 21 March 1959, 24: "In order to determine whether the examination of the grounds thus invoked is excluded from the jurisdiction of the Court for the reason alleged by the United States, … the Court does not, at the present stage of the proceedings, intend to assess the validity of the grounds invoked by the Swiss Government or to give an opinion on their interpretation, since that would be to enter upon the merits of the dispute. The Court will confine itself to considering whether the grounds invoked by the Swiss Government are such as to justify the provisional conclusion that they may be of relevance in this case and, if so, whether questions relating to the validity and interpretation of those grounds are questions of international law."

[77] *Case Concerning Certain German Interests in Polish Upper Silesia*, Preliminary Objections, Judgment of 25 August 1925, PCIJ Ser A No 6 (1925) 1, at 15.

those issues which are strictly necessary for that purpose. Restraint can also be important to avoid allowing arguments on the merits to hijack the preliminary stage of the proceedings and unduly delay the adjudicatory process.[78]

3.4.3 Alternative 3: definitively concluding on the issue related to the merits at the preliminary stage

On the other hand, if a tribunal has jurisdiction and it is clear that it has before it all the necessary facts to make a decision on the preliminary issue involving questions of fact entangled with the merits, and if this decision is not prejudicial to the parties' right to be heard, the tribunal may also take a step further and provide an early decision on the issue of merit at the preliminary stage – not in the form of a provisional conclusion, but as a definitive one. In this sense, tribunals have yet another possible course of action when they face factual issues related to preliminary questions bound with issues of merit: rather than postponing the decision on the preliminary question to the merits stage, tribunals may anticipate the decision on the question of merit during the preliminary stage.[79] The availability of this option depends on the tribunal's certainty with regard to the fulfillment of the procedural prerequisites for a judgment on the merits,[80] but such possibility should not be ruled out.[81] Thus, in the ICSID arbitration in *Salini* v. *Morocco*, Morocco objected to the jurisdiction *ratione personae* of the tribunal, arguing that the

[78] See Article 79(7), ICJ Rules of Court ("The statements of facts and law in the pleadings referred to in paragraphs 4 and 5 of this Article, and the statements and evidence presented at the hearings contemplated by paragraph 6, shall be confined to those matters that are relevant to the objection"); and ICJ Practice Direction VI ("Where objections of lack of jurisdiction or of inadmissibility are being considered, oral proceedings are to be limited to statements on the objections").

[79] See also *Territorial and Maritime Dispute (Nicaragua* v. *Colombia)*, 13 December 2007, paras. 50–1 (where the ICJ recognizes the possibility); Rule 41(5), ICSID Arbitration Rules (whereby a party may file an objection that the claim is manifestly without legal merit). See *Trans-Global Petroleum Inc.* v. *Jordan*, ICSID Case No ARB/07/25, Decision on the Respondent's Objection under Rule 41(5) of the ICSID Arbitration Rules, 12 May 2008.

[80] Conceivably, specific constituent instruments might also authorize the tribunal to terminate proceedings with regard to substance before deciding definitively about the preliminary issues.

[81] In *Global Trading Resources Corp. and Globex International Inc.* v. *Ukraine*, ICSID Case No ARB/09/11, Award, 23 November 2010, a ruling referred to below under ICSID Arbitration Rule 41(5), the Tribunal raised a question that is also relevant in this context: "[W]hat other materials might either Party … bring to bear if the question at issue were to be postponed until a later stage in the proceedings?"

acts claimed against Morocco by the respondent were not attributable to Morocco.[82] The tribunal did have jurisdiction, since the claimants had directed their claims against Morocco and had based them on the Italy–Morocco BIT. Therefore, a decision on the issue of attribution was indeed an issue related to the merits, rather than a jurisdictional issue. But according to the tribunal, the parties had a legitimate expectation that it decide the question of attribution at that stage.[83] As a result, the tribunal decided that the actions at stake were attributable to Morocco, even at the preliminary stage.[84]

ICSID arbitral tribunals' pragmatic inclination to avoid a hard-and-fast split between decisions on preliminary issues or issues of merit from a chronological perspective, as indicated in *Salini*, is also reflected in the emerging case law on Rule 41(5) of the ICSID Arbitration Rules. Rule 41(5), established in a 2006 review, sets forth an expedited procedure for objections that a claim is manifestly without "legal merit."[85] Based on the wording of this provision alone, which applies to claims manifestly without legal merit, one could be inclined to say that it does not cover preliminary objections that are distinct from the merits. A case could then be made that Rule 41(5) targets cases that are manifestly hopeless regarding the claims made as to their merits. Such interpretation would arguably find support in Article 36(6) of the ICSID Convention, which authorizes the Secretary General not to register a request for arbitration in the event that the dispute is manifestly outside the jurisdiction of the Centre.[86] After all, if the Secretary General has found that a dispute *is not* manifestly outside the jurisdiction of the Centre it may seem redundant to establish another expedited procedure for

[82] *Salini Construttori SpA and Intalstrade SpA* v. *Kingdom of Morocco*, ICSID Case No ARB/00/4, Decision on Jurisdiction, 16 July 2001, paras. 28–35.

[83] *Ibid.*, para. 30. [84] *Ibid.*, para. 35.

[85] Rule 41(5), ICSID Arbitration Rules: "Unless the parties have agreed to another expedited procedure for making preliminary objections, a party may, no later than 30 days after the constitution of the Tribunal, and in any event before the first session of the Tribunal, file an objection that a claim is manifestly without legal merit. The party shall specify as precisely as possible the basis for the objection. The Tribunal, after giving the parties the opportunity to present their observations on the objection, shall, at its first session or promptly thereafter, notify the parties of its decision on the objection. The decision of the Tribunal shall be without prejudice to the right of a party to file an objection pursuant to paragraph (1) or to object, in the course of the proceeding, that a claim lacks legal merit."

[86] Article 36(3), ICSID Convention: "The Secretary-General shall register the request unless he finds, on the basis of the information contained in the request, that the dispute is manifestly outside the jurisdiction of the Centre. He shall forthwith notify the parties of registration or refusal to register."

a tribunal to find whether the same dispute *is* manifestly outside the jurisdiction of the Centre. Yet, interestingly, an emerging consensus among ICSID tribunals is that Rule 41(5) applies both to manifest lack of jurisdiction and to manifest lack of merit. This interpretation highlights the protective function of Rule 41(5) and is in line with the recognition that manifest lack of jurisdiction, manifest lack of admissibility, and manifest lack of merit all enable justifications to avoid unnecessary prolongation of proceedings from a chronological perspective.[87]

Thus, the arbitral decision in *Brandes* v. *Venezuela*[88] established that the expression "legal merit" in Rule 41(5) "covers all objections to the effect that the proceedings should be discontinued at an early stage because, *for whatever reason*, the claim can manifestly not be granted by the Tribunal"[89] – hence, encompassing both "jurisdictional questions" and "questions of merit."[90] The tribunal pointed out that there is no objective reason why the intent behind Rule 41(5) – not burdening the parties with long and costly proceedings about patently unmeritorious claims – should be limited to questions of merit and exclude an examination of questions of jurisdiction.[91] While this approach blurs the notions of preliminary questions and questions of merit, it emphasizes the protective function underlying Article 41(5) of the ICSID Arbitration Rules and can be used to foster procedural economy. Indeed, if claims are manifestly outside the jurisdiction of a tribunal, there are strong reasons to support the termination of the proceedings at the earliest opportunity. Two other decisions made public at the end of 2010 follow a similar approach.[92]

If Arbitration Rule 41(5) does apply to a manifest lack of jurisdiction, the ICSID machinery's approach to jurisdiction can be described as a

[87] See also Antonio Parra, 'The Development of Regulations and Rules of the International Centre for Settlement of Investment Disputes,' 41 *Int'l Lawyer* (2007), 47; and Aurelia Antonietti, 'The 2006 Amendments to the ICSID Rules and Regulations and the Additional Facilities Rules,' 21 *ICSID Rev* (2006) 427, at 439.

[88] *Brandes Investment Partners, LP* v. *Venezuela*, ICSID Case No ARB/08/3, Decision on the Respondent's Objection to Jurisdiction under Rule 41(5) of the ICSID Arbitration Rules, 2 February 2009.

[89] *Ibid.*, para. 55 (emphasis added). According to the Tribunal, the wording "legal merit," "by itself, does not provide a reason why the question whether or not a tribunal has jurisdiction and is competent to hear and decide a claim could not be included in the very general notion that the claim filed is '*without legal merit*'" (at para. 50). See also Aurelia Antonietti, 'The 2006 Amendments,' at 439–40.

[90] *Brandes* v. *Venezuela*, para. 50. [91] *Ibid.*, para. 52.

[92] *Global Trading* v. *Ukraine*; *Rachel S. Grynberg, Stephen M. Grynberg, Myriam Z. Grynberg, and RSM Production Corporation* v. *Grenada*, ICSID Case No ARB/10/6, Award of 30 November 2010.

"belts and braces" one. In practice, a manifest lack of jurisdiction in the ICSID arbitration context can be addressed at two different levels even before the respondent triggers the traditional procedure on preliminary objections under Article 41(1) of the Arbitration Rules.[93] At a first level, as explained before, Article 36(3) of the ICSID Convention authorizes the Secretary General to not register a request for arbitration if the dispute is manifestly outside the jurisdiction of the Centre.[94] This screening power of the Secretary General under Article 36(3) of the ICSID Convention has led to formal denials to register these requests.[95] For example, Ibrahim Shihata and Antonio Parra report that the Secretary General's power has been used in relation to a request arising from a sale of goods – which manifestly could not be considered an investment protected under the ICSID Convention, despite the fact that the request allegedly was made on the basis of the relevant BIT. Another request, made by an individual who was a national of both states which were party to a BIT, was denied on the basis that Article 25(2)(a) of the ICSID Convention excluded from the Centre's jurisdiction disputes between a state and natural persons with the nationality of that same state, without exceptions.[96] According to Shihata and Parra, moreover, in most instances of unregistrable requests, the requesting parties themselves withdraw the request in order to prevent the ICSID's Secretary General from formally refusing it.[97] Considering that account, it would be misleading to assume that Article 36(3) is not of practical importance based solely on the fact that there have been relatively few formal refusals of registration under that provision.[98] In any

[93] Or, as the Tribunal in *Brandes* v. *Venezuela* put it: "there are actually three levels at which jurisdictional objections could be examined. First by the Secretariat, and if the case passes that level, it would then be under Rule 41(5), and if it passes that level, it might still be under Rule 41(1)." *Brandes* v. *Venezuela*, Rule 41(5) of the ICSID Arbitration Rules, para. 53. In fact, however, there are four such levels, since jurisdictional questions can also be examined in the merits award where the timeline-related effect of jurisdictional objections is not present.

[94] Article 36(3), ICSID Convention is reproduced in n. 60 above.

[95] See *Asian Express Int'l PTE Limited* v. *Greater Colombo Economic Commission*, as reported in 2 *News from ICSID* (1985, Winter), at 3 and 2 *News from ICSID* (1985, Summer), at 3: "The Secretary-General finds that the dispute is 'manifestly outside of the jurisdiction of the Centre' and accordingly notifies the parties of his refusal to register the request."

[96] Ibrahim Shihata and Antonio Parra, 'The Experience of the International Centre for the Settlement of Investment Disputes,' 14 *ICSID Rev* (1999) 299, at 308.

[97] *Ibid.*, 308–9.

[98] In practice, parties consult with the Centre and have the option to either supplement or withdraw the request after they have submitted it. See also Christoph

event, the screening power of the Secretary General may serve to prevent the clearest cases where the request for ICSID arbitration is outside the jurisdiction of the Centre.

At a second level, as explained above, Article 41(5) of the ICSID Arbitration Rules establishes an expedited strikeout procedure that may be triggered based on a perceived manifest lack of jurisdiction. One might argue, therefore, that Article 36(3) of the ICSID Convention and Arbitration Rule 41(5) are duplicative procedures that make the adjudication of investor claims more complex. Nonetheless, Article 36(3) of the ICSID Convention and Arbitration Rule 41(5) are different on at least three accounts. First, Rule 41(5) is broader than Article 36(3) in that the former arguably addresses preliminary questions and questions of merit broadly, and the latter addresses only jurisdictional issues *stricto sensu* related to the Centre – as opposed to the jurisdictional issues related to the tribunals. Second, whereas under Article 36(3) the decision of the Secretary General is made "on the basis of the information contained in the request,"[99] Rule 41(5) grants the respondents a chance to object, and the decision is based on the "observations on the objection" by both parties. After both parties have argued their cases, something which was not "manifest" in the context of the registration of a request – to which Article 36(3) applies – may well become "manifest" in the context of a decision under Rule 41(5). Third, unlike in the case of Article 41(5), the application of Article 36(3) does not lead to an arbitral award or decision with a similar legal effect, but to a decision by the Secretary General.[100]

At any rate, one should be careful to avoid the risk that reluctant respondents' use of Arbitration Rule 41(5) may unduly delay and further increase the cost of ICSID arbitration. The tribunal in *Brandes* v. *Venezuela* was mindful of this possibility, but it considered that the proceeding was "not overly burdensome and if it can avoid cases to go ahead if there is a manifest absence of jurisdiction, it can clearly fulfill the basic objectives of this Rule which is to prevent the continuation of a procedure when the claim is without legal merit."[101] Notwithstanding the tribunal's considerations, it remains the case that both Article 36(3)

Schreuer, *The ICSID Convention: A Commentary* (Cambridge University Press, 2001), at 458–65. Note, furthermore, that the Secretary General has not refrained to use his powers to request further information from claimants on the question of the Centre's jurisdiction, as part of his attributions under Article 36(3) of the ICSID Convention. See *BIVAC* v. *Paraguay*, paras. 22–5.

99 See also *Brandes* v. *Venezuela*, para. 51.

100 See also *Trans-Global* v. *Jordan*, para. 92.

101 *Brandes* v. *Venezuela*, para. 54.

of the ICSID Convention and Article 41(5) of the ICSID Arbitration Rules embrace a similarly worded "manifest lack" standard. Therefore, if Article 41(5) of the Arbitration Rules encompasses jurisdictional issues, it does partially overlap with Article 36(3) of the ICSID Convention. To an objecting respondent's dismay, both the Secretary General and arbitral tribunals may be reluctant not to register requests or to discontinue proceedings where controversial questions of law or fact have to be decided. As the tribunal in *Trans-Global* v. *Jordan* synthesized it, the "manifest" standard "requires the respondent to establish its objection clearly and obviously, with relative ease and dispatch. The standard is thus set high..."[102] But whereas setting a high bar is important to balance the protective and enabling functions in ICSID adjudication, this time, to aggrieved investors' dismay, the several layers of proceedings available to address preliminary objections may result in the prolongation of the proceedings (and make them considerably more costly). In order to allow tribunals to avoid the potentially negative consequences of Article 41(5) of the Arbitration Rules and reap the procedural economy objectives of the rule, it is suggested that the proceedings under that article be administered as flexibly as possible.[103] Moreover, ICSID tribunals' apportioning costs relative to success at that stage of the proceedings might provide some disincentive for the frivolous use of the mechanism under Article 41(5) of the Arbitration Rules.

Other international dispute settlement mechanisms outside the context of investment arbitration explicitly foresee screening or accelerated strikeout procedures that may apply to preliminary questions and questions of merit (the latter when the claims are *prima facie* unfounded or manifestly groundless). Article 294 of the UNCLOS, for instance, establishes a procedure for addressing claims that may constitute an abuse of process or be *prima facie* unfounded.[104] This procedure

[102] *Trans-Global* v. *Jordan*, para. 97. See also para. 90: "the rule is directed only at clear and obvious cases"; *Brandes* v. *Venezuela*, paras. 63–4; and *Global Trading* v. *Ukraine*, para. 35.

[103] In *Global Trading* v. *Ukraine*, for instance, it was agreed that the first session of the Rule 41(5) procedure would be held in conjunction with the first session of the Tribunal (para. 18), potentially avoiding the convening of a session exclusively on Rule 41(5).

[104] Article 294, UNCLOS: "1. A court or tribunal ... shall determine at the request of a party, or may determine *proprio motu*, whether the claim constitutes an abuse of legal process or whether *prima facie* it is well founded. If the court or tribunal determines that the claim constitutes an abuse of legal process or is *prima facie* unfounded, it shall take no further action in the case... 3. Nothing in this article

is without prejudice to a party's right to make preliminary objections in accordance with the applicable rules of procedure, as Article 294(3) makes clear. Analogously to the discussion of ICSID Arbitration Rule Article 41(5), it is suggested that Article 294 of the UNCLOS could be interpreted as a procedure for addressing abuse of process or manifest lack of foundation for a claim for "whatever reason," be it preliminary or substantive. Along those lines, both the American and the European Conventions on Human Rights provide for procedures to assess preliminary (e.g., inadmissibility due to lack of exhaustion of local remedies, time-bars, *lis pendens* or *res judicata*)[105] and substantive (e.g., manifestly ill-founded claims)[106] aspects that may prevent further examination of a case.

Another example is Article 92(1) of the ECJ Rules of Procedure, which establishes a strikeout procedure in the event of either clear lack of jurisdiction or manifest inadmissibility.[107] In yet another context, Article 38(5) of the ICJ Rules of Court can also be considered as a filter against the registration of cases where jurisdiction is lacking. That provision disciplines the administration of applications where the jurisdictional title is nonexistent at the time of the application. In those cases, although the respondent may agree to appear before the Court under the doctrine of *forum prorogatum*, there is clearly no specific jurisdiction toward the respondent invested in the Court at the moment when the application is submitted. Therefore, the case cannot enter the general list, nor can the Court take any action in the proceedings, "unless and until the State against which such application is made consents to the Court's jurisdiction for the purposes of the case."[108] Before the 1978 revision of the ICJ Rules of Court and under the previous version of current Article 38(5), the Court treated an application based on consent yet to be given by the respondent in the same way as any other application. Thus, the Court's registry would issue the usual notifications and the case would be included on the general list, even if specific jurisdiction toward the respondent

affects the right of any party to a dispute to make preliminary objections in accordance with the applicable rules of procedure."

105 Article 35(1) and (2), ECHR; Articles 46, 47(a) and (d), ACHR.

106 Article 35(3), ECHR; Article 47 (b) and (c), ACHR.

107 See Article 92(1), Consolidated Version of the Rules of Procedure of the Court of Justice, Official Journal of the European Union, C177/1, 2 June 2010 (ECJ Rules of Procedure). The wording and location of the provision seem to confine it to actual preliminary questions.

108 Article 38(5), ICJ Rules of Court.

clearly did not exist. Further, the ICJ could only remove the case from the list if the respondent explicitly rejected the Court's jurisdiction to entertain it. The Court then had to list cases where jurisdiction plainly did not exist,[109] and respondents had to request delisting. Now, except for the transmission of the application to the potential respondent, no further action is taken by the Court and the potential respondent is free to answer as it sees fit.[110]

Provisions establishing screening mechanisms and strikeout procedures can certainly comfort wary respondents in cases where there is manifestly no jurisdiction vested in the tribunal (a preliminary question), or that the case is legally hopeless (a question of merit that can nonetheless be addressed at an early stage in the proceedings). They also provide a clearer legal foundation on which to base an expedited strikeout in the present stage of development of international adjudication. Still, considering that a tribunal must satisfy itself as to its jurisdiction *ex officio* before deciding on the merits of a case,[111] it is suggested that a strikeout power against applications where there is manifestly no jurisdiction is embedded in the principle of *la compétence de la compétence*. In this sense, the explicit recognition of a strikeout power in cases of manifest lack of jurisdiction at the first opportunity to do so would be declaratory: provided that the question is ripe for a decision, a specific procedure for early strikeouts is not necessary. This consideration might explain the inclination of ICSID tribunals to address procedural questions under Rule 41(5) in addition to questions of merit – notwithstanding the fact that the Rule's text mentions claims "manifestly without legal merit," as discussed above.

Further support for this proposition can be found in the ICJ decision to remove from the general list the *Legality of Use of Force* cases against Spain and the United States by means of orders related to a request for provisional measures.[112] In both cases, the Court found that

109 See *Treatment in Hungary of Aircraft and Crew of United States of America (United States of America* v. *Hungary)*, Order of 12 July 1954, 99; *Treatment in Hungary of Aircraft and Crew of United States of America (United States of America* v. *Union of Soviet Socialist Republics)*, Order of 12 July 1954, 103.

110 See *Certain Questions of Mutual Assistance in Criminal Matters (Djibouti* v. *France)*, Judgment of 4 June 2008, para. 63 (where the Court discusses the review of Article 38(5) of the ICJ Rules of Court).

111 See discussion in Chapter 5.

112 *Case Concerning Legality of Use of Force (Yugoslavia* v. *Spain)*, Provisional Measures, Order of 2 June 1999; *Case Concerning Legality of Use of Force (Yugoslavia* v. *United States of America)*, Provisional Measures, Order of 2 June 1999.

the titles of jurisdiction invoked by Yugoslavia against Spain and the United States were insufficient to reach even the lower *prima facie* jurisdictional threshold that is applicable to requests for provisional measures.[113] The Court, noting that it manifestly lacked jurisdiction in the event, considered that "to maintain the General List a case upon which it appears certain that the Court will not be able to adjudicate on the merits would most assuredly not contribute to the sound administration of justice."[114] Accordingly, it terminated the proceedings and removed the cases from the list. Note that under Article 38(5) of the ICJ Rules of Court discussed above, where the applicant is not able to identify a jurisdictional title the case cannot even enter the general list. In *Legality of Use of Force*, however, Yugoslavia had indicated potential jurisdictional titles, and as a result, the cases against Spain and the United States entered the Court's general list. In those circumstances, removing the cases from the list while still at the provisional measures stage freed Spain and the United States from having to continue arguing a case that was doomed not to go forward and respected the fact that there had been no delegation of jurisdiction to the ICJ. In sum, it is suggested that tribunals have a power of preliminary dismissal for cases of manifest lack of jurisdiction. This power may be used to address flawed forum selection strategies, highlighting the protective function of procedural norms.

3.5 Concluding remarks

Preliminary questions refer to prerequisites to the existence and development of an adjudicatory process. Preliminary objections are actions by a party, notably the respondent, that raise these prerequisites for the existence and development of the adjudicatory process. This chapter presented and discussed the above working concepts of preliminary questions and objections. In doing so, it referred to the distinction between procedural questions and questions of merit as a starting

[113] See *Legality of Use of Force (Yugoslavia* v. *Spain)*, paras. 23–5 (discussing a twelve-month limitation on Spain's declaration of acceptance as a bar to jurisdiction under Article 36(2) of the Statute), 28–33 (discussing Spain's reservation to Article IX of the Genocide Convention), and 34–5 (referring to Spain's refusal to accept jurisdiction for that specific case); *Legality of Use of Force (Yugoslavia* v. *United States)*, paras. 21–5 (discussing the United States' reservation to Article IX of the Genocide Convention), and paras. 26–8 (referring to the United States' refusal to accept jurisdiction for that specific case).

[114] *Ibid.*, para. 29.

point. Considering that such distinction is contextual, this chapter proposed that the basic parameter for classifying a question as either one of merits or procedure is the object of the request.

The concepts of preliminary questions and objections herein anchor on their material character (i.e., to be logically assessed before the merits) and on their material effect (i.e., to potentially prevent or postpone a decision of merit). This perspective contrasts to strictly time-based definitions of preliminary questions that focus on the fact that preliminary objections are submitted *in limine litis* and prevent or interrupt further proceedings. The latter approach may be fit for certain cases before some international tribunals, such as the ICJ, where a preliminary question presented in accordance with Article 79 of the Rules of Court results in the opening of a separate stage in the proceedings, and generally avoids further pleadings on questions of merit. However, from a more general perspective, a so-called "preliminary" stage is not necessary for a given question to qualify as preliminary. Indeed, before some adjudicatory bodies and in certain cases there is no such "preliminary" stage. Moreover, even where there is a preliminary stage, a preliminary question can still be entertained after such stage. On the other hand, in certain cases, questions of merit can be addressed at a "preliminary" stage. By focusing on the material character and effect of preliminary questions and objections, an overall assessment of the technique of preliminary objections as it operates before international adjudicatory bodies in general is permitted. The following discussion refers to a number of such bodies. Because the definition of preliminary objections presented here is based on general features, it is claimed that this definition may be used in future general and comparative studies of procedure before international tribunals.

4 The source and contours of international tribunals' authority to rule on preliminary questions

4.1 Introduction

While Chapter 3 presented the concept of preliminary questions and objections, this chapter turns to the power of international tribunals to rule on them. Imagine an international tribunal constituent instruments of which make no reference to preliminary objections. There is a simple dispute-resolution clause stating that the tribunal shall decide all the disputes submitted to it by either *A* or *B* against each other, concerning the interpretation or application of provision X. This means that *A* or *B*, acting as a complaining party, will have the right to a ruling on a dispute concerning the interpretation or application of *X* against the counterpart. Now assume that *A* files with the tribunal a complaint against *B* over a given application of provision *X* and that *B* advances a preliminary objection requesting that the tribunal not decide the merits of *A*'s complaint. Three questions that arise are:

(i) Does the tribunal have the power to refrain from deciding the complaint on the merits, despite the fact that such power is not mentioned in its constitutive instrument, or should the tribunal rather ignore the preliminary objection and continue? This question refers to the *existence* and the *source* of the authority of international tribunals to rule on preliminary questions.

(ii) Does it make any difference whether the objection is grounded on the very constituent instruments of the tribunal or on any other treaty independent from them? The answer to this question relates to the *scope* of the authority to rule on preliminary questions in international adjudication.

(iii) Finally, if the tribunal decides the issue, what is the effect of its decision on the parties, on the specific proceeding at stake, and on other potential proceedings? Answering this question clarifies the *effect* of an international tribunal's decision on a preliminary question.

The examples referred to in Chapter 3 illustrate that international tribunals do verify whether the requirements for an adjudicatory process before them have been fulfilled. Yet, better defining the source of the power to assess preliminary questions in international tribunals also helps to clarify the scope and effect of that power. The question of scope is particularly important for the present book, because addressing forum shopping in the context of autonomous tribunals may rest on respondents' and adjudicators' ability to rely on norms applicable across those tribunals. The issue of effect, on the other hand, is important because international tribunals are tribunals of limited, delegated jurisdiction and cannot bind the parties or other international tribunals beyond that limited jurisdiction.

This chapter argues that (i) the power to rule on preliminary questions is an inherent power of international tribunals; (ii) the pool of procedural norms that adjudicators may apply goes beyond the pool of substantive norms under which a claim before the same adjudicators must fall; and (iii) decisions on preliminary questions may have the quality of *res judicata* across international tribunals or a stabilizing effect that is specific to the proceedings at stake, depending on the ambit of jurisdiction that authorizes the decision. To that effect, Section 4.2 disentangles the concept of adjudicatory jurisdiction in international law. It depicts adjudicatory jurisdiction (a power) with reference to two spheres (the ambit of this power), namely: (i) principal jurisdiction, a fixed sphere which refers to the claims or class of claims a tribunal is entitled to decide; and (ii) incidental jurisdiction, a context-dependent sphere which refers to a broader authority vested in the tribunal to decide issues in the circumstances of a specific case. Applying this concept to the power to rule on preliminary questions, Section 4.2 argues that such power is inherent, derives from adjudicatory jurisdiction, and is located in the sphere of incidental jurisdiction. Drawing on the concepts outlined in Section 4.2, and on the distinction between principal jurisdiction and applicable law, Section 4.3 explains that preliminary objections based on norms beyond the principal jurisdiction of a tribunal can also be entertained. It argues that the existence of both principal and incidental jurisdiction lends support to a broad stance on applicable law, even before specialized tribunals such as the WTO adjudicative bodies (i.e., painting the determination of the applicable law as a question of incidental jurisdiction). Section 4.4 then discusses the effects of decisions on preliminary questions. In particular, it argues that the distinction between principal and incidental jurisdiction leads to another distinction between the effects of decisions made in the exercise of principal jurisdiction (which may acquire the full force of *res judicata*) vis-à-vis those flowing from decisions made in the exercise of incidental jurisdiction (which are specific to the proceeding at stake). This difference accommodates a possible contention that incidental jurisdiction could undermine the consensual character of jurisdiction in international law or impose new obligations on litigants not intended by the framers of an adjudicatory regime. Section 4.5 presents the chapter's concluding remarks.

4.2 Adjudicatory jurisdiction, principal jurisdiction, incidental jurisdiction, and the inherent power to rule on preliminary objections

4.2.1 Disentangling the concept of adjudicatory jurisdiction

Jurisdiction is a chameleon buzzword. It is indiscriminately employed as a shortcut to the existence and boundaries of authority, and to the exercise of authority, whether such authority is political, legislative, or adjudicatory in function,[1] or whether in the context of domestic or international law. A common feature in the diverse uses of the term *jurisdiction* is that it refers to a power to do something (e.g., to police, to legislate on matter, to decide a case). As Hugh Thirlway famously noted in the context of the adjudicatory jurisdiction of the International Court of Justice (ICJ), when speaking of jurisdiction one must always ask: "[J]urisdiction to do what?"[2]

Jurisdiction, in its broadest sense as applied to the work of international tribunals, connotes the power to state the law in relation to

[1] The use of the word "jurisdiction" is more limited in certain countries following the Roman tradition, where it normally refers to the specific power vested in tribunals to "state the law" in concrete disputes (*juris-dictio; jus-dicere*). For instance, in French-, Spanish-, or Portuguese-speaking countries, *juridiction*, *juridicción*, or *jurisdição* normally connote authority which is adjudicatory in nature. As Michael Reisman notes, "[W]hile the term 'jurisdiction' in some languages refers solely to judicial competences, the international usage of the term ... encompasses the exercise of official power by the full range of legislative, executive and judicial institutions by which states purport to make and apply the law." Michael Reisman, 'Introduction,' in Michael Reisman (ed.), *Jurisdiction in International Law* (Aldershot: Ashgate, 1999), xi, at xiii.

[2] Hugh Thirlway, 'The Law and Procedure of the International Court of Justice 1960–89: Part Nine,' 68 *BYBIL* (1998) 1, at 6.

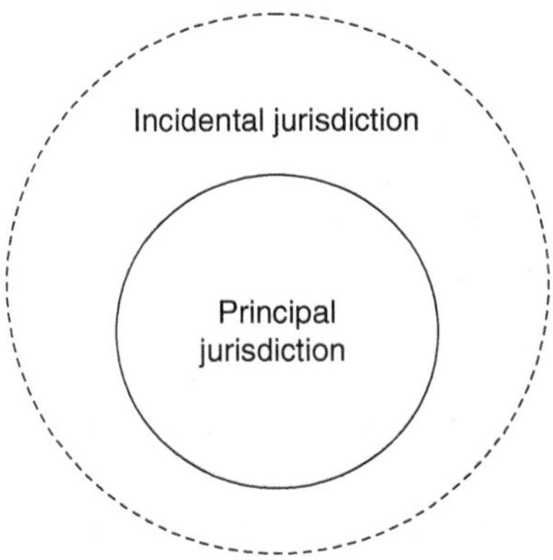

Figure 1 Adjudicatory jurisdiction

disputed claims by opposing parties. This power translates as a function: *adjudicatory jurisdiction*. As Chapter 2 pointed out, the international adjudicatory function is delegated, inert, and substitutive. This function is circumscribed by two spheres, graphically represented in Figure 1 as principal jurisdiction and incidental jurisdiction. The narrower sphere in Figure 1 is referred to herein as *principal jurisdiction*. It determines the class of disputed claims a tribunal is entitled to hear and dispose of with finality. In other words, principal jurisdiction defines the framework within which a claim must be formulated in order for a tribunal to be entitled to rule on it with finality for the parties to the case. This sphere has also been called primary jurisdiction, field jurisdiction, or *compétence* in French.[3] It is also often described through reference to the personal, the material, the temporal, and the territorial elements of jurisdiction (jurisdiction *ratione personae*, *ratione materiae*, *ratione*

[3] The term *compétence*, in the domestic law of countries following the Roman tradition, is often used as the "unity of measure" of jurisdiction, which is pictured as a unified power emanating from the state. However, this distinction between jurisdiction (*juridiction*) and competence (*compétence*) common in legal systems with a top-down division of labor amongst tribunals (with different "competencies") is arguably less pertinent for international law, where there is no unified authority and each tribunal can be normally thought of as comprising one "independent jurisdiction." See, for example, *Prosecutor* v. *Dusko Tadic a/k/a "Dule,"* Case No IT-9A-1-AR72, Defense Motion for Interlocutory Appeal on Jurisdiction, ICTY Appeals Chamber, Decision of 2 October 1995, para. 20: "International law, because it lacks a centralized structure, does not provide for an integrated judicial system operating an orderly division of labour among a number of tribunals, where certain aspects or components of jurisdiction as a power could be centralized or vested in one of them but not the others. In international law, every tribunal is a self-contained system (unless otherwise provided). This is incompatible with a narrow concept of jurisdiction, which presupposes a certain division of labour."

temporis, and *ratione loci*). A tribunal only has the authority to dispose directly of an issue with the authority of *res judicata* if each of those elements of jurisdiction, as conferred on the tribunal, is fulfilled in a concrete instance.[4] In sum, the principal jurisdiction of a tribunal is expressly determined. It is fixed and defines the set of issues which the tribunal may decide with the force of *res judicata*.

For example, in the WTO context, the principal jurisdiction of adjudicative bodies is limited first to disputes under WTO-covered agreements.[5] This is the WTO's adjudicative bodies' *general principal jurisdiction*, as defined in their constituent instruments, like the ICJ's general jurisdiction under the ICJ Statute,[6] or ICSID's general jurisdiction under the ICSID Convention.[7] Second, the principal jurisdiction of WTO adjudicative bodies is limited to the terms of reference of the specific panel endorsed by the WTO Dispute Settlement Body,[8] as the ICJ's jurisdiction is limited to the relevant jurisdictional bond established by the optional clause,[9] compromissory clause,[10] or acceptance by *forum prorogatum*,[11] or as the ICSID arbitral tribunal's jurisdiction is normally defined under a BIT.[12] This is these bodies' *special principal jurisdiction*. Consequently, WTO panels can only decide on the merits of claims submitted both under the WTO-covered agreements (general principal jurisdiction) and within the specific panel's terms of reference as endorsed by the WTO Dispute Settlement Body (specific principal jurisdiction). Likewise, the ICJ and an ICSID arbitral tribunal can only decide on the merits of claims submitted to them falling under *both* the general (ICJ Statute, ICSID Convention) and the specific instruments of delegation (e.g., the compromissory clauses in international treaties).

[4] See Gerald Fitzmaurice, *The Law and Procedure of the International Court of Justice*, vol. II (Cambridge: Grotius, 1986), at 436.

[5] Article 1(1) of the DSU.

[6] Articles 35(1), 35(2), 36(1), ICJ Statute. For the concepts of general and special jurisdiction (*compétence générale* and *compétence spéciale*) as applied to the ICJ, see Georges Abi-Saab, *Les exceptions préliminaires dans la procédure de la Cour Internationale* (Paris: Pedone, 1967), at 61–3.

[7] Article 25, ICSID Convention.

[8] Article 7, DSU.

[9] Article 36(2), ICJ Statute.

[10] Articles 36(1), 37, ICJ Statute.

[11] See, for example, *The Corfu Channel Case (United Kingdom* v. *Albania)*, Preliminary Objections, Judgment of 25 March 1948, 26–9; *Certain Questions of Mutual Assistance in Criminal Matters (Djibouti* v. *France)*, Judgment of 4 June 2008, paras. 60–97.

[12] Article 25(1), ICSID Convention. For the concept of general and special jurisdiction as applied to ICSID arbitration, see *Abaclat and others* v. *Argentina*, ICSID Case

Importantly, however, principal jurisdiction is not the end of the matter; the adjudicatory jurisdiction of WTO panels as well as that of other international tribunals is characterized by the presence of broader elements of authority than principal jurisdiction. The broader and traced sphere in Figure 1 is referred to here as *incidental jurisdiction*. It is principal jurisdiction's necessary supplement, exercised with a view to guaranteeing the proper discharge of the adjudicatory jurisdiction conferred upon the tribunal.[13] Some instances of incidental jurisdiction are expressly foreseen in the constituent instruments of international tribunals. Notice the ICJ's and the ITLOS's incidental jurisdiction to issue provisional measures,[14] or WTO panels' authority to seek information and technical advice from any individual or body which they deem appropriate.[15] Nevertheless, constituent instruments do not necessarily address certain important parts of incidental jurisdiction. This does not mean those parts are nonexistent; they may be latent in tribunals' adjudicatory jurisdiction as inherent components. Such inherent components derive from the existence of international tribunals, which confers upon them the prerogatives that are considered necessary for the exercise of their adjudicatory function. In other words, incidental jurisdiction may refer to explicit powers - such as the ICJ's or the ITLOS's authority to issue provisional measures or WTO panels' authority to seek information - or to inherent powers.

4.2.2 Inherent powers (or inherent jurisdiction) in international tribunals

The inherent components of incidental jurisdiction find practical recognition under the doctrine of inherent powers, which can also be described as a doctrine of inherent jurisdiction.[16] Under this doctrine, some inherent jurisdiction is a necessary element of adjudicatory

No ARB/07/5, Decision on Jurisdiction and Admissibility, Dissenting Opinion, 28 October 2011, para. 12.

13 See also Ibrahim Shihata, *The Power of the International Court to Determine its Own Jurisdiction* (The Hague: Martinus Nijhoff, 1965), at 169.

14 Article 41, ICJ Statute, Article 290(5), UNCLOS.

15 Article 13(1), DSU.

16 For a review of the literature on the doctrine of inherent powers, see Chester Brown, 'The Inherent Powers of International Courts and Tribunals,' 76 *BYIL* (2005) 195; Paola Gaeta, 'Inherent Powers of International Courts and Tribunals' in Lal Vohrah *et al.* (eds.), *Man's Inhumanity to Man: Essays on International Law in Honour of Antonio Cassese* (The Hague: Kluwer, 2003) 353; Herbert Briggs, 'The Incidental Jurisdiction of the International Court of Justice as Compulsory Jurisdiction,' in K. Zemanek *et al.* (eds.), *Völkerrecht und Rechtliches Weltbild: Festschrift für Alfred Verdross*

jurisdiction in international tribunals. This is significant because in international law there is often no mechanism for a tribunal to refer any issue outside its principal jurisdiction to another tribunal which would, in turn, enjoy principal jurisdiction to decide that issue. Therefore, in the event that a preliminary or antecedent question *A* affects the response to claim *B*, the international tribunal must possess some authority to dispose of question *A*.[17] If this incidental jurisdiction did not exist, then every time such a situation arose, the tribunal would either be automatically deprived of its adjudicatory jurisdiction (i.e., under the hypothesis that it lacked the authority to decide any issue beyond its principal jurisdiction), or it would only be able to exercise its adjudicatory jurisdiction in a partial manner (i.e., under the hypothesis that the tribunal would be obliged *a priori* to ignore the issue beyond its principal jurisdiction, thus acting in a biased manner against the party raising the issue). In short, inherent jurisdiction is an enabling accessory to, and derives from, the adjudicatory jurisdiction of international tribunals.

Inherent jurisdiction is considered to stem from the very essence of international tribunals as courts of law.[18] The basic rationale for the doctrine is that when subjects of international law establish an

(Berlin: Springer, 1960) 87; Elihu Lauterpacht, 'Partial Judgments and the Inherent Jurisdiction of the International Court of Justice,' in Vaughan Lowe and Malgosia Fitzmaurice (eds.), *Fifty Years of the International Court of Justice* (Cambridge University Press, 1996) 465; Michèle Buteau and Gabriel Oosthuizen, 'When the Rules Are Silent: The Inherent Powers of the Tribunal,' in R. May and G. Kirk McDonald (eds.), *Essays on ICTY Procedure and Evidence in Honour of Gabrielle Kirk McDonald* (London: Kluwer Law International, 2001) 65; Danesh Sarooshi, 'The Powers of the United Nations International Criminal Tribunals,' 2 *Max Planck YB UN L* (1998) 141; I. H. Jacob, 'The Inherent Jurisdiction of the Court,' 23 *Curr Leg Probs* (1970) 23; Isabelle van Damme, 'Inherent Powers of and for the WTO Appellate Body,' CTEI Working Paper (2008); Andrew Mitchell and David Heaton, 'The Inherent Jurisdiction of WTO Tribunals: The Selective Application of Public International Law Required by the Judicial Function,' 31 *MJIL* (2010) 558.

[17] See also *Prosecutor* v. *Dusko Tadic*, para. 20, reproduced in n. 3 above.

[18] See *Nuclear Tests Case (New Zealand* v. *France)*, Judgment of 20 December 1974, para. 23 ("such inherent jurisdiction derives from … the mere existence of the Court as a judicial organ"); *Hrvatska Elektroprivreda dd* v. *Slovenia*, ICSID Case No ARB/05/24, Ruling of 6 May 2008, para. 33 ("as a judicial formation governed by public international law, the tribunal has an inherent power"); Appellate Body Report, *Mexico – Tax Measures on Soft Drinks and Other Beverages*, WT/DS308/AB/R, adopted 24 March 2006, para. 45 ("WTO panels have certain powers that are inherent in their adjudicative function"); *Rio Grande Irrigation and Land Company (United Kingdom* v. *United States)*, Arbitral Award of 28 November 1923, 6 *UNRIAA* (2006) 131, at 135–6 ("there is inherent in this and in every legal Tribunal a power").

international judicial body, they *ipso facto* endow this body with certain enabling capabilities.[19] These need not all be spelled out expressly in the constituent instrument, and a provision which states an inherent power in so many words is declaratory in nature (although it may provide a shortcut for the power's exercise).[20] To return to the concept of jurisdiction just described, the establishment of adjudicatory jurisdiction means attributing more jurisdiction than simply principal jurisdiction to an international tribunal: it means also attributing to it a degree of incidental jurisdiction that, further, includes elements of inherent jurisdiction.

4.2.3 *Limitations to inherent jurisdiction*

The recognition of inherent jurisdiction provides no *carte blanche* for international tribunals to assert whatever power one could think of. First, inherent powers require a relationship of necessity between the authority to be asserted or exercised on the one hand, and the performance of the adjudicatory function conferred upon the international tribunal on the other hand.[21] The performance of the adjudicatory

[19] In turn, the notion of "inherent powers of international tribunals" cannot apply as such to entities that cannot qualify as "judicial," "tribunals," or "courts of law." See Friedl Weiss, 'Inherent Powers of National and International Courts,' in Federico Ortino and Ernst-Ulrich Petersmann (eds.), *The WTO Dispute Settlement System 1995–2003* (The Hague: Kluwer, 2004) 177 (arguing against WTO panels' and the Appellate Body's exercise of inherent powers based on their alleged non-judicial nature, but recognizing the potential influence of those bodies in the evolution of their own powers). In any event, the doctrine of inherent powers finds a functional equivalent for "political bodies" in the doctrine of implied powers. On the doctrine of implied powers, see Krzysztof Skubiszewski, 'Implied Power of International Organizations,' in Yoram Dinstein and Mala Tabory (eds.), *International Law at a Time of Perplexity: Essays in Honour of Shabtai Rosenne* (The Hague: Kluwer, 1989) 855.

[20] See *Nottebohm (Liechtenstein* v. *Guatemala)*, Preliminary Objection, Judgment of 18 November 1953, 120, where the ICJ stated that its judicial character and the rule of general international law recognizing competence-competence were "sufficient to establish that the Court is competent to adjudicate on its own jurisdiction," even though that competence is also expressly provided for in Article 36(6) of the ICJ Statute. See also Christoph Schreuer, *The ICSID Convention: A Commentary* (Cambridge University Press, 2001), 683.

[21] *Nuclear Tests Case (New Zealand* v. *France)*, para. 23 (indicating that inherent jurisdiction empowers the Court to make findings *necessary* for guaranteeing that its established jurisdiction over the merits is not frustrated, to provide for the orderly settlement of all matters in dispute, to ensure the observance of inherent limitations on the exercise of the judicial function, and to maintain its judicial character); *Hrvatska Elektroprivreda* v. *Slovenia*, para. 33 (quoting *Prosecutor* v. *Fatmir Limaj, Haradin Bala and Isak Musliu*, Case No IT-03-66, ICTY Trial Chamber Contempt Allegations (Beqa Beqaj), Judgment of 27 May 2005, paras. 9–10, which reads: "[T]here is an inherent

function requires a decision on issues of fact and law that are necessarily antecedent to the solution of an issue under a tribunal's principal jurisdiction.[22] These issues include both preliminary questions and questions antecedent to the merits of a claim. Bin Cheng explains it thus: "[w]here a tribunal has jurisdiction in a particular matter, it is also competent with regard to all relevant incidental questions, subject to express provision to the contrary."[23] Indeed, the exercise of inherent jurisdiction when it comes to both procedural and substantive matters is well established. Hence, in discussing the validity of a preliminary objection that a panel considered to have been untimely submitted, the Appellate Body stated that "as a matter of due process, and the *proper exercise of the judicial function*, panels are *required to address* issues that are put before them by parties to a dispute."[24] In the same sense, although the arbitral tribunal in *World Duty Free Company Limited* v. *Kenya* under the ICSID Convention had no jurisdiction over a former president of Kenya, it nonetheless had to assess whether the former president had corruptly favored an investor in securing a contract, on the basis of the evidence adduced and the submissions of the parties to the case, in order to determine the admissibility of the investor's request.[25] These examples show that, upon necessity, incidental jurisdiction extends beyond the principal jurisdiction of tribunals in the context of preliminary questions.

power of an international court to deal with any issues necessary for the conduct of matters falling within its jurisdiction"); *Prosecutor* v. *Tihomir Blaskic*, ICTY Appeals Chamber, Request of the Republic of Croatia for the Review of the Decision of the Trial Chamber II of 18 July 1997, Judgment of 29 October 1997 (at para. 33, describing an inherent power as one that the tribunal must possess to make a determination that is necessary for the exercise of its primary jurisdiction).

22 See also *Case Concerning Certain German Interests in Polish Upper Silesia*, PCIJ Ser A No 6 (1925), 5, at 18: "[T[he interpretation of other international agreements is indisputably within the competence of the Court if such interpretation must be regarded as incidental to a decision on a point in regard to which it has jurisdiction."

23 Bin Cheng, *General Principles of Law as Applied by International Courts and Tribunals* (Cambridge University Press, 1953, 2006) 266. At 266–7, Cheng refers to arbitral practice in support of his claim. He also reproduces the following passage from the arbitration on *Compagnie pour la construction du chemin de fer d'Ogulin à la frontière, S.A.* (1926): "Incidental questions arising in the decision of a case ought to be examined by the judge competent to decide on the principal issue, unless the law provides otherwise … "

24 Appellate Body Report, *Mexico – Anti-Dumping Investigation of High Fructose Corn Syrup (HFCS) from the United States – Recourse to Article 21.5 of the DSU by the United States*, WT/DS132/AB/RW, adopted 21 November 2001, para. 36 (emphasis added).

25 *World Duty Free Company Limited* v. *Kenya*, ICSID Case No ARB/00/7, Award of 4 October 2006, para. 3.

Incidental jurisdiction covering substantive questions is also readily recognized. For example, the WTO panel in *Continued Suspension* considered that, in order to decide on the European Communities' claim that the United States violated Article 22.8 of the DSU, it was necessary to examine issues under the Agreement on Sanitary and Phytosanitary Measures (SPS Agreement). Such issues were flagrantly outside its terms of reference. Still, the panel's incidental jurisdiction came into play as necessary for the panel's findings under its established principal jurisdiction.[26] In yet another case, the ICJ assessed objections to Security Council and General Assembly Resolutions in the *Namibia* opinion, even though the Court did not consider it had powers of judicial review or appeal over decisions of United Nations' political organs. The Court made its assessment "before determining any legal consequences arising from those resolutions," "in the exercise of its judicial function and since objections ha[d] been advanced."[27] Hence, if necessary, incidental jurisdiction also extends beyond principal jurisdiction when it comes to substantive issues.

A caveat to the proposition that incidental jurisdiction extends beyond principal jurisdiction is this: when the very subject matter of the required decision on issues of fact and law that would otherwise be permitted in the exercise of incidental jurisdiction entangles the legal position of a state non-party to the proceedings, the tribunal cannot exercise inherent powers.[28] Chapter 6 further discusses this limitation,

[26] Panel Report, *United States – Continued Suspension of Obligations in the EC – Hormones Dispute*, WT/DS320/R, adopted 14 November 2008, as modified by Appellate Body Report WT/DS320/AB/R, for instance, at para. 7.272, stating that it "should address the compatibility of [Directive 2003/74/EC] with the provisions of the SPS Agreement referred to by the parties to the extent necessary to determine, with respect to the claim relating to Article 22.8, whether the measure found to be inconsistent in the *EC – Hormones* case has been removed"; and at para. 7.276, stressing that "in reviewing the EC claims of violation … our intention is not to substitute ourselves for a compliance panel under Article 21.5 of the DSU. We will make findings … with the only purpose to reach a conclusion on the violation of the provisions referred to in those claims." The Appellate Body upheld this approach. See Appellate Body Report, *US – Continued Suspension*, para. 332. For an earlier instance where incidental jurisdiction was deemed broader than principal jurisdiction in the context of the determination of remedies, see *Brazil – Export Financing Programme for Aircraft (Recourse to Arbitration by Brazil under Article 22.6 of the DSU and Article 4.11 of the SCM Agreement)*, WT/DS46/ARB, circulated 28 August 2000, paras. 3.16–3.17.

[27] *Legal Consequences for States of the Continued Presence of South Africa in Namibia (South West Africa) Notwithstanding Security Council Resolution 276* (1970), Advisory Opinion of 21 June 1971, para. 89.

[28] *Case Concerning East-Timor (Portugal* v. *Australia)*, Judgment of 30 June 1995, para. 28; *Case of the Monetary Gold Removed from Rome in 1943 (Italy* v. *France, United Kingdom and*

which international adjudication's consensual background justifies: after all, third parties that have not delegated principal jurisdiction cannot have implicitly delegated incidental jurisdiction. In sum, whereas necessity justifies the exercise of incidental jurisdiction *ratione materiae*, the limitations to incidental jurisdiction *ratione personae* are stricter.

A second limitation to inherent jurisdiction is that its assertion or exercise must not contradict or be inconsistent with the relevant constituent instruments.[29] This limitation is also embedded in the consensual background of international adjudication. Along these lines, the WTO Appellate Body has refused to accept the argument that reasons of judicial propriety would justify panels' declining to rule on the "entirety of the claims" before them. According to the Appellate Body, this would imply a modification of the rights and obligations in the DSU and would prevent a panel from fulfilling its functions under Article 11 of the DSU.[30] In another example, an ICSID Annulment Committee called to exercise inherent powers refused to inquire whether a Grenadian authority had behaved corruptly during the negotiations that led to an investment contract, an issue which had not been decided in the original proceedings. According to the Committee, such an inquiry in the scope of an annulment proceeding would be inconsistent with the structure of the ICSID Convention.[31]

4.2.4 The power to rule on preliminary questions as inherent jurisdiction

The power of international tribunals to rule on preliminary questions can be thus described as an inherent power rooted in their incidental

United States of America), Preliminary Question, Judgment of 15 June 1954, 32. See discussion in Chapter 6 on the "essential third party" rule as a brake on joint forum shopping.

[29] *RSM Corporation* v. *Grenada*, ICSID Case No ARB/05/14 (Annulment Proceeding), RSM Production Corporation's Application for a Preliminary Ruling of 29 October 2009, Decision of 7 December 2009 (at para. 20, stating that there are limitations to inherent powers, including that such powers cannot be inconsistent with the relevant constituent instrument); Appellate Body Report, *Mexico – Taxes on Soft Drinks*, para. 46 (citing, with approval, Appellate Body Report, *India – Patent Protection for Pharmaceutical and Agricultural Chemical Products*, WT/DS50/AB/R, adopted 16 January 1998, para. 92, where the Appellate Body stated that nothing in the DSU gives a panel the authority to disregard or modify explicit provisions of the DSU); *Heathrow Airport User Charges (United States* v. *United Kingdom)*, Decision No 23 of the Tribunal, Decision of 1 November 1993, 24 *UNRIAA* (2006) 335, para. 2.26.

[30] Appellate Body Report, *Mexico – Taxes on Soft Drinks*, para. 46.

[31] *RSM* v. *Grenada* (Annulment Proceeding). The Committee pointed in particular to Article 52 (which states the grounds for annulment of decisions) and Article 53

jurisdiction.[32] Its source is the nature of international tribunals as suppliers of an adjudicatory function. The adjudicatory function cannot be properly conceived without reference to the very idea of procedure or, conversely, without the notion that the tribunal is the third party who is responsible for guarding the integrity of the adjudicatory process and enforcing the conditions for its development.[33] The justification of the power to rule on preliminary objections is its inevitability for the proper discharge of adjudicatory jurisdiction and, where the preliminary question is overcome (since preliminary questions may well prevent a decision of merit), for the proper discharge of principal jurisdiction as well. Indeed, the necessity requirement discussed above in the context of inherent jurisdiction is easily met when it comes to preliminary objections: as Chapters 2 and 3 discussed, the assessment of given preliminary questions must take place in the context of the verification that the prerequisites for a ruling of merit have been met, and is therefore a condition upon the possibility of such ruling. It is accordingly submitted that a power to rule on preliminary questions must exist and, where applicable, be exercised, in order to enable international tribunals to perform their adjudicatory function.

4.3 The scope of the applicable law of preliminary objections

4.3.1 *Preliminary objections may draw on "all international law"*

That the authority to rule on preliminary questions is inherent and not located in the fixed sphere of tribunals' principal jurisdiction also helps to clarify the scope of potentially valid preliminary objections. Located in the contextual sphere of incidental jurisdiction, the power to rule on preliminary objections will be triggered depending on the

(which states that awards shall not be subject to appeal or any other remedy except as provided for in the Convention) of the ICSID Convention.

32 See also Briggs, 'Incidental Jurisdiction of the International Court.'

33 As Thirlway puts it: "A court or tribunal set up at the international level is expected to live up to its name, which means that it must conduct its work broadly according to norms that are generally recognized as applicable to judicial bodies." Hugh Thirlway, 'Dilemma or Chimera? Admissibility of Illegally Obtained Evidence in International Adjudication,' 78 *AJIL* (1984) 622, at 626. Or, as Kenneth Carlston observed in the context of international arbitration, "[a] State, in submitting its dispute with another to the decision of an international tribunal, has certain fundamental rights which it may expect in full confidence will be respected... The tribunal must respect the law governing its creation and defining its powers as laid down in the *compromis*, and it must likewise observe certain other established rules of a fundamental character which inherently, under the generally accepted rules of

parties' opposing allegations of fact and law, and exercised depending on the extent necessary to guarantee the performance of the tribunal's adjudicatory function. Accordingly, this power extends to any international norm that governs the existence and development of the adjudicatory process, that applies to the relationship between the disputing parties, and the invocation of which calls for a decision that must be made in the exercise of the adjudicatory function as an incidental question. In practical terms, this means that an exclusive jurisdiction clause such as Article 344 (formerly Article 292) of the Treaty on the Functioning of the EU can apply before an UNCLOS Annex VII Arbitral Tribunal; it also means that a fork-in-the-road clause such as Article 1.2 of the Olivos Protocol can prevent a MERCOSUR member from receiving a judgment on the merits of its claim at the WTO.[34]

4.3.2 *Deriving the scope of preliminary objections in WTO adjudication from the scope of applicable law, and vice versa*

The notion that any jurisdictional or procedural norm is capable of justifying a preliminary objection may sound superfluous where the relevant constituent instrument specifies "all international law" as the potentially applicable law – which is often the case.[35] However, certain constituent instruments do not expressly state the boundaries of applicable law or specify the conditions for the application of norms that go beyond the principal jurisdiction of the tribunal. In such cases, the precise scope of the power to rule on preliminary objections might be subject to debate. The WTO DSU offers an intriguing example. As this book sees it, the DSU establishes neither the scope of applicable law nor of preliminary objections in WTO adjudication – although some scholars do interpret certain provisions as limiting the reach of applicable law.[36] This fact, coupled with the ever-increasing importance of WTO adjudicative bodies in international law and dispute settlement,

law and justice, regulate the conduct of any judicial body." Kenneth Carlston, *The Process of International Arbitration*, (Westport: Greenwood Press, 1946), at 38.

[34] Article 1.2, The Olivos Protocol for the Settlement of Disputes in MERCOSUR, 2251 *UNTS* 288 (Olivos Protocol).

[35] See Article 38(1) ICJ Statute; Article 293(1) UNCLOS; Article 42(1) ICSID Convention.

[36] See, against the position on applicable law espoused here, Joel Trachtman, 'Jurisdiction in WTO Dispute Settlement,' in Rufus Yerxa and Bruce Wilson (eds.), *Key Issues in WTO Dispute Settlement: the First Ten Years* (Cambridge University Press, 2005), 136. See also Joel Trachtman, 'The Domain of WTO Dispute Resolution,' 40 *HILJ* (1999) 333; and Gabrielle Marceau, 'A Call for Coherence in International Law: Praises for the Prohibition Against "Clinical Isolation" in WTO Dispute Settlement,' 33 *JWT* (1999) 87.

has prompted a lively debate over the possibility of applying "non-WTO law" in the context of WTO dispute settlement.

That debate has clear implications also for WTO respondents' ability to battle against forum shopping and for WTO adjudicative bodies' capacity to guarantee some degree of protection to those respondents. To imagine just one potential situation, reference can be made to the *Automotive Leather* dispute between the United States and Australia.[37] In that case, after the adoption of the original panel report, the parties bilaterally agreed on how to proceed with the dispute under Articles 21 and 22 of the DSU. Part of the deal was that "[b]oth Australia and the United States will unconditionally accept the review Panel report [under Article 21(5) of the DSU] and there will be no appeal of that report."[38] Later, the report of the panel under Article 21(5) found in favor of the United States. Australia never appealed, in accordance with the bilateral agreement. However, had Australia appealed that report, could the United States have relied on the bilateral agreement? If so, could or should the Appellate Body have considered the bilateral agreement and abstained from ruling on the merits of the appeal, or could or should it have only ignored the agreement and proceeded to a decision on the merits of the appeal? The discussion brings to mind the balance between the enabling and protective function of procedural norms, and that concerning the system- versus regime-based approaches to international adjudication. The answer on the scope of applicable law before WTO adjudicative bodies influences the answer on the scope of potentially valid preliminary objections to some extent. For instance, if the Appellate Body can refer exclusively to DSU rules, then it would be difficult to apply a provision of the bilateral agreement in *Automotive Leather*. More broadly, this argument could be applied to any potential jurisdictional overlap between the WTO machinery and other international tribunals.[39]

Regardless of the debate over the applicable law, in practice, a forum-shopped WTO member could still rely on an indirect application of the non-WTO procedure-regulating norm through a direct application of

[37] Panel Report, *Australia – Subsidies Provided to Producers and Exporters of Automotive Leather – Recourse to Article 21.5 of the DSU by the United States*, WT/DS126/RW and Corr.1, adopted 11 February 2000.

[38] WTO doc. WT/DS126/8, 4 October 1999.

[39] For this view, see Kyung Kwak and Gabrielle Marceau, 'Overlaps and Conflicts of Jurisdiction between the World Trade Organization and Regional Trade Agreements,' in Lorand Bartels and Federico Ortino (eds.), *Regional Trade Agreements and the WTO Legal System* (Oxford University Press, 2006) 465.

a WTO rule. First, the respondent could frame its procedural objection under Article 3(10) of the DSU, streamlining the preliminary objection into the narrower view that the applicable law of WTO adjudicative bodies is limited to the covered agreements.[40] Article 3(10) of the DSU obliges WTO members to engage in dispute settlement procedures in good faith. The Appellate Body has considered that obligation to cover "the entire spectrum of dispute settlement, from the point of initiation of a case through implementation."[41] Hence, Article 3(10) governs resort to and insistence on the WTO as a forum of choice. To be successful in its preliminary objection, the respondent would have to prove that the insistence on the WTO proceedings is contrary to the obligation of good faith. To that effect, it would be grounded in the procedure-regulating norm agreed to elsewhere as a "fact" that proves an abusive exercise of the right to bring claims under the DSU. In this sense, the Appellate Body has recognized the doctrine of abuse of rights as one application of the general principle of good faith.[42] According to the Appellate Body, the doctrine of abuse of rights "prohibits the abusive exercise of a state's rights and enjoins that whenever the assertion of a right 'impinges on the field covered by [a] treaty obligation, it must be exercised bona fide, that is to say, reasonably.'"[43] Moreover, in the view of the Appellate Body, "an abusive exercise by a Member of its own treaty right thus results in a breach of the treaty rights of the other Members and, as well, a violation of the treaty obligation of the Member so acting."[44] This reasoning arguably applies to the obligation of good faith under Article 3(10) of the DSU. From this perspective, in our hypothetical example, had Australia appealed the

[40] See also Mitchell and Heaton, 'Inherent Jurisdiction of WTO Tribunals' at 615–18.

[41] Appellate Body Report, *European Communities – Export Subsidies on Sugar*, WT/DS265/AB/R, WT/DS266/AB/R, WT/DS283/AB/R, adopted 19 May 2005, para. 312.

[42] Appellate Body Report, *United States – Import Prohibition of Certain Shrimp and Shrimp Products*, WT/DS58/AB/R, adopted 6 November 1998, para. 158.

[43] *Ibid*. The Appellate Body cites Cheng, *General Principles of Law*, at 125: "A reasonable and bona fide exercise of a right in such a case is one which is appropriate and necessary for the purpose of the right (*i.e.*, in furtherance of the interests which the right is intended to protect). It should at the same time be fair and equitable as between the parties and not one which is calculated to procure for one of them an unfair advantage in the light of the obligation assumed. A reasonable exercise of the right is regarded as compatible with the obligation. But the exercise of the right in such a manner as to prejudice the interests of the other contracting party arising out of the treaty is unreasonable and is considered as inconsistent with the bona fide execution of the treaty obligation, and a breach of the treaty."

[44] Appellate Body Report, *United States – Import Prohibition of Certain Shrimp and Shrimp Products*, para. 158.

panel report in *Automotive Leather* in violation of the procedural agreement with the United States, this could be considered an unreasonable, and therefore objectively abusive, exercise of the right of appeal under the DSU. Thus, by framing its objection under Article 3(10) of the DSU, the United States would have been able to avoid the applicable law debate and still argue that Australia was precluded from appealing. This would allow the Appellate Body to safeguard the integrity of the WTO adjudicatory process directly, under "WTO rules only."

Another possible way for the United States to proceed with the *Automotive Leather* hypothesis would be to use Article 3(10) as a vehicle to import the notion of estoppel into the WTO proceedings, relying on the procedural agreement with Australia indirectly. The rule of estoppel may afford a basis to a preliminary objection with the effect of a binding preclusion.[45] Nevertheless, if the applicable law is restricted, estoppel would not apply as such, but again, preclusion would nevertheless result as an expression of the principle of good faith expressly enshrined in Article 3(10) of the DSU. Indeed, estoppel, like the prohibition on abuse of rights, is normally recognized as a particularization of the principle of good faith.[46] An estoppel is premised on (i) sufficiently clear acts or declarations by a party and (ii) reliance upon those acts or declarations by the other party to its own detriment or prejudice or to the advantage of the party acting or declaring otherwise.[47] In our *Automotive Leather* hypothesis, then, the procedural agreement with the United States whereby Australia committed not to appeal the panel report would be tantamount to a declaration on which the United States had relied to its own detriment, now that it would face an appeal, and to the advantage of Australia, who would have a second

[45] Here, the rule of estoppel is basically restricted to the notion which in common law comprises the concepts of *estoppel by deed* and *estoppel in pais* (generally, estoppel by conduct). The rationale for that principle stems from the maxim *allegans contraria non audiens est* which, in civil law countries as well, gives rise to a preclusion on inconsistent positions. See generally David Bowett, 'Estoppel before International Courts and Tribunals and its Relation to Acquiescence,' 33 *BYBIL* (1957) 176.

[46] See, for example, Robert Kolb, 'Aperçus sur la bonne foi en droit international public,' 54 *RHDI* (2001) 1; Andrew Mitchell, 'Good Faith in WTO Dispute Settlement,' 7 *Mel JIL* (2006) 340.

[47] *Case Concerning the Land, Island and Maritime Frontier Dispute (El Salvador/Honduras)*, Application of Nicaragua for Permission to Intervene, Judgment of 13 September 1990, para. 63. See also *Case Concerning Land and Maritime Boundary between Cameroon and Nigeria (Cameroon* v. *Nigeria)*, Preliminary Objections, Judgment of 11 June 1998, para. 57; *North Sea Continental Shelf Cases (Germany* v. *Denmark; Germany* v. *The Netherlands)*, Judgment of 20 February 1969, para. 30.

shot that the parties had agreed beforehand not to have. In light of those facts, a violation of the good faith requirement under Article 3(10) of the DSU could arguably be sustained.

At any rate, even though streamlining a preliminary objection based on non-WTO law into strict DSU terms may be an attractive alternative for individual WTO respondents in light of the debate about the scope of the applicable law in WTO dispute settlement, this book maintains that a better solution for the WTO system would be to more openly recognize other international norms, such as procedure-regulating norms from non-WTO law, as law on an equal footing with WTO law. Instead of indirectly applying those norms as mere "facts" through the backdoor of WTO provisions, WTO adjudicators would preserve the content of their own norms, but recognize that those norms do not discipline all the eventualities that may take place in the WTO adjudicatory process.

In fact, a principled rationale for the application of preclusion techniques across international tribunals, related to the enabling and protective functions of procedure-regulating rules, does not depend on the terms of explicit governing instruments such as the DSU. The principle of good faith – and estoppel and the prohibition of abuse of rights as two of its operational manifestations – are general principles of law as such. May a complainant seize a forum against a respondent who relies in good faith on a previous commitment by the complainant that there would be no such seizing? How can an international tribunal responsible for the integrity of the adjudicatory process between two parties turn a blind eye to an alleged violation of a previous commitment and allow an adjudicatory process to move forward notwithstanding the violation of a previous commitment by one party, to the detriment of the other? *Ex injuria jus non oritur*,[48] the old maxim goes. In light of the prohibition on the abusive exercise of rights by states,[49] which includes

48 See, for example, *Legal Status of Eastern Greenland*, Judgment of 5 April 1933, PCIJ Ser A/B No 53 (1933) 21, Dissenting opinion of Judge Anzilotti, at 95: "an unlawful action cannot serve as the basis of an action at law." See also *Gabcikovo-Nagymaros Project (Hungary* v. *Slovakia)*, Judgment of 25 September 1997, para. 133 (denying the possibility that facts flowing from wrongful conduct determine the law and recognizing the principle of *ex injuria jus non oritur*). It is submitted that the principle applies equally to substantive and procedural matters.

49 See Cheng, *General Principles of Law*, 121–36; Michael Byers, 'Abuse of Rights: An Old Principle, a New Age', 47 *McGill LJ* (2002) 389. On the application for questions of forum shopping, see also Vaughan Lowe, 'Overlapping Jurisdictions in International Courts and Tribunals', 20 *Australian YBIL* (1999) 191, at 203.

the right of action conferred by an international instrument, a complainant may not seize a forum in violation of its counterpart rights. As Cheng, to whom the Appellate Body has turned, explains, rights and obligations are interdependent and the assumption of every obligation may limit the exercise of another right to a certain extent. It follows that a state's rights must be exercised in a manner compatible with its various obligations, whether they arise from a treaty or a set of treaties, or from general law.[50] This naturally applies to a situation where a complainant attempts to evade a preclusive norm. This good faith-based reasoning places the parties on an equal footing in their procedural relationship and safeguards the integrity of the adjudicatory process by enforcing party autonomy. Incidental jurisdiction covers this type of situation in order to allow a proper exercise of the adjudicatory function.

The present study adopts the broader position that the applicable law in WTO adjudication encompasses all international law, provided that: (i) such norms are invoked as objections or defenses, that there is a conflict between the non-WTO and the WTO norm, and that the non-WTO norm prevails over the relevant WTO provision pursuant to the general rules of conflict;[51] or (ii) such norms are invoked as objections or defenses and there is no specific regulation of the matters under WTO norms. Indeed, the DSU does not address,[52] let alone limit, the applicable law in WTO dispute settlement.[53] The provisions which one might interpret as indicating such a limitation are actually devoted to clarifying the adjudicatory jurisdiction of WTO adjudicative bodies

[50] Cheng, *General Principles of Law*, at 123–31.

[51] Joost Pauwelyn, *Conflict of Norms in Public International Law: How WTO Law Relates to Other Rules of International Law* (Cambridge University Press, 2003). See also Lorand Bartels, 'Applicable Law in WTO Dispute Settlement Proceedings' 35 *JWT* (2001) 499 (Bartels' position differs from Pauwelyn's, however, mainly in that Bartels pictures Article 3(2) of the DSU as a conflict rule granting superior status to WTO law in the context of WTO dispute settlement).

[52] In the context of Article 7, DSU, just return to the decision by the panel in *US – Continued Suspension*. Nowhere in the panel's terms of reference could one find a reference to the SPS Agreement; however, the panel had exercised (incidental) jurisdiction in addressing issues under the SPS Agreement. This approach is irreconcilable with the isolationist perspective to Article 7(1). Moreover, Article 7(2) mentions "covered agreement or agreements cited by the parties," and those "agreements cited by the parties" may include other, non-WTO agreements cited by the respondent.

[53] Panel Report, *Korea – Measures Affecting Government Procurement*, WT/DS163/R, adopted 19 June 2000, approaches Article 3(2) of the DSU in this manner, at para. 7.96: "[W]e can see no basis here for an *a contrario* implication that rules of international

or to explicitly defining their principal jurisdiction, a question to be distinguished from the issue of applicable law. With regard to the Marrakesh Agreement, the general statement in Article XVI:1 would not justify the view that the WTO "contracts out" of international law, especially in light of the fundamental changes from the GATT to the WTO days.[54]

As an empirical issue, WTO adjudicative bodies have avoided taking clear sides on the issue of the applicability of non-WTO law to the maximum extent possible.[55] Nevertheless, panels and the Appellate Body have inescapably applied non-WTO law in concrete instances.

law other than rules of interpretation do not apply. The language of 3.2 in this regard applies to a specific problem that had arisen under the GATT to the effect that, among other things, reliance on negotiating history was being utilized in a manner arguably inconsistent with the requirements of the rules of treaty interpretation of customary international law."

[54] See Pauwelyn, *Conflict of Norms*.

[55] The Appellate Body recognizes the distinction between interpretation and application. See Appellate Body Report, *United States – Definitive Anti-dumping and Countervailing Duties on Certain Products from China*, WT/DS379/AB/R, adopted 25 March 2011, para. 316. But the line is often elusive, and this, together with the use of the *arguendo* technique, has offered a window for WTO adjudicators to avoid ruling on the issue openly. In practice, WTO adjudicative bodies have preferred to import non-WTO law into the WTO agreements by anchoring the issues in the context of a WTO provision first, and then referring to non-WTO principles and norms in the context of that provision. This exercise is often labeled "interpretation of WTO law" rather than "direct application of non-WTO law." See, for example, Panel Report, *European Communities and Certain Member States – Measures Affecting Trade in Large Civil Aircraft*, WT/DS316/R, adopted 1 June 2011, as modified by Appellate Body Report, para. 7.46; Appellate Body Report, *US – Shrimp*, paras. 128–32. However, this approach may not be possible in all cases – first, by reason of textual limitation, such as in the case of rules on burden of proof, as discussed below. Second, in the case of law binding specifically on parts of the WTO membership or the disputing parties exclusively, relying solely on "interpretation" may be insufficient as a means to avoid the debate, at least if one agrees with the approach adopted in the Panel Report, *European Communities – Measures Affecting the Approval and Marketing of Biotech Products*, WT/DS291/R, WT/DS292/R, WT/DS293/R, Add.1 to Add.9, and Corr.1, adopted 21 November 2006, paras. 7.68–7.70 (holding that Article 31(3)(c) of the VCLT would require consideration of those rules of international law which are applicable in the relationship of all parties to the treaty which is being interpreted). Note, however, that the Appellate Body recently recognized the possibility that norms agreed by subsets of the WTO membership influence the interpretation of WTO norms, a potentially relevant development regarding systemic integration. See Appellate Body Report, *EC and EC Member States – Large Civil Aircraft*, para. 845. Article 31(3)(c), VCLT does not specify whether, in determining relevance and applicability, one shall consider all parties to the treaty in question, only the disputing parties, or another subset of "parties." See generally, Campbell McLachlan, 'The Principle of Systemic Integration and Article 31(3)(c) of the Vienna Convention,' 54 *ICLQ* (2005) 279.

Two examples – the application of rules on burden of proof that appear nowhere in the DSU[56] and of rules of attribution under the international law of state responsibility – immediately come to mind.[57] Therefore, at least to a certain extent, the notion that the applicable law in WTO dispute settlement is broader than exclusively WTO law has already proved correct.

Moreover, since the debate on the scope of applicable law is still ongoing, it is submitted that the concept of jurisdiction just presented and the focus on preliminary objections adopted here lend further support, on three interrelated levels, to the position that non-WTO law may conditionally apply in WTO dispute settlement. First, on a more practical level, the concept of jurisdiction presented here indicates that the explicit provisions of the DSU do not exhaust the incidental jurisdiction of WTO adjudicative bodies. This responds to a mainstream reaction of WTO complainants to preliminary objections or defenses of merit based on non-WTO law: to assert or imply that panels' terms of reference determine a closed list of agreements that a panel may address. That argument confuses WTO adjudicative bodies' (special) principal jurisdiction and their incidental jurisdiction. Take the recent panel report on the dispute involving *Large Civil Aircraft* between the United States (as complainant) and the European Communities (as respondent). The EC asked for a preliminary ruling, arguing that a 1992 bilateral agreement with the United States had grandfathered government-supporting measures to Airbus prior to 1992, and that this agreement would have excluded those measures from WTO dispute settlement.[58] The United States did not limit itself to opposing the grandfathering argument by the EC; it further argued that the 1992 bilateral agreement could not apply.[59] Among its arguments on the issue of applicable law, the United States recalled that the covered agreements which it had cited in its request for the establishment of a panel included the DSU, the GATT 1994, and the SCM Agreement, but not the 1992 agreement. Further, the United States noted that the definition of "covered agreements" was a closed list which did not include the 1992 agreement. It also submitted that

[56] See Appellate Body Report, *United States – Measure Affecting Imports of Woven Wool Shirts and Blouses from India*, WT/DS33/AB/R, adopted 23 May 1997, and Corr.1, at 14.

[57] See Panel Report, *Turkey – Restrictions on Imports of Textile and Clothing Products*, WT/DS34/R, adopted 19 November 1999, as modified by Appellate Body Report WT/DS34/AB/R, paras. 7.33–7.43.

[58] Panel Report, *EC and Certain Member States – Large Civil Aircraft*, paras. 7.71–7.76.

[59] *Ibid.*, paras. 7.78–7.81.

the 1992 agreement was not one of the instruments otherwise incorporated into the GATT. As a result, the United States emphasized that the SCM Agreement and the GATT 1994, and not the 1992 agreement, contained the relevant obligations of the parties to that dispute.[60] The panel, for its part, did examine the question of whether the 1992 agreement could have undermined the invocation of provisions of the SCM Agreement in relation to measures of government support to civil aircraft prior to 1992. However, it used the *arguendo* technique to reject the European Communities' defense on its substance. The panel held that even if the 1992 agreement applied, it could not be construed in the way the EC argued. Thus, there was no need for the Panel to resolve the question of the applicability of non-WTO law in WTO dispute settlement, and the question remained open.[61]

The distinction between principal and incidental jurisdiction demonstrates that arguments to the effect that the terms of reference define the boundaries of applicable law, such as the United States' argument in *Large Civil Aircraft*, miss the point.[62] Terms of reference – which are documents normally based on panel requests which, in turn, are drafted exclusively by the complainant – contain only the signposts of the WTO claims to be dealt with.[63] The terms of reference establish the special principal jurisdiction of panels; but they do not anticipate the whole matter in dispute, which only comes into being after the respondent draws its line of defense.[64] As a result, terms of reference

[60] *Ibid.*, para. 7.78.

[61] *Ibid*, paras. 7.92–7.98. The EC did not reiterate this position in the same terms on appeal and, therefore, the Appellate Body did not address the question, which remained open as the panel left it. On appeal, the EC argued that the 1992 agreement was a relevant rule of international law applicable in the relations between the parties in the sense of Article 31(3)(c), VCLT. The Appellate Body, while recognizing the possibility that a treaty involving a subset of the WTO membership might fall under Article 31(3)(c), ultimately avoided the question concerning the 1992 agreement, by holding that it was not "relevant" in the circumstances. See Appellate Body Report, *EC and Certain Member States – Large Civil Aircraft*, paras. 846–51.

[62] See also the discussion in n. 26 above and accompanying text on *US – Continued Suspension*.

[63] See, for example, Panel Report, *India – Quantitative Restrictions on Imports of Agricultural, Textile and Industrial Products*, WT/DS90/R, adopted 22 September 1999, upheld by the Appellate Body, at para. 5.19, where the panel states that a respondent is not restricted in the provisions of the WTO Agreement that it can invoke in its defense (although the case makes the point discussed here, it does not deal with "non-WTO law").

[64] See also Veijo Heisnaken, 'Dealing with Pandora: The Concept of "Merits" in International Commercial Arbitration,' 22 *Arb Int'l* (2006) 597.

cannot be invoked as a means to restrict preliminary objections and defenses brought by the respondent, which are normally not included therein.

Second, on the level of legal interpretation, emphasis on the power to rule on preliminary objections as an inherent power located in the sphere of incidental jurisdiction supports a presumption that, except to the extent that there has not been explicit derogation from non-WTO law, such norms continue to apply in WTO dispute settlement. The present approach therefore shifts the immediate focus from the specific language in specific provisions of the DSU, to seeing WTO panels and the Appellate Body as the guarantors of the adjudicatory process at the WTO. This too has implications for the debate on the applicability of non-WTO law, especially because the main arguments against the application of non-WTO law are based on the specific language of certain DSU provisions.[65] Granted, this is not a claim that the text of the DSU is not important or that it must not remain the major signpost for one's answer: as discussed above, constituent instruments may limit the extension of otherwise inherent powers. But the question is one of interpreting the DSU provisions. The present approach recognizes the existence of incidental jurisdiction (part of which is inherent, as the Appellate Body has recognized)[66] and leads one to conclude, in the absence of a definition in the WTO DSU, that the applicable law in WTO dispute settlement is broader than the principal jurisdiction of WTO adjudicative bodies. Under the perspective of (inherent) incidental jurisdiction, one would first inquire about the function of panels and the Appellate Body; second, verify the necessity of applying non-WTO law for the exercise of that function, depending on the specific circumstances of the case at hand; and third, ask whether the DSU would lead to a change in the conclusion. That shift places the adjudicators as guarantors of their own judicial integrity in assessing the parties' litigation strategies and behavior. This is all the more important in the context of permanent dispute settlement systems of a largely automatic and permanent character, such as the WTO dispute settlement system.[67]

65 See Trachtman, 'Jurisdiction in WTO Dispute Settlement'; Trachtman, 'Domain of WTO Dispute Resolution.'

66 See Appellate Body Report, *Mexico – Taxes on Soft Drinks*, para. 45.

67 As the ICJ held with respect to the interpretation of constituent instruments of international organizations in *Legality of the Use by a State of Nuclear Weapons in Armed Conflict*, Advisory Opinion of 8 July 1996, para. 19: "[Constituent instruments] can raise specific problems of interpretation, owing, *inter alia*, to their character which is

Third, focusing on preliminary objections pushes the discussion forward in a procedural front that complements the heated debate concerning the connections between trade and so-called "non-trade" law. The latter field is where the debate on the scope of applicable law has been primarily conducted.[68] The example just drawn from the agreement between Australia and the United States in *Automotive Leather* is on point. Rather than leading to a major accommodation or clash between two different regimes advancing potentially conflicting fundamental values (such as trade liberalization, sustainable development, freedom of speech, or labor conditions, to name just a few), the preclusion of a member's right to receive findings on the merits of its claims when that member has itself committed not to ask for a finding in the first place seems much more trivial an example stemming from the notion of party autonomy.

If forum shopping takes place, the application of procedure-regulating norms outside the WTO is a means for WTO adjudicators to safeguard the WTO system itself, not as against other regimes, but from party conduct that would tarnish the integrity of the WTO adjudicatory process. Put this way, the question is farther from a major clash of regimes or tribunals and closer to a question of making parties stick to their agreed choices. Noticeably, even Joel Trachtman, one of the leading voices among those who argue that non-WTO law cannot apply in WTO dispute settlement, concedes that "other international law may be used in construction in order to complete the procedural structure of the DSU itself and to ensure an 'objective assessment of the matter' under Article 11 of the DSU."[69] It is argued that the application

conventional and at the same time institutional; the *very nature* of the organization created, the objectives which have been assigned to it by its founders, the *imperatives associated with the effective performance of its functions*, as well as its own practice, are all elements which may deserve special attention when the time comes to interpret constituent instruments" (emphasis added). Although this remark is directed to the interpretation of constituent instruments of international organizations, it is also apposite for interpreting constituent instruments of permanent international adjudicatory mechanisms. See also John Jackson, *Sovereignty, the WTO and Changing Fundamentals of International Law* (Cambridge University Press, 2006), at 386.

68 See Pauwelyn, *Conflict of Norms*; Gabrielle Marceau, 'Conflicts of Norms and Conflicts of Jurisdictions: The Relationship between the WTO Agreement and MEAs and other Treaties,' 35 *JWT* (2001) 1081.

69 Trachtman, 'Jurisdiction in WTO Dispute Settlement,' at 136. It should be noted that Trachtman makes a clear distinction between construction and interpretation. See, in this regard, Trachtman, 'Domain of WTO Dispute Resolution,' at 337: "[I]nterpretation refers to the determination of the meaning of words contained in

of procedural norms beyond the DSU as conditions to the admissibility of a WTO complaint, in certain cases, is the only conclusion that conforms to basic notions of impartiality toward the disputing parties in the adjudicatory process. Bringing the debate to those terms might make it easier to convey the message that the real judicial activism on the part of panels and the Appellate Body would not lie in applying rules beyond the covered agreements, under certain circumstances and conditions, such as in the context of preliminary objections. Rather, it would lie in choosing to altogether ignore all the relevant rules which normally apply to a given relationship between two disputing parties, permitting the use of the WTO system to circumvent procedural norms expressly agreed to by WTO members.

4.4 The stabilizing effect of a decision on a preliminary question

The remaining question to be addressed in this chapter refers to the effect of decisions on preliminary questions. Answering this question requires one to distinguish first between a decision made within the scope of principal jurisdiction and a decision made outside the scope of principal jurisdiction. Second, it is important to distinguish between a decision on procedural grounds and a decision on substantive grounds. These two distinctions lead to the conclusion that, first, decisions on preliminary questions beyond the scope of principal jurisdiction have effects that are exclusive to the proceedings at stake, and second, that they do not prejudice the merits of the case. These two conclusions accommodate the contention that the exercise of authority to rule on a preliminary objection may undermine the consensual authority of international adjudication.

4.4.1 Decisions within principal jurisdiction versus decisions beyond principal jurisdiction

Decisions within the scope of principal jurisdiction, to the extent that they are part of an operative clause or are "necessarily entailed in the decision," regarding the circumstances in which the judgment

a contract, statute or treaty while construction refers to the determination of the intent of the parties in connection with a matter not specifically addressed in the text of the document." Now, if one agrees that the DSU does not address the issue of applicable law explicitly and based on the concept of incidental jurisdiction and the adjudicatory function of WTO panels and the Appellate Body, this would lead to the position that this book adopts.

was given, have the character of *res judicata*.[70] This means that the question will have been finally decided, that the decision should be implemented, and that the issue will be protected from re-litigation. By contrast, international tribunals, being tribunals of delegated jurisdiction, cannot state the law with finality outside their principal jurisdiction. Therefore, decisions made in the exercise of incidental jurisdiction beyond principal jurisdiction simply cannot constitute *res judicata*.[71]

Nonetheless, this does not mean that issues decided in the exercise of incidental jurisdiction remain open without exception. A procedural relationship develops during the course of the proceedings through sequentially linked, interrelated acts and stages, and a decision affecting or determining the procedural relationship precludes re-litigation of issues that have already been decided in the course of the same proceedings. This preclusion enables the procedural relationship to stabilize and move forward in the first place. However, this is a practical and organizational need that may require balancing the circumstances of each case with other considerations related to the conduct of the parties and, potentially, developments outside the specific proceeding. Accordingly, decisions on preliminary questions beyond principal jurisdiction serve to stabilize the procedural relationship and may become definitive only in the sense that they cannot be overturned in the course of the same proceeding.[72] In other proceedings, they are assessed *de novo* – even if, from a material perspective, the tribunal assessing a similar question may justifiably opt to defer to the prior decision or refer to it as persuasive authority.

[70] See *Application of the Convention on the Prevention and Punishment of the Crime of Genocide (Bosnia and Herzegovina* v. *Serbia and Montenegro)*, Judgment of 26 February 2007, paras. 123–6. The application of this standard to the question of what issues are covered as *res judicata* is not without difficulties in practice. See generally Leonardo Brant, *L'autorité de la chose jugée en droit international public* (Paris: LGDJ, 2003).

[71] See also Cheng, *General Principles of Law*, at 355. It is one thing to recognize that the judicial function authorizes or even requires tribunals to decide a question in the exercise of their incidental jurisdiction (as argued here). It is a different question whether the judicial function attaches to every given action by the tribunal – even those outside its field-jurisdiction – the character of finality, including finality before other tribunals (which is not the case).

[72] See also Article 46, 1899 Convention for the Pacific Settlement of International Disputes; Article 71, 1907 Convention for the Pacific Settlement of International Disputes: "[Agents and counsel] have the right to raise objections and points. The decisions of the Tribunal on those points are final, and cannot form the subject of any subsequent discussion."

The definitive character of decisions on preliminary objections within principal jurisdiction is made particularly evident in cases where they constitute a separate judgment, such as in most cases before the ICJ. Hence, the Court has held that its judgments on preliminary objections are final and not subject to appeal pursuant to Articles 59 and 60 of the ICJ Statute, just like any other judgment on the merits.[73] Moreover, the Court has emphasized that the exclusive possibility for reviewing a judgment on preliminary objections is provided for in Article 61 of the Statute.[74] But again, in light of the fact that the procedure moves forward sequentially, separate judgments on preliminary objections such as in most ICJ cases are not required for a decision on a preliminary objection to be considered definitive in the specific proceeding, as described above. Therefore, regardless of the moment when the decision takes place, or of the instrument within which it is incorporated, this book regards a decision on a given preliminary objection, at a minimum, as a stabilizer with respect to that objection: unless compelling reasons require a modification of the decision, it should be considered definitive. For that reason, in a WTO case, say, where a panel issues preliminary findings upholding or dismissing a preliminary objection, the decision should be respected by the parties and the panel during the remainder of the proceeding.

However, to the extent that decisions on preliminary objections beyond principal jurisdiction may be definitive, they remain circumscribed to the proceedings in which they are made.[75] This preclusive character is distinguishable from – and more limited than – the

[73] See *Genocide (Bosnia v. Serbia)*, paras. 113–20; *Request for the Interpretation of the Judgment of 11 June 1998 Concerning the Land and Maritime Boundary between Cameroon and Nigeria (Nigeria v. Cameroon)*, Judgment of 25 March 1999, paras. 12–17. Neither Article 59 nor Article 60 distinguishes judgments on preliminary objections from judgments of merit. On the other hand, the ICJ Statute does not foresee preliminary objections at all, which are only dealt with under the Rules of Court. Therefore, it would be awkward if the Statute itself drew a distinction between judgments on preliminary issues and judgments on the merits. From this perspective, the ICJ's straightforward reasoning that a separate judgment on preliminary objections constitutes *res judicata* just like judgments on the merits would be subject to qualification.

[74] *Genocide (Bosnia v. Serbia)*, Judgment of 26 February 2007, para. 117: "Article 61.1 of the ICJ Statute also does not distinguish between judgment on preliminary objections and on the merits." But see the above note on the fact that the ICJ Statute does not foresee preliminary objections at all. In the light of this fact, the ICJ explanation is arguably anachronistic.

[75] It is submitted that such preclusive character refers to the set of proceedings including the judgments on preliminary objections and the merits, as well as

preclusive character that underlies the protection of *res judicata* as a principle of law.[76] Put differently, the definitive character of a decision on preliminary questions beyond principal jurisdiction refers to the *decision* on the issue, taken as a *procedural* act, and not to the overall dispute. The decision on preliminary objections, as a procedural act, determines a moment as of which a question can no longer be discussed in the given proceeding at stake. Because the adjudicatory process is a sequence of procedural acts materialized in the proceeding, one procedural act (e.g., a decision on a preliminary objection) may lead to the closing of the issue in the course of the proceeding. However, using the proceeding as a benchmark, this is an internal effect only, to be distinguished from *res judicata*, which also has external effects.

The lack of external preclusive effects in decisions on preliminary objections beyond principal jurisdiction answers the potential contention that, in deciding an issue beyond the tribunal's principal jurisdiction, the tribunal would impinge upon the jurisdiction of another tribunal or adjudicate a dispute outside its principal jurisdiction. Instead, by deciding on a preliminary question implicating a norm beyond its principal jurisdiction, the tribunal is merely deciding on a specific procedural relationship as a matter of incidental jurisdiction. That decision is not determinative of a dispute beyond the principal jurisdiction of the tribunal and does not, as such, create further rights or obligations for the parties outside the context of the proceeding at stake.

4.4.2 *Decisions on preliminary questions (procedural* res judicata*) and decisions on the merits (substantive* res judicata*)*

There is also a distinction in the coverage of "procedural" versus "substantive" *res judicata*. This distinction stems from a functional distinction between procedure and substance, or preliminary questions and questions of merit, discussed in Chapters 2 and 3. A decision on a preliminary question, being a decision on the requirements of process, has no bearing on the substantive dispute. Hence, a decision on a preliminary question cannot constitute *res judicata* as to any question of

applicable incidental proceedings, which could be regarded as being within the context of a single principal procedural relationship.

[76] Chapter 7 discusses the broader notion of *res judicata* in further detail. *Res judicata* does not attach to all decisions, but only to judgments. Moreover, *res judicata* is opposable in other proceedings, even before a different tribunal. The notions of preclusion and *res judicata* are often used interchangeably, but the distinction is important for present purposes.

merit, which will remain undecided where a preliminary question is upheld and leads to the termination of the proceeding.[77]

On the other hand, the distinct coverage of decisions on preliminary questions and decisions on questions of merit does not mean there is a distinction between the requirements for *res judicata* to apply to either type of decision. As Chapter 3 illustrated, controverted positions on preliminary questions can be interpreted as a "mini-dispute." This "mini-dispute" refers to specific parties, a specific cause (in this case, a "cause of process," that is, the facts and law referring to the requirements of process), and specific requests (i.e., for the complainant, that the prerequisites for a process are fulfilled; for the respondent, that those prerequisites are not fulfilled). These three elements provide the outer limits of the "procedural" *res judicata*. Accordingly, changes in the underlying "cause of process" – a condition analogous to the "cause of action" when *res judicata* refers to the merits – may lead to a new procedure in a narrow sense, even between the same parties and referring to the same underlying dispute.

This is the reason why the peremptory or dilatory effect of decisions on preliminary questions is a relative matter. Decisions on preliminary questions may have a peremptory effect which terminates the proceedings and prevents new proceedings between the same parties relating to the same underlying dispute. They may also have a more modest, dilatory effect which only postpones a decision of merit within the same proceedings; or, even when they might lead to the termination of the proceedings, they may not prevent further proceedings between the same parties and referring to the same underlying dispute. In other words, the peremptory effect of a preliminary objection will depend not on the decision itself, but rather on the nature of the objection. In that sense, an objection based, for example, on the rules governing the attribution of nationality may be peremptory (to the extent that the lack of nationality cannot be remedied by the complaining party), while an exception based on the lack of exhaustion of local remedies or the lack of previous consultations could be simply dilatory, to the

[77] This distinction reminds one of the notions of "formal *res judicata*" (narrower) and "material *res judicata*," which are used in certain domestic legal systems, such as in Germany, Italy, and Spain. See Institut de Droit Comparé Edouard Lambert, '*L'étendue de l'autorité de chose jugée en droit comparé*,' (manuscript). The doctrine of *res judicata* in common law would encompass broader preclusive effects through the different applications of estoppel. See, for an early work, George S. Bower, *The Doctrine of* Res Judicata (London: Butterworth, 1924).

extent that local remedies are exhausted or consultations are held and the action is reintroduced in different proceedings. Upholding a dilatory preliminary objection leads simply to the end of a given *proceeding* or its postponement. To this extent, the previous decision does not directly and as such affect the complainant's ability to act in subsequent proceedings.

4.5 Concluding remarks

This chapter examined the source, scope, and effect of the power of international tribunals to rule on preliminary objections. It has been argued that the source of this power is the judicial character of international tribunals, and that this power is a matter of inherent jurisdiction, which is exercised incidentally where necessary and applicable. Moreover, the power to rule on preliminary objections covers any international norm binding on the relationship between the two disputing parties. Finally, exercises of this power beyond principal jurisdiction have effects which are internal to the given proceedings and which do not, as such, determine the overall legal relationship between the disputing parties. They merely govern the procedural relationship at stake.

Applying the contours of the power to rule on preliminary objections to the issue of forum shopping, one may conclude that international adjudicators are in a position to address any party behavior adhering to or deviating from any norm of international law applicable to the relationship between the disputing parties, provided that the issue (i) is put before them by the parties themselves and (ii) requires an incidental decision in the course of the adjudicatory process. Therefore, where applicable, forum-shopped parties are advised to push their objection forward and place it as a disputed issue the resolution of which restricts the continuation of the adjudicatory process. The decision on the issue may be limited to the proceeding at stake. But it will correspond to a tribunal's engaging or disengaging from deciding the request on the merits, regarding other tribunals' potential principal jurisdictions and the fulfillment of any other procedural requirements by the parties.

5 Jurisdiction and admissibility

5.1 Introduction

Chapter 4 argued that the power to rule on preliminary objections in the exercise of incidental jurisdiction inheres in international tribunals. It posited that the power to address preliminary objections extends to the whole of the law applicable to the relationship between the parties to a dispute, to the extent that the procedural matters need to be resolved incidentally in order to reach the merits of a case. This recognition is essential for procedural coordination to be effectively implemented across different international tribunals.

The present chapter addresses the categorization of preliminary questions into questions of jurisdiction and admissibility so as to decode their application to forum shopping strategies. It submits that procedural coordination may take place through a direct model of coordination under the notion of jurisdiction, and an indirect model of coordination under the notion of admissibility. These two different models of coordination supplement each other. In the direct model, the coordinating tribunals have a direct jurisdictional link that commands coordination. In the indirect model, autonomous international tribunals may address forum shopping even in the absence of an explicit and direct jurisdictional link between them, through the use of objections to admissibility. The notion of admissibility permits coordination of different proceedings mediated by general principles of law and preclusion norms regardless of whether a full-fledged jurisdictional system is in place. As a category of prerequisites to the development of the adjudicatory process that extends beyond jurisdictional requirements themselves, admissibility further attests that the inquiry of an international tribunal need not necessarily stop at its own jurisdictional clauses and constituent instrument. It is thus a channel to apply procedure-regulating norms across international tribunals as a matter of incidental jurisdiction. Moreover, as a matter of incidental jurisdiction, and thus as an area which takes place within existing jurisdiction, admissibility questions may be resolved pending a stay, rather than invariably requiring full-blown termination of the proceedings. Finally, the requirement that the aggrieved party explicitly raise a given admissibility question lest it not be entertained explains why, in several past cases where the parties neglected to specifically raise objections to tackle forum shopping, procedural coordination was neither possible nor warranted. In sum, recognizing jurisdiction and admissibility as different categories of preliminary questions, along with their different consequences, is significant for autonomous tribunals implementing procedural coordination.

Four sections follow. In the next section, this chapter explains the relevance of a dual categorization of preliminary questions into questions of jurisdiction and admissibility, which takes on increased importance with the rise in forum shopping (Section 5.2). The chapter then sketches and discusses three typical approaches to the dual jurisdiction–admissibility categorization: (i) indifference, (ii) objectivism, and (iii) conventionalism–residualism. It is argued that the "conventionalist–residualist" approach best reflects current international law and adjudication (Section 5.3). Subsequently, the chapter derives the two mutually reinforcing models of procedural regulation and coordination latent in international law: a direct model and an indirect model (Section 5.4). Concluding remarks close the chapter (Section 5.5).

5.2 A distinction that makes a difference

Preliminary questions essentially fall into two alternative categories: jurisdiction and admissibility. There may be discussion about other categories of preliminary objections, but the classic jurisdiction-versus-admissibility categorization is generally sufficient for present purposes and reflects the vast majority of the case law.[1] The categorization

[1] The ICJ has occasionally hinted at a possible third category of preliminary objections. For instance, in *Case Concerning Territorial and Maritime Dispute (Nicaragua v. Colombia)*, Preliminary Objections, Judgment of 13 December 2007, para. 51, recalling its previous *Nuclear Tests* decisions, the Court stated that "while examining questions of jurisdiction and admissibility, it is entitled, and in some circumstances may be required, to go into other questions which may not strictly be capable of classification as

developed originally in the practice of the PCIJ and the ICJ and is now incorporated in the practice of several international tribunals.[2] It is a product of practice that has achieved the status of a general feature of international adjudication, and which multiple procedural instruments have progressively incorporated.[3] The categorization could usefully apply to international tribunals that have not openly referred to

matters of jurisdiction or admissibility but are of such a nature as to require examination before the merits." However, in the context of that observation, the Court examines factual and legal issues with the objective of deciding on its *jurisdiction* under the Pact of Bogotá. The issue in *Nuclear Tests* was the existence of a dispute. See *Nuclear Tests Case (New Zealand* v. *France)*, Judgment of 20 December 1974, paras. 58–61. But the question of the existence of a dispute falls under the binary categorization, although its classification is ambiguous. The requirement can be depicted either as a requirement to the exercise of adjudicatory jurisdiction (since adjudicatory jurisdiction is substitutive as Chapter 2 explained), or to the admissibility of an application, under the notion of mootness of a request. The farthest that the Court has gone regarding a potential "third category" of preliminary objections was to hold that the field of application of Article 79 of the Rules of Court is not limited to objections to jurisdiction and admissibility. See *Case Concerning Questions of Interpretation and Application of the 1971 Montreal Convention Arising from the Aerial Incident at Lockerbie (Libyan Arab Jamahiriya* v. *United Kingdom)*, Preliminary Objections, Judgment of 27 February 1998, para. 47. Article 79 of the ICJ Rules mentions objections to the jurisdiction of the Court or to the admissibility of the application or any "other objection the decision upon which is requested before any further proceedings on the merits." However, as discussed in Chapter 3, Article 79 does not conceptualize preliminary objections in a *material* sense. Rather, it provides for the timeline character and effect of preliminary objections. Indeed, in *Lockerbie*, the Court emphasized the formal character of Article 79 of the Rules, in line with timeline-based definitions of preliminary objections. Moreover, the specific objection discussed there properly falls under the binary categorization (i.e., the mootness of the Libyan application due to subsequent Security Council resolutions). For recent arbitral decisions that hint of a threefold categorization of preliminary objections, see *Hochtief AG* v. *Argentina*, ICSID Case No ARB/07/31, Decision on Jurisdiction, 24 October 2011, para. 90; *ICS Inspection and Control Services Limited* v. *Argentina*, Award on Jurisdiction under UNCITRAL Rules, PCA Case No 2010–09, 10 February 2010, paras. 252–5.

[2] The PCIJ referred to the distinction for the first time in *Case Concerning Certain German Interests in Upper Silesia (Poland* v. *Germany)*, PCIJ Ser A No 6 (1925) 5, at 18. It first upheld a preliminary objection to admissibility (based on the lack of exhaustion of local remedies) in *The Panevezys-Saldutiskis Railway Case (Estonia* v. *Lithuania)*, PCIJ Ser A/B No 76 (1939). For detailed analysis of the PCIJ practice, see Georges Abi-Saab, *Les exceptions préliminaires dans la procédure de la Cour Internationale* (Paris: Pedone, 1967).

[3] The ICJ Statute, the ITLOS Statute, and the ICSID Convention do not refer explicitly to jurisdiction and admissibility. In the ICJ and ITLOS contexts, the distinction was referred to in procedural rules elaborated by the tribunals themselves, based on practice. See Article 79(1), ICJ Rules of Court; Article 97(1), International Tribunal for the Law of the Sea, Rules of the Tribunal, ITLOS/8, (ITLOS Rules of the Tribunal). Under Article 30(1), ICJ Statute and Article 16, ITLOS Statute (Annex VI to the UNCLOS), the tribunals shall frame rules for carrying out their functions. In particular, they shall lay down rules of procedure.

the distinction between jurisdiction and admissibility, such as WTO panels and the Appellate Body.[4] It is suggested that true recognition of the twofold categorization in WTO litigation would represent a procedural development to be welcomed.[5]

[4] As in the context of other tribunals, the lack of explicit mention of the two categories in the WTO DSU is no reason to disregard them out of hand. The Appellate Body's power to determine its rules of procedure under Article 17(9) of the DSU is akin to that of the ICJ and the ITLOS. Although panels are normally required to follow standard working procedures, they may decide otherwise after consulting the parties, pursuant to Article 12(1) of the DSU. With regard to the specific use of admissibility as a category of objections, the panel in *Japan – DRAMs* correctly referred to the question of whether certain claims by Korea were presented in a sufficiently clear manner in Korea's panel request as an issue related to the admissibility of Korea's claims. See Panel Report, *Japan – Countervailing Duties on Dynamic Random Access Memories from Korea*, WT/DS336/R, adopted 17 December 2007, as modified by Appellate Body Report WT/DS336/AB/R, para. 7.22 (these findings were not reviewed by the Appellate Body). The panel's general reasoning sits well with the notion of admissibility, but the panel found that the "inadmissible" claims were outside the terms of reference. Yet, the issue was not that the claims were outside the terms of reference, but rather that they were inadmissible because of a deficiency in the panel request. The panel's categorization of the issue as one of admissibility is important because the claims could be the object of a ruling on the merits if: (i) Korea had elaborated on the claims during the proceeding, and (ii) Japan had not raised the issue of admissibility explicitly. See also Panel Report, *Colombia – Indicative Prices and Restrictions on Ports of Entry*, WT/DS366/R and Corr.1, adopted 20 May 2009. At para. 7.47, the panel examines the question of whether a measure fell under its terms of reference as a question of jurisdiction. By contrast, the section on a claim arguably included in the terms of reference, but not developed in the first written submission, was correctly called "Admissibility of Panama's second claim under Article I:1 of the GATT 1994" (para. 7.55). However, the panel errs when it states that the question was whether that claim was part of its "mandate" (which evokes the notion of jurisdiction, at para. 7.59). The panel did not rule on the latter issue, since it found violations of other provisions and employed judicial economy (paras. 8.4 and 8.6).

[5] Interestingly, the assessment of questions of admissibility in the sense discussed here by WTO panels and the Appellate Body – without them explicitly being called questions of admissibility – stands in marked contrast with the approach under GATT dispute settlement. GATT panels rejected the premise that they were entitled to rule on the admissibility of claims if the issue was not expressly covered in their terms of reference. See GATT Panel Reports, *Korea – Restrictions on Imports of Beef*, L/6505 – 36S/202, L/6504–36S/232, L/6505–36S/268, 24 May 1989, adopted 7 November 1989, paras. 6–10. In reaching this conclusion, the panels emphasized that the respondent agreed with the terms of the request. In the WTO context, as in the GATT context, terms of reference do not normally provide the power to rule on questions of admissibility. However, unlike in the GATT context, an examination has become routine. Regarding the requirements for panel requests, indeed, the Appellate Body has stated that, since the requests are normally not subjected to detailed scrutiny by the DSB, it is incumbent upon panels to verify them very carefully to ensure their compliance with both the letter and the spirit of the DSU. See Appellate Body Report, *European Communities – Regime for the Importation, Sale and Distribution of Bananas*, WT/DS27/AB/R, adopted 25 September 1997, para. 142.

To be sure, the terminology used with regard to preliminary questions is far from uniform. Moreover, the distinction between jurisdiction and admissibility may not be of practical importance in every case, and tribunals are not necessarily supposed to follow academically minded, general concepts in the context of every dispute they decide.[6] Furthermore, distinguishing between jurisdiction and admissibility is not always easy. The distinction is contingent, can be subtle, and can become even more complex depending on how parties structure the case and how the tribunal structures its decision. All these factors help to explain why, in the absence of anything close to an international code of procedure, the terminology used by international tribunals in practice may be hard to organize and understand as a coherent whole.

Terminological confusion in law is unsatisfactory for aesthetic and pedagogical reasons, but it is most unfortunate for analytical and practical reasons. While there is still confusion concerning the notions of jurisdiction and admissibility when the case law of various tribunals is analyzed together, a common grammar in this area would serve many purposes. Harmonic, consistent, and precise use of terminology normally fosters communication, facilitates understanding, and improves decision-making, potentially reducing transaction costs and promoting legal certainty. Moreover, an understanding of preliminary questions from the twofold perspective of jurisdiction and admissibility has practical implications; and if practical consequences ensue from the use of these concepts, then keeping and understanding them as a matter of theory becomes indispensable.

Specific reasons that justify the categorization of preliminary questions into questions of jurisdiction and admissibility can be discussed in two groups for present purposes. A first, more traditional group of reasons refers to: (i) the order of analysis of preliminary questions; (ii) the consequence of non-fulfillment of a procedural requirement in terms of a stay or termination of the proceedings; (iii) the relevance of the distinction for the reviewability of decisions; and (iv) the differentiated burden to raise questions of admissibility. A second, emerging

[6] For example, in *Mavrommatis Palestine Concessions*, PCIJ Ser A No 2 (1924), at 10, the Court stated that it "has not to ascertain what are, in the various codes of procedure and in the various legal terminologies, the specific characteristics of such an objection; in particular it need not consider whether 'competence', and 'jurisdiction', *incompétence* and *fins de non recevoir*, should invariably and in every connection be regarded as synonymous expressions." See also *Certain German Interests in Upper Silesia*, at 19.

group of reasons to keep the dual categorization relates to the rise in forum shopping activity, since explicitly recognizing admissibility paves the way for horizontal procedural coordination in the noncentralized structure of international adjudication.

5.2.1 Traditional reasons for a dual categorization

Why bother to ask whether a party or tribunal should call a question one of jurisdiction or admissibility? The answer is, well, it depends. Neatly distinguishing between jurisdiction and admissibility may not be essential in every case, but it will be relevant in some of them. Seizing the contours of jurisdictional and admissibility issues is of interest in these latter cases. Essentially, there have been four "traditional" general reasons to distinguish between jurisdiction and admissibility. While these reasons do not necessarily apply in all cases, let alone before all tribunals with the same force, they are significant practical reasons for the application of a dual categorization.

A first reason for distinguishing between jurisdiction and admissibility stems from the inescapably consensual structure of international adjudication. Given the delegated nature of jurisdiction in international law, jurisdiction should be established in order for a tribunal to move forward and assess whether other "nonjurisdictional" or "admissibility-related" prerequisites for the development of the adjudicatory process are also fulfilled. Thus, on a basic level, the distinction determines a tribunal's order of analysis and disposal of given preliminary questions. It is in this sense that international tribunals[7] and their procedural rules[8] at times expressly point out that a question of admissibility should come into play only after jurisdiction is established.[9] This is also how practice normally goes. Although it is true that adjudicators have not always followed this order of analysis and have terminated proceedings or denied sequence to claims on a clear and narrow basis related to admissibility without definitively

[7] See, for example, *Case Concerning Armed Activities on the Territory of Congo (New Application: 2002) (Democratic Republic of the Congo* v. *Rwanda)*, Jurisdiction and Admissibility, Judgment of 3 February 2006, paras. 4, 17, 52.

[8] International Criminal Court, Rules of Procedure and Evidence (3–10 September 2002), Official Records ICC-ASP/1/3 (Part. II-A), Rule 58(4): "The Court shall rule on any challenge or question of jurisdiction first and then on any challenge or question of admissibility."

[9] See also Gerald Fitzmaurice, *The Law and Procedure of the International Court of Justice*, vol. II (Cambridge: Grotius, 1986), at 438–9; Ian Brownlie, *Principles of Public International Law*, 5th edn (Oxford University Press, 1998), at 479.

concluding on their jurisdiction,[10] this course of action has clearly been exceptional. All in all, if the end result is exactly the same, that is, termination of the proceedings, albeit on a logically subsequent basis in relation to jurisdiction (i.e., based on admissibility-related considerations), one might justify a reversal in the order of analysis for reasons of procedural economy.[11] From that perspective, sequencing considerations may not be decisive in all cases, and the dual categorization of preliminary questions may be more of a guideline or a pedagogical tool than an absolute requirement as far as this aspect is concerned. Nonetheless, one should also bear in mind that many objections to admissibility – such as the objection that local remedies have not been exhausted – may be remedied, permitting resubmission. If that is the case, the distinction between jurisdiction and admissibility regains significance even for the order of analysis dealt with here, since terminating the proceedings based on inadmissibility may leave the door open for the case to be brought again, whereas a finding of lack of jurisdiction could be conclusive.[12]

A second reason for the distinction is closely related to the first one discussed above: the fact that admissibility operates within existing jurisdiction, and should thus be assessed in the event that jurisdiction is established, embeds a further distinction as to the measures that the tribunal may adopt in reaction to nonfulfillment of a procedural requirement. As the arbitral tribunal explained in *ICS* v. *Argentina*, "[o]nce a tribunal has conclusively determined that it has no jurisdiction, it is rendered *functus officio* and ceases to exist and act in relation to the dispute."[13] By contrast, admissibility is an area in which tribunals enjoy "some discretion as to how to deal with its non-fulfillment, such as by staying instead of terminating the proceedings."[14] Thus,

[10] Thus, in some cases, a claim has been found to be inadmissible while the objections to jurisdiction had not been thoroughly disposed of. See, for example, *Interhandel (Switzerland* v. *United States)*, Preliminary Objections, Judgment of 21 March 1959, 8–9.

[11] See also Hugh Thirlway, 'Preliminary Objections,' in *Max Planck Encyclopedia of Public International Law* (Oxford University Press, 2007, electronic version), para. 15.

[12] See, for example, Judge Lauterpacht's remarks in *Interhandel*. The objection to admissibility that the ICJ eventually referred to in that case was the non-exhaustion of local remedies in the United States. As Judge Lauterpacht argued, if local remedies were exhausted and Switzerland came back to the Court, and the Court then denied that it lacked jurisdiction, the first proceeding would have been a waste of time and judicial resources. *Interhandel (Switzerland* v. *United States)*, Dissenting Opinion of Judge Lauterpacht, at 95–102.

[13] *ICS* v. *Argentina*, para. 255.

[14] *Ibid.*, para. 256.

successful objections to jurisdiction should lead a tribunal to terminate the proceedings, while successful objections to admissibility need not necessarily require termination. This is especially so if the question leading to inadmissibility can be solved pending a stay.[15] In this case, a tribunal's remaining seized of the case may be justified as an exercise of procedural economy and efficiency, and by the possibility that the tribunal will monitor the resolution of the issue. If a tribunal has jurisdiction, this monitoring may be warranted. Here, the different consequences of lack of jurisdiction (termination) versus lack of admissibility (suspension) flow from the idea that jurisdiction is a threshold question – akin to the sequencing considerations discussed above. Consequently, if jurisdiction exists and the admissibility issue is curable, in some cases tribunals may opt for a stay pending a solution to the question of admissibility.[16]

A third reason to distinguish between jurisdiction and admissibility refers to the reviewability of decisions. Decisions of commercial and investment arbitrators on jurisdictional questions, for instance, are often definitely subject to review by controlling authorities, such as the courts of the seat of arbitration[17] or annulment committees.[18] This is arguably not the case (and in any event not necessarily the case) if the decision refers to admissibility. As Jan Paulsson summarizes, "[d]ecisions of tribunals which do not respect jurisdictional limits may be invalidated by a controlling authority. But if parties have consented to the jurisdiction of a given tribunal, its determinations

[15] See generally John Collier and Vaughan Lowe, *The Settlement of Disputes in International Law* (Oxford University Press, 1999), at 155–6: "[L]ack of jurisdiction means that the Court cannot hear a particular case at all, whereas non-admissibility means sometimes that the Court could have heard the case at one time, but cannot do so now, or that it cannot hear it now, but could do so in the future."

[16] Chapter 6 discusses the importance of stays in the context of forum shopping strategies. The discussion there is intentionally broader, and refers to stays in light of doubts regarding determinations of jurisdiction, admissibility, or even merits (i.e., stays as a measure stemming from adjudicatory jurisdiction and targeted at procedure in a narrow sense, to facilitate the determination of a question). The issue here is narrower and refers to terminations and stays as a consequence of a successful objection (i.e., stays as a consequence of a determination of inadmissibility).

[17] See Article 34(2)(A)(iii), UNCITRAL Model Law on International Commercial Arbitration; Article 67, English Arbitration Act (1996); Article 1502, French Code of Civil Procedure; Articles 190(2)(b), 190(2)(c), Swiss Private International Law Statute; Article 32(iv), Brazilian Arbitration Statute. See Zachary Douglas, *The International Law of Investment Claims* (Cambridge University Press: 2009), 146.

[18] Article 52, ICSID Convention.

as to the admissibility of claims should be final."[19] As a consequence, treating jurisdictional questions as questions of admissibility narrows the scope for challenging awards. Conversely, treating admissibility-related questions as jurisdictional may unjustifiably enhance a party's ability to reopen issues that have already been decided. In this case, serial litigation will be incentivized, and the finality of awards will be relativized.

The stricter standard of review when it comes to jurisdictional questions tends to implicate higher stakes in the context of investment arbitration than elsewhere, given the express possibility of annulment provided for in Article 52 of the ICSID Convention. In fact, the distinction between jurisdiction and admissibility may directly influence one's approach to the possibility of annulling arbitral awards under Article 52(1)(b) of the ICSID Convention. That provision permits either party to request the annulment of an ICSID arbitral tribunal's award on the grounds "that the Tribunal has manifestly exceeded its powers." But what does "manifest" excess of powers mean with regard to jurisdictional questions? As Zachary Douglas argues, when a tribunal lacks jurisdiction, basically any decision that fails to recognize this and any logically subsequent decision that the case is admissible or decision over the merits will necessarily meet the "manifest excess of power" standard.[20] With reference to a given claim, either a tribunal has jurisdiction or it does not, and in the latter case it cannot move forward with the analysis at all. It is, in a nutshell, hard to think of anything short of a "manifest excess of power" when a tribunal wrongly asserts jurisdiction. However, when the arbitral tribunal is vested with jurisdiction and correctly asserts it, then the tribunal's decision regarding any other question (of either admissibility or merits) should be reviewable under Article 52(1)(b) only to the extent that it constitutes a manifest excess of power concerning the other question. Here, the "manifest excess of power" standard requires more than "any" excess.[21] In summary: for jurisdictional questions, any excess of power will be manifest; for

[19] Jan Paulsson, 'Jurisdiction and Admissibility,' in Gerald Aksen *et al.* (eds.), *Global Reflections on International Law, Commerce and Dispute Resolution.* (Paris: ICC Publishing, 2005) 601, at 601.

[20] See Douglas, *International Law of Investment Claims*, at 146–8.

[21] An analogous argument might be made for review under Article 52(1)(d), ICSID Convention, which permits requests for annulment in the event that "there has been a serious departure from a fundamental rule of procedure." Jurisdictional rules are arguably fundamental in any event, and most departures from them will be serious; admissibility-related rules are not necessarily fundamental and

questions related to admissibility and merits only a manifest excess of power should lead to an annulment under Article 52.

A fourth reason to keep the distinction between jurisdiction and admissibility – particularly important for present purposes – is the fact that a party's burden to raise a preliminary objection varies depending on the category of question at stake.[22] As Judge McNair explained with reference to ICJ procedure, "an international tribunal cannot regard a question of jurisdiction solely as a question *inter partes*. That aspect does not exhaust the matter. The Court itself, acting *proprio motu*, must be satisfied that any State which is brought before it ... has consented to the jurisdiction."[23] In the context of WTO disputes, the Appellate Body has indicated that panels should sort out the issue of jurisdiction for themselves, while parties must explicitly raise other potential legal impediments at an early opportunity in order to avoid preclusion.[24] The Appellate Body's distinction between "jurisdiction" and "other legal impediments" and the related distinction concerning the burden to raise each type of question dovetail with the categorization of preliminary questions as questions of jurisdiction and admissibility by other tribunals. ICSID arbitral tribunals – which are expressly authorized to consider issues of jurisdiction at any time on their own initiative under the Arbitration Rules[25] – have adopted a similar reasoning,[26]

departing from them will not necessarily be serious. Of course, this is not to say that admissibility or procedural requirements should be treated lightly and easily sidestepped, since they are also mandatory.

22 There is no contradiction between the fact that tribunals have an inherent power to rule on preliminary questions and the fact that the parties may have a burden to trigger the exercise of that power by raising an objection. Affirming the existence of a power does not mean that this power is unconditionally exercised.

23 *Anglo-Iranian Oil Co. Case (United Kingdom* v. *Iran)*, Preliminary Objections, Judgment of 22 July 1952, Individual Opinion of Judge McNair, at 116. On the burden to raise objections to admissibility, see also Chittharanjan Amerasinghe, *Jurisdiction of International Tribunals* (The Hague: Kluwer, 2003), at 286–7.

24 See Appellate Body Report, *Mexico – Anti-Dumping Investigation of High Fructose Corn Syrup (HFCS) from the United States – Recourse to Article 21.5 of the DSU by the United States*, WT/DS132/AB/RW, adopted 21 November 2001, paras. 37, 50, 53, 64.

25 Rule 41(2), ICSID Arbitration Rules. See also Douglas, *International Law of Investment Claims*, at 141.

26 Contrast *Bernardus Henricus Funnekottre and others* v. *Zimbabwe*, Award of 22 April 2009, ICSID Case No ARB/05/6, para. 94, where the tribunal explicitly assesses the question of jurisdiction despite the agreement of the parties on such question, with *Bureau Veritas, Inspection, Valuation, Assessment and Control (BIVAC BV)* v. *Paraguay*, ICSID Case No ARB/07/9, Decision of the Tribunal on Objections to Jurisdiction, 29 May 2009, para. 157, where the tribunal implies that issues of admissibility must be argued in order to be taken into consideration: "Although that award [*Noble Ventures*]

as have other arbitral tribunals,[27] including state-to-state ones.[28] The ICSID tribunal in *Hochtief* v. *Argentina* put it bluntly: "defects in admissibility can be waived or cured by acquiescence: defects in jurisdiction cannot."[29]

A caveat must naturally be added for the situation where a constituent instrument specifically regulates the burden to raise objections. For instance, Article 19(1) of the Rome Statute of the International Criminal Court provides that the court "shall satisfy itself that it has jurisdiction" and "may, on its own motion, determine the admissibility of a case."[30] The provision on jurisdiction thus indicates that the ICC must assess jurisdictional questions in all cases. However, for admissibility-related questions the text is cast in terms of an authorization rather than an obligation. Therefore, the ICC may have discretion to raise admissibility issues on its own motion, whether a party explicitly objects to the admissibility of a case or not. A different example is found in Article 189(4)(d) of the EU–Chile Free Trade Agreement, which establishes an explicit burden to raise certain objections to jurisdiction *in limine litis*.[31]

Applying an objectivist perspective to the categorization of preliminary questions into jurisdiction- or admissibility-related,[32] the burden to raise the latter type of question would reflect the very nature of a lack of jurisdiction versus the inadmissibility of a claim. From such a perspective, lack of jurisdiction concerns the tribunal's authority to decide the issue. It is well established that international tribunals, whose authority is delegated, must sort this out for themselves, even if neither party raises the question, in order to avoid acting *ultra*

dealt with the meaning and effect of an umbrella clause, there is no indication that the underlying contract included an exclusive jurisdiction clause *or that there was any argument as to admissibility*. Accordingly that award can provide no assistance to BIVAC" (footnote omitted, emphasis added).

27 See, for example, *Larsen/Hawaiian Kingdom*, Arbitral Award of 5 February 2001.

28 See, for example, *Iron Rhine Railway (Belgium* v. *Netherlands)*, Award of 24 May 2005.

29 *Hochtief* v. *Argentina*, para. 95.

30 Article 19(1), Rome Statute of the International Criminal Court, 2187 *UNTS* 90 (ICC Statute).

31 Article 189(4)(d), Agreement Establishing an Association between the European Community and its Member states, of one part, and the Republic of Chile, of the other part, Official Journal of the European Union, L352, 30 December 2002 (EU–Chile FTA): "Any question on the jurisdiction of the arbitration panels established under this Title shall be raised within 10 days of the establishment of the panel, and shall be settled by a preliminary ruling of the panel within 30 days of the establishment of the panel."

32 See discussion in Section 5.3 below.

vires.[33] Inadmissibility, on the other hand, relates to the action or procedure in a narrow sense. In this sense, the analysis of admissibility is subject to implied waiver and acquiescence.

The relevance of this distinction for practicing lawyers is self-evident. It has particular implications for forum shopping objectors and tribunals confronting forum shopping strategies: depending on whether one qualifies *res judicata*, collateral estoppel, *lis pendens*, *forum non conveniens*, forum-election clauses, or preclusion clauses in outside treaties as relating to the admissibility of a claim or to the jurisdiction of a tribunal, the parties may be required to raise the objection (admissibility), or the tribunal must consider the matter on its own initiative (jurisdiction). Indeed, the distinction outlined here becomes relevant for explaining several cases of jurisdictional overlaps involving the WTO and preferential trade-dispute settlement, and investor-state tribunals and national courts, where preclusion clauses were not at stake – arguably due to the lack of a specific objection based thereon.

[33] See, for example, *Case Concerning Military and Paramilitary Activities in and against Nicaragua (Nicaragua* v. *United States of America)*, Jurisdiction and Admissibility, Judgment of 26 November 1984, para. 80; Appellate Body Report, *Mexico – Corn Syrup (Article 21.5 – US)*, paras. 37, 50, 53; Appellate Body Report, *United States – Anti-Dumping Act of 1916*, WT/DS136/AB/R, WT/DS162/AB/R, adopted 26 September 2000, para. 54; *Milicom International Operations BV and Sentel GSM SA* v. *Senegal*, ICSID Case No ARB/08/20, Decision on the Jurisdiction of the Tribunal, 16 July 2010, para. 60. Note, however, that the ICJ allows for the possibility that upon an unambiguous waiver by the respondent the Court be granted jurisdiction under the doctrine of *forum prorogatum*. See *The Corfu Channel Case (United Kingdom* v. *Albania)*, Preliminary Objections, Judgment of 25 March 1948, 26–9; *Certain Questions of Mutual Assistance in Criminal Matters (Djibouti* v. *France)*, Judgment of 4 June 2008, paras. 60–97. Note also that there may be pragmatic reasons for "overlooking" a preliminary question of jurisdiction which could be unilaterally remedied by the applicant, in order to foster procedural economy. Thus, defects in the application that may be easily and unilaterally remedied may not lead to a dismissal of the case, even when it comes to jurisdictional matters. See *Case Concerning Application of the Convention on the Prevention and Punishment of the Crime of Genocide (Bosnia and Herzegovina* v. *Yugoslavia)*, Preliminary Objections, Judgment of 11 July 1996, para. 26. The "hands-off" approach at the ICJ is not normally echoed at the WTO, where a complainant's omission to include a provision or a measure in the panel request has led to dismissals of claims, even if a WTO complainant, of course, could just adjust its case and resubmit a request for the establishment of a panel. See Appellate Body Report, *European Communities – Regime for the Importation, Sale and Distribution of Bananas*, WT/DS27/AB/R, adopted 25 September 1997, para. 143: "[i]f a *claim* is not specified in the request for the establishment of a panel, then a faulty request cannot be subsequently 'cured' by a complaining party's argumentation …" The contrast in approaches may be explained by the fact that WTO panels' terms of reference, which establish their special principal jurisdiction, are under the responsibility of the DSB, and not of the parties directly.

At the WTO, NAFTA choice-of-forum provisions could have been at issue in *Periodicals*, *Taxes on Soft Drinks*, and *Tuna and Tuna Products*, but they were not.[34] Crucially, neither Canada, in *Periodicals*, nor Mexico, in *Taxes on Soft Drinks*, nor the United States, in *Tuna and Tuna Products*, ever raised NAFTA choice-of-forum provisions as specific objections to the admissibility of the claims made by the United States. In *Taxes on Soft Drinks*, although the Appellate Body was fully aware of the potential overlap, it explicitly noted "that Mexico has expressly stated that the so-called 'exclusion clause' of Article 2005(6) of the NAFTA had not been 'exercised'" and expressly left the issue of the applicability of Article 2005(6) of the NAFTA open.[35] The approach in *Periodicals*, *Taxes on Soft Drinks*, and *Tuna and Tuna Products* contrasts with the panel's willingness to openly entertain Argentina's preliminary objections in *Poultry Anti-Dumping Duties*.[36] In that case, Argentina did raise objections to the admissibility of Brazil's attempt to relitigate facts that had already been adjudicated by a MERCOSUR arbitral tribunal, based on the principles of good faith and estoppel. These arguments were ultimately unsuccessful, but their "merits" were openly discussed.[37] The contrast between *Periodicals*, *Taxes on Soft Drinks*, and *Tuna and Tuna Products*, on the one hand, and *Poultry Anti-Dumping Duties* on the other hand, confirms that where potential or actual procedural overlaps are at stake, either the parties raise specific objections to admissibility, which then become issues that must be decided, or the parties do not raise the objections and the tribunal does not normally deal with the issues.

Analogous considerations apply to investor-state arbitration. Take the *Lauder/CME*[38] set of cases that August Reinisch considers the

[34] See Appellate Body and Panel Reports, *Mexico – Tax Measures on Soft Drinks and Other Beverages*, WT/DS308/AB/R, adopted 24 March 2006; Appellate Body Report, *Canada – Certain Measures Concerning Periodicals*, WT/DS31/AB/R, adopted 30 July 1997, DSR 1997:I, 449; Panel Report, WT/DS31/R and Corr.1, adopted 30 July 1997, as modified by Appellate Body Report WT/DS31/AB/R; Appellate Body Report, *United States – Measures Concerning the Importation, Marketing and Sale of Tuna and Tuna Products*, WT/DS381/AB/R, Panel Report, WT/DS381/R, adopted 13 June 2012, as modified by Appellate Body Report WT/DS381/AB/R.

[35] Appellate Body Report, *Mexico – Taxes on Soft Drinks*, para. 54.

[36] Panel Report, *Argentina – Definitive Anti-Dumping Duties on Poultry from Brazil*, WT/DS241/R, adopted 19 May 2003.

[37] *Ibid.*, paras. 7.33–7.42. The panel did resort to the *arguendo* technique with regard to the objection based on estoppel, but nevertheless addressed Argentina's argument in full.

[38] See *Lauder* v. *Czech Republic*, Arbitral Tribunal under UNCITRAL Rules, 3 September 2001; *CME Czech Republic B.V. (The Netherlands)* v. *Czech Republic*, Arbitral Tribunal

"ultimate fiasco in investment arbitration."[39] There, the respondent expressly opted not to rely on *res judicata* or *lis pendens* considerations, and the tribunals' remarks on those principles can be considered as *obiter dicta*.[40] Moreover, the respondent expressly refused to accept any form of coordination between the parallel proceedings that were at stake.[41] In that context, should the arbitral tribunals have "discovered" general principles of law or another reason to coordinate as a matter of incidental jurisdiction if the respondent, the party itself affected by multiplicative litigation, opted not to rely on those principles? With the hindsight of the decisions in light of the dual categorization of preliminary objections, while the outcome of the cases may indeed be described as a fiasco, the burden to raise the issue and the respondent's insistence on keeping the two proceedings in splendid isolation from one another are key factors explaining the fiasco.

More broadly, the burden to expressly raise issues of admissibility draws an implicit balance for parties and for adjudicators in the context of alleged forum shopping strategies, taking into account party autonomy on the one hand, and the enabling, protective, and allocative functions of procedure-regulating rules on the other hand. It is difficult to draw definitive guidance as to when a tribunal should decline from ruling on the merits of a claim because of a procedural norm which would lead to inadmissibility. In those circumstances, one may expect judicial caution, especially given that the tribunal that is considering the issue of admissibility does indeed have jurisdiction to decide the case. Relatedly, one should expect the aggrieved party to come forward and state its case clearly on the matter. But if neither party raises a specific question of admissibility, then retaining the case seems to be the simplest and most reasonable solution. For, in that situation, there is no question related to the protective function of jurisdictional rules arising from the overlaps (i.e., the respondent itself is ready to fight the case on the merits), and the balance is directly

under UNCITRAL Rules, Partial Award, 13 September 2001, Final Award, 14 March 2003.

[39] August Reinisch, 'The Proliferation of International Dispute Settlement Mechanisms: The Threat of Fragmentation vs. the Promise of a More Effective System? Some Reflections from the Perspective of Investment Arbitration,' in I. Buffard *et al.* (eds.), *International Law between Universalism and Fragmentation: Festschrift in Honour of Gerhard Hafner* (The Hague: Brill, 2008) 107, at 116.

[40] See *CME* v. *Czech Republic*, Partial Award, paras. 430–1.

[41] *Ibid.*, para. 412; Final Award, 14 March 2003, paras. 426–9. See discussion in Chapter 7.

between party autonomy (i.e., both parties agree on the forum) and the systemic function of jurisdictional rules. Nonetheless, if the question refers to admissibility, there is no strict jurisdictional system to be concerned about. In that case, it is submitted that party autonomy should normally prevail over systemic considerations. On the other hand, a specific objection to admissibility indicates that party autonomy in the sense of agreement on a specific forum may not be present in the first place. In that case, thorough assessment of the issue appears to be warranted.

International law is still largely based on the notion of "bilateralism," and especially so when it comes to international adjudication. As in most types of private claims under domestic laws, in most international disputes between states or between states and other legal persons, the parties can be placed at two basic opposing poles: one complaining, the other responding. The parties can decide jointly whether to opt for judicial settlement and where to take their case. Hence, an agreement to plead a case before a tribunal is an exercise governed largely by the notion of party autonomy, as contractual freedom to choose the forum or to acquiesce on a forum.[42] From this perspective, the obligation to raise issues of admissibility lest the case proceed to a decision of merit places international tribunals at the service of the parties and allows acquiescence to effectively operate in international adjudication. By acting under this guideline, tribunals' exercise of incidental jurisdiction fully respects the course of action chosen by both parties.

5.2.2 *The dual categorization and forum shopping*

The binary categorization of preliminary questions addressed here gains relevance with the rise in forum shopping. The category of objections to admissibility speaks by implication to the fact that a party can raise more objections than those based on the jurisdictional title as such. As a result, the category of admissibility – a complement to the category of jurisdiction – is the usual channel for preliminary objections based on the broader set of norms governing the procedural rights and obligations of the parties. While the bases for that were discussed in Chapter 4, it is important to note that the category of admissibility further attests that the governing law of procedural coordination across international tribunals goes beyond each specific jurisdictional instrument, as applied by each corresponding tribunal in isolation

[42] See discussion in Chapter 4.

from other tribunals. This recognition is crucial to implementing and fostering coordination.

It is well known (i) that international tribunals are normally independent from one another, each one being the ultimate arbiter of its own jurisdiction (*la compétence de la compétence*), and (ii) that the jurisdiction of international tribunals over certain issues may overlap. In the basically horizontal context of international law, jurisdictional rules often exclusively govern the relationship (of authority) between the tribunal being granted jurisdiction and the parties. These rules may not themselves address the broader context of where international tribunals operate, especially due to the fact that international law expands through an incremental process. Because international tribunals are independent entities with *la compétence de la compétence*, the fact that a tribunal *has* jurisdiction over some issues does not mean that other tribunals *lack* or *are deprived of* jurisdiction over the same or substantially equivalent issues. Hence, if jurisdiction were the end of the story, the ability of tribunals and interested parties to call for and promote procedural coordination would be severely limited, since coordination would need to be explicitly provided for as a matter of *jurisdiction*.[43] Therefore, in order to make procedural coordination more effective, one must go beyond a purely jurisdictional approach. The existing category of admissibility adds that further dimension. As such, an objection to admissibility leaves untouched the jurisdiction of a tribunal to decide the case and is fully compatible with the logic underlying the principle of *la compétence de la compétence*. In fact, if a tribunal refuses to examine claims based on their inadmissibility, the tribunal is, by definition, exercising jurisdiction, albeit to decline to rule on the merits of the claims. Accordingly, even though the question of whether a tribunal has been deprived of jurisdiction may not be answered in the affirmative, a tribunal may exercise its jurisdiction so as to recognize the inadmissibility of claims and stop the proceeding without reaching the merits.

In order to emphasize that recognizing admissibility as a category of preliminary questions does make a difference for procedural coordination, contrast the ICSID arbitral tribunals' approaches in *SGS* v. *Pakistan*[44] – where the distinction between jurisdiction and admissibility

[43] This argument resonates with the deadlock argued by some scholars when it comes to jurisdictional overlaps involving the WTO. See discussion in Chapter 7.

[44] *Société Générale de Surveillance* v. *Pakistan*, ICSID Case No ARB/01/13, Decision of the Tribunal on Objections to Jurisdiction, 6 August 2003.

was not resorted to – and *SGS* v. *Philippines*[45] – where the distinction was employed. Both tribunals grappled with the similar question of whether an umbrella clause in the BIT gave them jurisdiction over contractual claims. In both cases, the investment contracts directed the dispute to commercial arbitration, not ICSID arbitration. In *SGS* v. *Pakistan*, the tribunal considered that, while it had jurisdiction over the BIT claims, it did not have jurisdiction over contractual claims, notwithstanding the presence of an umbrella clause.[46] One of the reasons given by the tribunal to interpret the umbrella clause narrowly was that if the tribunal had jurisdiction over contractual claims, the umbrella clause would override the contractual choice of forum by the parties and, arguably, the jurisdiction of the arbitral tribunal under the contractual arbitration clause.[47] According to the tribunal, the general description in the umbrella clause at issue could not be interpreted to that effect. The *SGS* v. *Pakistan* approach, therefore, recognized only a limited effect for an umbrella clause, partly in order to preserve the contractual choice of forum. In *SGS* v. *Philippines*, by contrast, the tribunal found that it had jurisdiction over contractual claims by virtue of the umbrella clause in the BIT.[48] However, in the opinion of the tribunal, the fact that it possessed jurisdiction did not mean that the umbrella clause nullified the contractual choice of forum. Rather, the contractual choice-of-forum clause represented a bar to the admissibility of the contractual claims before the ICSID tribunal.[49] As it turned out, by resorting to the distinction between jurisdiction and admissibility, the tribunal was able to give effect to (i) the umbrella clause, (ii) the contractual forum choice, and (iii) its own jurisdiction. In short, while the *SGS* v. *Pakistan* "jurisdiction-only" approach limited the reach of the umbrella clause, partly in order to respect the contractual choice of forum, the *SGS* v. *Philippines* "jurisdiction and admissibility" approach both preserved the reach of the umbrella clause and respected the contractual choice of forum.[50]

On the theoretical side, the notion of admissibility sheds light on the broader debate over jurisdictional overlaps among international

[45] *Société Générale de Surveillance* v. *Philippines*, ICSID Case No ARB/02/6, Decision of the Tribunal on Objections to Jurisdiction, 29 January 2004.

[46] *SGS* v. *Pakistan*, paras. 155, 162.

[47] *Ibid.*, para. 168.

[48] *SGS* v. *Philippines*, para. 135.

[49] *Ibid.*, para. 154.

[50] The latter approach, by incorporating the distinction between jurisdiction and admissibility, takes into account a distinction between the effect of an umbrella clause and the preclusion of the possibility to invoke the umbrella clause by a forum election clause in the contract. As the ICSID tribunal noted in *BIVAC BV* v.

tribunals. Recognizing that most questions of coordination focus on the procedural relationship between the parties and involve admissibility, rather than direct allocation of authority, which is normally a question of jurisdiction,[51] moves the debate a step away from the "clash of legal regimes" or "conflicts of jurisdiction" perspective. To date, the scholarly debate has focused more on procedural coordination as being squarely a problem of jurisdiction than on its being a problem of admissibility.[52] This perspective emphasizes questions of delegation and allocation under the function of jurisdictional regulating rules, while undermining questions stemming from the enabling and protective function of such rules. Instead, focusing on the procedural question of admissibility frames the question of forum shopping and jurisdictional overlaps in terms of an assessment of the legal conditions linked to the specific action or procedure before a particular tribunal and to the preclusive effects of party conduct. This brings in a more open, contingent-cooperation mode, mediated by the whole of international law. It paves the way for a cosmopolitan perspective on procedure across international tribunals[53] based on party autonomy. In short, focusing on questions of admissibility signals that coordination can be made effective while the jurisdiction of each international tribunal and the architecture of the international judiciary are left untouched. Under this perspective, one avoids abstract and aprioristic judgments as to which tribunal should necessarily prevail over another as a "supreme arbiter."[54] Focusing on admissibility puts all tribunals on an equal footing, but it also underscores the need for a case-by-case assessment of the conditions underlying adjudication. The supreme arbiter can be

Paraguay, para. 142: "The effect of an umbrella clause is one issue; a different issue is whether such a clause may be invoked in circumstances where the parties have clearly agreed on an exclusive jurisdiction for the resolution of contractual disputes that may fall within the terms of the umbrella clause."

51 See generally Tomer Broude and Yuval Shany, *The Shifting Allocation of Authority in International Law: Considering Sovereignty, Supremacy and Subsidiarity* (Oxford: Hart Publishing, 2008).

52 See Nicolaos Lavranos, *Jurisdictional Competition: Selected Cases in International and European Law* (Groningen: Europa Law, 2009); Joost Pauwelyn, 'How to Win a World Trade Organization Dispute Based on Non-World Trade Organization Law? Questions of Jurisdiction and Merits,' 37 *JWT* (2003), 997.

53 See generally Campbell McLachlan, Lis Pendens *in International Litigation* (Leiden: Martinus Nijhoff, 2009).

54 See Nicolaos Lavranos, 'The MOX Plant and IJzeren Rijn Disputes: Which Court is the Supreme Arbiter?' 19 *LJIL* (2006) 223.

anyone. While the final balance will depend on the specific normative context, it will stem chiefly from the specific procedural choices parties make within that context.

From a party-focused perspective, a principled rationale for the application of preclusion techniques across international tribunals as a matter of admissibility, primarily related to the enabling and protective functions of procedure-regulating rules, flows from the principle of good faith and two of its operational manifestations: estoppel and the prohibition of abuse of rights.[55] A complainant may not seize a forum against a respondent who relies in good faith on a previous commitment by the complainant that there would be no such seizing: *allegans contraria non est audiendus*. This follows the logic of estoppel,[56] based on the requirement to perform international obligations in good faith. In turn, an international tribunal responsible for the integrity of the adjudicatory process between two parties cannot endorse the violation of a previous commitment by allowing the adjudicatory process to move forward notwithstanding the violation of a previous commitment by one party, to the detriment of the other: *ex injuria jus non oritur*.[57] Moreover, in light of the prohibition on the abusive exercise of rights by states,[58] which includes the right of action conferred by an international instrument, a complainant may not seize a forum in violation of its counterpart rights. As Bin Cheng explains, rights and obligations are interdependent, and the assumption of every obligation may limit the exercise of another right to a certain extent. It follows that a state's rights must be exercised in a manner compatible with its various obligations, whether they arise from a treaty or set of treaties, or from general law.[59] This should apply to a situation where

[55] On the principle of good faith, see, for example, Robert Kolb, 'Aperçus sur la bonne foi en droit international public,' 54 *RHDI* (2001) 1.

[56] See generally David Bowett, 'Estoppel before International Courts and Tribunals and its Relation to Acquiescence,' 33 *BYBIL* (1957) 176.

[57] See, for example, *Legal Status of Eastern Greenland*, Judgment of 5 April 1933, PCIJ Ser A/B No 53 (1933) 21, Dissenting opinion of Judge Anzilotti, at 95 and *Gabcikovo-Nagymaros Project (Hungary* v. *Slovakia)*, Judgment of 25 September 1997, para. 133 as discussed in n. 48, Chapter 4.

[58] See Bin Cheng, *General Principles of Law as Applied By International Court and Tribunals* (Cambridge University Press: 1953, 2006), 121–36; Michael Byers, 'Abuse of Rights: An Old Principle, a New Age,' 47 *McGill LJ* (2002) 389. On the application for questions of forum shopping, see also Vaughan Lowe, 'Overlapping Jurisdictions in International Courts and Tribunals,' 20 *Australian YBIL* (1999) 191, at 203.

[59] Cheng, *General Principles of Law*, at 123–31.

a complainant attempts to evade a preclusive norm. Indeed, a good faith-based reasoning places the parties on an equal footing in their procedural relationship and safeguards the integrity of the adjudicatory process. Chapter 4 has shown that incidental jurisdiction covers this type of situation in order to allow a proper exercise of the adjudicatory function. Preclusion techniques become thereby applicable as a matter of admissibility.

5.3 Three typical approaches to jurisdiction versus admissibility

Having argued that a dual categorization of preliminary questions has both explanatory and practical impact – including on the ability to address forum shopping strategies – it is necessary to try to seize that categorization. Ask a bunch of international lawyers interested in procedure what admissibility is, and those who actually attempt to answer your question[60] are likely to give you one of three answers.[61] One camp will conceive admissibility as a mere consequence of the fact that all procedural requirements have been fulfilled, regardless of their potential classification as jurisdictional or admissibility-related. They will explicitly or implicitly define admissibility as a synonym to acceptability, without further technical implications. These will adhere, in short, to an "indifference" approach.

[60] Distinguished authors in leading treatises assume the distinction and approach it by looking at the different consequences of a finding of lack of jurisdiction or inadmissibility, rather than looking for a conceptual distinction. See, for example, Fitzmaurice, *The Law and Procedure*, at 438–9; Brownlie, *Principles of Public International Law*, at 479; Collier and Lowe, *Settlement of Disputes*, at 155–6.

[61] In addition to the three approaches sketched here, a fourth approach separates jurisdiction and merits, then links admissibility to merits rather than jurisdiction. This approach, however, blurs preliminary questions and questions of merit, and does not define admissibility from the perspective of preliminary objections in the sense discussed in this book. For instance, in a piece whose title inspired the title of Section 5.2 above, Ian Laird argues (from a big-picture perspective, in my view, quite off the mark) that "ultimately a challenge to admissibility is not a 'question of procedure.'" See Ian Laird, 'A Difference Without a Distinction? An Examination of the Concepts of Admissibility and Jurisdiction in *Salini v. Jordan* and *Methanex v. USA*,' in Todd Weiler (ed.), *International Investment Law and Arbitration: Leading Cases from the ICSID, NAFTA, Bilateral Treaties and Customary International Law* (New York: Cameron May, 2005) 200, at 221. This book argues within the framework of a contextual difference between preliminary and merits' questions and does not elaborate further on the alternative approach that links admissibility to questions of merit. This particular approach is seldom adopted or argued for. But see, for example, Article 35(3), ECHR; Article 47, ACHR. Article 35 of the ECHR deals with questions of procedure and substance indistinctively as "admissibility criteria." Thus, Article 35(3)

The second and third camps will consider admissibility to refer to procedural requirements that are not jurisdictional. However, there may be disagreement when you ask the subsequent question of what exactly "not jurisdictional" is. Some lawyers will highlight the objective character of admissibility by defining it as the mode of exercise of the action and procedural requirements *stricto sensu*, whereas jurisdiction refers to the existence of a power to adjudicate. From this "objectivist" perspective, jurisdiction is an attribute of tribunals and admissibility is an attribute of claims. Another group, however, will highlight the residual character of admissibility when compared to jurisdiction: they will link jurisdiction to consent and define admissibility as a residual category of preliminary questions. These will speak from a "conventionalist-residualist" perspective.

Traits of the three approaches suggested here can be found in the decisions of international tribunals and writings of scholars. Although these approaches are not always neatly presented as caricaturized here for the sake of exposition, grasping them as ideal types helps to decode the grammar of preliminary objections, and to understand how it applies or may apply to forum shopping strategies. It is argued that the third approach best reflects the structure of international adjudication and the predominant case law on the distinction between jurisdiction and admissibility – although this approach offers no magic potion. Even if objectivism is helpful, this book leans toward a "conventionalist-residualist" approach as part of the framework to address forum shopping.

5.3.1 *The indifference approach: jurisdiction and admissibility as acceptability*

A first approach to the distinction between jurisdiction and admissibility is to neglect it. For this reason, one may call it the indifference approach. When the word admissibility is employed in the context

states: "The Court shall declare inadmissible any individual application submitted under Article 34 if it considers that: (a) the application is incompatible with the provisions of the Convention or the Protocols thereto, manifestly ill-founded, or an abuse of the right of individual application; or (b) the applicant has not suffered a significant disadvantage, unless respect for human rights as defined in the Convention and the Protocols thereto requires an examination of the application on the merits and provided that no case may be rejected on this ground which has not been duly considered by a domestic tribunal." Note that "manifest" questions may indeed be answered early (even at a preliminary stage) – for instance, in the form of a power to strike out applications summarily. See discussion in Chapter 3. But such a dismissal, if one adheres to a distinction between preliminary questions and questions of merit, would be on substantive rather than procedural grounds.

of the indifference approach, it is merely a synonym to acceptability. Admissibility can indeed be synonymous with acceptability. But it may also have a meaning beyond that, which refers to acceptability in light of particular procedural requirements – as discussed below in the context of the other approaches. The indifference approach neglects the more specific meaning of admissibility as a particular category of preliminary questions. From the standpoint of indifference, admissibility is simply a consequence of having fulfilled any requirement and receiving approval for it. Indeed, if one focuses on the objective of any preliminary objection, which is to prevent or postpone findings on the merits, it is not immediately evident why a twofold categorization into jurisdiction and admissibility is necessary. Thus, early works on preliminary objections referred to any procedural requirements indiscriminately and broadly as questions of admissibility.[62]

In strong mode, the indifference approach explicitly denies relevance and recognition to a twofold categorization of preliminary questions. The arbitral tribunal in *Enron and Ponderosa* v. *Argentina*, for instance, stated that "the distinction between jurisdiction and admissibility does not appear to be necessary in the context of the ICSID Convention, which deals only with jurisdiction and competence."[63] Yet, apart from a few investor-state cases,[64] it is exceptional to find relevant recent instances of tribunals rejecting the dual categorization discussed here. More frequently, the indifference approach appears in soft mode, such as in cases where adjudicators do not rigorously apply the distinction, while refusing to reject it. Indifference toward the distinction may be justified by a perceived lack of need for it in the concrete circumstances at stake.[65] In this sense, while not denying the

[62] See J. Witenberg, 'La recevabilité des réclamations devant les juridictions internationales,' 41 *Recueil des Cours* III (1932) 1, at 9; Maarten Bos, *Les conditions du procès en droit international public* (Leiden, Brill: 1957), at 2 (considering that a condition of process is a condition of admissibility).

[63] *Enron Corporation and Ponderosa Assets, LP* v. *Argentina*, ICSID Case No ARB/01/3, Decision on Jurisdiction, 14 January 2004, para. 33.

[64] *Ibid.*; see also *CMS Gas Transmission Company* v. *Argentina*, ICSID Case No ARB/01/8, Decision of the Tribunal on Objections to Jurisdiction, 17 July 2003, para. 41.

[65] See, for example, *The Pajzs, Csáky, Esterházy Case*, PCIJ Ser A/B 68, Judgment of 16 December 1936, at 30; *Case Concerning the Northern Cameroons (Cameroon* v. *United Kingdom)*, Judgment of 2 December 1963, at 27; *Activities in and against Nicaragua (Nicaragua* v. *United States)*, para. 84; *Pan American Energy LLC, and BP Argentina Exploration Company* v. *Argentina*, ICSID Case No ARB/03/13, Decision on Preliminary Objections, 27 July 2006, para. 54.

general value of the distinction as such, tribunals sometimes take the objections as the parties plead them.[66]

Actually, in the event that the parties actively raise all preliminary questions as objections, a major practical reason to apply the distinction is not present (i.e., the respondent's burden to raise objections to admissibility). In that case, if the other reasons for the distinction do not apply, the worst consequence of the indifference approach would be to add terminological confusion to the field. On the other hand, as suggested above, correctly understanding the notion of admissibility is helpful to understand that procedure-regulating norms apply across international tribunals.[67] Therefore, for present purposes, indifference will not do. In conclusion, the indifference approach has it right that, if one focuses on the material objective of any preliminary objection – which is to prevent or postpone findings on the merits – it is not readily obvious why a dual categorization of preliminary questions should be important. Nonetheless, in addition to contributing to the terminological slip-up, the indifference approach misses the actual implications of a dual categorization. As a result, the approaches that recognize jurisdiction and admissibility as complementary categories of preliminary questions should be preferred.

5.3.2 The objectivist approach: jurisdiction as a tribunal-centered concept, admissibility as a claim-centered concept

A second perspective to the dual categorization of preliminary questions starkly contrasts with the indifference approach. Proponents of this approach uphold a distinction between jurisdiction and admissibility and, crucially, consider the distinction to be objectively established. This approach is herein referred to as objectivism. Adherents of objectivism consider the distinction between jurisdiction and admissibility as a pre-established lens to categorize preliminary questions independently of the specific structure of the conventional instruments at stake. The classic scholarly articulation of the objectivist approach is George Abi-Saab's 1967 book, where he adopts a particularly strong objectivist perspective and argues that the nature of conditions of admissibility

[66] See, for example, *Activities in and against Nicaragua (Nicaragua* v. *United States)*, para. 84; *Pan American and BP* v. *Argentina*, para. 54.

[67] It is interesting to note that precisely in WTO adjudication, where the twofold categorization explained here has not been explicitly endorsed, arguments for the application of preclusion clauses across international tribunals face more resistance.

would remain the same regardless of whether the jurisdictional title incorporates them.[68] Abi-Saab adopts a threefold concept of procedure substantially similar to the one espoused in this book. Moreover, he links objections to jurisdiction (*exceptions d'incompétence*) to the field of a tribunal's power, and objections to admissibility (*exceptions de recevabilité*) to the modalities of exercise of that power. Specifically, admissibility covers the notions of action (*l'action, fins de non-recevoir* in French law) and procedure in a narrow sense (*l'instance, exceptions de procédure* in French law).[69] This is, in the present author's view, still a sound articulation of the general tenets of the twofold category of preliminary questions.

An inclination toward objectivism is a recognizable trend in the scholarship, especially for the purpose of explaining the contours of jurisdiction versus admissibility.[70] The general argument is that objections to jurisdiction take aim at the authority of the tribunal as such (i.e., the existence of adjudicatory power), whereas objections to admissibility target the specific request and claims at stake (i.e., the exercise of adjudicatory power in the specific circumstances). A basic question would be: does the objection take aim at the tribunal, or at the claim?[71] In the latter case, the question or objection would refer to admissibility, and in the former, to jurisdiction. Article 79(1) of the ICJ Rules of Court – which reflects the ICJ *acquis* as a champion of the dual categorization of preliminary questions – squarely suggests both the above

[68] Abi-Saab, *Les exceptions préliminaires*, at 177. But see Abi-Saab's recent stance as an arbitrator in *Abaclat and others* v. *Argentina*, ICSID Case No ARB/07/5, Decision on Jurisdiction and Admissibility, 4 August 2011, Dissenting Opinion, 28 October 2011 as Section 5.3.3 discusses.

[69] *Ibid*. Abi-Saab further divides the category of admissibility questions under this perspective, classifying thus: (i) questions of admissibility related to the action as questions of material admissibility (*recevabilité matérielle*) and (ii) questions of admissibility related to intrinsic procedural requirements as questions of formal admissibility (*recevabilité formelle*). He also suggests a third category of questions of admissibility, which he calls general admissibility (*recevabilité générale*), related to the question of propriety in exercising jurisdiction over the merits of a dispute. The issue of propriety is dealt with in Chapter 6 below and is considered to relate to adjudicatory jurisdiction (adjudicatory power itself) as defined in Chapter 4.

[70] See, for example, Paulsson, 'Jurisdiction and Admissibility,' at 616; Douglas, *International Law of Investment Claims*; John Grant and J. Craig Barker, *Parry and Grant Encyclopaedic Dictionary of International Law*, 2nd edn (Oxford University Press, 2003).

[71] Paulsson, 'Jurisdiction and Admissibility,' at 616; Douglas, *International Law of Investment Claims*, at 141, 148. See also Joost Pauwelyn and Luiz Eduardo Salles, 'Forum Shopping before International Tribunals: (Real) Concerns, (Im)Possible Solutions,' 42 *Cornell ILJ* (2009) 77, at 94–5; *Waste Management, Inc.* v. *United Mexican States*, ICSID Case No ARB(AF)/98/2, Award of 2 June 2000, Dissenting Opinion of Keith Highet, paras. 56–8.

question and its answer: "Any objection by the respondent to the *jurisdiction of the Court* or to the *admissibility of the application* ..."[72] In fact, the tribunal-versus-claim question suggested above has been implied at least since the first case where the PCIJ dealt with a question that it expressly referred to as pertaining to admissibility. Thus, in *Certain German Interests in Upper Silesia*, the PCIJ drew a distinction between its jurisdiction and "whether the *suit* c[ould] be entertained," speaking of the latter in terms of the "admissibility *of the suit*."[73]

A recent and clear illustration of the objectivist approach is the decision on preliminary objections in the investor-state arbitration *Hochtief* v. *Argentina* – with the necessary qualification that the decision stands for a threefold rather than a twofold categorization of preliminary questions. This point calls for a short digression. In that case, the tribunal distinguished between questions of jurisdiction (i.e., taking aim at the tribunal), questions of admissibility (i.e., taking aim at the action or claim), and questions of receivability (i.e., taking aim at procedure in a narrow sense or, in the tribunal's formulation, *seisin*).[74] The tribunal's objective threefold categorization of preliminary questions mirrors a threefold concept of procedure analogous to the one adopted in this book, and links that threefold concept of procedure to a threefold categorization of preliminary objections. Nevertheless, the tribunal's use of the term "receivability" can cause confusion, because "receivability" in French (*recevabilité*) is used precisely to refer to traditional objections to admissibility. Moreover, whereas a default threefold categorization along the lines suggested by the arbitral tribunal could contribute to an understanding of preliminary questions in the light of a threefold concept of procedure, the tribunal's fine distinction between "admissibility" and "receivability" – or better, between objections to the action (admissibility) and objections to procedure in a narrow sense (receivability) – is seldom made in the practice of international tribunals. Furthermore, this distinction was not relevant for the decision, which

[72] Article 79(1), ICJ Rules of Court (emphasis added).

[73] *Certain German Interests in Upper Silesia*, at 13 (emphasis added).

[74] *Hochtief* v. *Argentina*, para. 90: "Jurisdiction is an attribute of a tribunal and not of a claim, whereas admissibility is an attribute of a claim but not of a tribunal. A distinction may also be drawn between questions of admissibility and questions of receivability. A tribunal might decide that a claim of which it is seised and which is within its jurisdiction is inadmissible (for instance, on the ground of *lis alibi pendens* or *forum non conveniens*); or it might refuse then to receive and become seised of a claim that is within its jurisdiction because of some fundamental defect in the manner in which the claim is put forward."

revolved around the traditional jurisdiction-versus-admissibility divide. This threefold distinction that *Hochtief* v. *Argentina* suggests will therefore not be further pursued here.[75]

Returning to the case, Hochtief resorted to arbitration under the Argentina–Germany BIT without having previously litigated the dispute for at least eighteen months before Argentinean courts. Argentina then objected to the jurisdiction of the tribunal, arguing that Hochtief had not complied with the requirement of eighteen months of domestic litigation expressly provided for in Article 10 of the applicable BIT. The tribunal held that the requirement at issue referred to the manner in which Hochtief's existing right to arbitration was to be exercised rather than to the existence of a new, independent right to arbitration. According to the tribunal, the distinction between an independent right to arbitrate and the manner in which this right should be exercised mirrored the distinction between jurisdiction and admissibility, which it then elaborated in the objective terms explained above. The tribunal concluded that the prior litigation requirement was linked to admissibility, not jurisdiction. Since the question was one of admissibility, the tribunal reasoned that Argentina could waive the requirement or acquiesce to its nonfulfillment. This Argentina had done, according to the tribunal, by virtue of the more favorable treatment afforded to investments and investors in a comparable BIT,[76] to which Hochtief was eligible in light of the Argentina–Germany BIT's most-favored-nation (MFN) clause.

In short, the tribunal reclassified the Argentinean objection to jurisdiction as an objection to the admissibility of the case, and then rejected the objection. The tribunal's objectivist approach to the categorization of preliminary questions was crucial for the result, given the tribunal's own reasoning that the MFN clause applied to the exercise of rights and duties actually secured by the BIT (an existing right to arbitration, a matter of admissibility),[77] but not to rights in other BITs (such as an independent, new right to arbitration). Since the MFN clause served neither to grant nor to expand jurisdiction according to the tribunal, had the domestic litigation requirement been considered a jurisdictional requirement, the tribunal would not have been able to assert jurisdiction.

[75] See also discussion in note 1 above.

[76] The Argentina–Chile BIT requires no prior domestic litigation in Argentina.

[77] *Hochtief* v. *Argentina*, paras. 81, 86.

Objectivism is clearly superior to the indifference approach in terms of explanatory reach. The recognition of admissibility not only makes objectivism more precise to address well-established practice recognizing a binary categorization; it also captures the practical consequences which stem from that categorization. Traits of objectivism can be found in several decisions and in the text of procedural rules such as Article 79(1) of the ICJ Rules of Court, referred to above. Moreover, objectivism is doctrinally attractive due to its simplicity and potential for generalization, a virtue that might explain scholars' inclination toward this approach when they seek to explain the distinction between jurisdiction and admissibility.

Significantly, objectivism permits preliminary objections to be classified abstractly, notwithstanding the specific structure of the jurisdictional instruments. Thus, to use a common example, from an objectivist perspective questions stemming from the non-exhaustion of local remedies give rise to objections of admissibility – as do analogous questions arising in connection with mandatory quiet periods, negotiation periods, and consultation requirements. In the same vein, from an objectivist perspective, most preliminary questions stemming from forum shopping strategies would arise under the notion of admissibility, through reference to procedural rules of other international tribunals or notions of estoppel, *lis pendens*, *res judicata*, or collateral estoppel. These questions would not take aim at the authority of the tribunal before which they are invoked, but rather at the exercise of the action by the forum shopper, and would therefore qualify as admissibility-related.

However, objectivism's simplicity and generality sometimes may come at unbearable cost. Despite its attractiveness for pedagogical purposes, objectivism should not be stretched too far – especially if international law's bottom-up construction by states defies it. Thus, depending on the structure of the instruments that adjudicators are bound to interpret and apply, objectivism may need tempering. Noticeably, in his blistering dissenting opinion in *Abaclat*, Abi-Saab – who so clearly stated in his 1967 book that the nature of a question of admissibility would remain unchanged regardless of whether the admissibility requirement at stake was included in a jurisdictional title – went through the following ostensible change of heart:

> It is true that, under general international law, the two requirements [eighteen-month domestic litigation and negotiations] in question are considered as conditions of admissibility. But when such conditions are included in the

jurisdictional title, they condition, like any other reservation inserted in the jurisdictional title, the consent of the party or parties making them, to submit to the jurisdiction of the judicial or arbitral organ, and limit by that much the exercise by the organ of its jurisdiction. In other words, in this case these conditions become conventionally jurisdictional, in addition to being admissibility conditions by their legal nature.[78]

The above remark tempers objectivism in light of the dominant approach to the classification of preliminary questions into jurisdiction and admissibility, referred to herein as conventionalism–residualism. Conventionalism–residualism places the specific instruments under interpretation first, and therefore values party autonomy over and above a quest for the essence of a preliminary question. Given international law's flat and by-and-large malleable structure, it is submitted that this approach is the most appropriate one among the three approaches outlined here.

5.3.3 The "conventionalist–residualist" approach: jurisdiction as consent, admissibility as a residual category

The dominant approach to the distinction between jurisdiction and admissibility conceptualizes jurisdiction with reference to consent ("conventionalism") and considers other procedural requirements as admissibility-related ("residualism"). The conventionalist–residualist approach shares objectivism's adherence to the dual categorization of preliminary questions, but it adopts a contingent perspective to it, in which consent is the main signpost to differentiation. Many among the more recent decisions explicitly addressing the categorization incorporate this approach. The ICJ, for instance, offered its most extensive collegiate explanation to date of the categorization of preliminary objections into jurisdiction and admissibility in its *Croatia Genocide* judgment:

> A distinction between the two kinds of objections is well recognized in the practice of the Court. In either case, the effect of a preliminary objection to a particular claim is that, if upheld, it brings the proceedings in respect of that claim to an end, so that the Court will not go on to consider the merits of the claim. If the objection is a jurisdictional objection, then since the jurisdiction of the Court derives from the consent of the parties, this will most usually be because it has shown that no such consent has been given by the objecting State to the settlement by the Court of the particular dispute. A preliminary objection to admissibility covers a more disparate range of possibilities.

[78] *Abaclat* v. *Argentina*, Dissenting Opinion, 28 October 2011, para. 23.

> ... Essentially, such an objection [to admissibility] consists in the contention that there exists a legal reason, even when there is jurisdiction, why the Court should decline to hear the case or, more usually, a specific claim therein. Such a reason is often of such a nature that the matter should be resolved *in limine litis*, for example where without examination of the merits it may be seen that there has been a failure to comply with the rules as to nationality of claims; failure to exhaust local remedies; the agreement of the parties to use another method of pacific settlement; or mootness of the claim.[79]

The Court indicates therein three elements of demarcation that pave the way for a method to draw the line between objections to jurisdiction and objections to admissibility, and thus to conceptualize admissibility. First, "the effect of a preliminary objection to a particular claim is that, if upheld, it brings the proceedings in respect of that claim to an end." Here, the Court underscores the common (potential) effect of a preliminary objection, which is to prevent an assessment of the merits of the claim. Accordingly, by relying on a distinction between preliminary questions (procedure) and merits (substance), one may draw a first demarcation line, namely between preliminary questions and questions of merit.[80]

Second, "[i]f the objection is a jurisdictional objection, then since the jurisdiction of the Court derives from the consent of the parties, this will most usually be because it has shown that no such consent has been given by the objecting State to the settlement by the Court of the particular dispute." The Court, therefore, links objections to jurisdiction with the consent of the parties. Now, having defined objections to jurisdiction, and having defined preliminary objections in contradistinction to the merits, one may draw a second demarcation line between questions of jurisdiction on the one hand, and questions of merit on the other hand. Logically, if the categorization of preliminary objections is twofold and comprises objections to jurisdiction or admissibility, then one may draw consequential lines between questions of jurisdiction, questions of merit, and questions of admissibility (the residual category of preliminary objections).

Third, the remaining question is whether there are preliminary objections other than objections to admissibility. The Court seems to indicate that there are none: "Essentially, such an objection consists in

[79] *Case Concerning the Application of the Convention on the Prevention and Punishment of the Crime of Genocide (Croatia* v. *Serbia)*, Preliminary Objections, Judgment of 18 November 2008, para. 120.

[80] See discussion in Chapter 3.

the contention that there exists a legal reason, even when there is jurisdiction, why the Court should decline to hear the case or, more usually, a specific claim therein." Hence, the Court indicates that preliminary objections to admissibility comprise essentially a residual category of preliminary objections, whereby a party contends that there is a legal reason not to hear the case, notwithstanding the Court's jurisdiction being established. Consequently, one may draw the line between objections to jurisdiction – to the Court's authority to decide, which stems from consent – and objections to admissibility – nonjurisdictional preliminary objections.

Subsequently, in *Application of CERD*, the ICJ confirmed its current preference for conventionalism–residualism. In that case, Georgia seized the Court with an application against Russia invoking Article 22 of the Convention on the Elimination of All Forms of Racial Discrimination (CERD) as a basis of jurisdiction. The provision establishes that "[a]ny dispute ... which is not settled by negotiation or by the procedures expressly provided for in this Convention, shall, at the request of any of the parties to the dispute, be referred to the [ICJ] ..."[81] The Court found that it lacked jurisdiction to try the case because it could not find any genuine attempt to negotiate related to the subject matter of the dispute by either party prior to Georgia's seizing the Court.[82] It construed the requirement of negotiations as a precondition for its *seisin* linked to jurisdiction. It noted that "it is not unusual in compromissory clauses conferring jurisdiction on the Court and other international jurisdictions to refer to resort to negotiations" and, subsequently, that "prior resort to negotiations or other methods of peaceful dispute settlement performs an important function in indicating the limit of consent given by States."[83] In sum, the ICJ emphasized that the requirement of negotiations had been linked to the expression of consent by CERD drafters, construing it to be a question of jurisdiction, not admissibility. The Court's reasoning emphasizes the crossroads where strong objectivists and conventionalist–residualists part ways. Although in many cases adherents of both camps will agree, for strong objectivists, a requirement of prior negotiations would take aim at the exercise of

[81] Article 22, International Convention on the Elimination of All Forms of Racial Discrimination, 660 *UNTS* 195 (CERD).

[82] *Case Concerning Application of the Convention on the Elimination of All Forms of Racial Discrimination (Georgia* v. *Russia)*, Preliminary Objections, Judgment of 1 April 2011, paras. 161–2.

[83] *Ibid.*, para. 131.

the action, or at the claims, thus raising a question of admissibility – even if this requirement were part of the jurisdictional clause. Under conventionalism–residualism, although prior negotiations refer to admissibility as a matter of principle, the requirement in CERD Article 22 is (or becomes) jurisdictional by virtue of its link to consent.[84]

Decisions within a conventionalist–residualist framework can also be found in the context of specialized tribunals. Consider the *ICS* v. *Argentina* and *Daimler* v. *Argentina* investor-state arbitral tribunals' interpretations of the requirement to submit the dispute for at least eighteen months to domestic courts in Argentina prior to arbitration, pursuant to the Argentina–UK and Argentina–Germany BITs. In these tribunals' view, the requirement was very much jurisdictional, because it had been agreed to by states in the BITs as conditions precedent to their consent to a particular dispute being submitted to arbitration.[85] Noticeably, in the *Daimler* tribunal's view, all BIT-based dispute resolution provisions are strictly jurisdictional because they are founded upon the consent of the contracting parties to the BIT:

> The mere fact of their inclusion in a bilateral treaty indicates that they are a reflection of the sovereign agreement of two States – not the mere administrative creation of arbitrators. They set forth conditions under which an investor-State arbitral tribunal may exercise its jurisdiction with the contracting state parties' consent, much in the same way in which legislative acts confer jurisdiction upon domestic courts.[86]

The conventionalism of *ICS* and *Daimler* can be contrasted with the objectivist approach adopted in *Hochtief* – which, as discussed above, considered the local litigation requirement to be a matter of admissibility because it referred to the manner in which an existing right to arbitrate was to be exercised, notwithstanding the fact that the requirement was expressly provided for in the BIT.

In the UNCLOS context, *Saiga* offers another illustration. That dispute was originally submitted to an arbitral tribunal under Annex VII of the UNCLOS, but the parties agreed to transfer the case to the ITLOS on the basis of an agreement which stated that "[t]he dispute shall be deemed to have been submitted to the International Tribunal for the Law of the Sea on the 22 December 1997, the date of the Notification by

[84] See also *Armed Activities on the Territory of Congo (DRC* v. *Rwanda)*, para. 88.

[85] *ICS* v. *Argentina*; *Daimler Financial Services AG* v. *Argentina*, Award, ICSID Case No ARB/05/11, 22 August 2012.

[86] *Daimler* v. *Argentina*, para. 193.

St. Vincent and the Grenadines."[87] The ITLOS found that the agreement between the parties, together with Articles 286, 287, and 288 of the UNCLOS, established its jurisdiction. The agreement specified:

> the written and oral proceedings before the International Tribunal for the Law of the Sea shall comprise a single phase dealing with all aspects of the merits (including damages and costs) and the objection as to jurisdiction raised in the Government of Guinea's Statement of Response dated 30 January 1998.[88]

On the basis of the agreement, Saint Vincent and the Grenadines argued before the ITLOS that objections to admissibility which Guinea raised had been precluded. The ITLOS, however, held the right to raise objections to admissibility to be a "general right"[89] and proceeded to consider a number of objections, such as an objection to Saint Vincent and the Grenadines' standing to bring the claims and an objection that local remedies had not been exhausted. In sum, the ITLOS upheld a distinction between its jurisdiction, established by the agreement between the parties together with Articles 286–8 of the UNCLOS (conventionalism), and the admissibility of Saint Vincent and the Grenadines' claims, a question which was to be examined as a matter of "general right" (residualism).

In the WTO context, although the Appellate Body has not expressly referred to the distinction between jurisdiction and admissibility in so many words, it has reasoned along the lines of residualism with regard to admissibility. For instance, in *Taxes on Soft Drinks*, the Appellate Body drew an implicit distinction between the jurisdiction of panels versus other "legal impediments to the exercise of jurisdiction," in line with the residual nature of admissibility as interpreted by the ICJ and other tribunals.[90] On the other hand, the Appellate Body expressed no view on the applicability of those other "legal impediments" in WTO dispute settlement; this was not an issue in that case because Mexico did not construe the case as a question of a legal impediment, but as a question of inherent "discretion" for WTO adjudicative bodies to abstain from exercising jurisdiction.

Conventionalism–residualism reflects the consensual foundation of jurisdiction in international law. In this sense, it is hardly escapable for present purposes, for it takes into account states' right to regulate

[87] *The M/V "Saiga" (No 2) Case (Saint Vincent and the Grenadines* v. *Guinea)*, Judgment of 1 July 1999, para. 41.

[88] *Ibid.*, para. 47. [89] *Ibid.*, para. 51.

[90] Appellate Body Report, *Mexico – Taxes on Soft Drinks*, para. 54.

resort to dispute settlement in line with the notion of party autonomy. Objectivism provides an impressionistic framework from which to seize the distinction between jurisdiction and admissibility from a general standpoint, and may be used as guidance to categorize preliminary questions. But it breaks if pushed to its limits, since it may lose sight of specific configurations in its ambitions of generality. On the other hand, the classification of a preliminary objection within a conventionalist–residualist framework is objection-specific, and requires deciphering among given procedural requirements at stake: those which would refer to consent to jurisdiction and those which would refer to "other reasons" not to hear a claim. Unless one is ready to accept that all treaty-based procedural requirements are jurisdictional since they flow from consent,[91] classification will often not be straightforward. Judge Fitzmaurice's synthesis in *Northern Cameroons* is somewhat helpful in offering practical guidance, while generally capturing the conventionalist–residualist line of reasoning:

> [T]he real distinction and test would seem to be whether or not the objection is based on, or arises from, the jurisdictional clause or clauses under which the jurisdiction of the tribunal is said to exist. If so, the objection is basically one of jurisdiction. If it is founded on considerations laying outside the ambit of any jurisdictional clause, and not involving the interpretation or application of such a provision, then it will normally be an objection to the receivability of the claim.[92]

All in all, the crux of classification refers to the proximity of a question to the jurisdictional grant. In conclusion, although one may try to draw generalizations about the distinction between jurisdiction and admissibility as in the objectivist approach, the specific text of the instruments being invoked must always be carefully scrutinized in deciding whether an issue relates to jurisdiction or admissibility.

5.4 Addressing forum shopping strategies through preliminary questions: jurisdiction or admissibility?

Due to international law's malleable and flat structure, as recognized in the conventionalist–residualist approach to jurisdiction and admissibility, a procedural framework for addressing forum shopping strategies

[91] See n. 85 above and accompanying text.

[92] *Northern Cameroons (Cameroon* v. *United Kingdom)*, Separate Opinion of Judge Fitzmaurice, at 102–3.

in practice should be contingent upon the model of procedural organization embedded in the jurisdictional instruments or clauses governing the forum that is examining the preliminary question. This is to say, in a nutshell, that the same procedure-regulating norm may found a question of jurisdiction before a given tribunal and a question of admissibility before another. It further means that the application of one and the same procedure-regulating norm may lead to different consequences depending on the strength of the link between the norm and the authority of the norm-applying tribunal.

First, a forum shopping strategy may raise a jurisdictional question. This will happen where the jurisdictional instruments or clauses of the forum that is examining the question expressly regulate the procedural relationship between the forums at stake (as an issue of jurisdiction). In this situation, states themselves have chosen a direct model of jurisdictional organization for the tribunal before which the matter is at issue. Second, a forum shopping strategy may raise a question of admissibility. This will take place where procedural organization is indirect – the result of the application of a written procedure-regulating norm unrelated to the authority of the tribunal examining the question, or of a general principle of law.

5.4.1 Forum shopping raises jurisdictional questions: the direct model of jurisdictional organization/procedural coordination

Forum shopping strategies raise jurisdictional questions under procedural requirements connected to consent to the authority of the tribunal before which the preliminary issue is at stake. This will most likely be the case when the objection is litigated before the tribunal whose establishment led to the possibility of forum shopping in the first place (the tribunal established subsequently in time). Pursuant to Judge Fitzmaurice's test in *Northern Cameroons*, the preliminary question would be based on, or arise from, the jurisdictional clauses upon which the authority of that tribunal is founded.

Take the case where an UNCLOS-based tribunal under Part XV of the Convention faces the preliminary question of whether the parties to the dispute have agreed to another procedure that entailed a binding decision. Article 288 of the UNCLOS, located in Part XV, provides that a court or tribunal referred to in Article 287 "shall have jurisdiction over any dispute concerning the interpretation or application of this Convention which is submitted to it in accordance with this Part." However, Article 282 of the UNCLOS, also located in Part XV, establishes the subsidiarity of

UNCLOS dispute settlement in relation to other procedures that entail a binding decision for a dispute.[93] As a result of the combination of Articles 282 and 288 of the UNCLOS, a preliminary question arising under Article 282 before a court or tribunal referred to in Article 287 shall be dealt with as a jurisdictional question. The lack of another mechanism to decide the dispute with binding force is a prerequisite for UNCLOS-Part XV-based tribunals to exercise their jurisdiction over the merits of a dispute. Thus, in *MOX Plant*, Article 292 of the EC Treaty led to an objection to the jurisdiction of an UNCLOS arbitral tribunal based on Article 282, read together with Article 288 of the UNCLOS.[94] The UNCLOS therefore brings other agreements into its own jurisdictional scheme. By incorporating those agreements, it expressly commands UNCLOS-Part XV-based tribunals to tackle forum shopping strategies employed before them – integrating UNCLOS and procedural norms agreed to elsewhere (i.e., "other procedures entailing a binding decision"). From the standpoint of an UNCLOS-Part XV-based tribunal, the Convention provides for *direct* procedural organization and coordination. The link between UNCLOS-Part XV-based tribunals and other procedures is immediate and is indicative of a jurisdictional system strictly speaking.

In the direct model of jurisdictional organization, the particular consequences stemming from lack of jurisdiction – as opposed to inadmissibility – apply. Thus, an UNCLOS-Part XV-based tribunal is arguably required to assess the question on its own motion.[95] Furthermore, if lack of jurisdiction is identified, the UNCLOS-based tribunal should terminate the case before addressing any matter of admissibility.[96] Moreover, the jurisdictional decision of an UNCLOS-Part XV-based

[93] Article 282, UNCLOS: "If the States Parties which are parties to a dispute concerning the interpretation or application of this Convention have agreed, through a general, regional or bilateral agreement or otherwise, that such dispute shall, at the request of any party to the dispute, be submitted to a procedure that entails a binding decision, that procedure shall apply in lieu of the procedures provided for in this Part, unless the parties to the dispute otherwise agree."

[94] *MOX Plant Case (Ireland* v. *United Kingdom)*, Terminated 6 June 2008, further discussed in Chapter 7.

[95] This observation is subject to a caveat in light of the text of Article 282. Article 282, UNCLOS seems to expressly allow waiver and acquiescence, considering that parties may agree to adjudicate the dispute before the UNCLOS even where they have previously agreed on other procedures.

[96] Note that the arbitral tribunal in the *MOX Plant Case* opted for a stay pending the resolution of the jurisdictional question, as discussed in Chapter 6, since the determination of the jurisdictional question would be aided by the ECJ consideration of the case. The proceedings were terminated by Ireland's withdrawal of the claim.

tribunal referring to a preclusion clause in another treaty may have the quality of *res judicata* (since the jurisdictional decision will be based on Articles 282 and 288, which are within the principal jurisdiction of UNCLOS tribunals). More broadly, a direct jurisdictional link such as the one established in the UNCLOS reflects an underlying option by the parties to the Convention to establish a jurisdictional system, strictly speaking, from the perspective of UNCLOS-based tribunals.

5.4.2 Forum shopping raises questions of admissibility: the indirect model of procedural coordination

Considering their residual character, admissibility questions may first arise under provisions which do not directly relate to consent to adjudication before the tribunal where the question is raised. This will most likely be the case of preclusion clauses in the instrument of a "younger" tribunal, litigated before an "older" tribunal. Second, admissibility questions may arise under general principles of law that regulate resort to international adjudication. These two possibilities are indicative of an *indirect* model of procedural interaction, where the basis for coordination has no bearing on the authority as such of the tribunal facing the preliminary question. Rather, it focuses on the parties' undertakings with regard to their ability to sue. In light of international law's flat and noncentralized structure, the indirect model of procedural interaction is the default one for international tribunals.

The international judiciary's bottom-up construction is such that there is no overarching, direct jurisdictional link between international tribunals. As a matter of general international law, even indirect links are scant, as reflected in strictures of the principles of *res judicata* and *lis pendens*, further discussed in Chapter 7. On the other hand, indirect procedural links between "older" and "younger" tribunals can be created by agreement, for instance, when the "younger" tribunal is established. Through the rearview mirror, the existence of plural adjudicators can be better taken into account, and parties may normally regulate the procedural relationship between these plural adjudicators as they see fit. This possibility is firmly embedded in the principle of party autonomy and fits nicely with international law's expansion by accretion.

It is difficult to abstractly categorize preliminary questions arising from written norms, because categorization requires a definition about the relationship between that norm and consent to adjudicate – thus begging a distinction between jurisdiction and admissibility in the first place. Nonetheless, it is possible to distill potential situations that may facilitate categorization. First, with regard to unwritten norms, that is, when the basis for a preliminary objection is a general principle of law not anchored in specific provisions, the matter refers to admissibility. For instance, arguments related to the concept of *lis pendens* have long been employed to raise questions of admissibility before international tribunals.[97] Second, when it comes to written norms, if the immediate basis for the objection is a procedure-regulating norm outside the purview of the principal jurisdiction of the tribunal facing the question, the matter is one of admissibility. Thus, a bilateral agreement between Australia and the United States along the lines of the *Automotive Leather* example in Chapter 4 may give rise to an objection to admissibility, not jurisdiction, before the WTO Appellate Body.[98] Likewise, Article 1(2) of the Olivos Protocol, a fork-in-the-road clause applicable in adjudication between MERCOSUR members, can only give rise to a question of admissibility before WTO panels. Third, in order to categorize a preliminary objection against an alleged forum shopper, one may ask whether or not the opposing parties in the dispute have a direct bearing on the tribunal's jurisdiction, as a bilateral matter between those parties only. For instance, in the investor-state context, the *SGS* v. *Philippines* tribunal reasoned that jurisdiction established by treaty (state-state) could not be abrogated by contract (state-investor), unless expressly provided otherwise. From this angle, choice-of-forum clauses in investor-state contracts may give rise to questions of admissibility, not jurisdiction.[99] Finally, although this is not absolute, Judge Fitzmaurice's test may be framed *a contrario sensu*: where the preliminary question is based on, or arises from, a clause upon which the tribunal facing the preliminary question is not founded (i.e., a "non-jurisdictional clause"), the question will refer to admissibility.[100]

[97] See, for example, *Certain German Interests in Upper Silesia*, at 19, discussing whether previous action by a company before a Germano-Polish Mixed Arbitral Tribunal should mean the suspension of the action at the PCIJ until judgment in the first action had been given as a matter related to the "admissibility of the suit."

[98] See discussion in Chapter 4.

[99] See *SGS* v. *Philippines*, para. 154.

[100] See also *Daimler* v. *Argentina*, para. 193, cited above. According to the tribunal, all BIT-based dispute resolution provisions refer to jurisdiction because they comprise BIT parties' consent. From this perspective, all prerequisites to adjudication established under a treaty establishing a given dispute settlement mechanism would be considered to give rise to jurisdictional questions before that dispute-settlement mechanism. As for other dispute-settlement mechanisms, the provisions would give rise to jurisdictional questions to the extent that they are expressly incorporated by the governing instruments of the other tribunal. Otherwise, they would give rise to admissibility-related questions.

5.5 Concluding remarks

This chapter discussed the binary categorization of preliminary questions as questions of jurisdiction or admissibility. It argued that this categorization has practical and analytical importance. On the practical front, the distinction between jurisdiction and admissibility influences, for instance, a tribunal's ability to react to forum shopping strategies in terms of a necessary termination of the proceedings (lack of jurisdiction) versus a possible stay in the proceedings (resolvable lack of admissibility). Second, it determines a party's burden to raise a preliminary objection concerning matters of admissibility. On the analytical front, the fact that admissibility questions go beyond a given tribunal's general authority to adjudicate speaks to the fact that jurisdictional coordination is not necessarily a question of deference by one tribunal to another. Coordination may be required in order to make the parties stick to the procedural requirements they themselves have entered into.

The line between jurisdiction and admissibility may be difficult to draw or may not really matter in all cases. Yet, where a preliminary objection does not rely on the constituent instrument of the tribunal receiving it, recognizing both jurisdiction and admissibility as two complementary categories is key to driving home the point that independent international tribunals of limited principal jurisdiction with authority to decide on a claim or claims, and equipped with *la compétence de la compétence*, may still engage in procedural coordination (i.e., through admissibility objections). More broadly, the direct and the indirect models of procedural coordination which capture the distinction between jurisdiction and admissibility place relatively different emphases on certain of the functions of procedural norms. While both jurisdiction- and admissibility-related objections refer to the allocative function of procedural norms in the context of forum shopping strategies, jurisdictional issues evoke questions closely related to the delegation function of procedural norms, and admissibility issues tend to suggest questions linked to those norms' enabling and protective functions.

The fact that the same norm may fall to be assessed under different categories of preliminary questions attests to the contingency of the distinction between jurisdiction and admissibility. It further reflects the noncentralized, malleable character of international law, which expands through accretion. Thus, a WTO adjudicator would assess a preclusion clause in a preferential trade agreement's dispute settlement procedure, such as Article 1(2) of the Olivos Protocol, as a question of admissibility. It would do so, from a WTO-based perspective, under an indirect model of procedural coordination, focusing on the allocative, enabling, and protective functions of the MERCOSUR rule for WTO complainants and respondents. However, the same Article 1(2) may be considered to give rise to jurisdictional challenges in MERCOSUR litigation, given this Article's proximity to consent to adjudication within MERCOSUR, and, for that matter, MERCOSUR members' ability to establish a jurisdictional system between them, under a direct model of jurisdictional organization.

6 International tribunals' discretion to (not) exhaust principal jurisdiction and forum shopping

6.1 Introduction

This book has so far contextualized the rise in forum shopping in international adjudication; presented the concepts of procedure and preliminary questions; discussed the source, scope, and effect of international tribunals' power to rule on preliminary objections to tackle forum shopping strategies; and presented two models of procedural coordination available with reference to the distinction between jurisdiction and admissibility. An underlying assumption has been that the preliminary objections are grounded in specified legal norms, which is the most frequent situation. Those legal norms may be called *preclusion* clauses, doctrines, or techniques – that is, principles and rules that either take away the jurisdiction of a tribunal in favor of another tribunal or preclude a complaint before a given tribunal, as a matter of admissibility.[1] In those cases, a decision to uphold an objection leads the tribunal not to exhaust its principal jurisdiction over a claim or case. Importantly, such a decision is *not* discretionary in a meaningful way, since there is a preclusion norm applicable to the situation at hand that prevents a ruling on the merits. Chapter 7 will return to a consideration of preclusion techniques as they apply to parallel and serial litigation or strategic forum selection.

This chapter pauses to investigate the nature of the adjudicatory power, and the question of whether situations of forum shopping may be addressed regardless of a specific procedural norm being applicable to that situation. It examines whether international tribunals may refuse to exhaust validly established principal jurisdiction over admissible

[1] Joost Pauwelyn and Luiz Eduardo Salles, 'Forum Shopping Before International Tribunals: (Real) Concerns, (Im)Possible Solutions,' 42 *Cornell ILJ* (2009) 77, at 86.

claims, based on reasons of propriety – and the extent to which they may do so.[2] That is, assuming that the tribunal would have principal jurisdiction to rule on the merits of admissible claims, can it still refuse to exhaust that jurisdiction? To answer that question, one needs to delve into the issue of discretion as an element of the adjudicatory jurisdiction of international tribunals. This chapter does that primarily from an empirical and doctrinal standpoint.

The techniques used in the context of tribunals' discretion not to exercise validly established jurisdiction can be called *abstention* doctrines or techniques.[3] When a preliminary question about the propriety of exercising jurisdiction is raised, the interested party implies that there is an element of discretion inherent in the international tribunal's adjudicatory jurisdiction.[4] In this sense, preliminary questions implicating an issue of propriety refer to adjudicatory jurisdiction. Unlike standard questions of jurisdiction that refer to the scope of authority granted to a tribunal to decide cases with finality, these questions refer to the adjudicatory jurisdiction of the tribunal as such: the propriety of exercising its power to adjudicate in the circumstances, notwithstanding the question of whether the matter falls under the jurisdictional ambit of the tribunal.[5]

[2] Granted, even in this case the tribunal's decision would still be grounded in a legal norm or a set of legal norms, which authorized the tribunal to decide based on propriety. But this norm would rather postulate discretion as an element of adjudicatory jurisdiction in international law than be the basis for the objection.

[3] Pauwelyn and Salles, 'Forum Shopping Before International Tribunals,' at 86.

[4] See, for example, *Case Concerning Land and Maritime Boundary between Cameroon and Nigeria (Cameroon* v. *Nigeria)*, Preliminary Objections, Judgment of 11 June 1998, para. 72; *Case Concerning Certain Phosphate Lands in Nauru (Nauru* v. *Australia)*, Preliminary Objections, Judgment of 26 June 1992, para. 37; Appellate Body Report, *Mexico – Tax Measures on Soft Drinks and Other Beverages*, WT/DS308/AB/R, adopted 24 March 2006, para. 42.

[5] See also Georges Abi-Saab, *Les exceptions préliminaires dans la procédure de la Cour Internationale* (Paris: Pedone, 1967) 146–7. Abi-Saab uses the term "general admissibility" to classify objections based on reasons of propriety, which refer to adjudicatory jurisdiction. Judge Fitzmaurice, in his opinion in *Case Concerning the Northern Cameroons (Cameroon* v. *United Kingdom)*, Preliminary Objections, Judgment of 2 December 1963, categorized those questions as questions of admissibility, even though for him those questions were "of a wholly antecedent or, as it were, pre-preliminary character" (at 103). Fitzmaurice did so based on a distinction between questions of *principal* jurisdiction and questions of admissibility. As explained in Chapter 4, however, the concept of jurisdiction includes both the adjudicatory power itself and the scope of that power. Therefore, objections targeted at the adjudicatory power as such would normally fall under the category of objections to jurisdiction, not admissibility, subject to the specific instruments at stake.

The significance of discretion in the exercise of jurisdiction depends on the dimension of discretion under survey. Section 6.2 identifies several dimensions of discretion, of which two – namely, discretion to dismiss and discretion to stay proceedings – are directly relevant for present purposes. Section 6.3 shows that discretion to dismiss claims or cases without a decision of merit is very limited. Propriety considerations have been used to justify not ruling on claims or cases only with reference to the purpose of the judicial function and of a judicial decision, not as a question of opportunity or convenience. In this context, discretion cannot do much in terms of reactions to forum shopping, except as a means to avoid frivolous claims or where judicial economy applies. On the other hand, as Section 6.4 demonstrates, discretion to dismiss finds a partly functional equivalent in discretion to stay proceedings. This possibility provides a window of opportunity for tribunals to foster coordination in relation to forum shopping. It permits considerations of comity akin to the common law doctrine of *forum non conveniens* to play a role in international adjudication, under which new principles and doctrines to enable coordination may develop. Section 6.5 discusses the role of abstention doctrines as a means to tame forum shopping. Section 6.6 closes the chapter.

6.2 Discretion and its dimensions

The notion of discretion suggests, above all, an idea of choice.[6] As Maurice Rosenberg synthesized:

> If the word discretion conveys to legal minds any solid core of meaning, one central idea above all others, it is the idea of *choice*. To say that a court has discretion in a given area of the law is to say that it is not bound to decide the question one way rather than another. In this sense, the term suggests that there is no wrong answer to the questions posed – at least, there is no officially wrong answer.[7]

[6] See generally David Shapiro, 'Jurisdiction and Discretion,' 60 *NYULR* (1985) 543; Henry Friendly, 'Indiscretion about Discretion,' 31 *Emory LJ* (1980) 747.

[7] Maurice Rosenberg, 'Judicial Discretion of the Trial Court, Viewed from Above,' 22 *Syracuse LR* (1971) 635, at 636. Rosenberg distinguishes between a primary type of discretion, which refers to the "margin of choice as to what he [the adjudicator] decides, free from constraints which characteristically attach whenever legal rules enter the decision process" (at 636), and a secondary type of discretion, which relates to the degree of finality and authority a lower court's decision enjoys in higher courts. Discretion, in this chapter, refers to Rosenberg's primary type of discretion.

In this broad sense, discretion as an element of the adjudicatory jurisdiction of international tribunals can be discussed from several dimensions. Two such dimensions are directly relevant for present purposes, and a third dimension is pervasive throughout this book.[8]

To begin with, discretion can be analyzed in connection with a choice to adjudicate the merits of given claims. In this context, two dimensions of discretion linked to preliminary questions come into play: first, *discretion to dismiss* claims or cases without a decision on their subject matter or, in other words, discretion to terminate the proceedings with regard to given claims or the whole suit; and second, *discretion to stay* proceedings before deciding on the merits of the case. These are the two key dimensions where the notion of discretion relates to the possibility of addressing forum shopping through preliminary issues, and they are thus directly relevant for present purposes. Sections 6.3 and 6.4 discuss these two dimensions in turn.

A third dimension of discretion relates to the interpretation and qualification of facts and the application and interpretation of rules to the issues in dispute. This, of course, is a pervasive dimension of adjudication, including international adjudication[9] - even though there are structural principles, textual constraints, shared perceptions, and rules of interpretation which restrict such discretion.[10] Discretion to

[8] In addition to the three dimensions discussed here, discretion can be addressed as an element of adjudicatory jurisdiction in connection to the collection, assessment, and handling of evidence, and to the power to decide based on equity considerations (decisions *ex aequo et bono*), for example. These other dimensions will not be further pursued here. On evidence and its treatment, see generally Mojtaba Kazazi, *Burden of Proof and Related Issues: A Study on Evidence before International Tribunals* (The Hague: Kluwer, 1996). On the authority to decide *ex aequo et bono*, see, for example, Article 38(2), ICJ Statute; Article 42(3), ICSID Convention. Decisions *ex aequo et bono* may take place "outside" the realm of law, upon authorization of the parties. See, for example, *Chaco Arbitral Award (Bolivia* v. *Paraguay)*, Arbitral Award of 10 October 1938, 3 *UNRIAA* (2006) 1817; *Atlantic Triton Company* v. *Guinea*, ICSID Case No ARB/84/3, Award of 21 April 1986, 3 *ICSID Rep* (1985) 17. Equity *ex aequo et bono* is distinguishable from other forms of equity, such as equity *infra legem* (see, for example, *North Sea Continental Shelf Cases (Germany* v. *Denmark; Germany* v. *The Netherlands)*, Judgment of 20 February 1969, para. 91; *Case Concerning the Frontier Dispute (Burkina Faso* v. *Mali)*, Judgment of 22 December 1986, paras. 27–8) and equity *praeter legem* (power to fill *lacunae*). See generally Paul Reuter, 'Quelques réflexions sur l'équité en droit international' 15 *RBDI* (1980) 165.

[9] See generally Christopher Ford, 'Judicial Discretion in International Jurisprudence: Article 38(1)(c) and "General Principles of Law",' 5 *Duke J Comp&Int'l L* (1994) 35.

[10] Articles 31–3; Vienna Convention on the Law of Treaties (VCLT). These Articles are considered to reflect customary international law. They refer to the interpretation of treaties and, being focused on the interpretation of texts, cannot apply, as such,

interpret and apply the law stems from the relative indeterminacy of rules. Rules may be more or less open-textured, and facts may be more or less malleable. Interpretation is a function of multiple inter-subjective factors in which some margin of flexibility is inevitable.[11] This dimension of discretion is implicit throughout this book – more obviously, but not exclusively, when Chapter 7 discusses the application and interpretation of procedural norms. But again, this is not to say that anything goes.[12] Adjudicators are meant to apply the law, and discretion when it comes to legal interpretation in general is not, as such, the object of this study.

Returning to the two first dimensions of discretion suggested above, choice, of course, is a matter of degree. As a general proposition, the more discretion tribunals enjoy, the more they will be capable of engaging in or disengaging from the adjudication of a dispute in a concerted manner, enabling coordination where parties ask for it or the tribunals consider it suitable. By contrast, the less discretion tribunals have, the more they will depend upon the existence and applicability of specific rules and principles that require coordination. In several cases, however, such rules and principles are not readily available. Discretion to dismiss or to stay proceedings would thus contribute to procedural coordination by allowing tribunals to fine-tune their exercise of adjudicatory jurisdiction when the forum shopping strategy at stake is not explicitly regulated. Discretion might therefore pave the way for implementing coordination in practice, encouraging litigation before appropriate forums and mitigating the potential effects of parallel proceedings.[13]

As Chapter 5 discussed, the distinction between jurisdiction and admissibility embeds a difference as to the discretion a tribunal

to the interpretation of unwritten norms. There is abundant literature on the rules of interpretation in international law (most of which are focused on treaty interpretation); for recent works, see, for example, Richard Gardiner, *Treaty Interpretation* (Oxford University Press, 2008); Ulf Linderfalk, *On the Interpretation of Treaties: The Modern International Law as Expressed in the 1969 Vienna Convention on the Law of Treaties* (Dordrecht: Springer, 2007); Isabelle Van Damme, *Treaty Interpretation by the WTO Appellate Body* (Oxford University Press, 2009).

11 See generally Hans-Georg Gadamer, *Truth and Method*, 2nd edn (London: Sheed & Ward, 1989).

12 See discussion in Chapter 2.

13 See, for example, Yuval Shany, *The Competing Jurisdictions of International Courts and Tribunals* (Oxford University Press, 2003); Nicolaos Lavranos, *Jurisdictional Competition: Selected Cases in International and European Law* (Groningen: Europa Law, 2009); Pauwelyn and Salles, 'Forum Shopping Before International Tribunals.'

possesses to either dismiss a case or stay the proceedings. This is especially so if the question that gives rise to the objection of admissibility can be resolved during a stay. Although this is a relevant distinction, it simply means that the consequences of a finding of inadmissibility versus a lack of jurisdiction may be different. It does not mean that objections to admissibility are a matter for discretion, while objections to jurisdiction have a mandatory character. One may thus disagree with the approach pursued by the majority in *Abaclat* v. *Argentina*. In that case, the arbitral tribunal's majority viewed the requirements of prior negotiations and eighteen months of domestic litigation in the Argentina–Italy BIT as being related to "the conditions for the implementation of Argentina's consent to ICSID jurisdiction and arbitration" as opposed to the "fundamental question of whether Argentina consented." In the view of the tribunal, noncompliance with such requirements could not lead to lack of jurisdiction "and only – if at all – [to] a lack of admissibility."[14] The tribunal then basically read the requirements out of the text. It considered a consultation requirement as a mere "expression of good will of the parties to try to settle the dispute in an amicable way."[15] Concerning the eighteen-month litigation requirement, the majority held that regardless of non-compliance, the claimant's interest in an efficient dispute resolution prevailed in the circumstances.[16] In sum, the tribunal first approached the treaty-based requirements of prior negotiations and domestic litigation as potentially leading "only – if at all" to a lack of admissibility; and second, it softened the requirements' mandatory character, importing an element of optionality into them.

While jurisdiction and admissibility are distinguishable for a number of reasons, requirements pertaining to both categories are binding.[17] At

[14] *Abaclat and others* v. *Argentina*, Decision on Jurisdiction and Admissibility, ICSID Case No ARB/07/5, 4 August 2011, para. 496.

[15] *Ibid*., para. 564. [16] *Ibid*., para. 590.

[17] The present book does not find or suggest a distinction between jurisdiction and admissibility in terms of the discretionary or dispositive character of each requirement. Normally, requirements related to both jurisdiction and admissibility are mandatory. See, *contra*, Shabtai Rosenne, 'International Courts and Tribunals, Jurisdiction and Admissibility of Inter-State Arbitration,' in *Max Planck Encyclopedia of Public International Law* (Oxford University Press, 2008, electronic version). This, however, is not to say that any futile requirement may necessarily prevent adjudication. Futility may indeed be a reason to reject a given preliminary objection, but this is not related to whether the objection refers to jurisdiction or admissibility. See, for example, the discussion in *ICS Inspection and Control Services Limited* v. *Argentina*, PCA Case No 2010–09, Award on Jurisdiction under UNCITRAL Rules, 10 February 2010, paras. 263–73.

any rate, the question that this chapter addresses is not whether there is discretion to dismiss or stay proceedings depending on whether the question refers to inadmissibility or lack of jurisdiction. The question here is whether discretionary elements in adjudicatory jurisdiction justify an abstention to exercise jurisdiction for reasons of propriety. As Section 6.4 discusses, tribunals normally have a power to stay proceedings, to be exercised under their discretion as case managers.[18] This is different from whether a response to a preliminary question of jurisdiction or admissibility itself entails a discretionary approach.

6.3 Discretion to dismiss

6.3.1 Stating the obvious: tribunals are meant to decide on the merits of admissible claims under their jurisdiction

A discretionary dismissal of a claim or case before a decision on its merits represents a refusal to exhaust adjudicatory jurisdiction. It is a most trite proposition that a tribunal with validly established jurisdiction over admissible claims should exhaust this jurisdiction. Deciding on claims duly brought before them is the *raison d'être* of international tribunals.[19] Accordingly, their power to decide a case must be correlative to an obligation to decide.[20] As the ICJ put it in *Libya/Malta Continental Shelf*, "the Court must not exceed the jurisdiction conferred upon it by the Parties, but it must also exercise that jurisdiction to its full extent."[21] Likewise, the WTO panel in *Mexico – Taxes on Soft Drinks*, called by Mexico to exercise an alleged inherent jurisdiction to decline from ruling because the proper forum to decide the whole sugar dispute with United States would be the NAFTA, concluded that "under the DSU, it had no discretion to decide whether or not to exercise its jurisdiction in a case properly before it."[22] Indeed, tribunals' picking and choosing the

[18] In other words: adjudicatory jurisdiction implies control over procedure in a narrow sense, or over procedural requirements *stricto sensu*. A threefold classification of preliminary questions would aid in the visualization of this idea.

[19] See, for example, Article 38(1), ICJ Statute: "The Court, *whose function is to decide* in accordance with international law *such disputes as are submitted to it* …" (emphasis added).

[20] See also Prosper Weil, 'The Court Cannot Conclude Definitively … : *Non-Liquet* Revisited' 36 *Colum J Transnat'l L* (1998) 119.

[21] *Case Concerning the Continental Shelf (Libyan Arab Jamahiriya/Malta)*, Judgment of 3 June 1985, para. 19.

[22] Panel Report, *Mexico – Tax Measures on Soft Drinks and Other Beverages*, WT/DS308/R, adopted 24 March 2006, as modified by Appellate Body Report WT/DS308/AB/R,

cases they receive would be incompatible with the idea of the impartial adjudicator and would contradict the delegation and enabling function of procedural norms. It should therefore come as no surprise that even those who advocate that a margin of discretion not to decide a case based on reasons of judicial propriety does exist emphasize that such discretion ought to be exercised only in limited circumstances.[23]

One of the most powerful confirmations of the notion that questions of opportunity must not prevent a tribunal from adjudicating on the subject matter of disputes is the outright and consistent rejection of the doctrine of "political questions" by the ICJ. In various instances, the Court has been asked by respondents not to decide cases due to their political impact, especially in situations of ongoing hostility or armed conflict between the parties. Yet, never in a contentious case has the ICJ refused to exercise validly established jurisdiction over admissible claims based on political considerations.[24] Indeed, in rejecting an objection by Honduras based on the political questions doctrine in *Border and Transborder Armed Actions*, the Court squarely confirmed the principle that it must decide on admissible claims under its jurisdiction:

> [T]he Court is aware that political aspects may be present in any legal dispute brought before it. The Court, as a judicial organ, is however only concerned to establish, first, that the dispute before it is a legal dispute, in the sense of a dispute capable of being settled by the application of principles and rules of international law, and secondly, that the Court has jurisdiction to deal with it, and that that jurisdiction is not fettered by any circumstance rendering the application inadmissible.[25]

More broadly, in discussing the potential obstacle of "political and historical" questions in the *Hostages* case, the Court emphasized that "no

paras. 7.1 and 7.18. See also Appellate Body Report, *Taxes on Soft Drinks*. The Appellate Body upheld the panel's finding, but carefully construed its reasoning to leave it clear that it upheld the panel's ruling that "under the DSU, it ha[d] no discretion to decline to exercise its jurisdiction in the case that ha[d] been brought before it" (para. 57) and that it was "unnecessary to rule in the circumstances of this appeal on the propriety of exercising such discretion" (*ibid.*).

[23] See, for example, *Northern Cameroons (Cameroon* v. *United Kingdom)*, Preliminary Objections, Separate Opinion of Judge Gerald Fitzmaurice, at 101.

[24] See *Case Concerning Border and Transborder Armed Actions (Nicaragua* v. *Honduras)*, Jurisdiction and Admissibility, Judgment of 20 December 1988, para. 52; *Case Concerning Military and Paramilitary Activities in and against Nicaragua (Nicaragua* v. *United States of America)*, Jurisdiction and Admissibility, Judgment of 26 November 1984 para. 96; case concerning *Diplomatic and Consular Staff in Tehran (United States of America* v. *Iran)*, Judgment of 24 May 1980, para. 37.

[25] *Border and Transborder Armed Actions (Nicaragua* v. *Honduras)*, para. 52.

provision of the Statute or Rules contemplates that the Court should decline to take cognizance of one aspect of a dispute merely because that dispute has other aspects, however important."[26] The holding, which was formulated as a general statement, may also apply to the issue of procedural coordination in the event of forum shopping. It suggests that the ICJ would not abdicate from exercising its adjudicatory jurisdiction just because a dispute under its principal jurisdiction had aspects which would be under the principal jurisdiction of another international tribunal, unless there were a specific norm requiring this result.[27]

6.3.1.1 The prohibition of *non liquet* and discretion not to exhaust principal jurisdiction

The prohibition of *non liquet* may support or weaken a tribunal's discretion to dismiss, depending on the scope attributed to the prohibition. In relative terms, the broader one conceives the prohibition of *non liquet*, the smaller the room for discretionary dismissals. *Non liquet* is normally understood as a requirement that adjudicators decide cases before them even when the law is lacunary, indeterminate, or unclear.[28] The prohibition of *non liquet* is founded on a premise of completeness of the law that governs the operation of legal systems.[29] Applied to the question of discretion to dismiss, if the prohibition of *non liquet* were

[26] *Diplomatic and Consular Staff in Tehran (United States of America v. Iran)*, para. 36.

[27] That such a rule may prevent a judgment of merit was affirmed by the PCIJ in the very first instance where preliminary objections were invoked before it. See *Mavrommatis Palestine Concessions*, Judgment of 30 August 1924, PCIJ Series A No 2 (1924), at 29–30: "If a state has recourse to the Court under a clause establishing the latter's jurisdiction, it must be prepared for the contingency that the other party may cite agreements entered into between the opposing Parties which may prevent the exercise of the Court's jurisdiction."

[28] See, for example, Daniel Bodansky, '*Non Liquet* and the Incompleteness of International Law,' in Laurence Boisson de Chazournes and Philippe Sands (eds.), *International Law, the International Court of Justice and Nuclear Weapons* (Cambridge University Press, 1999) 153; Weil, 'The Court Cannot Conclude Definitively'; Hersch Lauterpacht, 'Some Observations on the Prohibition of "*Non Liquet*" and the Completeness of the Law,' in Elihu Lauterpacht (ed.), *International Law: Collected Papers of Sir Hersch Lauterpacht*, vol. II (Cambridge University Press, 1975) 216; Gerald Fitzmaurice, 'The Problem of *Non-Liquet*: Prolegomena to a Restatement,' in Charles Rousseau and Suzanne Bastid (eds.), *Mélanges Offerts à Charles Rousseau* (Paris: Pedone, 1974) 92.

[29] See, for example, Article 42(2), ICSID Convention, for explicit textual recognition of the prohibition. See generally Niklas Luhmann, *Law as a Social System* (Cambridge University Press, 2004). It must be noted that the premise of completeness in international law need not be based on the notion of sovereignty as a basis to a so-called

to entail an absolute and irrevocable obligation to decide all admissible claims under the jurisdiction of a tribunal, then there would be no role at all for such discretion.

This book adheres to the view that the prohibition against *non liquet* derives from the very notion of law and of the adjudicatory function to settle disputes in accordance with the law.[30] The scope of the prohibition of *non liquet* covers lack of clarity or silence in both procedural and substantive law. In my view, therefore, an anticipated or actual lack of clarity or silence in the law does not permit tribunals to dismiss claims or cases,[31] regardless of whether the unclear or silent law is procedural or substantive.[32] In practice, the limited discretionary dismissals that may be said to have taken place were not based on *non liquet* considerations, as the discussion below illustrates.

In a more limited view of the prohibition against *non liquet*, certain scholars appear to consider that it is restricted to the law on the merits of claims, as opposed to procedural requirements.[33] From that perspective, a tribunal's dismissing claims or cases based on discretionary procedural grounds would be distinct from the question of a *non liquet*.

"residual rule of freedom," or the "Lotus principle." See *The Case of the SS "Lotus,"* Judgment of 7 September 1927, PCIJ Ser A No 10 (1927) 2. The presumption of completeness of international law follows from the operative closeness of the law as a system. It merely recognizes that the basic commands of the law are binary – legal/illegal – and that there is a solution to every case within the operative structure of the system, because of the duties placed on adjudicators to decide (the prohibition against *non liquet*). See also Marcelo Kohen, 'L'avis consultatif de la CIJ sur la licéité de la menace ou de l'emploi d'armes nucléaires et la fonction judiciaire,' 8 *EJIL* (1997) 336.

30 See, for example, Lauterpacht, 'Some Observations,' at 217; Kohen, 'L'avis consultatif de la CIJ,' at 348. See, *contra*, Julius Stone, '*Non Liquet* and the Function of Law in the International Community, 35 *BYBIL* (1959) 124.

31 In the context of the advisory function of the ICJ, the *Legality of Nuclear Weapons* Opinion provides a good example. Certain scholars and judges consider the opinion to be a *non liquet*. Several judges have appended individual opinions to the Court's opinion, considering whether the lack of clarity in both the question posed to the Court and the answer given by the Court would have justified the Court's using its discretion not to render an opinion. See *Legality of the Threat or Use by a State of Nuclear Weapons in Armed Conflict*, Advisory Opinion, 8 July 1996, Individual Opinion of Judge Guillaume, paras. 1–2; Dissenting Opinion of Judge Schwebel, at 322; Dissenting Opinion of Judge Oda, at 332–74.

32 This position does not exhaust the question of whether there is any discretion to dismiss, as there remains the question of whether there may be other discretionary grounds for dismissals. See discussion below.

33 See, for example, Fitzmaurice, 'The Problem of *Non-Liquet*'; Daniel Bodansky, '*Non Liquet*,' in *Max Planck Encyclopedia of Public International Law* (Heidelberg: Oxford University Press, 2007, electronic version), para. 1.

In the case of a dismissal based on *non liquet* grounds, the dismissing tribunal would abstain because of silence or obscurity in the law governing the merits, whereas in a discretionary dismissal referring to procedural grounds, the tribunal would consider that it is not obliged to decide the case for some reason pertaining to jurisdiction or admissibility (separable from the lack of clarity or silence in the law on the merits). For instance, a tribunal might abstain from deciding because it is not the ideal forum to decide where legal issues under the principal jurisdiction of another tribunal are at stake. In this line of reasoning, discretionary dismissals for procedural reasons would conceivably lie outside the purview of the prohibition of *non liquet*. As a result, discretionary dismissals for procedural reasons might still be permitted, notwithstanding the prohibition against *non liquet* (which, according to this position, would be restricted to substantive law).

Another position would be that international law permits a proclamation of *non liquet*.[34] This would arguably make international tribunals' discretion not to rule on the merits of claims easier to discern. For instance, a tribunal might opt not to exhaust its adjudicatory jurisdiction because it anticipates a *non liquet*. Conversely, outright recognition of international tribunals' discretion not to exercise jurisdiction may imply a consequential recognition that *non liquet* considerations can play a role. For instance, it would be possible to conceive of judges who, in the context of their discretion, decide not to exercise jurisdiction based on the fact that the law regarding their jurisdiction or the admissibility of the claim is unclear or lacunary. Accordingly, those who accept *non liquet* in international adjudication are likely to recognize the possibility of discretionary dismissals.

6.3.2 Discretion to dismiss and the purpose of adjudication: a survey on discretion not to exhaust jurisdiction over admissible claims

In spite of the frequent indications by international tribunals that they must exhaust their jurisdiction, at times they do appear to ground dismissals in considerations of judicial propriety. Thus, Shabtai Rosenne argues that "the [International] Court possesses an element of discretion whether to entertain a case. That discretion must be exercised judicially and not capriciously."[35] Rosenne refers to the situations of

[34] See, for example, Stone, '*Non Liquet* and the Function of Law.'

[35] Shabtai Rosenne, *The Law and Practice of the International Court: 1920–2005*, vol. II, 4th edn (Leiden: Martinus Nijhoff, 2006) 532–3.

"mootness" in *Interhandel*,[36] *Northern Cameroons*,[37] and *Nuclear Tests*[38] in support of his position.[39] Gerald Fitzmaurice, who agrees with the existence of a discretionary power not to exercise jurisdiction,[40] refers to the *Monetary Gold*[41] case. By contrast, Chittharanjan Amerasinghe considers that the ICJ's judgments on the questions of mootness or the "essential third party" do not constitute examples of discretionary dismissals.[42]

This book's reaction to that debate is nuanced. In fact, the ICJ has never pronounced in so many words that it was exercising discretion when dismissing a claim. *Monetary Gold* and its pedigree would afford very limited support for the proposition that tribunals have any discretion to abstain from ruling on the merits of a case.[43] On the other hand, *Northern Cameroons* and a series of WTO precedents support the position that tribunals possess discretion to dismiss to a limited extent. The survey below indicates that the notion of discretion to dismiss, in practice, is restricted to situations where a decision is not capable

[36] *Interhandel Case (Switzerland* v. *United States of America)*, Preliminary Objections, Judgment of 21 March 1959, 29. In that case, the "mootness" of an objection of jurisdiction by the respondent, not a claim by the applicant, was at stake. However, while the Court mentioned that the objection was without object "at the present stage of the proceedings," it reached that conclusion having regard to the fact that the Court had found the application to be inadmissible (26), and based on the recognition by the respondent that the respondent's objection had become "somewhat academic" and "somewhat moot." Moreover, although the Court's approach could be criticized as a reversal of the order in which the Court should have decided the objections – first, those related to jurisdiction; next, those related to admissibility – *Interhandel* does not offer an example of a discretionary dismissal because, if the subsequent stage of the proceedings were to take place, the Court would actually have had to decide the outstanding issue of its jurisdiction, unless the "mootness" of the jurisdictional question itself were confirmed.

[37] *Northern Cameroons (Cameroon* v. *United Kingdom)*, 33, 38.

[38] *Nuclear Tests Case (New Zealand* v. *France)*, Judgment of 20 December 1979, para. 23.

[39] Rosenne, *Law and Practice*, at 533–7.

[40] Gerald Fitzmaurice, *The Law and Procedure of the International Court of Justice*, vol. II (Cambridge: Grotius, 1986) 448.

[41] *Case of Monetary Gold Removed from Rome in 1943 (Italy* v. *France, United Kingdom and United States of America)*, Preliminary Question, Judgment of 15 June 1954.

[42] Chittharanjan Amerasinghe, *Jurisdiction of International Tribunals* (The Hague: Kluwer, 2003), at 238.

[43] For applications of the "essential third party" rule, discussed in Section 6.3.2.1, see *Larsen/Hawaiian Kingdom*, Arbitral Award of 5 February 2001, paras. 11.8–12.19; *Case Concerning East-Timor (Portugal* v. *Australia)*, Judgment of 30 June 1995, paras. 28–35. See also *Phosphate Lands in Nauru (Nauru* v. *Australia)*, paras. 48–55; *Case Concerning the Land, Island and Maritime Dispute (El Salvador/Honduras)*, Application of Nicaragua for Permission to Intervene, Judgment of 13 September 1990, para. 56; *Activities in and against Nicaragua (Nicaragua* v. *United States)*, Jurisdiction and Admissibility, para. 88.

of effective application, rendering adjudication frivolous. A related development is the doctrine of judicial economy. Applied to potential forum shopping strategies, the survey demonstrates that discretion to dismiss has a limited impact at best. It can be used as a reaction to frivolous claims,[44] as objections to (adjudicatory) jurisdiction, or under the notion of judicial economy, as an issue-avoidance technique that may apply to forum shopping strategies.

6.3.2.1 The "essential third party" rule: discretionary or peremptory dismissal?

Monetary Gold offers a first example of what has been described as a discretionary type of dismissal.[45] However, this study suggests a different perspective. In *Monetary Gold*, Italy instituted proceedings against France, the United Kingdom, and the United States regarding certain monetary gold German forces had removed from Rome during the Second World War. The gold was then held by a commission formed by the respondents, which had been advised that the gold belonged to Albania. The respondents agreed that the gold would be handed to the United Kingdom in partial satisfaction of the *Corfu Channel* judgment, with which Albania had allegedly not complied, provided that neither Italy nor Albania applied to the ICJ regarding that decision. Italy did apply. The principal issue that Italy submitted to the Court was whether the respondents should deliver the gold to Italy, in partial satisfaction of damages that Albania had allegedly caused to Italy in the 1940s. The Court considered that the incidental question of Albanian responsibility toward Italy formed the "very subject-matter"[46] of the decision and the "vital issue to be settled." The Court concluded that "although Italy and the three Respondent states ha[d] conferred jurisdiction upon the Court, it c[ould] not exercise this jurisdiction."[47] Such recognition by the Court that the parties had conferred jurisdiction upon it underlies the notion that *Monetary Gold* offers an example of a discretionary declination to exercise jurisdiction.

[44] The notion of frivolous claims addressed here refers to the futility of an exercise of the adjudicatory function by reason of the claims being devoid of purpose in the sense that a judicial decision would not have a practical application. The adjudicatory function is by nature substitutive. If settlement is or becomes unnecessary, the exercise of jurisdiction itself becomes devoid of purpose, even if principal jurisdiction is formally established. This meaning of "frivolous" is not necessarily identical to "frivolous litigation" for obvious lack of legal merit. See discussion in Chapters 2 and 3.

[45] Fitzmaurice, *Law and Procedure*, at 448.

[46] *Monetary Gold*, at 32. [47] *Ibid.*, at 33.

Nevertheless, the decision regarding Italy's first claim in *Monetary Gold* illustrates that neither the principal nor incidental jurisdiction of international tribunals extends to states that have not consented to adjudicatory jurisdiction and that are not parties to the proceedings, where the "very subject-matter" or "vital issue" of the exercise of incidental jurisdiction implicates a determination on the lawfulness of the absent third party's conduct. It is suggested that this is not a matter for discretion. As Chapter 4 explains, incidental jurisdiction does extend more broadly than principal jurisdiction, depending on the circumstances of the case. However, states that are parties to a dispute have no right to implicate a non-party state in the judgment without the latter's consent to adjudicatory jurisdiction. If the adjudicatory jurisdiction of the ICJ over Albania did not exist at all for that case, no adjudicatory jurisdiction over Albania could be exercised. The absence of Albania thus represented a peremptory obstacle to the exhaustion of jurisdiction over the parties. The Court found that "the jurisdiction conferred upon it by the common agreement of France, the United Kingdom, the United States of America and Italy does not, in the absence of the consent of Albania, *authorize it* to adjudicate upon the first Submission."[48] This limitation recognizes the role of state consent in ICJ dispute settlement,[49] and is not discretionary. Furthermore, to the extent that the non-party to the proceeding could not even be heard by the tribunal, the limitation also flows from fundamental notions of due process, which caution against *ex parte* judgments (under the maxim *audi alteram partem*). This due process angle supports the view that the question was not one of discretion, but of a peremptory limitation to the exercise of adjudicatory jurisdiction. Therefore, where incidental jurisdiction requires a determination on the lawfulness of the behavior of a state non-party to the proceedings, which has not consented to adjudicatory jurisdiction, the tribunal cannot exhaust its principal jurisdiction over the merits.

[48] *Ibid.*, at 34 (emphasis added). See also *East-Timor (Portugal* v. *Australia)*, para. 38: "[I]t cannot in the present case exercise the jurisdiction conferred upon it by the declarations made by the Parties … to adjudicate upon the dispute referred to it by the Application …"

[49] See also *Larsen/Hawaiian Kingdom*, para. 11.17: "That rule applies with at least as much force to the exercise of jurisdiction in international arbitral proceedings. While it is the consent of the parties which brings the arbitration tribunal into existence, such a tribunal, particularly one conducted under the auspices of the Permanent Court of Arbitration, operates within the general confines of public international law and, like the International Court, cannot exercise jurisdiction over a State which is not a party to its proceedings."

A link between the essential third party rule and forum shopping can be established in situations where two parties jointly submit a case for adjudication entangling the legal position of a third party and, by doing so, attempt to circumvent the lack of consent of the third party to the adjudication. This is a type of "joint forum shopping" that exceeds the limits of party autonomy, and that international adjudicators should bar. Since tribunals must satisfy themselves that they have jurisdiction before proceeding to a decision on the merits of a case, such a situation should be addressed as a preliminary issue regardless of whether the third party takes part in the proceedings. For instance, A and B may concede that C has violated a certain obligation, but submit a dispute restricted to the consequences of C's violation to the relations between A and B. In such a case, should the tribunal decide the subject matter of the dispute? If the legal interests of C constitute the subject matter of the decision, the answer would be no.

An example on point is the arbitral decision in *Larsen/Hawaiian Kingdom*. In that case, Mr Larsen, a Hawaiian resident, and the "Hawaiian Kingdom by its Council of Regency" had concluded an agreement to arbitrate a dispute concerning the alleged violation of international law by the Hawaiian Kingdom's allowing the "unlawful imposition of American municipal laws over claimant's person within the territorial jurisdiction of the Hawaiian Kingdom."[50] The parties agreed that Mr Larsen's rights as a Hawaiian subject "were being violated as a result of the prolonged occupation of the Hawaiian Islands by the United States," but disagreed as to whether Mr Larsen was entitled to any redress against the Hawaiian Kingdom (not against the United States).[51] In that circumstance, given the absence of the United States as a party to the proceedings, the tribunal resorted to the essential third party principle established by the ICJ in *Monetary Gold*. It found that "[t]he principle of consent in international law would be violated if this Tribunal were to make a decision at the core of which was a determination of the legality or illegality of the conduct of a non-party,"[52] and thus, that it was precluded from considering the issues the parties had raised.[53] *Larsen/Hawaiian Kingdom*, therefore, illustrates that even where parties jointly resort to arbitration, if the subject matter of the dispute revolves around or assumes the legal position of a state not party to the proceedings, a tribunal will refuse to decide the case. That

[50] *Ibid.*, para. 2.1. [51] *Ibid.*, para. 6.2.
[52] *Ibid.*, para. 11.17. [53] *Ibid.*, point (b) of the Award.

outcome prevents the parties-in-name to the dispute from circumventing the lack of consent of an essential third party.

Indirectly, by enforcing the principle of consent in favor of the essential non-party, this outcome preserves the asymmetrical judicialization of international law, since the lack of consent of the essential party shields that party from adjudication. In order to avoid this encumbrance on adjudication of disputes where the third party has locked in its full consent to adjudicatory jurisdiction, say, in a treaty that establishes a permanent tribunal with automatic jurisdiction, it is submitted that, because the principle of consent would not apply with the same force there, the essential third party rule could be relaxed as well.

6.3.2.2 Mootness, declaratory judgments, and the outer limits of discretion to dismiss

The notion of mootness connotes the "hypothetical or academic" nature of an issue and its lack of "practical significance." It depicts "a matter in which a controversy no longer exists, a case that presents only an abstract question."[54] Mootness relates to the purpose of adjudicatory jurisdiction as a function: to settle extant disputes. The existence of a dispute is a minimum requirement for the exercise of contentious adjudicatory jurisdiction as such. From this perspective, one cannot consider dismissals based on the non-existence of a dispute to be discretionary. Either there is a dispute that must be decided, as long as the tribunal has jurisdiction and the claims are admissible; or there is no dispute, and there is nothing to be decided in the first place. Thus, in the *Nuclear Tests* cases, the ICJ found that a unilateral commitment by France to halt atmospheric nuclear testing in the South Pacific had accomplished the objective sought by the applicants.[55] Noting that the dispute had "disappeared,"[56] and that "[t]he Court, as a court of law, is called upon to resolve existing disputes,"[57] the ICJ found that the claim "no longer has any object and that the Court is therefore not called upon to give a decision thereon."[58] This study argues that *Nuclear Tests* does not offer an example of discretionary dismissal. The Court was convinced that a dispute in the objective sense did not exist, which it made clear throughout the judgment, and stated that it was not called

[54] *Black's Law Dictionary*, 9th Deluxe Edn (2009), 1099.
[55] See, for example, *Nuclear Tests (New Zealand v. France)*, paras. 54–5.
[56] *Ibid.*, para. 59. [57] *Ibid.*, para. 58. [58] *Ibid.*, para. 65.

upon to decide on the claims, based on its interpretation of the issue at stake.

Nonetheless, in certain cases mootness considerations have gone beyond the question of the existence of a dispute. Classically understood, the existence of a dispute is asserted by means of an objective examination of whether there is "a disagreement on a point of law or fact, a conflict of legal views or of interests between two persons."[59] This examination does not require an inquiry into the use that the parties may intend to make of the decision or, in other words, the potential practical application of a decision. In particular, a party may desire a judgment to obtain moral satisfaction or as a building block in a broader strategy to seek compensation from the opposing party.[60] Can tribunals second-guess complainants' desires? If they can, under the notion that the judgment would have no particular application or that the decision would be unnecessary, one may then say that there is at least some discretion to dismiss under international law.[61] This possibility would, in turn, offer a brake to forum shopping for frivolous claims.

Tribunals have indeed declined to exhaust principal jurisdiction where there is a dispute in the legal sense between the parties, but where such a dispute would lead at best to a purely declaratory judgment, incapable of effective application. It is suggested that tribunals have thereby asserted a discretionary power not to adjudicate. It is further suggested that the situation of purely declaratory judgments constitutes the outer limit of what tribunals consider to be their discretion to dismiss. Discretion to dismiss, therefore, can be described as a margin of appreciation related to the function and relevance of adjudication as a method for settling a concrete dispute by means of a judgment. In the ICJ context, the situation arose most evidently in *Northern Cameroons*. In that case, the United Nations General Assembly had terminated the trusteeship agreement with respect to Northern Cameroon. The dispute concerned the interpretation and application of that trusteeship agreement, which was no longer in force. The Court

[59] *Mavrommatis Palestine Concessions*, at 11.

[60] See discussion below on *Northern Cameroons (Cameroon* v. *United Kingdom)*, Preliminary Objections.

[61] This seems to be a reasonable interpretation of Article 92(2) of the ECJ Rules of Procedure, which states that: "The Court may at any time of its own motion, after hearing the parties … declare that the action has become devoid of purpose and that there is no need to adjudicate on it; it shall give its decision in accordance with Article 91(3) and (4) of these Rules."

held that there could be no opportunity for a future act of interpretation or application of that treaty in accordance with any judgment, and concluded that adjudication would thus be devoid of purpose. Since no purpose would be served by undertaking an examination of the merits in the case,[62] the Court found that it could not adjudicate upon the merits of Cameroon's application.[63]

In a controversial separate opinion, Judge Fitzmaurice explained that "underlying the judgment of the Court there are clear considerations of propriety."[64] The Court, for its part, premised the dismissal on the incapacity of effective application of a judgment on the merits, which made adjudication devoid of purpose.[65] However, the reasoning of the Court in *Northern Cameroons* contrasts with the recognition of satisfaction as a remedy to international wrongs. As the International Law Commission put it in its *Commentaries to the Draft Article on State Responsibility*, "[o]ne of the most common modalities of satisfaction provided in the case of moral or non-material injury to the State is a declaration of the wrongfulness of the act by a competent court or tribunal."[66] The ICJ in fact had clearly affirmed the utility of satisfaction as a remedy in *Corfu Channel*.[67] Against this backdrop, the crux of *Northern Cameroons* is indeed the question of propriety, as reflected in the separate opinion of Judge Fitzmaurice. Although Cameroon had explicitly sought a declaratory judgment and did not make an actual claim for satisfaction, such a declaratory judgment could be used by Cameroon to obtain the remedy of satisfaction, or even other remedies. If the Court knew that satisfaction is one of the possible forms of reparation in international law (which it clearly did, as *Corfu Channel* illustrates), it also knew that the judgment was capable of having an effect in the legal relations between the parties. To this extent, Cameroon's application was not and could not be considered completely devoid of purpose. In conclusion, while the Court's judgment in *Northern Cameroons* is unclear, it arguably consists of a dismissal based on propriety considerations. It is submitted

62 This summary is based on the ICJ's interpretation of *Northern Cameroons* in *Land and Maritime Boundary (Cameroon* v. *Nigeria)*, para. 72.

63 See *Northern Cameroons (Cameroon* v. *United Kingdom)*, 39.

64 *Ibid.*, separate Opinion of Judge Gerald Fitzmaurice, at 100.

65 *Ibid.*, at 33–9.

66 International Law Commission, 'Draft Articles on Responsibility of States for Internationally Wrongful Acts with Commentaries' (2001), UN doc. A/56/10, Commentary to Article 37, 'Satisfaction,' at 266.

67 *The Corfu Channel Case (United Kingdom* v. *Albania)*, Merits, Judgment of 9 April 1949, at 35–6.

that this type of discretion could find broader application in addressing frivolous claims where the result of the judgment would be too remotely connected with a practical application.

6.3.2.3 Confirming discretion to dismiss in the context of purely declaratory judgments in the WTO context: measures revoked or modified after the panel request

Without any reference to *Northern Cameroons*, WTO dispute settlement has echoed the above discussion on discretion to dismiss in connection with the purpose of a judicial decision. The examples on point are related first to panels' established discretion to take into account subsequent modifications or repeals of measures after a panel request has been submitted, but before the panels' deliberations;[68] and second, to the doctrine of judicial economy. The Appellate Body has affirmed "it to be within the discretion of the panel to decide how it takes into account subsequent modifications or a repeal of the measures at issue."[69] Since the Appellate Body's recognition of discretion is framed in broad terms, it is useful to distinguish between three types of situation that have arisen from repeals or modification of measures after the panel request: (i) where the measure terminated or modified still affects the operation of a covered agreement; (ii) where the measure's termination or modification constitutes a mutually agreed-upon solution or operates as a result thereof; and (iii) where the measure's termination or modification leads to the mootness of any recommendation to bring the measure into conformity with WTO obligations.[70]

[68] Most of the past cases on this topic have dealt with measures terminated after the *establishment of the panel* and during the panel procedures. However, there should be no difference in approach in situations where the measures are terminated after the *panel request* has been submitted. The incumbency on panels to examine their terms of reference is not different in these two situations. The Appellate Body has refused to distinguish between the situations or measures repealed before or after the establishment of panels, or before or after the initiation of the adjudicatory process. See, for example, Appellate Body Report, *European Communities – Regime for the Importation, Sale and Distribution of Bananas – Second Recourse to Article 21.5 of the DSU by Ecuador*, WT/DS27/AB/RW2/ECU, adopted 11 December 2008, and Corr.1, para. 269, where it stated that: "if the DSU does not exclude from the scope of consultations, or from the scope of panel proceedings, a measure that was no longer in force when the dispute was initiated, then, *a fortiori*, a panel is not precluded from making findings with respect to measures that expire during the course of the proceedings."

[69] *Ibid.*, para. 270.

[70] The question of expired measures may also be assessed from the perspective of remedies. However, like questions of mootness where the judgment would find

6.3.2.3.1 *Measures terminated or modified that still affect the operation of a WTO-covered agreement*

First, in certain cases, the modified or discontinued measure may still affect the operation of a WTO-covered agreement. Examples are measures that have lingering effects after their termination (such as subsidies disbursed in the past whose effects may go forward),[71] or cosmetic modifications that maintain the essence of the old measure (and potentially, the same WTO violations).[72] In those cases, since the measures still affect the operation of a WTO-covered agreement, it would not be appropriate to speak of any discretion not to exercise jurisdiction. Instead, panels must address the claims against such measures on their merits, provided that they have jurisdiction to do so, that the claims are admissible,[73] and, last, that the panel cannot exercise judicial economy over the claims concerning that measure. Not to address such claims would be to abdicate panels' adjudicatory function and the aim of WTO dispute settlement: to secure a positive solution to the dispute.[74]

no practical application, the question pertains to adjudicatory jurisdiction, to the extent that it implicates the substitutive character of jurisdiction.

[71] This is, more evidently, the case where the adverse effects of subsidies whose financial contributions may have been disbursed in the past, and for which the legislative basis may have even expired, are at stake. This was the case with production flexibility contract payments and market loan assistance payments at issue in *United States – Upland Cotton*. See Appellate Body Report, *United States – Subsidies on Upland Cotton*, WT/DS267/AB/R, adopted 21 March 2005, paras. 256–74. But the examples are not restricted to subsidies cases. See also Panel Report, *European Communities and its member States – Tariff Treatment of Certain Information Technology Products*, WT/DS375/R, WT/DS376/R, WT/DS377/R, adopted 21 September 2010, paras. 7.1159–7.1160 (where the complainants submitted evidence that French customs authorities relied on regulations and other national customs authorities within the European Communities used a "conversion table" relating back to pre-existing tariff headings no longer in place).

[72] See, for example, Appellate Body Report, *Chile – Price Band System and Safeguard Measures Relating to Certain Agricultural Products*, WT/DS207/AB/R, adopted 23 October 2002, paras. 126–44.

[73] In the hypothesis of modifications to an original measure, this requires an assessment of whether the modifications would fall under the specific terms of reference. Complainants, in order to protect themselves from the modification of measures, should include potential modifications and amendments to a measure explicitly in the panel request. See *ibid.*, paras. 135, 144. Moreover, panels, in order to protect complainants from cosmetic modifications to measures as a bar to their adjudication, should assess whether the measure, as modified, is essentially the same, instead of whether the measure is identical. See *ibid.*, paras. 139, 144.

[74] Article 3(7), DSU.

6.3.2.3.2 Measures terminated or modified that constitute a mutually agreed-upon solution between the disputing parties, or that are a result of such a solution

Second, the termination or modification of a measure prior to the panel's deliberations may lead to the termination of the dispute underlying the adjudicatory exercise. This would certainly be the case where the parties achieve a mutually agreed-upon solution, in accordance with Article 3(6) and (7) of the DSU. In such cases, the panel report is confined to a brief description of the case and to reporting that a solution has been reached.[75] The absence of a ruling on the merits of the claims due to a mutually agreed-upon solution is not discretionary in any meaningful sense. Rather, it is explicitly provided for by the DSU.[76]

6.3.2.3.3 Measures terminated or modified that lead to the mootness of the recommendation

Third, as is often the case, parties may maintain their dispute over the terminated measure, even if a recommendation focused on the measure would not be capable of effective application. This is the situation that is analogous the ICJ's approach in *Northern Cameroons*, and it is where the discretion recognized by the Appellate Body really enters into the picture. At first glance, since the foremost remedy in WTO dispute settlement is a member's prospectively bringing the WTO-inconsistent measure into compliance with WTO obligations,[77] the termination of a measure before the panel's deliberations would normally turn a WTO ruling into a purely declaratory one, incapable of effective application.[78] However, the Appellate Body has drawn a clear distinction between the preliminary question of whether a panel can address claims against an expired measure and the potential for a recommendation to bring the measure into conformity with WTO obligations.[79]

[75] See, for example, Panel Report, *Japan – Import Quotas on Dried Laver and Seasoned Laver*, WT/DS323/R, 1 February 2006, paras. 14–17.

[76] Article 3(7), DSU. [77] Article 19(1), DSU.

[78] Thus, no recommendation to bring the measure into conformity would be issued in such cases. See, for example, Appellate Body Report, *United States – Import Measures on Certain Products from the European Communities*, WT/DS165/AB/R, adopted 10 January 2001, para. 82; *European Communities – Regime for the Importation, Sale and Distribution of Bananas – Recourse to Article 21.5 of the DSU by the United States*, WT/DS27/AB/RW/USA and Corr.1, adopted 22 December 2008, para. 479.

[79] Appellate Body Report, *US – Upland Cotton*, para. 272.

Previous GATT panels had ruled on expired measures that were included in their terms of reference as a matter of course.[80] This is not surprising, since GATT panels normally did not even consider themselves empowered to scrutinize their terms of reference.[81] Moreover, GATT parties normally did not object to the fact that an expired measure was under consideration.[82] By contrast, objections to panels' ruling on terminated and modified measures are frequently encountered in WTO dispute settlement. Consider the early *Argentina – Textiles* dispute. In that case, Argentina explicitly objected to the panel's consideration of a claim by the United States against a specific duty on footwear that had been terminated after the panel request, but before the panel establishment.[83] According to Argentina, the revocation of the measure turned the United States' claim on that measure into an abstract one.[84] For its part, the United States insisted that the panel rule on the measures, since they had been included in the terms of reference and Argentina might decide to reinstate them.[85] The panel sided with Argentina, noting that it must assume that Argentina would fulfill its treaty obligations in good faith. It concluded that it should not consider the US claim on the measure that had been revoked absent clear evidence that Argentina would reinstate the measure in an attempt to evade panel consideration.[86]

The "good-faith assumption" made by the panel in *Argentina – Textiles* has been softened by subsequent panels. For instance, in *India – Additional Duties*, the panel had to decide whether it would rule on claims against additional duties on liquor imposed by India, based on the original configuration of the measure as included in its terms of reference, or whether the panel should take into account the fact that the measure had been suspended after the panel's establishment.[87] India expressly indicated that it had no intention of

[80] See, for example, GATT Panel Report, *EEC – Measures on Animal Feed Protein*, L/4599, 25S/49, adopted 14 March 1978, para. 2.4.

[81] See discussion in Chapter 5.

[82] GATT Panel Report, *EEC – Measures on Animal Feed Protein*, para. 2.4. See also GATT Panel Report, *United States – Prohibition of Imports of Tuna and Tuna Products from Canada*, L/5198–29S/91, adopted 22 February 1982, para. 4.3. This, again, would be no surprise, for GATT parties had to agree on the panels' terms of reference.

[83] Panel Report, *Argentina – Measures Affecting Imports of Footwear, Textiles, Apparel and Other Items*, WT/DS56/R, adopted 22 April 1998, as modified by Appellate Body Report WT/DS56/AB/R, paras. 6.4–6.15 (the panel's findings on the issue were not appealed).

[84] *Ibid.*, para. 6.8. [85] *Ibid.*, para. 6.9. [86] *Ibid.*, para. 6.14.

[87] Panel Report, *India – Additional and Extra-Additional Duties on Imports from the United States*, WT/DS360/R, adopted 17 November 2008, reversed by Appellate Body Report WT/DS360/AB/R, paras. 7.56–7.70.

reintroducing the *status quo ante*. However, India did not expressly recognize that the suspension of the duties was in order to address a perceived WTO inconsistency.[88] The panel eventually ruled on the original measure, considering that it had not been revoked and that the previous legal situation could be reinstated easily and quickly.[89] In short, the *Additional Duties* panel was less prompt to recognize the mootness of a WTO claim on a terminated measure than was the earlier *Textiles* panel. It is this type of margin of appreciation that the Appellate Body recognized when it asserted panels' discretion to address terminated and modified measures, in light of the purpose of WTO adjudication.

6.3.2.4 Confirming discretion to dismiss in the context of purely declaratory judgments in the WTO context: judicial economy

The application of the doctrine of judicial economy is the other major example of the recognition of WTO panels' discretion not to rule on the merits of certain claims.[90] The doctrine of judicial economy entitles a WTO panel "to refrain from making multiple findings that the same measure is inconsistent with various provisions when a single, or a certain number of findings of inconsistency, would suffice to resolve the dispute."[91] The starting point of judicial economy is the notion that "a panel need only address those claims which must be addressed in order to resolve the matter in issue in the dispute."[92] While it has cautioned panels not to exercise "false judicial economy" – that is, not ruling on issues that must be resolved to allow sufficiently precise recommendations and rulings by the DSB and, in turn, to ensure effective

[88] *Ibid.*, paras. 7.67, 7.69. [89] *Ibid.*, para. 7.70.

[90] See Jan Bohanes and Andreas Sennekamp, 'Reflections on the Concept of "Judicial Economy" in WTO Dispute Settlement,' in Giorgio Sacerdoti *et al.* (eds.) *The WTO at Ten: The Contribution of the Dispute Settlement System* (Cambridge University Press, 2006) 424. See also Alberto Alvarez-Jiménez, 'The WTO Appellate Body's Exercise of Judicial Economy,' 12 *JIEL* (2009) 393.

[91] Appellate Body Report, *Canada – Measures Relating to Exports of Wheat and Treatment of Imported Grain*, WT/DS276/AB/R, adopted 27 September 2004, para. 133. The practice of judicial economy was carried over from GATT panels. WTO practice has elaborated on the potential uses of the practice. For an overview, see Bohanes and Sennekamp, 'Reflections on Judicial Economy.'

[92] Appellate Body Report, *United States – Measures Affecting Imports of Woven Wool Shirts and Blouses from India*, WT/DS33/AB/R, adopted 23 May 1997, and Corr.1, at 19.

resolution of disputes[93] – the Appellate Body has indicated that the use of judicial economy is a matter falling under panels' discretion (since panels can exercise it, but are not obliged to do so).[94]

The fact that judicial economy is a discretionary doctrine of abstention that panels may exercise in light of the aim of WTO dispute settlement also fits nicely with the notion that jurisdiction may not be exhausted where adjudication is considered to be devoid of purpose. As discussed below, this possibility of not exhausting jurisdiction under judicial economy can be strategically used to justify tribunals' not ruling on specific claims in order to avoid potential concerns arising from parallel or serial litigation.

6.3.3 *Partial conclusion: the limited role of discretion to dismiss in relation to forum shopping*

The survey presented above indicates that the existence of discretion to dismiss claims or cases before making findings of merit has been limited to considerations related to the purpose of a decision or its ability to be of practical application, in connection with the notion of mootness. International tribunals have been wary of asserting any kind of discretion to abstain from ruling on admissible claims under their established jurisdiction, except where they have recognized that adjudication would not have a purpose. From an empirical perspective, therefore, lack of purpose of a judicial decision seems to constitute the outer limit of a court's discretion to not exhaust principal jurisdiction. In this sense, discretion connotes a margin of appreciation to assess why a judicial decision is triggered in a given circumstance before proceeding to such a decision.[95]

Applied to the issue of forum shopping, discretion to dismiss – limited as it may be – could be used in two principal ways. First, discretionary

[93] Appellate Body Report, *Australia – Measures Affecting Importation of Salmon*, WT/DS18/AB/R, adopted 6 November 1998, para. 223.

[94] Appellate Body Report, *United States – Imposition of Countervailing Duties on Certain Hot-Rolled Lead and Bismuth Carbon Steel Products Originating in the United Kingdom*, WT/DS138/AB/R, adopted 7 June 2000, para. 71 (rejecting the argument by the United States that panels may not rule on further claims after they have resolved the dispute between the parties).

[95] See generally Georges Abi-Saab, 'On Discretion: Reflections on the Nature of the Consultative Function of the International Court of Justice,' in Laurence Boisson de Chazournes and Philippe Sands (eds.), *International Law, the International Court of Justice and Nuclear Weapons* (Cambridge University Press, 1999) 36.

dismissals may avoid rulings on the merits of frivolous claims. Forum shopping could then be limited by means of discretionary dismissals when the forum shopping strategy does not bring forward the prospect of a judicial decision that serves a concrete purpose for the party requesting it. One potential application for this reasoning would be in cases of expired or revoked trade-distorting measures that no longer affect the operation of a WTO agreement and that are unlikely to be reinstated in the near future, before a panel's deliberation on the specific measure. Under those conditions, the Appellate Body's recognition of panels' discretion on whether to decide the corresponding claim or case in light of the purpose of WTO adjudication may be fit to protect respondents from the burden of litigation. Another potential application would be in situations of parallel and serial litigation where one tribunal has already been seized of or decided a dispute and another tribunal is seized subsequently. Arguably, if the aggrieved party would definitely not be able to obtain different or additional remedies before the second tribunal, even if the requirements for the application of a preclusion doctrine would not be present, the second tribunal may still be able to dismiss the case, based on the lack of purpose of the second proceeding. To prevent a dismissal by the second tribunal from prejudicing the complainant before it in cases of parallel litigation, the second tribunal could first suspend the proceedings and wait for the development of the first proceedings. Then, after it has made sure that there is no possibility of harm to the complainant, the second tribunal could terminate the proceedings.

Second, discretion to dismiss may be used as an issue-avoidance technique by resorting to judicial economy. Indeed, scholars have pictured judicial economy as a means for WTO panels to avoid controversial questions and thereby appease the parties or the broader membership of the organization.[96] Judicial economy has also been considered to be an important means of stimulating compliance with WTO rulings, by injecting a degree of flexibility in dispute settlement.[97] By the same token, judicial economy could be used by international tribunals as an issue-avoidance

[96] See William Davey, 'Has the WTO Dispute Settlement System Exceeded its Authority? A Consideration of Deference Shown by the System to Member Government Decisions and its Use of Issue-Avoidance Techniques,' 4 *JIEL* (2001) 79; Marc Busch and Peter Krzysztof, 'The Politics of Judicial Economy at the World Trade Organization,' 64 *IO* (2010) 257.

[97] Davey, 'Has the WTO Dispute Settlement System Exceeded its Authority?'; Busch and Krzysztof, 'The Politics of Judicial Economy at the World Trade Organization.'

technique to leave undecided questions that overlap with issues under adjudication in other forums, or issues only remotely connected to a panel's principal jurisdiction. Imagine a case where a MERCOSUR and a WTO dispute between Brazil and Argentina partially overlap, and where a WTO panel's deciding a number of claims would be a sufficient solution for the dispute. If some of the WTO claims overlap with claims before the MERCOSUR tribunal, the WTO panel may make use of the doctrine of judicial economy in order to avoid a decision on the overlapping claims under adjudication at the MERCOSUR dispute-settlement system. Of course, this possibility is subject to the requirements for employing judicial economy in the specific circumstance. But it should not be ruled out. This approach, limited as it may prove to be, can also have some influence when addressing forum shopping strategies.

6.4 Discretion to stay: a window of opportunity

6.4.1 Discretionary stays as case management: survey of procedural rules

Whereas tribunals' discretionary power to dismiss is significantly restricted, their discretion to temporarily stay proceedings is much easier to discern. A stay or suspension of the proceedings is a temporary measure which the tribunal can reverse *ex officio* or based on a request by either party. It is thus more flexible than a full-blown termination of the proceedings. Thus, situations warranting discretionary stays should arise more frequently than those justifying discretionary dismissals. Most tribunals' rules of procedure are indeed flexible when it comes to the administration of procedural timetables pursuant to the needs identified in a particular case. Notably, ECtHR rules go as far as stating that the ECtHR may *derogate* from the rules of procedure for the consideration of a particular case.[98] A similar approach is followed by the WTO DSU, where panels must follow standard working procedures unless they decide otherwise.[99]

Granted, there is a common quest across international tribunals to avoid undue delays and to facilitate the expeditious resolution of disputes.[100] However, provided that there are sufficient reasons

[98] Rule 31, ECtHR Rules of Court.

[99] Article 12(2), DSU. This possibility is subject to respecting the DSU.

[100] See, for example, Articles 44(4) and 48, ICJ Rules of Court; Articles 46 and 49, ITLOS Rules of the Tribunal; Article 12(2) WTO DSU; Rule 101, International

warranting a stay (e.g., tackling a forum shopping strategy of concern in the specific case), it is suggested that the consequent delay in the proceedings may not be *undue* in the first place. To that effect, tribunals need to balance the need for a ruling and their readiness to rule, on the one hand, and the inescapable fact that the proceedings will be delayed if a stay is executed, on the other hand.[101] Consequentially, tribunals should factor the estimated period of the suspension (and the continued justification for the proceedings to remain suspended) into their analysis of whether to grant and to keep a stay. ICC Rules of Procedure and Evidence candidly summarize that balance by directing the ICC to set time limits with "regard to the need to facilitate *fair and expeditious proceedings*, bearing in mind in particular the rights of the defence and the victims."[102] In turn, the ICSID Convention grants arbitral tribunals the power to decide on any question of procedure not covered by the Convention, the Arbitration Rules, or rules agreed upon by the parties.[103] As a complement, the ICSID Arbitration Rules provide that "[t]he Tribunal shall make the orders required for the conduct of the Proceeding"[104] and authorize the tribunal to fix and extend time limits.[105] Along the same lines, the ICJ and ITLOS rules establish that the president will ascertain the views of the parties with regard to questions of procedure.[106] In light of the information received thereby, the ICJ and the ITLOS determine, inter alia, the number and the order of filing of the pleadings and the time limits within which the pleadings must be filed.[107] Further, both the ICJ and ITLOS may extend time

Criminal Court, Rules of Procedure and Evidence (3–10 September 2002), Official Records ICC-ASP/1/3 (Part. II-A) (ICC Rules of Procedure and Evidence); Article 17(1), UNCITRAL Arbitration Rules (as revised in 2010).

[101] See generally *Eureko BV* v. *Slovakia*, PCA Case No 2008–13, Award on Jurisdiction, Arbitrability and Suspension, 26 October 2010, para. 292 (denying a suspension in the face of alleged pending proceedings before EU courts: "[W]hile the tribunal wishes to organize its proceedings with full regard for considerations of mutual respect and comity as regards other courts and institutions, it does not consider that the questions in issue in the infringement case are so far coextensive with the claims in the present case that it is appropriate to suspend its proceedings now. Should it become evident at a later stage that the relationship between the two sets of proceedings is so close as to be a cause of procedural unfairness or serious inefficiency, the Tribunal will reconsider the question of suspension").

[102] Rule 101, ICC Rules of Procedure and Evidence (emphasis added).

[103] Article 44, ICSID Convention. [104] Rule 19, ICSID Arbitration Rules.

[105] Rule 26(1) and (2), ICSID Arbitration Rules.

[106] Article 31, ICJ Rules of Court; Article 45, ITLOS Rules of the Tribunal. See also Rule 20(1)(c), ICSID Arbitration Rules.

[107] Article 44, ICJ Rules of Court; Article 59, ITLOS Rules of the Tribunal. Note that, already under the Rules of Court of the PCIJ, the Court fixed and could extend

limits at the request of a party, as long as there is adequate justification.[108] ECJ Rules of Procedure also explicitly foresee the possibility of stays, including, but not limited to, discretionary stays when parallel proceedings are running before the General Court.[109] In conclusion, based on the above examples, flexibility is a clear trend in relation to time limits, in the interest of justice. This opens a door for the possibility of justified discretionary stays as a matter of case management.

6.4.2 Discretionary stays and the WTO DSU time limits

At first glance, the WTO DSU is peculiar in that it specifies stricter limits for the circulation of panel and Appellate Body reports. Article 3(3) of the DSU recognizes as a general statement that the prompt settlement of disputes "is essential to the effective functioning of the WTO and the maintenance of a proper balance between the rights and obligations of Members." More specifically, according to Article 12(8) of the DSU, "in order to make the procedures more efficient," the period of panel examination "from the date that the composition and terms of reference of the panel have been agreed upon until the date the final report is issued to the parties to the dispute, shall, as a general rule, not exceed six months."[110] Whereas Article 12(9) does authorize panels to exceed the six-month period, in those cases panels "shall inform the DSB in writing of the reasons for the delay together with an estimate of the period within which it will issue its report." Moreover, "*in no case should* the period from the establishment of the panel to the circulation of the report to the Members exceed nine months."[111] Referring to Article 12(8) and (9) of the DSU, Yuval Shany suggests that WTO

time limits. *Prince Von Pless* provides an early example of the possibility to adjust the timetable of proceedings to take into account developments before another (domestic) tribunal. According to the Court, "it will certainly be an advantage to the Court, as regards the points which have to be established in the case, to be acquainted with the final decisions of the Supreme Polish Administrative Tribunal upon the appeals brought by Prince Von Pless and now pending before that Tribunal; and as the Court must therefore manage its procedure … to ensure that this will be possible." *Case Concerning Prince Von Pless Administration*, PCIJ Ser. A/B No 52 (1933) 10, at 16. See also Article 33, Permanent Court of International Justice, Rules of Court, as amended until 21 February 1931.

[108] Article 44(3), ICJ Rules of Court; Article 59(3), ITLOS Rules of the Tribunal.

[109] Article 82a, ECJ Rules of Procedure; Article 54, Protocol No 3 on the Statute of the Court of Justice of the European Union.

[110] Article 12(8), DSU. Pursuant to Article 12(8), in cases of urgency, including those relating to perishable goods, the panel shall aim to issue its report to the parties to the dispute within three months.

[111] Article 12(9), DSU (emphasis added).

panels would appear to lack sufficient discretion to stay proceedings.[112] Furthermore, whereas Article 12(12) authorizes panels to suspend their work at the request of the complaining party, it limits such suspensions to a maximum of twelve months, lest the authority for establishment of the panel shall lapse. With regard to Appellate Body proceedings, Article 17(5) of the DSU provides that they shall not, as a general rule, exceed sixty days from the notice of appeal to the circulation of the report. As is the case with panels, the Appellate Body must inform the DSB of the reasons for any delay and provide an estimate of the period within which the report will be submitted. Finally, Article 17(5) states that "*in no case shall* the proceedings exceed 90 days" (emphasis added). In sum, the DSU expresses a clear concern for celerity.

Nonetheless, in effect, the procedural rules of the DSU are not significantly different from those of other international tribunals, and the WTO dispute-settlement system does afford a certain degree of flexibility to discretionary stays. Support for this position can be found, for example, in the *Section 301* panel's interpretation that most of the time limits in the DSU are "indicative only."[113] At any rate, it is important to note that the possibility of discretionary stays, if correctly explored, would be more pertinent to the panel stage than to the appellate stage. Because appeals must be limited to issues of law covered in the panel report and legal interpretations developed by the panel,[114] a situation warranting a potential stay should be resolved before the end of the panel stage, so that it can be properly dealt with on appeal if necessary.

Interestingly, there is a contrast in the language regarding time limits at the panel stage (which "in no case *should*" exceed nine months) and the appeal stage (which "in no case *shall*" exceed ninety days). In contrast to the time limit applicable to panels, the Appellate Body's time limit is cast in unambiguous fashion. Based on the text of the DSU, therefore, it is suggested that the panel stage may exceed the nine-month period under Article 12(9) of the DSU, provided that this démarche is made to ensure a high-quality panel report and does not unduly delay the panel process. This position finds further support

[112] Yuval Shany, *Competing Jurisdictions*, at 265.

[113] Panel Report, *United States – Sections 301–310 of the Trade Act of 1974*, WT/DS152/R, adopted 27 January 2000, para. 7.31. Time limits here refer to the conduct of proceedings by adjudicators rather than to requirements affecting the relationship between the parties to the dispute, such as mandatory quiet periods or consultation requirements that a party must fulfill before resorting to adjudication.

[114] Article 17(6), WTO DSU.

in the fact that panels do exceed the nine-month period indicated in Article 12(9) of the DSU[115] while reporting to the DSB on their delays. A recent example is offered by the *Large Civil Aircraft* case. In informing the DSB of two repeated delays, the chairman of the panel referred to the six-month limit in the general rule under Article 12(8) and to the panel's obligation to notify the DSU under Article 12(9); however, he only left implicit that he was also not accomplishing the nine-month period under Article 12(9).[116] Only in his last communication – which he made after the panel had issued its interim report to the parties – did the chairman state, in general terms, why the panel had not been able to complete the work within the nine-month period specified in Article 12(9).[117] Moreover, he did so retrospectively (after a prolonged delay), rather than before the nine months had expired. In this sense, the panel did not seek authorization by the parties or the DSB to exceed the nine-month limit in Article 12(9). This indicates that the panel did not consider itself to be unconditionally bound by that period. And, while pragmatism may well dictate the panel's approach to the nine-month limitation, this approach does give effect to the textual difference between Articles 12(9) and 17(5) of the DSU.

115 See, for example, Panel Report, *European Communities and Certain Member States – Measures Affecting Trade in Large Civil Aircraft*, WT/DS316/R, adopted 1 June 2011, as modified by Appellate Body Report WT/DS316/AB/R, paras. 1.5; 1.9. The panel was constituted on 17 October 2005, suspended by request of the parties on 1 March 2006 and resumed upon request by the complainant on 4 September 2006. The interim report was issued to the parties on 4 September 2009 (thirty-six months after the resumption of the proceedings) and the final report was not issued to the parties until 23 March 2010. Interestingly, the report makes no mention at all of Articles 12(8) or 12(9) of the DSU.

116 Communication from the Chairman of the Panel on *EC and Certain Member States – Large Civil Aircraft*, WTO doc. WT/DS316/9, 14 December 2007 (stating that the panel would not be able to complete its work within six months of the composition due to, inter alia, the substantive and procedural complexities involved in the dispute, and that the panel expected to complete its work in 2008). See also Communication from the Chairman of the Panel on *EC and Certain Member States – Large Civil Aircraft*, WTO doc. WT/DS316/10, 20 October 2008 (this time, stating that the panel expected to complete its work in 2009).

117 Communication from the Chairman of the Panel on *EC and Certain Member States – Large Civil Aircraft*, WT/DS316/11, 7 December 2009 (stating that the interim report had been issued to the parties in September 2009 – thirty-six months after the proceedings had resumed and almost four years after the panel had been composed – and that the panel expected to complete its work before the end of April 2010. Stating, moreover, that "[i]t has not been possible for the Panel to complete its work within the time provided for in Article 12.9 of the DSU, due to, inter alia, the substantive and procedural complexities and the volume of materials involved in this dispute").

By contrast, the imperative language in Article 17(5) of the DSU leads to the conclusion that appellate proceedings cannot last beyond ninety days. This makes it difficult to accept that stays may take place at the appeal stage, at least without the specific agreement of the parties to the dispute. It is true that, in practice, the Appellate Body has also exceeded the period within which it must submit its reports.[118] As justifications to exceed the time limit for submission of the report, the Appellate Body has pointed, for instance, to the complexities of the case and the difficulties in scheduling a hearing,[119] to the time needed to translate the parties' submissions upon request of the participants in the appeal,[120] and to its exceptional workload.[121] More to the point, in the *Continued Suspension* dispute, the Appellate Body justified its delay based on the need to decide on a preliminary issue arising in the proceedings (in that case, the possibility of hearings being open to the public).[122] Yet, in each case where it submitted a belated report, the Appellate Body used to carefully register the agreement of the parties to deem the report to have been circulated pursuant to Article 17(5) of the DSU. This practice contrasted with panels' approach – for instance, in the *Large Civil Aircraft* dispute where the panel did not indicate any agreement from the parties concerning the delay. The difference in these approaches supports the distinction between Article 12(9) and 17(5) suggested here.

However, the Appellate Body's practice toward Article 17(5) has changed recently. Beginning with the *US – Cool* appeal through 2012, when the ninety-day deadline was passed, the Appellate Body has neither

[118] See Appellate Body Report, *United States – Continued Suspension of Obligations in the EC – Hormones Dispute*, WT/DS320/AB/R, adopted 14 November 2008, para. 29; Appellate Body Report, *United States – Subsidies on Upland Cotton – Recourse to Article 21.5 of the DSU by Brazil*, WT/DS267/AB/RW, adopted 20 June 2008, para. 14; Appellate Body Report, *Mexico – Definitive Anti-Dumping Measures on Beef and Rice, Complaint with Respect to Rice*, WT/DS295/AB/R, adopted 20 December 2005, para. 7; Appellate Body Report, *European Communities – Export Subsidies on Sugar*, WT/DS265/AB/R, WT/DS266/AB/R, WT/DS283/AB/R, adopted 19 May 2005, para. 7; Appellate Body Report, *US – Upland Cotton*, para. 8; Appellate Body Report, *Thailand – Anti-Dumping Duties on Angles, Shapes and Sections of Iron or Non-Alloy Steel and H-Beams from Poland*, WT/DS122/AB/R, adopted 5 April 2001, para. 7; Appellate Body Report, *European Communities – Measures Affecting Asbestos and Asbestos-Containing Products*, WT/DS135/AB/R, adopted 5 April 2001, para. 8; Appellate Body Report, *US – Lead and Bismuth II*, para. 8.

[119] See, for example, Appellate Body Report, *US – Upland Cotton (Article 21.5 – Brazil)*, para. 14.

[120] See, for example, Appellate Body Report, *Mexico – Anti-Dumping Measures on Rice*, para. 7.

[121] See, for example, Appellate Body Report, *Thailand – H-Beams*, para. 7.

[122] See, for example, Appellate Body Report, *US – Continued Suspension*, para. 29.

consulted with the parties nor obtained their agreement to receive the reports as having been circulated pursuant to Article 17(5) of the DSU.[123] Article 17(5) expresses a goal cast in obligational language, but does not spell out a consequence for its unfulfilment and is arguably severable from other DSU provisions. Based on that, and considering the reverse-consensus rule for the adoption of Appellate Body reports, this change of practice is not likely to affect the adoption of reports. If anything, the procedural pragmatism of the Appellate Body further attests to that adjudicative body's flexible approach to the administration of time limits, despite the noticeable search for expeditious resolution of disputes in its constituent instrument. Yet, it is submitted that, in light of the unconditional text in Article 17(5), there would be less room to envision the application of discretionary stays by the Appellate Body than to panels, unless participants to appeals agree to the stay, or where both the stay and the report remain within the ninety-day limit for issuance of the report – which seems highly unlikely.

In conclusion, if panels are not bound by the nine-month period for issuing the report to the parties, then it is possible to conceive discretionary stays also in the panel stage of WTO dispute settlement. True, stays requested by the complaining party are explicitly regulated under Article 12(12) of the DSU and therefore cannot exceed twelve months. However, nowhere does the DSU regulate stays requested by the respondents or determined *ex officio* by panels where circumstances warrant the stay. In this context, it is suggested that panels can approach the issue on a case-by-case basis, in the exercise of their established discretion.[124] On the other hand, in the context of a reform of the DSU, it is suggested that WTO members consider ameliorating the text of Articles 12(8), 12(9), and 17(5) to clarify or consolidate their position with regard to the time limits provided therein.[125]

123 Appellate Body Report, *United States – Certain Country of Origin Labelling (Cool) Requirements*, WT/DS384/AB/R, adopted 23 July 2012, para. 16. See also Minutes of the DSB Meeting of 23 July 2012, WTO doc. WT/DSB/M/320, paras. 81–110. This change of practice and its impacts have been significantly debated at the DSB.

124 See, for example, Appellate Body Report, *European Communities – Measures Concerning Meat and Meat Products (Hormones)*, WT/DS26/AB/R, WT/DS48/AB/R, adopted 13 February 1998, para. 152, footnote 138: "[T]he DSU, and, in particular, its Appendix 3, leave panels a margin of discretion to deal, always in accordance with due process, with specific situations that may arise in a particular case and are not explicitly regulated."

125 This might also be achieved under the interpretative function of the Ministerial Conference and the General Council under Article IX(2) of the Agreement Establishing the World Trade Organization.

6.4.3 Discretionary stays and forum shopping: examples from practice

The above overview demonstrates that there is a place for discretionary stays in international adjudication. It is submitted that such stays can be used as a reaction to forum shopping strategies, in connection with preliminary questions related to the appropriateness or ripeness of adjudication before a given forum. Again, the difference between stays and dismissals is that if, as time goes by, the tribunal's concern over the issue of appropriateness or ripeness of a decision changes, the stay can be lifted and the proceedings can go forward normally. Alternatively, the proceedings may be terminated if the dispute is resolved by another tribunal or settled by the parties. Finally, if the stay refers to one specific question within a larger dispute, the proceedings can also be resumed and the decision of the other tribunal can be taken into account. In this sense, discretion to stay provides a partial functional equivalent to discretion to dismiss and is an avenue that can be explored in developing procedural coordination.

Support for this position can be found in the approach of the arbitral tribunals in the *Pyramids*, *MOX Plant*, and *SGS* v. *Philippines* cases. In *Pyramids*, an arbitral tribunal under the ICSID Convention confronted a preliminary objection by Egypt, the respondent, that the parties had agreed in the investment contract to submit the dispute to arbitration under the auspices of the International Chamber of Commerce.[126] That question had been the object of previous arbitral proceedings under the contract,[127] but the award had been set aside after Egypt appealed to the Paris Court of Appeal.[128] The claimant then appealed the decision of the Paris Court of Appeal to the French Court of Cassation.[129] The ICSID tribunal found that it was entitled to resolve the issue of whether the dispute must be decided under the International Chamber of Commerce.[130] Nevertheless, it recognized that the same question

[126] *Southern Pacific Properties (Middle East) Limited* v. *Egypt*, ICSID Case No ARB/84/3, Decision on Jurisdiction, 27 November 1985, 3 *ICSID Rep* (1995) 101.

[127] *SPP (Middle East) Limited and Southern Pacific Properties Limited* v. *Egypt and Egyptian General Company for Tourism and Hotels*, ICC Arbitration No YD/AS No 3493, 11 March 1983, 3 *ICSID Rep* (1995) 45.

[128] *Egypt* v. *Southern Pacific Properties Limited and Southern Pacific Properties (Middle East) Limited*, Cour d'appel, Paris (First Additional Chamber), 12 July 1984, 3 *ICSID Rep* (1995) 79 (1984, France).

[129] *Egypt* v. *Southern Pacific Properties Limited and Southern Pacific Properties (Middle East) Limited*, France, Cour de cassation, Paris (First Civil Chamber), 6 January 1987, 3 *ICSID Rep* (1995) 96 (1987, France).

[130] *SPP* v. *Egypt* (ICSID, 1985), para. 81.

was pending before the Court of Cassation. In those circumstances, the ICSID tribunal noted that the jurisdictional *question préalable* involving the same issue and the same parties could lead to conflicting decisions or a denial of justice.[131] The tribunal, then, in the exercise of its discretion, opted for a stay in the proceedings, pending resolution of the issue before the French judiciary. In deciding for the stay, the ICSID tribunal stated that "every court has an inherent power to stay proceedings when justice so requires, and this tribunal's discretion to do so is established by Article 44 of the [ICSID] Convention."[132] According to the tribunal:

> 83. While the concurrent pursuit of a remedy in different jurisdictions might be justified to protect legitimate interests of a claimant, it nevertheless entails certain problems of international judicial administration, since it invites a clash between competing exercises of jurisdiction. This may result, not only in the concurrent exercise of jurisdiction by different tribunals, but also in a tribunal declining jurisdiction on the assumption, which later proves invalid, that another tribunal was the competent one to deal with the case.
> 84. When the jurisdictions of two unrelated and independent tribunals extend to the same dispute, there is no rule of international law which prevents either tribunal from exercising its jurisdiction. However, in the interest of international judicial order, either of the tribunals may, in its discretion and as a matter of comity, decide to stay the exercise of its jurisdiction pending a decision by the other tribunal.[133]

Subsequently, the French Court of Cassation decided that the parties had not agreed to submit the dispute to arbitration under the auspices of the International Chamber of Commerce. The ICSID proceedings were then resumed, and the ICSID tribunal asserted jurisdiction over the claims by the complainant.[134] Therefore, by staying the proceedings, the ICSID tribunal implicitly recognized that the appropriate mechanism for resolving the issue of the parties' potential choice of forum by contract was defined in the contract itself. Only after the choice of forum under the contract was held to be invalid, did the ICSID tribunal decide on its own jurisdiction.

In *MOX Plant*, the United Kingdom raised a preliminary objection arguing that the dispute was subject to the exclusive jurisdiction of

[131] *Ibid.*, para. 82. [132] *Ibid.*, para. 87. [133] *Ibid.*, paras. 83–4.

[134] *Southern Pacific Properties (Middle East) Limited v. Egypt*, ICSID Case No ARB/84/3, Decision on Jurisdiction, 14 April 1988, 3 *ICSID Rep* (1995) 131.

the ECJ.[135] Having been informed that the European Commission was examining whether to institute proceedings against Ireland for violation of Article 292 of the EC Treaty, the arbitral tribunal under UNCLOS' Annex VII noticed that its jurisdiction could be entirely precluded depending on the ECJ decision, pursuant to Article 282 of the UNCLOS.[136] It recognized the risk of delay and the possibility that certain UNCLOS provisions might not fall under the exclusive jurisdiction of the ECJ, but considered it inappropriate to proceed with the merits, and decided on a stay.[137] The tribunal, bearing in mind considerations of "mutual respect and comity which should prevail between judicial institutions,"[138] stayed its hand to avoid the risk of a decision that might conflict with a foreseeable determination by the ECJ that Ireland had violated the ECJ's own exclusive jurisdiction. Curiously, none of the parties had expressly asked for a stay. Indeed, agents for both Ireland and the United Kingdom later said, informally, that they were surprised by the suspension of the proceedings.[139] For its part, the tribunal based the stay on Article 8 of its rules of procedure, according to which the tribunal may, subject to its other procedural rules, "conduct the arbitration in such manner as it considers appropriate, provided that the parties are treated with equality and that at any stage of the proceedings each Party is given a full opportunity to be heard and present its case."[140] The tribunal's approach limited the odds of contrary decisions under the UNCLOS and the law of the European Communities while at the same time allowing for continuous supervision of the dispute. Afterwards, the ECJ decided that Ireland had violated Article 292 of the EC Treaty.[141] Ireland then withdrew its claims before the arbitral tribunal, and the proceedings were terminated.[142]

Finally, in *SGS* v. *Philippines*,[143] the ICSID tribunal upheld the parties' forum selection by contract to determine the amount payable to SGS by

[135] *MOX Plant Case (Ireland* v. *United Kingdom)*, Arbitral Tribunal under ITLOS Annex VII, Order No 3, 24 June 2003, para. 20.

[136] *Ibid.*, paras. 21–3. [137] *Ibid.*, paras. 25–30. [138] *Ibid.*, para. 28.

[139] Oral intervention by Philippe Sands and Michael Wood at PICT, *Conference on International Courts and Tribunals in the 21st Century: The Future of International Justice* (2007), The Hague, 30 November 2007.

[140] Article 8, Rules of Procedure for the Tribunal Constituted under Annex VII to the United Nations Convention on the Law of the Sea Pursuant to the Notification of Ireland dated 25 October 2001.

[141] *Commission* v. *Ireland*, C-459/2003, Judgment of the Court, 30 May 2006.

[142] *MOX Plant Case (Ireland* v. *United Kingdom)*, Order No 6, Termination of Proceedings, 6 June 2008.

[143] *SGS Société Générale de Surveillance* v. *Philippines*, ICSID Case No ARB/02/6, Decision of the Tribunal on Objections to Jurisdiction, 29 January 2004.

the Philippines. Because, according to the ICSID tribunal, the amount payable was to be determined under the contractual choice of forum, the claims on the amount payable based on the umbrella clause were inadmissible.[144] However, SGS had also raised a claim under the fair and equitable treatment clause in the Philippines–Switzerland BIT, for an allegedly unjustified refusal by the Philippines to pay its contractual debt. This was held to be a treaty claim over which the ICSID tribunal had jurisdiction. But as a treaty claim, it was not certain that it could be addressed by the contract forum.[145] Yet the tribunal was convinced that a decision on the fair and equitable treatment claim by SGS would still depend on the determination of the amount payable under the contract, a question for the contract forum to decide. As a result, the ICSID tribunal decided that the fair and equitable treatment claim was "premature and must await the determination of the amount payable in accordance with the contractually-agreed process."[146] Therefore, the tribunal, referring to Article 19 of the ICSID Arbitration Rules and Article 44 of the ICSID Convention, opted for a stay in the proceedings pending the determination of the amount payable.

Curiously, the *SGS* v. *Philippines* tribunal stayed the proceedings not only with respect to the fair and equitable treatment claim; the stay comprised also the claim under the umbrella clause, which the tribunal had found to be inadmissible because of the contractual choice of forum. One may question the option to preserve the proceedings with respect to the inadmissible claim under the umbrella clause, since the choice of forum under the contract was mandatory. Indeed, toward the end of the award, the tribunal appears to conflate the issue of admissibility under the contract claim allegedly covered by the umbrella clause, with the issue of the claim's ripeness based on fair and equitable treatment.[147] The two issues raise different problems that could have been kept distinct. Therefore, one might have expected that the finding of inadmissibility of the umbrella clause claim would lead the tribunal to dismiss the claim.[148] On the other hand, the specific inadmissibility of

[144] *Ibid.*, para. 154.

[145] *Ibid.*, paras. 162–4. Note that the tribunal did not consider it necessary to address the question of whether the "treaty claims" could be decided by the contract forum, since a decision on the claims based on fair and equitable treatment would depend, in any event, on a determination of the amount payable under the contract, a question which, in the tribunal's view, should be determined by the contract forum.

[146] *Ibid.*, para. 163. [147] *Ibid.*, paras. 174–6.

[148] See, for example, the discussion in *Bureau Veritas, Inspection, Valuation, Assessment and Control (BIVAC BV)* v. *Paraguay*, ICSID Case No ARB/07/9, Decision of the Tribunal on Objections to Jurisdiction, 29 May 2009, para. 154.

the umbrella clause claim in *SGS* v. *Philippines* was only dilatory, in that after the determination of the amount payable or in the event that a determination was not forthcoming, the claimant could request that the ICSID proceedings be resumed. In that circumstance, to permit the tribunal to monitor the situation and reactivate the proceedings at any time advances the interest of the claimant. Respondents may feel hard-pressed to collaborate with the expeditious resolution of the dispute by the forum of choice by both parties, if the forum seized by the complainant is monitoring the situation.[149] As discussed in Chapter 5, it is possible to stay proceedings as a consequence of a finding of inadmissibility if the matter may be resolved pending a stay. On the other hand, tribunals remaining seized of claims declared to be inadmissible for violations of forum selection clauses may provide incentives for claimants to test the waters and resort directly to their forum of unilateral choice, notwithstanding the previous and common choice of the parties. This increases costs for respondents. All in all, the approach of the tribunal in *SGS* v. *Philippines* seems to be both pragmatic and cautious with respect to an issue (the role of the umbrella clause) which is still unsettled.[150] Moreover, the tribunal did have jurisdiction over the fair and equitable treatment claim by SGS which would arguably be admissible after the determination of the amount payable. Hence, the tribunal would have remained seized of a part of the dispute anyway.

Stays may also apply where there is clearly a more appropriate forum available to try an admissibility issue. For instance, in the WTO *Tuna and Tuna Products* dispute between Mexico and the United States, a NAFTA panel would arguably have been the best forum to decide on the applicability and effect of NAFTA Article 2005 as to the WTO dispute, had the United States raised an objection to that effect.[151] In such a situation, the WTO panel could have suspended its work until the

[149] Note, in this respect, the tribunal's reference to the "substantial efforts" by the claimant to settle the dispute through negotiations. *SGS* v. *Philippines*, paras. 173–4.

[150] See, for example, *BIVAC* v. *Paraguay*, paras. 157–61. In that case, the tribunal found the claim under the umbrella clause to be inadmissible because of the forum election in the contract. However, absent a discussion between the parties on the consequence to follow inadmissibility, the tribunal considered "that the most prudent approach is to join to the merits the limited issue of whether the Tribunal should *either* dismiss the claim under Article 3(4) of the BIT *or* stay the exercise of jurisdiction indefinitely or for some other period of time or until some other circumstances pertain."

[151] *United States – Measures Concerning the Importation, Marketing and Sale of Tuna and Tuna Products*, WT/DS381. See United States Trade Representative, 'United States Requests

NAFTA panel decided the issue. The suspension would have favored the United States as the WTO respondent, but the suspension would be justified by the fact that there seems to be an argument for NAFTA as the forum of choice under NAFTA Article 2005(4), the solution of which is by no means straightforward. This position would be subject to at least two caveats, however. First, the United States should have explicitly raised an objection to the admissibility of Mexico's WTO claims, based on NAFTA Article 2005, which it did not. Second, possible delaying tactics of the United States before the NAFTA panel ought to be carefully monitored by the WTO panel, since the United States would benefit from the delay caused by the suspension of the WTO proceedings.

6.5 Abstention doctrines in international adjudication: a potential way forward?

It is suggested that the distinction between discretion to dismiss and discretion to stay, as discussed above, opens a way for the development of abstention techniques adapted to the specificities of international adjudication. Although abstention is hard to square with international tribunals' obligation to decide cases under their principal jurisdiction, it has been demonstrated that temporary stays may be used within tribunals' discretion to administer the timetable of proceedings. A temporary stay may allow time for the resolution of an issue by the appropriate forum and the decision on that issue may then be taken into consideration by the tribunal that stayed the proceedings. Put differently, discretionary stays may be used to implement adjudicatory comity in procedures in a narrow sense, enhancing tribunals' ability to address systemic and party-related concerns arising from strategic forum selection and parallel litigation.

In the context of US foreign relations, comity connotes "neither a matter of absolute obligation, on the one hand, nor of mere courtesy and good will, upon the other," but the "recognition which one nation allows within its territory to the legislative, executive, or judicial acts of another nation."[152] Based on this traditional notion of comity, comity in international adjudication would consist of the mutual recognition of international tribunals' principal jurisdictions. Adjudicatory comity

Dispute Settlement Panel in NAFTA Choice of Forum Dispute,' (Press Release, September 2010).

[152] *Hilton* v. *Guyot*, 159 US 113, at 163–4 (1895, United States).

and the deferential approach it calls for can apply both to questions about the merits and about preliminary issues related to the propriety of exercising adjudicatory jurisdiction. In both cases, the tribunal resorting to comity considerations would accept determinations of fact and law by another body regarding a similar or identical matter[153] or endorse the legal reasoning of the other body in resolving interpretative questions on the same topic of the law, especially within the other body's area of expertise.[154]

As pointed out above, in opting for a discretionary stay, a tribunal balances the need for a speedy ruling and its readiness to rule on the one hand, against the effects of the delay on the parties on the other hand. Considerations akin to the notion of *forum non conveniens* may enter that balancing exercise, especially in the first part of the balance. *Forum non conveniens* is an abstention doctrine rooted in adjudicatory comity and applied by common law legal systems. It allows the court first seized of a case the discretion not to exhaust jurisdiction because the interests of justice are best served if the trial of at least one issue takes place in another court.[155] The ultimate goal of the *forum non conveniens* analysis is to direct the litigation of an issue to the most appropriate tribunal. To that effect, tribunals adopt a "convenience-suitability approach,"[156] which can be synthesized as follows:

> [A] stay will only be granted on the ground of forum non conveniens where the court is satisfied that there is some other available forum, having competent

[153] See, for example, *Review of the Final Determination of the Antidumping Investigation on Imports of High Fructose Corn Syrup Originating from the United States of America*, NAFTA Case Mex-USA-98-1904-01, 3 August 2001, Courtesy Translation, Public Version, paras. 372–9 (applying comity and accepting certain previous determinations by a previous WTO panel: Panel Report, *Mexico – Anti-Dumping Investigation of High Fructose Corn Syrup (HFCS) from the United States*, WT/DS132/R, adopted 24 February 2000).

[154] See, for example, *Case Concerning Application of the Convention on the Prevention and Punishment of the Crime of Genocide (Bosnia and Herzegovina* v. *Serbia and Montenegro)*, Judgment of 26 February 2007, paras. 402–4, where the ICJ highlights the expertise of specialized bodies in their specific field of competence and signals a predisposition to defer to their interpretations in that regard, but emphasizes its preeminent role in interpreting questions of general international law and calls for deference to ICJ interpretations in general matters by other international tribunals.

[155] See generally, Ronald Brand and Scott Jablonski, Forum Non Conveniens: *History, Practice and Future under the Hague Convention on Choice of Court Agreements* (Oxford University Press, 2007); Arnaud Nuyts, *L'exception de forum non conveniens: étude de droit international privé comparé* (Brussels: Bruylant, 2003).

[156] Arthur von Mehren, *Adjudicatory Authority in Private International Law: A Comparative Study* (Leiden: Martinus Nijhoff, 2007) 326. One exception seems to be Australia, where an "abuse-of-process" approach or "clearly inappropriate" test is used. In

jurisdiction, which is the appropriate forum for trial of the action, i.e., in which the case may be tried more suitably for the interests of all the parties and the ends of justice.[157]

Broadly, the *forum non conveniens* analysis revolves around two main sets of preoccupations. First, there must be another forum available that is clearly more appropriate than the seized forum to try the issue. Second, if the question of appropriateness is answered in favor of the other forum, reasons of justice should not prevent the stay from being granted.[158] The second part of the analysis may require the balancing of the interests of the parties in connection with the whereabouts of the litigation,[159] and even with the interests of the administration of justice.[160]

The same set of preoccupations may arise in international law. Take the potential relevance of NAFTA Article 2005 for the *Tuna and Tuna Products* WTO dispute as an example.[161] Related to the first part of the analysis, assuming that the United States raised NAFTA Article 2005 before the WTO panel, should the WTO panel decide the issues under that Article? Is a NAFTA panel available and if so, is it not clearly a more appropriate forum to try the dispute?[162] Related to the second part of the analysis, are there reasons of justice not to wait for the analysis of the NAFTA panel, such as the "defects" in the NAFTA dispute-settlement mechanism or a significant delay of a WTO decision on the Mexican request? It is suggested that a NAFTA panel would clearly be the more appropriate forum to try the issue of whether Mexico respected NAFTA Article 2005 in bringing the case to the WTO. Initially, there would be no equitable reasons not to wait for the NAFTA panel analysis, as long as the United States proved that it was undertaking its best efforts to

Australia, the issue is whether the complainant's forum of choice leads to vexation or oppression to the respondent. See *Oceanic Sun Line Special Shipping Co. Inc.* v. *Fay*, 165 CLR 197 (1988, Australia) and Ronald Brand and Scott Jablonski, Forum Non Conveniens, at 87–100.

157 *Spiliada Maritime Corp.* v. *Cansulex Ltd.*, AC 460 (1987, United Kingdom), at 476.

158 *Ibid.*, at 478.

159 See, for example, *Gulf Oil Corporation* v. *Gilbert*, 330 US 501 (1947, United States), at 508–9.

160 *Ibid.*, at 509.

161 US *Tuna and Tuna Products*.

162 The representative of the United States at the WTO DSB meeting in which Mexico's request for the establishment of the panel was approved, for instance, argued that the WTO would not be the best place to discuss the meaning of NAFTA provisions. See World Trade Organization, Minutes of the DSB Meeting of 20 April 2009, WTO doc. WT/DSB/M267.

initiate the case and obtain an expeditious settlement. If a concern over NAFTA dispute settlement arose in those circumstances, it would be because Mexico was giving cause to delay at NAFTA. In that context, Mexico should not be rewarded for this conduct by a WTO ruling of merit. In sum, it is suggested that a *forum non conveniens* analysis would be possible and pertinent also in international adjudication, in the limited context of discretionary stays.

Yet the prevailing view among international lawyers is that the doctrine of *forum non conveniens* cannot apply, as such, to international adjudication.[163] There are four main reasons for this. The first two speak to the inapplicability of the doctrine as such, whereas the third and the fourth reasons make the doctrine (as it is traditionally conceived in common law) harder to square with international adjudication. First, as illustrated above, international tribunals have very limited discretion to dismiss admissible cases within their jurisdiction. Therefore, they cannot normally dismiss cases based on propriety-related considerations. Second, *forum non conveniens* is difficult to sell as a general principle of law. It is a doctrine originating in the common law, and what is more, a doctrine which the civil law tradition tends to abhor, because it openly imports an element of discretion to adjudicatory jurisdiction.

Third, to decide both on the relative appropriateness of the forums and whether justice will be served in a concrete instance if a *forum non conveniens* stay is granted, common-law tribunals generally place a heavy weight on claims of hardship to the defendant that are linked to territoriality-based connecting factors between the parties, the dispute, and the allegedly inappropriate forum. The standard case is an individual or corporation being sued before a foreign court and that court declaring that forcing a foreign defendant to defend itself before it is unduly burdensome (evidence must be moved, witnesses transported, experts in foreign law hired, and so on). However, in interstate disputes before international tribunals, such geographical factors are often irrelevant.[164]

[163] Vaughan Lowe, 'Overlapping Jurisdictions in International Tribunals,' 20 *Australian YBIL* (1999) 191, at 198–202; Kyung Kwak and Gabrielle Marceau, 'Overlaps and Conflicts of Jurisdiction between the World Trade Organization and Regional Trade Agreements,' in Lorand Bartels and Federico Ortino (eds.), *Regional Trade Agreements and the WTO Legal System* (Oxford University Press, 2006) 465, at 479–80. See also Andrea Gattini, 'Un regard procédural sur la fragmentation du droit international,' 110 *RGDIP* (2006) 303, at 320–6.

[164] As Vaughan Lowe points out, "In inter-state disputes, the lawyers prepare the case; they get on the plane; they get off and they litigate. Where they do it is a matter of little legal significance." Lowe, 'Overlapping Jurisdictions,' at 201.

Fourth, a court will generally declare itself an "inconvenient" forum in a case where the alternative, foreign court would have jurisdiction to decide the whole dispute before it.[165] But the division of labor between international tribunals is not territorial. Rather, it is drawn along treaty lines. As a result, the potentially alternative forum may not have jurisdiction to decide the whole dispute before the other forum, and there may be a risk that a *forum non conveniens* declination amounts to a denial of justice.[166] For instance, the ITLOS may consider that a dispute under its jurisdiction is better settled at the WTO; yet at present, the WTO could never deal with the dispute's claims of violation of the UNCLOS; hence, to refer the case from ITLOS to the WTO based on the principle of *forum non conveniens* as it is known in domestic law would be impossible.

Based on the two first reasons explained above (tribunals' limited discretion and *forum non conveniens* being restricted to the common law), this book agrees that *forum non conveniens* as commonly understood cannot apply to international adjudication as a self-standing principle. Still, it is suggested that underlying features of the doctrine can apply in the limited context of stays as steps to address systemic and party concerns related to strategic forum selection and parallel litigation. From this perspective, there is room for a progressive development of principles to direct litigation of specific issues to their natural forum. Reference can be made, again, to the *Tuna and Tuna Products* dispute taken to the WTO by Mexico. As suggested above, a NAFTA panel would be the natural forum to decide on the potential applicability of NAFTA Article 2005 to the Mexican choice of forum, but Mexico took the dispute to the WTO. However, assume that the United States objected to the Mexican forum selection before the WTO panel, arguing that the dispute should have been taken to the NAFTA. In that circumstance, the WTO panel would have incidental jurisdiction to decide on the United States' preliminary objection, independent of the NAFTA decision – should there be one. Nonetheless, the appropriateness of the NAFTA panel to decide on the issue regarding Article 2005

[165] See, for example, *Gulf* v. *Gilbert*, at 506–7: "In all cases in which the doctrine of *forum non conveniens* comes into play, it presupposes at least two forums in which the defendant is amenable to process; the doctrine furnishes criteria for choice between them." One exception to this consideration would be Australia. See Brand and Jablonski, Forum Non Conveniens.

[166] Giles Cuniberti, 'Parallel Litigation and Foreign Investment Dispute Settlement,' 21 *ICSID Rev* (2006) 381, at 421.

would be justified by the principal jurisdiction of the NAFTA versus the incidental jurisdiction of the WTO. In other words, even though the WTO panel may be empowered to decide the issue in the exercise of its incidental jurisdiction, if a NAFTA panel were available to decide the question, given the complex and novel legal issues that would need to be considered, the NAFTA panel would be the proper forum to try the NAFTA-related issue.

Crucially, as a doctrine applicable to transnational litigation across legal systems, *forum non conveniens* may also apply across inherently different international tribunals that may not be related. As for the fact that territoriality-based concerns traditionally dominate the application of *forum non conveniens* (the third reason pointed to above), this fact is contingent upon the structure within which the doctrine operates in domestic law (transnational adjudication across states). Importantly, whereas common-law *forum non conveniens* tends to focus on geographic factors, it also considers broader appropriateness-related demands in the administration of justice. These include references to the overall connections the competing adjudicators have to the dispute. As hinted in connection with the *Tuna and Tuna Products* discussion above, it is submitted that the reference to the principal versus incidental nature of jurisdiction in relation to the question at stake could be a first factor to be taken into consideration when deciding on the natural forum to try an issue. In this sense, the closer that an issue is to a tribunal's principal jurisdiction, the more appropriate it would be for that tribunal to decide the question.

Moreover, even though *forum non conveniens* traditionally (with the exception of United States law) excludes a comparison of the "merits" of the procedural laws of each adjudicator, the skills of the judges, or the substantive quality of the justice provided (including remedies and enforceability) may be worth looking at for overlaps between international tribunals – especially given the diverse stages of development, institutional contexts, expertise, and levels of legitimacy or support that surround today's panoply of international courts and tribunals.[167] Thus, William Davey and Andre Sapir have argued with regard to the relationship between WTO dispute settlement and preferential trade agreements' dispute settlement, for example, that preferential agreements would be more political and generally have no second-tier review.

[167] *Ibid.*, at 424. See also Ernest Young, 'Institutional Settlement in a Globalizing Judicial System,' 54 *Duke LJ* (2005) 1143, at 1236–43.

According to Davey and Sapir, such agreements therefore should not be thought of as producing superior decisions worthy of deference.[168] Another suggestion that may be assimilated to the type of assessment discussed here is Peter Drahos's position on the question of "single-breaches" and "double-breaches."[169] In Drahos's view, a single-breach – that is, a situation where a state allegedly breaches an obligation under either a preferential trade agreement or the WTO – could be taken to either forum. However, when it comes to double-breaches – namely, alleged violations of similar obligations in both settings – Drahos argues that such disputes should be taken to the WTO. One reason to prefer the WTO could be, for example, the fact that it has more expertise and experience on disputes involving double-breaches, given that WTO dispute settlement seems to be far more commonly used than regional dispute settlement.

Finally, the requirement that there be an alternative, appropriate forum to try the issue should not mean that this other forum should have jurisdiction over the whole dispute if the claims or specific questions to be addressed before the other forum can be separated from the claims or specific questions to be addressed in the "referring" forum: a *forum non conveniens*-applying court need not limit itself to declining to exercise jurisdiction over the merits of an entire dispute. In particular, the *forum non conveniens*-referring court may retain or reassume and exhaust its jurisdiction over particular aspects of the dispute which the *forum non conveniens*-receiving court does not or cannot decide.[170] Especially in the context of temporary stays, therefore, a referring international tribunal would retain control over the effect of the developments before the receiving court with regard to the referring court's own proceedings and decisions.[171] To return to the *Tuna and Tuna Products* WTO dispute as an example, a NAFTA panel would decide on the choice of forum issue; and if it found in

[168] William Davey and Andre Sapir, 'The *Soft Drinks* Case: The WTO and Regional Trade Agreements,' 8 *WTR* (2009) 5, at 16–17.

[169] Peter Drahos, 'Weaving Webs of Influence: The United States, Free Trade Agreements and Dispute Resolution,' 41 *JWT* (2007) 191.

[170] See Brand and Jablonski, Forum Non Conveniens, at 57: "While the doctrine of forum non conveniens most often is used to seek full dismissal of all aspects of an action before a court, nothing in that doctrine (or in the doctrine of international comity) prevents a court from dismissing part of the case and retaining other parts of the case when it is appropriate to do so."

[171] See von Mehren, *Adjudicatory Authority in Private International Law*, at 391: "A common law jurist does not see granting a *forum non conveniens* stay as a court's refusal

favor of Mexico, the WTO panel would then proceed to decide on Mexico's substantive claims. Moreover, while a stay could allow time for a NAFTA panel to decide on the choice of forum by Mexico under Article 2005, if the United States obstructed a NAFTA panel decision in order to buy time at the WTO, the WTO panel could fully determine that issue for itself.

The above-described examples in *Pyramids*, *MOX Plant*, and *SGS* v. *Philippines* drive the point home: in none of these cases did the tribunal opting for the stay lose control over its own proceedings and decisions, nor did it simply refuse to exercise jurisdiction. Rather, in all those cases the tribunals administered their own proceedings in such a way that enabled them to coordinate their own exercise of jurisdiction with what they perceived to be the appropriate forums to try specific questions, taking into account that other tribunal's principal jurisdiction (be it jurisdiction under a contractual forum of choice, as in *Pyramids* and *SGS* v. *Philippines*, or jurisdiction under EU law, as in *MOX Plant*).[172]

Finally, there is a common quest across legal systems for the *forum conveniens* or the natural forum to decide specific disputes,[173] often defined as the adjudicator "with which the action has the most real and substantial connection."[174] Common law systems focus on judicial discretion to manage unfair assertions of jurisdiction, whereas civil law countries endeavor to establish the natural forum through general jurisdictional organization and protect that forum through the individual guarantee of the independence and impartiality of the court consecrated in the principle of *le juge naturel*.[175] However, although one

to exercise its adjudicatory authority but as an effort to elicit another legal system's collaboration in the carrying out of that task. This effort may fail, in which event the court will exercise its full adjudicatory authority. Where the effort succeeds, in many cases the referring court will resolve certain aspects of the controversy either by decision or by requiring that stipulations be given on various issues. The court making a *forum non conveniens* referral does typically decide a significant part of the controversy with which it was seised."

172 The tribunal in *SGS* v. *Philippines* noticed the analogy with its discretionary stay and *forum non conveniens* stays (at para. 170, footnote 95).

173 See generally Andrew Bell, *Forum Shopping and Venue in Transnational Litigation* (Oxford University Press, 2003).

174 *Spiliada* v. *Cansulex*, at 478.

175 See, for example, *Dictionnaire de l'académie française dédié au roi* (Paris: Jean Baptiste Coignard, 1694): "à qui naturellement, ordinairement et de droit appartient la connaissance d'une affaire." See also International Commission of Jurists, *International Principles on the Independence and Accountability of Judges, Lawyers and Prosecutors: A Practitioners Guide* (Geneva: International Commission of Jurists, 2004), 7–11; Shimon Shetreet, 'Judicial Independence: New Conceptual Dimensions

must recognize that establishing *a priori* natural forums in domestic systems is hard, it may be even harder in international law because the latter generally lacks traditional connecting factors of a territorial character. Because the struggle for the international natural forum is likely to operate on the basis of the subject matter of the dispute, rather than the geographic origin of the relevant facts or the nationality of the parties – and will therefore vary case-by-case – some room for judges to define that natural forum in specific cases seems to be unavoidable. It is suggested that the connection between the specific issue in dispute and the principal jurisdiction of the adjudicator should be a key factor in searching for the natural forum in international adjudication.[176]

6.6 Concluding remarks

This chapter has shown that the discretion of international tribunals to dismiss cases without exhausting their jurisdiction is limited to considerations linked to the purpose of adjudication and of a judicial decision. Such discretion to dismiss has two principal, potential applications. First, discretion to dismiss can be used to avoid litigation of frivolous claims that are perceived to be devoid of purpose. Second, in certain situations, discretion to dismiss might be implemented under the doctrine of judicial economy – in particular, by WTO adjudicators seeking to avoid overlapping issues before other forums. While avoiding frivolous claims may help to protect defendants and avoid unnecessary litigation, and employing judicial economy may contribute to avoiding conflicting decisions, the practical applications of discretion to dismiss appear to be modest.

More importantly, where circumstances warrant, tribunals enjoy discretion to temporarily stay proceedings in order to allow the resolution of issues before another tribunal, prior to pursuing their own decisions. This authority with respect to case handling opens a door

and Contemporary Challenges,' in Shimon Shetreet and Jules Deschenes, *Judicial Independence: The Contemporary Debate* (Boston: Martinus Nijhoff, 1985) 590, at 619.

176 See Rosenne, *Law and Practice*, at 519 ("[T]he true nature of the dispute at hand is the real factor to determine to which court or tribunal a particular dispute should be submitted"). International tribunals possess the authority to "interpret the submissions of the parties" so as to "isolate the real issue in the case and to identify the object of the claim." See, for example, *Nuclear Tests*, para. 30; *Fisheries Jurisdiction Case (Spain* v. *Canada)*, Jurisdiction of the Court, Judgment of 4 December 1998, paras. 29–33.

to the implementation of adjudicatory comity considerations in international adjudication. To that effect, this chapter has argued that international tribunals may make considerations akin to the doctrine of *forum non conveniens* in considering a stay. The possibilities here are broader. Adjudicators, for instance, may stay proceedings or the assessment of part of the claims before them and wait for the resolution of a certain issue by another tribunal having principal jurisdiction over that issue. The staying tribunal can monitor the situation and resume the proceedings in the event that the reasons warranting the stay are no longer preponderant. In this sense, discretion to stay offers an avenue for adjudicators to engage in procedural coordination.

7 Principles and rules permitting procedural coordination through the prism of preliminary objections

7.1 Introduction

Chapter 6 focused on the extent to which international tribunals may decide not to exercise or stay the exercise of jurisdiction as a discretionary matter so as to address forum shopping. It surveyed *abstention* techniques and argued that discretionary stays as a measure of case management offer an avenue for adjudicators to engage in procedural coordination. This chapter turns principally to harder, *preclusion* techniques and their use with the objective of fostering procedural coordination. It takes a close look at the application of procedure-regulating norms through the prism of preliminary objections, putting together the transmission belts (preliminary objections) and that which is to be transmitted by the belt (procedure-regulating norms). As pointed out earlier, preclusion techniques either take away the jurisdiction of a tribunal in favor of another tribunal or preclude a complaint before a given tribunal as a matter of admissibility. Where the preclusion affects jurisdiction, under a direct model of coordination, it should be affirmed *ex officio* by the international judge. Where it relates to admissibility, under an indirect model of coordination, it is crucial that the interested party bring the objection forward clearly. As a secondary matter, this chapter also discusses *aggregation* techniques, which are principles and rules that combine issues pending in multiple proceedings before multiple tribunals, bringing them together in front of a single tribunal. Aggregation norms are seldom encountered for proceedings across different tribunals.

The remainder of this chapter discusses common preclusion techniques available for use through the prism of preliminary objections in the following sequence: exclusive jurisdiction clauses (Section 7.2), fork-in-the-road clauses (Section 7.3), subsidiary jurisdiction clauses (Section 7.4), preferential jurisdiction clauses (Section 7.5), *res judicata* and collateral estoppel (Section 7.6), and the protection of *lis pendens* (Section 7.7). Section 7.8 briefly addresses aggregation doctrines. Section 7.9 concludes.

7.2 Exclusive jurisdiction clauses

7.2.1 Exclusive jurisdiction clauses generally

Exclusive jurisdiction clauses establish a single mechanism as the forum responsible for disputes concerning the application or interpretation of a given set of rules. As promises to resort to the exclusive dispute-settlement mechanism for a given dispute, these clauses limit unilateral strategic forum selection as well as parallel and serial litigation before forums other than the exclusive jurisdiction. Exclusive jurisdiction clauses are frequently encountered in closely knit integration agreements and may be drafted in the affirmative, where they oblige the parties to submit certain disputes exclusively before one given forum, or in the negative, where they prohibit certain disputes from being submitted to other forums. An example of the affirmative type is Article 35 of the Protocol of Tegucigalpa to the Charter of the Organization of Central American States, which establishes that "[a]ny dispute concerning the implementation or interpretation of the provisions of this Protocol and other instruments referred to in the preceding paragraph shall be submitted to the Central American Court of Justice."[1] A frequently cited provision of the negative type is Article 344 of the Treaty on the Functioning of the EU (formerly Article 292, EC Treaty), which provides that "Member States undertake not to submit a dispute concerning the interpretation or application of this Treaty to any method of settlement other than those provided for therein,"[2] thus establishing the exclusive jurisdiction of the European courts for disputes between EU member states.

In the investment arbitration context, ICSID arbitral tribunals' exclusiveness may be a result of the combination of Article 26 of the ICSID Convention and the relevant expression of consent to ICSID arbitration

[1] Article 35, Protocol of Tegucigalpa to the Charter of the Organization of Central American States, 1695 *UNTS* 400.

[2] Article 344, Treaty on the Functioning of the EU. See also Article 33, Treaty Creating the Court of Justice of the Cartagena Agreement, 18 *ILM* 1203.

in the BIT. According to Article 26 of the ICSID Convention, consent of the parties under the convention "shall, unless otherwise stated, be deemed consent to such arbitration to the exclusion of any other remedy." Certain BITs limit the expression of consent to ICSID arbitration alone and thus establish ICSID's exclusiveness. This is the case, for instance, with provisions like Article 7 of France's 2006 Model BIT.[3] Other provisions when read in combination with Article 26 of the ICSID Convention provide a menu of options for arbitration for investors and therefore do not establish ICSID's exclusiveness.[4]

From a procedural perspective, exclusive jurisdiction clauses offer grounds for preliminary objections before tribunals seized of disputes that would fall under the exclusive jurisdiction of another tribunal. Under the distinction between jurisdiction and admissibility explained in Chapter 5 a clause establishing the exclusive jurisdiction of tribunal *A* in the governing instrument of tribunal *A* normally gives rise to a question of admissibility before tribunal *B*. A preliminary objection to admissibility based on the exclusive jurisdiction of tribunal *A* before tribunal *B*, then, brings to the attention of tribunal *B* a procedure-regulating norm that governs the resort to adjudication by the complainant. If the complainant does not comply with that provision, it should have no right to a ruling of merit. Generally, however, if the respondent does not invoke the procedure-regulating norm agreed to outside the purview of the principal jurisdiction of tribunal *B* (and within the purview of the exclusive jurisdiction – that is, tribunal *A*), the respondent acquiesces to the complaint's having been brought before the other tribunal and waives the admissibility issue that would otherwise have arisen. On the other hand, where a jurisdictional link between the two tribunals is present, exclusive jurisdiction clauses should be raised by the tribunals themselves. The establishment of a jurisdictional link, in this case, under a direct model of jurisdictional organization, underscores an allocative dimension which international tribunals are bound to respect.

Consider the *Iron Rhine Railway* arbitration.[5] That case involved the apportioning of costs between Belgium and the Netherlands to

[3] Article 7, France's Model BIT (2006), provides, in part, that: "... if this dispute has not been settled within a period of six months ... it shall be submitted at the request of either party to the arbitration of the [ICSID]."

[4] See, for example, Articles 24(3), United States' Model BIT (2012); Article 10(2) Germany's Model BIT (2008).

[5] *Iron Rhine Railway (Belgium v. The Netherlands)*, Award of 24 May 2005.

reactivate a railway along whose historical route nature reserves had been designated. The Arbitration Agreement mandated the tribunal to "render its decision on the basis of international law, including European Law if necessary, while taking into account the Parties' obligations under Article 292 of the EC Treaty."[6] The arbitral tribunal reasoned that the parties drew limits to its jurisdiction by their reference to Article 292.[7] For that reason, while it was clear that neither of the parties challenged the jurisdiction of the tribunal,[8] the tribunal examined provisions of European law that could be of relevance in the case.[9] The tribunal suggested a twofold measure of choice to assess preclusion under Article 292 of the EC Treaty. First, with respect to the jurisdictional limitation resulting from the reference to Article 292 in the Arbitral Agreement, the preclusion would ensue if the tribunal had to engage in the interpretation of rules of Community law which constituted neither *actes clairs* nor *actes éclairs* for the decision.[10] Put differently, if Community law could be applied straightforwardly, the tribunal would not recognize the preclusive force of Article 292. This element of the reasoning introduced a threshold which arguably was not included in the Arbitral Agreement and which, in effect, made it harder to recognize the preclusive effect of the ECJ's exclusive jurisdiction. Nevertheless, this measure of choice was actually irrelevant in the parts of the award dealing with European law, which makes one wonder why the tribunal decided to include it in the first place.

Second, and more importantly, the tribunal articulated a standard to assess the necessity of deciding issues of Community law in order to enable it to render its award. In my view, this is a relevant question for the preclusion based on Article 292 (now Article 344) to operate before non-European tribunals deciding disputes between EU members. The arbitral tribunal held that not every mention of Community law brought with it a duty to refer. Rather, reference to Community law should require the "interpretation" of Community law "in the sense of conclusiveness, or relevance."[11] The tribunal applied this standard to three potential areas where European law could have been relevant. First, it considered whether European law as applied to trans-European

[6] *Ibid.*, para. 97. The ECJ ruling in *Commission* v. *Ireland* was issued on 30 May 2006, whereas the arbitral tribunal in *Iron Rhine Railway* rendered its award on 24 May 2005. Thus, the Arbitral Tribunal could not use the former judgment as guidance to its interpretation of Article 292.

[7] *Ibid.*, para. 103. [8] *Ibid.*, para. 13. [9] *Ibid.*, para. 58.

[10] *Ibid.*, para. 103. [11] *Ibid.*, para. 106.

rail networks was relevant. It concluded that European law would not favor going beyond Belgium's transit rights which had been claimed based on the disputed 1839 Treaty of Separation.[12] Second, the tribunal examined the relevance of the European Habitats Directive. The tribunal noted the Netherlands' insistence that the issues at stake in fact resulted from its own domestic legislation. The tribunal also held that the Directive provided no more than a background in policies and law from which to interpret the Treaty of Separation. Therefore, the Directive did not meet the standard proposed by the tribunal.[13] Third, the tribunal assessed the potential role of Article 10 of the EC Treaty, but found no "dispute" between the parties therein; it thus held that Article 292 could not be triggered.[14]

So, where does *Iron Rhine Railway* leave us regarding an exclusive jurisdiction clause applied by a non-exclusive jurisdiction? First, as to the tribunal's obligation to address a preliminary question, the tribunal's approach confirms that jurisdictional limitations should be assessed *ex officio*. Second, the tribunal proposed as the test to trigger the preclusion that the exclusive jurisdiction's law (i) could not be clearly applied and (ii) was relevant or conclusive. The former part of the standard, it is argued, does not conform to the traditional text of exclusive jurisdiction clauses. On the other hand, where the application of the non-exclusive jurisdiction law is clear enough, the allocative concern of having another body pronouncing on the law is minimized. Further, if both parties have agreed to submit to the non-exclusive jurisdiction, the protective and enabling concerns are also minimized. From this perspective, the requirement that the exclusive jurisdiction's law be unclear does not seem, in practice, to raise a serious concern, except for those who consider any form of "intrusion" into exclusive jurisdiction to be a serious problem.[15] In my view, party autonomy should prevail, as it did in *Iron Rhine Railway*, as long as the exercise of jointly selecting another forum does not harm third parties. Although parties

[12] *Ibid.*, para. 117. [13] *Ibid.*, para. 136–7. [14] *Ibid.*, para. 140.

[15] See, for example, Nicolaos Lavranos, 'The MOX Plant and IJzeren Rijn Disputes: Which Court is the Supreme Arbiter?' 19 *LJIL* (2006) 223. This is the view espoused by the European Commission as a non-party to proceedings in investor-state cases. See, for example, *Eureko BV* v. *Slovakia*, PCA Case No 2008–13, Award on Jurisdiction, Arbitrability and Suspension, 26 October 2010, para. 184; and *Electrabel S.A.* v. *Hungary*, ICSID Case No ARB/07/19, Decision on Jurisdiction, Applicable Law and Liability, 30 November 2011. Both arbitral tribunals rejected the Commission's position that they lacked jurisdiction by virtue of a transfer of competences by member states to the European Union in investment matters.

to an exclusive jurisdiction instrument may have an interest (in a broad sense) that a given dispute be submitted to the exclusive forum set up by them, even when they are not parties to the dispute, this potential interest should arguably not as such prevail over the general international law right of parties to a dispute to agree on a method of settlement or forum that suits their specific dispute. After all, if two parties are free to bilaterally settle a dispute, provided that they do not prejudice the rights of third parties, it is difficult to see why they should not be free to bilaterally select an adjudicator to settle the dispute (without harming third parties).

The second part of the standard proposed by the arbitral tribunal (i.e., that the exclusive jurisdiction law be relevant or conclusive), by contrast, offers an interesting means to balance party autonomy with systemic concerns. Although expressed in vague terms, the application of this standard demonstrated essentially that (i) the exclusive jurisdiction's law must add value to the claims – otherwise there can be no preclusion and (ii) there must be a dispute about the exclusive jurisdiction's law; that is, there must be conflicting views as to the interpretation or application of the exclusive jurisdiction's law – otherwise there can be no preclusion. More generally, the fact that both parties jointly addressed the European Commission to express their commitment to comply with obligations under Article 292 of the EC Treaty[16] contributed to diluting concerns by European institutions. Finally, it is of note that the tribunal dedicated a considerable part of its reasoning to explaining why it did not consider Article 292 to be triggered in the circumstances, an approach that may have helped the parties justify their choice of forum to European institutions and certainly helps in the progressive definition of the contours of an international judiciary consisting of related – albeit autonomous and independent – tribunals.

The *Iron Rhine Railway* tribunal thus discussed but did not ultimately uphold a preclusive effect for the exclusive jurisdiction clause at stake. Preclusion is essentially a negative effect: you may not do something because of previous undertakings or occurrences. However, importantly, exclusive jurisdiction and other preclusion clauses potentially have positive effects as well, in that a party aggrieved by a violation of

[16] *Ibid.*, paras. 13–15. Belgium distinguished the dispute from the *MOX Plant* case that was pending before an UNCLOS Annex VII tribunal. In *Iron Rhine Railway*, the Netherlands had not objected to Belgium's references to EC law, and none of the parties contended that the other violated EC law.

such clauses may have a cause of action to fight the circumvention of the preclusion clause. From this perspective, if proceedings are under way before the non-exclusive tribunals in violation of the exclusive jurisdiction clause, the same clause operates as a cause of action[17] that, if successful, has effects analogous to those of an anti-suit injunction. *Commission* v. *Ireland*[18] offers an illustration. This case was decided just one year after *Iron Rhine Railway* and stands out as the most complete interpretation of the ECJ's exclusive jurisdiction to date by the ECJ itself. In that case, the European Commission alleged, inter alia, that Ireland had violated the exclusive jurisdiction of the ECJ by submitting the *MOX Plant* dispute to United Nations Convention on the Law of the Sea (UNCLOS) dispute settlement. In a nutshell, the ECJ held that the UNCLOS provisions on the prevention of maritime pollution relied on by Ireland before the arbitral tribunal came within the scope of the Community competence. And, since the Community elected to exercise such competence by becoming a party to the UNCLOS, the ECJ had exclusive jurisdiction to assess the compliance of those provisions in disputes between Community member states.[19]

That ECJ's finding effectively forecloses the possibility of forum shopping by individual European Union members against other members in matters involving the EU's competence. The ECJ explained that an "international agreement cannot affect the allocation of responsibilities defined in the Treaties and, consequently, the autonomy of the Community legal system."[20] The rationale is far reaching: if EU members cannot affect the allocation of responsibilities defined in the treaties, then, arguably, even two members acting jointly would be prohibited from taking their grievances to other mechanisms. Hence, if the reasoning in *Commission* v. *Ireland* is extended to cases where two EU member states jointly choose an alternative means of settlement like in *Iron Rhine Railway*, both states can be sued at the ECJ for violating the European courts' exclusive jurisdiction. Yet, under the framework that this book suggests, the applicability of that ECJ's reasoning to other tribunals *ex officio* would depend on the existence of direct jurisdictional organization involving the ECJ and the other tribunal in the governing instruments of the latter. Otherwise, the preclusion would require an objection to admissibility. However, it would be hard

[17] See discussion in Chapter 3.

[18] *Commission* v. *Ireland*, C-459/2003, Judgment of the Court, 30 May 2006.

[19] *Ibid.*, para. 121. [20] *Ibid.*, para. 123.

to imagine an admissibility objection if both parties jointly opt for, say, an arbitral forum created for specific purposes. Hence, notwithstanding the potential far-reaching implications of the ECJ reasoning, it is submitted that, in general, other tribunals are not invariably in a position to override an explicit agreement between two parties to refer disputes to them.

Two other caveats to extending the ECJ's reasoning are as follows. First, the premise in *Commission* v. *Ireland* was that the European Community was a party to the UNCLOS. According to the ECJ, this meant that, in ensuring respect for commitments arising from the UNCLOS, member states fulfill within the Community system an obligation in relation to the Community, which had assumed responsibility for the due performance of that agreement. As a result, Ireland's litigating the *MOX Plant* dispute outside the Community order, in the ECJ's view, affected the legal position of the Community, since it had the responsibility for performance of the treaty on behalf of member states. By contrast, where member states do not fulfill obligations over which the Community has assumed responsibility, states might arguably resort to other dispute-settlement mechanisms provided for by the relevant treaties. Second, the ECJ's precluding resort to dispute settlement by member states outside Community institutions is a "solution" for outside interference that is avoided even in most domestic legal systems, where alternative dispute resolution methods and arbitration, in particular, are accepted to varying extents. While the claim for power on behalf of Community or Union institutions may be legitimate within the European context and for integrationists, it is suggested from the outside that particular caution ought to be taken in extending this part of the ECJ ruling beyond *Commission* v. *Ireland*, and all the more so beyond the European Union context.

The latter caveat, even if it is not applicable to the ECJ exclusive jurisdiction in particular, is especially important for treaties among parties not even nearly as closely integrated as European Union members, such as the WTO Agreements. Generally speaking, it would not seem proper for an international tribunal to decline deciding a case over which the two disputing parties have granted it jurisdiction and where both parties agree that the tribunal must decide the dispute. From the perspective of the tribunal, other than the "exclusive jurisdiction," this is a joint exercise of party autonomy that international law does not subordinate to the exclusive jurisdiction clause in another treaty. In other words, *exclusive* jurisdiction should not mean *absolute* jurisdiction. The exercise of party autonomy to jointly opt for another forum would be legitimate and should be recognized, under the framework suggested here, provided that the disputing parties agree that the enabling function of jurisdictional rules should prevail in the circumstance (e.g., as in *Iron Rhine Railway*) and that such exercise does not affect the legal position of third parties in relation to the merits of the bilateral dispute (e.g., contrary to *MOX Plant*, where the position of the Community was affected as explained above). This is to say that exclusive jurisdiction clauses outside the context of close integration agreements would normally operate in a *relational* manner (as discussed in connection with Article 23 of the DSU, below) like most other international legal norms.

Admittedly, the position advocated here may raise a concern relative to the allocative function of jurisdictional rules, especially for those who consider that the non-exclusive jurisdiction is an intruder to the exclusive jurisdiction's legal order. Indeed, the more developed the allocative function is in the interactions between any two tribunals, the greater such concern, and this may well explain the ECJ's centripetal approach in *Commission* v. *Ireland*. In my view, however, allocative concerns based on the exclusive jurisdiction of given tribunals should not be overstated in the current context of international law, particularly if the disputing parties themselves have conscientiously established another tribunal and opted for a judgment by that tribunal which does not affect the legal position of third parties. If they have done so, it is because they understand that another means of settlement may be more suitable to their case. In such cases, it is doubtful whether an aprioristic systemic effort based on a preclusion type of reasoning should prevail over the parties' choice. (That, however, should not be an absolute impediment for consideration of soft abstention-type measures, discussed in Chapter 6.)

7.2.2 Is Article 23 of the DSU an exclusive jurisdiction clause, and does this really make the WTO an "absolute" jurisdiction?

The above discussion on exclusive jurisdiction clauses leads one to Article 23 of the DSU, paragraph 1 of which states:

> When Members seek redress of a violation of obligations or other nullification or impairment of benefits under the covered agreements or an impediment to the attainment of any objective of the covered agreements, they shall have recourse to, and abide by, the rules and procedures of this Understanding.

Article 23(1) of the DSU is drafted much like other typical exclusive jurisdiction clauses. A vexing question related to the above discussion on exclusive jurisdiction rules is whether the procedural effect of a choice-of-forum clause in a preferential trade agreement may ever be recognized through a preliminary objection to admissibility advanced at the WTO.[21] This question is central to the debate on overlaps between WTO and preferential trade agreements' dispute settlement, especially in light of the increase in preferential jurisdiction and fork-in-the-road clauses in recent preferential trade agreements.

Certain scholars and practitioners have espoused the view that Article 23 of the DSU would operate akin to Article 292 of the EC Treaty as interpreted in *Commission* v. *Ireland*: as an *absolute* jurisdiction clause.[22] From this perspective, Article 23 would resolutely bar preliminary objections based on preclusion clauses from outside the WTO agreements in WTO disputes. As Kyung Kwak and Gabrielle Marceau have put it:

> There could be overlaps or conflicts of jurisdiction between the dispute settlement mechanism of the WTO and RTAs [Regional Trade Agreements]. The wording of Article 23 and the quasi-automaticity process of the DSU makes it evident that a WTO adjudicating body always has the authority and even the obligation to examine claims of violation of WTO obligations … In addition, … in the context of a dispute between two WTO Members, involving situations covered by both an RTA and a WTO Agreement, any WTO Member that considers that any of its WTO benefits have been nullified or impaired has the *absolute right* to trigger the WTO dispute settlement mechanism and to request the establishment of a panel. Such a WTO Member *cannot be asked, and arguably cannot even agree, to take its dispute to another forum, even if that other forum appears to be more relevant or better equipped to deal with the problems at issue.* In so doing, the WTO Member may be in violation of an RTA but this matter is not for the WTO adjudicating body (under the existing WTO provisions). However, this WTO Member may risk RTA retaliation that could be WTO compatible.
>
> There appears to be no legal solution for a situation where two members are faced with two treaties that contain overlapping and potentially conflicting

[21] That question is the relevant one, for present purposes, as a dispute under WTO-covered agreements and agreements in other subject areas, such as the law of the sea or human rights, would not normally raise preclusion-type questions (although they may raise abstention-type questions, as pointed out in Chapter 6).

[22] See Kyung Kwak and Gabrielle Marceau, 'Overlaps and Conflicts of Jurisdiction between the World Trade Organization and Regional Trade Agreements,' in Lorand Bartels and Federico Ortino (eds.), *Regional Trade Agreements and the WTO Legal System* (Oxford University Press, 2006) 465. See also Fernando Piérola and Gary Horlick, 'WTO Dispute Settlement and Dispute Settlement in the "North-South" Agreements of the Americas: Considerations for Choice of Forum,' 41 *JWT* (2007) 885, at 893.

jurisdictions. Members remain obliged at all times to respect both treaties. However, this obligation on states may not suffice to stop a dispute settlement mechanism process triggered by a WTO Member contrary to its RTA obligations. [23]

Thus, for Kwak and Marceau, WTO panels are prevented from addressing forum shopping before the WTO, regardless of whether preferential agreements regulate the matter. Where the issue is regulated, the violation of a choice-of-forum or fork-in-the-road clause may give rise to a violation of the preferential agreement, and this may offer a cause of action under that agreement. However, the preclusion clause will not have the procedural effect of halting WTO litigation.[24] To give a concrete example, take the WTO *Tuna and Tuna Products* dispute between Mexico and the United States.[25] In Kwak and Marceau's view, even if the United States had advanced an objection to the admissibility of the Mexican case based on the NAFTA choice-of-forum clause, the WTO panel would be legally prevented under Article 23 of the DSU from declining to rule on the merits of the WTO case. By contrast, based on the NAFTA choice-of-forum clause, the United States could obtain a NAFTA ruling to the effect that Mexico had breached the NAFTA. Subsequently, based on the NAFTA ruling, the United States could be entitled to retaliate (under NAFTA) against Mexico's benefit arising from the WTO ruling, where the NAFTA choice-of-forum clause could not be considered in the first place. Kwak and Marceau would add that the NAFTA-authorized retaliation by the United States would be WTO compatible, since Article XXIV of the GATT allows the formation of free trade areas and customs unions by WTO members. In their view, assuming the compatibility of a preferential agreement with WTO rules, countermeasures are effective instruments for effective regional trade agreements and would therefore be WTO-compatible pursuant to Article XXIV.[26]

The scenario that Kwak and Marceau suggest may well take place under existing rules. However, in my view, this is not the only possible

23 Kwak and Marceau, 'Overlaps and Conflicts of Jurisdiction,' at 484 (emphasis added).

24 This covers two scenarios: (i) WTO adjudicators could not directly recognize a preclusion clause as a matter of incidental jurisdiction, and (ii) even if the preclusion clause were to offer a foundation for an anti-suit injunction before the other forum, such an injunction would be unrecognizable at the WTO.

25 *United States – Measures Concerning the Importation, Marketing and Sale of Tuna and Tuna Products*, WT/DS381.

26 Kwak and Marceau, 'Overlaps and Conflicts of Jurisdiction', at 483–4. This view is further developed in Julian Wyatt and Gabrielle Marceau, 'Dispute Settlement Regimes Intermingled: Regional Trade Agreements and the WTO,' 1 *JIDS* (2010) 67.

outcome, let alone the best one for a given case where a procedure-regulating norm from a preferential agreement is at stake. In addition to the good-faith arguments under Article 3(10) of the DSU that may lead a panel to decline from ruling based on a preclusion clause in a preferential trade agreement under WTO provisions,[27] two lines of argument are that: (i) Article XXIV of the GATT mandates recognition of both substantive and procedural norms in preferential trade agreements; and (ii) Article 23 of the DSU can be modified or revoked *inter partes* by the disputing parties. This study leans toward the view that the latter line of argument is more compelling, but the two lines are not mutually exclusive and recognition of a preclusion clause can take place under either of them.

Before addressing those arguments, it is important to briefly note some of the direct implications of denying effect to preclusion clauses in non-WTO agreements as a matter of principle: this approach unnecessarily extends the loop of litigation and allows WTO forum shoppers to circumvent previously negotiated preclusion clauses in preferential agreements. In general, it would be much simpler and more economical to (i) assess incidentally the violation of a preclusion clause in the WTO proceedings or (ii) eventually interrupt the WTO proceeding while the issue is assessed at the proper forum; rather than the alternative of (i) permitting the WTO proceeding to move forward, then (ii) having the respondent in the WTO proceeding initiate a different case before a different mechanism (akin to an anti-suit injunction) only to then (iii) examine the violation of the preclusion clause before a different mechanism. Crucially, if the bar to recognizing preclusion clauses were a matter of principle, even a duly identified violation of the preclusion clause under the preferential agreement would be unrecognizable at the WTO, the "absolute" jurisdiction (put shortly: the "anti-suit injunction" brought before a preferential trade agreement would not be recognizable at the WTO). This would potentially lead to (iv) an obligation to bring a measure into conformity with the WTO agreements by the WTO respondent which would be, in turn, arguably entitled to (v) resort to trade retaliation under the preferential agreement to cancel out the violation of the preclusion clause in the preferential agreement. The volume increase in litigation would be worrisome especially for developing and least developed countries with scarce legal resources. As Peter Drahos has pointed out, an obvious consequence of

[27] See discussion in Chapter 4.

a multiple-court trade regime is that it favors states with "the capacity to analyze its complex pathways and pick those that best suit their purposes."[28] This is all the more so where the multiplication of litigation is encouraged or remains uncontrolled – exactly where the lack of recognition of non-WTO clauses may lead.

For those who pursue a coordination agenda across international trade institutions, the lack of recognition of the effect of preclusion clauses in WTO dispute settlement endangers coordination.[29] On the other hand, the WTO dispute-settlement system would not necessarily be weakened by recognizing choice-of-forum and preclusion clauses in preferential agreements. Rather, it is argued that such recognition would be mutually beneficial for preferential agreements and the WTO dispute-settlement system. Concerns over weakening WTO dispute settlement are diminished as in practice the WTO system's comparative advantages make it naturally a magnet forum. When considering the advantages of the WTO, one may refer to the expertise and availability of the secretariat staff, multilateral surveillance and informal pressures for compliance, legitimacy of decisions, the possibility to appeal, strong rules-based orientation, and detailed jurisprudence offering greater legal security, among others.[30] In fact, noticeably fewer cases have been taken to preferential agreements than to WTO dispute settlement, whose resilience is well recognized.[31] While diminishing the importance of the WTO would be highly unlikely by recognizing preclusion clauses in preferential trade agreements, such recognition would lead to more conscientious choice of forum and increase the potential for procedural coordination. Furthermore, it would make functional dozens of preclusion clauses seriously negotiated by numerous different subsets of the WTO membership.

Having addressed some of the direct implications of the debate, it is possible to return to the reasons under existing law for recognizing

[28] Peter Drahos, 'Weaving Webs of Influence: The United States, Free Trade Agreements and Dispute Resolution,' 41 *JWT* (2007) 191, at 199.

[29] See Joost Pauwelyn, 'Legal Avenues to "Multilateralizing Regionalism": Beyond Article XXIV,' in Richard Baldwin and Patrick Low (eds.), *Multilateralizing Regionalism: Challenges for the World Trading System* (Cambridge University Press, 2008) 368.

[30] See, for example, William Davey, 'Dispute Settlement in the WTO and RTAs: A Comment,' in Bartels and Ortino (eds.), *Regional Trade Agreements and the WTO*, 343, at 344.

[31] *Ibid.*, at 354–6. See also Armand de Mestral, 'NAFTA Dispute Settlement: Creative Experiment or Confusion?' in Bartels and Ortino (eds.), *Regional Trade Agreements and the WTO*, 359, at 381.

the effect of preferential agreements' preclusion clauses before the WTO, notwithstanding the text of Article 23(1) of the DSU.[32] The first, more conservative avenue for recognition lies in Article XXIV of the GATT (or its equivalent in the GATS, Article V, or in the so-called enabling clause). As Kwak and Marceau rightly point out, Article XXIV of the GATT authorizes countermeasures under preferential trade agreements which, in turn, are considered compatible with the WTO. Indeed, Article XXIV authorizes the formation of free trade areas and customs unions and, hence, a departure from GATT/WTO rules. Consequently, it would be very awkward if developments under a permitted preferential agreement (such as countermeasures arising from dispute settlement under the preferential trade agreement) were suddenly prohibited by or blocked at the WTO. But this is exactly the point: Kwak and Marceau's logic is as compelling for authorized countermeasures as it must be for the operation of preclusion clauses before WTO panels. Given that WTO members are authorized to depart from GATT/WTO rules under GATT Article XXIV, they may establish a preferential agreement under Article XXIV and equip it with dispute-settlement machinery to then, notwithstanding Article 23 of the DSU, regulate forum election regarding that mechanism or the WTO. Just as countermeasures under preferential agreements are arguably authorized under Article XXIV of the GATT and would be recognized as *substantive* defenses in case the WTO member targeted by the preferential countermeasures complained at the WTO, *mutatis mutandis* procedure-regulating norms from preferential agreements should be recognized as *procedural*, admissibility objections in WTO dispute settlement. Or would it not be utterly strange if WTO panels were obliged to turn a blind eye to the circumvention of procedural rules under preferential agreements which are expressly permitted under Article XXIV? In sum, because the formation of preferential agreements is legal,

[32] An argument could also be made that Article 23 of the DSU is exclusively concerned with unilateral action, not with bilateral derogations of WTO provisions. The history of unilateral determinations of violations during the GATT and Article 23(2), DSU may support this interpretation. This question, in my view, has not been decided yet, since the focus of claims based on Article 23 of the DSU to date have all referred to unilateral action. See Appellate Body Report, *United States – Continued Suspension of Obligations in the EC – Hormones Dispute*, WT/DS320/AB/R, adopted 14 November 2008; Panel Report, WT/DS320/R, adopted 14 November 2008, as modified by Appellate Body Report WT/DS320/AB/R; Appellate Body Report, *United States – Import Measures on Certain Products from the European Communities*, WT/DS165/AB/R, adopted 10 January 2001.

departures from both WTO substantive and procedural rules are justifiable despite the ostensible WTO-exclusivity that Article 23 of the DSU otherwise engenders.

A second compelling reason to recognize a procedural effect for preferential agreement preclusion clauses is that subsets of WTO members are entitled to derogate from Article 23 in their specific relationship.[33] The refusal to recognize any preclusive effect to procedure-regulating rules from preferential agreements at the WTO stems from the view that Article 23 of the DSU establishes the absolute jurisdiction of the WTO over any and all WTO disputes. However, Article 23 stipulates a revocable obligation to have recourse to and abide by the DSU which is bilateral in nature (notwithstanding the fact that the obligation is provided for in a multilateral treaty). Article 23 incorporates a promise by each individual WTO member toward every other individual member that WTO disputes between these members will be settled with observance of DSU provisions. It creates a set of bilateral links rather than establishing a collective, integral obligation owed by all WTO members toward all WTO members that must prevail at whatever cost.[34] The object of Article 23 is to fix a forum of choice for WTO disputes. These disputes are almost fundamentally conceptualized as bilateral enterprises,[35] and several Articles within the DSU reflect the bilateral nature of WTO dispute settlement. Article 3(3), for instance, states:

> The prompt settlement of situations in which *a Member* considers that any benefits accruing to *it* directly or indirectly under the covered agreements are being impaired by measures taken *by another Member* is essential to the

[33] See Joost Pauwelyn, *Conflict of Norms in Public International Law: How WTO-Law Relates to Other Rules of International Law* (Cambridge University Press, 2003). The scope of the applicable law in WTO adjudication has been discussed in Chapter 4. The argument developed here addresses, more specifically, whether Article 23 of the DSU establishes the absolute jurisdiction of the WTO.

[34] On the nature of WTO obligations, see Joost Pauwelyn, 'A Typology of Multilateral Treaty Obligations: Are WTO Obligations Bilateral or Collective in Nature?' 14 *EJIL* (2003) 907. See generally Bruno Simma, 'Bilateralism and Community Interest in the Law of State Responsibility,' in Yoram Dinstein and Mala Tabory (eds.), *International Law at a Time of Perplexity: Essays in Honor of Shabtai Rosenne* (The Hague: Kluwer, 1989) 825.

[35] At a DSB meeting in 2003, the United States declared: "The concept *erga omnes* was squarely at odds with the fundamentally bilateral nature of WTO and GATT dispute settlement and with the notion that WTO disputes concerned nullification and impairment of negotiated benefits to a particular Member. WTO adjudicators were tasked with resolving disputes between specific complaining and defending parties. Adjudicators may not, through improper importation of the concept *erga omnes*,

effective functioning of the WTO and the maintenance of a proper balance between the rights and obligations of Members.[36]

It is true that solutions to disputes between given members should not nullify or impair benefits to the other members,[37] that a most-favored-nation (MFN) obligation regarding the implementation of WTO rulings potentially extends the benefits of a given dispute's resolution to the rest of the membership (since the removal or modification of the disputed measure will have to be made on an MFN basis),[38] and that third parties have certain defined procedural rights *stricto sensu* under Article 10 of the DSU. But this does not alter the bilateral character of WTO dispute-settlement proceedings. Hence, if Brazil brings a dispute against China and these two parties subsequently agree on a solution that satisfies both of them, or if Brazil gives up the case, the case is closed as a result. It falls for the other members to merely raise points on the mutually agreed-upon solution under Article 3(6) of the DSU or, if they wish, to bring another (bilateral) dispute against the same measure, even if they have participated as third parties in the proceedings opposing Brazil and China. The DSU, thus, subject to the specific rights of third parties which are recognized in the context of procedure in a narrow sense (or, as Article 10 of the DSU puts is, "during the panel process"), primes the concrete bilateral dispute between the parties to the proceedings over potential trade interests of the rest of the membership which are not parties to the dispute.

From this perspective, the paramount objective of Article 23 is to avoid unilateralism of *one member* as against *another member* in the context of WTO disputes.[39] Since Article 23 establishes bilateral obligations and

enforce WTO obligations on behalf of non-parties to a dispute." Minutes of the DSB Meeting of 7 May 2003, WTO doc. WT/DSB/M/149, para. 20.

[36] See also DSU Article 12(12) (which authorizes requests for suspensions by complainants and provides that if the suspension lasts more than twelve months the authority for the panel shall lapse); Article 17(4) (which explicitly restrict appeals to the parties to a dispute); Article 22(2) (which restricts the right to request authorization to suspend the application of concessions to the parties "having invoked the dispute settlement procedures"); Article 22(3) (permitting suspension of concessions by the complainant); Article 22(4) (stating that the level of suspension shall be equivalent to the level of nullification or impairment); Article 22(8) (which states that a mutually satisfactory solution regarding implementation prevents continued suspension of concessions); and Article 25 (which expressly permits bilateral arbitration of WTO disputes). All of these provisions, and others could be cited, attest to or imply the bilateral nature of WTO dispute settlement.

[37] Article 3(5), DSU.

[38] See, for example, Article 22(1), DSU.

[39] See, for example, the extensive discussion by twelve third parties and the European Communities in Panel Report, *United States – Sections 301–310 of the Trade Act of 1974*,

since the WTO does not prohibit modifications or revocations to it by subsets of the membership, the customary rules on treaty modification and suspension remain applicable to normative interactions between Article 23 of the DSU and non-WTO procedure-regulating norms. Such customary rules include, in particular, the default principles embodied in Articles 41(1)(b) on treaty modification and 58(1)(b) on suspension of treaty provisions of the Vienna Convention on the Law of Treaties (VCLT).[40] Both provisions confirm that preclusion clauses established by subsets of the WTO membership are permitted and have effect. In the exercise of their incidental jurisdiction, as Chapter 4 explained, WTO panels or the Appellate Body may refer to preclusion clauses from preferential agreements either by reference to Article 3(10) of the DSU or directly, by applying the preclusion clause from the other agreement.[41] The key conditions for the application of the preclusion clause would then be that (i) the respondent raised an objection based on the outside preclusion clause (since this would be a matter of admissibility) and that (ii) the preclusion clause prevailed over Article 23 of the DSU under the *lex posterior* or *lex specialis* principles.[42] As to the latter condition, most preclusion clauses in preferential trade agreements would indeed prevail as *lex posterior* or *lex specialis.*

Note, in this regard, the Appellate Body's recognition in *Continued Suspension* that a confidentiality provision in the DSU was "more properly understood as operating in a relational manner."[43] Granted, a confidentiality provision is not the same as an exclusive jurisdiction clause. However, the Appellate Body's reasoning is supportive of the underlying logic about the operation of procedure-regulating norms argued for here. In *Continued Suspension*, the disputing parties had asked that the Appellate Body's substantive hearing be made public. A number of third participants objected based on Article 17(10) of the DSU – which candidly establishes the confidentiality of appellate proceedings. The Appellate Body essentially agreed with those third participants on

WT/DS152/R, adopted 27 January 2000. See also the discussion held in a 1988 GATT Council Session on unilateralism during the GATT days, reproduced in GATT Council, Discussion on Unilateral Measures, 8–9 February 1989, GATT doc C/163, 16 March 1989.

[40] Article 41(1), VCLT is also discussed in Chapter 2 as a pro-party autonomy provision. Article 58(1)(b), VCLT is similarly drafted, but applies to suspensions rather than modifications of treaty provisions.

[41] It would also be possible to refer to the principles of good faith or estoppel independently of Article 3(10) of the DSU. See discussion in Chapter 4.

[42] See Pauwelyn, *Conflict of Norms.*

[43] Appellate Body Report, *US – Continued Suspension*, Annex VI, para. 6.

the existence of a confidentiality requirement applicable for hearings in Article 17(10) of the DSU. Notwithstanding that recognition, it held that the confidentiality requirement was not "absolute."[44] The Appellate Body's reasoning structure could apply to the recognition of procedural effect for preferential agreements' preclusion clauses:

> There are different sets of relationships that are implicated in appellate proceedings. Among them are the following relationships. First, a relationship between the participants and the Appellate Body. Secondly, a relationship between the third participants and the Appellate Body. The requirement that the proceedings of the Appellate Body are confidential affords protection to these separate relationships and is intended to safeguard the interests of the participants and third participants and the adjudicative function of the Appellate Body, so as to foster the system of dispute settlement under conditions of fairness, impartiality, independence and integrity. In this case, the participants have *jointly requested* authorization to forego confidentiality protection for their communications with the Appellate Body at the oral hearing. The request of the participants does not extend to any communications, *nor touches upon the relationship, between the third participants and the Appellate Body. The right to confidentiality of third participants vis-à-vis the Appellate Body is not implicated by the joint request*. The question is thus whether the request of the participants to forego confidentiality protection satisfies the requirements of *fairness and integrity* that are the essential attributes of the appellate process and define the relationship between the Appellate Body and the participants. If the request meets these standards, then the Appellate Body would incline towards authorizing such a joint request.[45]

The view espoused herein derives from the customary rules embodied in the VCLT. Under these rules, preclusion clauses may apply independently of any consideration based on Article XXIV of the GATT or analogous rules as to the permissibility of free trade areas or customs unions. As a consequence, even preclusion clauses not derived from preferential trade agreements could also apply in WTO dispute settlement.[46] Still, if there remains any doubt regarding the application of preclusion clauses from preferential trade agreements specifically, Article XXIV of the GATT or the rules analogous to it strongly supports

[44] *Ibid.*, para. 4. The Appellate Body found a workable solution to protect the interests of third parties while allowing public viewing of the hearing. The hearing was transmitted in closed circuit on the WTO premises, and interventions of third-party participants that did not agree to waive confidentiality of their statements were not transmitted. See *ibid.*, para. 11.

[45] *Ibid.*, para. 6 (emphasis added).

[46] See discussion in Chapter 2 regarding the principle of party autonomy.

the argument.[47] As discussed before, both substantive and procedural provisions permitted under Article XXIV of the GATT must be recognizable at the WTO.

In sum, while Article 23 is drafted as an exclusive jurisdiction clause, it operates in a relational manner. Preclusion clauses in preferential agreements may be thus recognized in WTO dispute settlement. What really matters is that Article 23 of the DSU is not an absolute jurisdiction clause, an insurmountable barrier for WTO panels to decline from ruling on the merits of a given case brought under WTO rules. In particular, if there is a non-WTO law preclusion clause and the issue is actively pleaded before a panel, a WTO complaint contrary to that clause can be held inadmissible.

7.3 Fork-in-the-road clauses

7.3.1 *Fork-in-the-road clauses generally*

So-called "fork-in-the-road" or *electa una via* clauses provide that once a party has opted to submit a dispute to a given forum, that choice is irreversible and the party is precluded from taking the dispute to another forum. Fork-in-the-road clauses assume considerable latitude for strategic forum selection, but once the choice is made, they offer grounds for preliminary objections against parallel and serial litigation. The key objective of fork-in-the-road clauses is to avoid the multiplication of litigation. Therefore, they are fit for coordinating dispute settlement within a subject area where international tribunals' jurisdiction is significantly juxtaposed. In this sense, fork-in-the-road clauses are typically less concerned about the allocative function of procedure-regulating norms, and more concerned about the balance between the enabling and protective functions, after the first forum is seized. They establish horizontal procedural organization: the multiple forums are deemed to be abstractly equivalent, but a second try is prevented.

Fork-in-the-road provisions are common in international investment agreements, where they normally provide for a definitive choice between national courts or arbitration; in preferential trade agreements, where the split roads are dispute settlement under the

[47] In this case, however, the basis for recognizing the modification would not be Article 41(1)(b) of the VCLT, but Article 41(1)(a), since the modification would be authorized under Article XXIV of the GATT.

preferential trade agreement or the WTO; and in human rights treaties, many of which preclude resort to more than one treaty body for the same matter. Their use in international investment agreements sits well with the objective of protecting investors while avoiding a multiplicity of actions before different forums. In international trade and human rights mechanisms, the large number of bodies and substantial similarity of obligations deriving from different treaties are particular reasons why states have explicitly included them.

A key challenge that frequently arises in applying fork-in-the-road clauses, as with other preclusion techniques, is to decide on the identity of matters or disputes for purposes of recognizing the preclusive effect. One way to dissect that challenge is to depict it as a twofold exercise. First, adjudicators determine the *type of identity* that they must seek to discern: either *substantive* or *formal* identity of the basis for the legal claims (cause of action) at stake in the parallel or serial proceedings. Second, adjudicators decide on the *degree of identity* they should ascertain: *substantial* or *strict* identity. These two steps determine the fate of a fork-in-the-road clause as a preclusion norm when the question of identity of disputes is at stake, and many preclusion clauses are drafted with identity of disputes as a background. Regarding the type of identity sought (substantive versus formal), it is suggested that, if fork-in-the-road clauses are to be given effect a formal assessment of the identity of legal claims would not be appropriate. There are cogent logic-juridical and policy reasons for this. From a logic-juridical perspective, a matter consists of the factual and legal aspects of the case (i.e., the claims and basis for the claims). Any given set of parallel or serial cases before different tribunals is practically fated to be formally different, for tribunals are often granted principal jurisdiction along specific treaty lines: WTO panels have jurisdiction over legal claims founded on WTO rules, a preferential trade tribunal would have jurisdiction over legal claims founded on the given preferential agreement. Hence, if the sole fact that a claim is based on a different instrument suffices as ground for distinguishing between a WTO case and a preferential trade agreement case, fork-in-the-road clauses will hardly ever apply.[48]

However, if that were the intention of treaty drafters, fork-in-the-road clauses (and indeed preclusion clauses) would be difficult to explain.

[48] For this view, see, for example, Gabrielle Marceau, 'Conflicts of Norms and Conflicts of Jurisdictions: The Relationship between the WTO Agreement and MEAs and other Treaties,' 35 *JWT* (2001) 1081.

Since treaty drafters must have intended to provide fork-in-the-road clauses the ability to produce effects when including numerous such clauses in agreements, these norms call for a *substantive* as opposed to a formal examination of identity in two sets of proceedings. From a policy perspective, looking for substantive as opposed to formal identity does not imply that coordination will be attempted and achieved at all costs. Rather, it merely leaves the window open for procedural coordination in case it is appropriate. The substantive perspective praised here has been confirmed by investment arbitral tribunals and human rights bodies, as discussed below. Streamlining the discussion on the need for a substantive examination of identity into the trade dispute settlement scholarly debate and practice would be important. Moreover, the call for a substantive as opposed to a formal assessment of identity is significant not only for fork-in-the-road clauses, but also for other principles and rules on preclusion, such as subsidiary jurisdiction rules, preferential jurisdiction rules, *lis pendens*, and *res judicata*, discussed below.

The second part of the assessment of identity refers to the degree of identity sought (*substantial* or *strict* identity). As with the type of identity, that exercise is relevant for the application of a number of other preclusion techniques. Generally, a determination about the degree of identity requires a thorough examination of the three traditional elements of identification: the identity of parties, matter, and requests. This book leans toward substantial identity of each of the three elements as a trigger to preclusion, as opposed to strict identity. Again, requiring strict identity would *ab initio* significantly narrow the potential to cope with forum shopping and to coordinate substantially similar sets of cases by means of preliminary objections. Nonetheless, it is difficult to draw hard lines to define substantial identity for present purposes. The number of potential situations, nuances, and complexities is enormous and justifies a case-by-case assessment.

7.3.2 Fork-in-the-road clauses in the investment arbitration context

In international investment agreements, fork-in-the-road clauses essentially have three styles. The simplest establish domestic courts versus international arbitration as alternative options for settling investment disputes without explicitly providing that the choice of forum cannot be altered. An example is Article 10(2) of the Albania–Greece BIT, interpreted as precluding parallel litigation before national courts of the host state and investment arbitral tribunals.[49] The provision states, in relevant part, that "either party may submit the dispute either to the competent court of the Contracting Party or to an international arbitral tribunal."[50] A second category of fork-in-the-road clauses explicitly provides that the claimant's choice between submitting the dispute to domestic courts of the host state or to international arbitration is definitive.[51] The Argentina–China BIT provides an example: "where an investor has submitted a dispute to the aforementioned competent tribunal of the Contracting Party where the investment has been made or to international arbitration, this choice shall be final."[52] A third type of fork-in-the-road clause applies to domestic courts versus international arbitration, and also to the specific international arbitration mechanism resorted to vis-à-vis other arbitration options available. For instance, Colombia's 2007 Model BIT allows investors to choose from among competent domestic tribunals of the host state, ad hoc arbitration under UNCITRAL rules, ICSID or ICSID Additional Facility's arbitration, or arbitration under any other arbitration institution or rules.[53] However, a fork-in-the-road clause thereafter makes the choice of procedure always final.[54]

Investor-state arbitration cases where fork-in-the-road clauses have been discussed basically revolve around an alleged choice of domestic courts by the investor as precluding arbitration. Arbitral tribunals have required a high degree of identity of parties and subject matter between the disputes and have frequently dismissed the objection based on the fork-in-the-road clause.[55] With support in a series of previous cases, Schreuer distills three elements for a preclusion to operate based on a fork-in-the-road clause: (i) domestic proceedings must have been instituted prior to the choice of arbitral tribunal, (ii) the disputes

[49] *Pantechniki S.A. Contractors & Engineers (Greece)* v. *Albania*, ICSID Case No ARB/07/21, Award of 28 July 2009.

[50] Article 10(2), Agreement between the Hellenic Republic and the Government of the Republic of Albania for the Encouragement and Reciprocal Protection of Investments (Albania–Greece BIT).

[51] See also Christoph Schreuer, 'Travelling the BIT Route: Of Waiting Periods, Umbrella Clauses and Forks in the Road,' 5 *JWIT* (2004) 231.

[52] Article 8(3), Agreement between the Government of the People's Republic of China and the Government of the Argentine Republic on the Promotion and Reciprocal Protection of Investments.

[53] Article IX(4), Colombia's Model BIT (2007).

[54] Article IX(7), Colombia's Model BIT (2007).

[55] See, for example, *Alex Genin, Eastern Credit Limited Inc and A.S. Baltoil* v. *Estonia*, ICSID Case No ARB/99/2, Award of 18 June 2001, paras. 330–4.

must be identical, and (iii) the parties must be identical.[56] He argues that a high degree of identity should be used as a threshold for preclusion essentially because investors may be dragged into domestic litigation for various reasons, and legal action for limited purposes related to the investment should not be tantamount to an option for domestic courts. Put briefly, the enabling function of jurisdictional rules would score high on this account, and one ought not to lightly presume an actual choice of forum based on the sole fact that the investor has litigated before domestic courts. By contrast, where the investor opts for one among multiple available international arbitral forums, concerns related to the enabling function would not be as strong. Hence, in those circumstances, it is the protective function of fork-in-the-road clauses to the host states that should not be assessed lightly.

In any event, one may question whether setting too high an identity threshold to give effect to a fork-in-the-road clause even in the domestic court versus international arbitration context may not, in practice, nullify the protective function of such norms to host states. Although the possibility to seek international remedies by investors should not lightly be curtailed, this is a question of interpretation of the relevant instruments and it is appropriate to consider the matter from a substantive perspective. An interesting decision along these lines is *Pantechniki* v. *Albania*. This appears to be the first time that a fork-in-the-road clause precluded an investor claim in the ICSID context. The case involved two contracts for the construction of roads and bridges. The contracts attributed the risk of losses for civil disturbances to Albania, the host state. In 2007, violent incidents resulted in the destruction or stealing of the investor's property. After an agreement between the investor and branches of the Albanian government was allegedly unfulfilled, Pantechniki attempted to enforce its alleged contractual right to compensation before Albanian courts. The claims were denied on essentially public policy grounds – according to Albanian courts, the clause attributing objective responsibility to Albania would be contrary to Albanian law. Pantechniki appealed to the Albanian Supreme Court, but before the conclusion of those proceedings turned to ICSID arbitration, withdrawing the pending appeal.

Whereas Albania objected to a ruling of merit based on the fork-in-the-road provision, Article 10(2) of the BIT, the investor relied on the traditional distinction between contract claims and treaty claims.

[56] Schreuer, 'Travelling the BIT Route,' at 248.

Pantechniki considered that the pursuit of compensation domestically had exclusively regarded its contractual rights and that the right to resort to arbitration for treaty-based rights remained intact. However, the arbitrator essentially upheld Albania's objection.[57] For him, it was common ground that the test was whether the "fundamental basis" of the claim brought before the arbitral forum was autonomous of claims to be heard elsewhere. Based on this premise, he rejected that formal identity was necessary for the fork-in-the-road clause to apply. He reasoned that the investor's argument was "reduced to the mere assertion that claims based on Treaty provisions are inherently different from those it pursued as a contractor. This is argument by labeling – not by analysis."[58] He thus assessed whether the "same purported entitlement" that the claimant had invoked "in the contractual debate" was being invoked through international arbitration. He answered that question in the affirmative and declined to rule on the merits of most claims by Pantechniki. Conversely, he proceeded to the analysis of merit for those claims which could be said to have an independent basis under the treaty and had not been necessarily involved in the Albanian court action – based on full protection and security and denial of justice grounds.[59] The *Pantechniki* approach is an interesting reminder that a mere formal lack of identity of disputes, say, because the source of the claim may be different (contract versus treaty, in that case), should not be a reason to automatically disregard a procedure-regulating norm out of hand (in that case, a fork-in-the-road clause in the investment treaty). Rather, to give practical effect to fork-in-the-road clauses, it is important to apply them based on the substantive identity of the matter.

Requesting a complete waiver of claims when investors opt for international arbitration over a measure by the host state is an interesting alternative approach to preclusion. This approach preserves some features of a fork-in-the-road approach, while taking into account the investors' ostensible preference for international arbitration. Requesting a waiver may afford the investor an opportunity to pursue domestic litigation, while international arbitration remains an option. However, when the investor opts for international arbitration, it should declare that such choice is final as a condition for arbitration to move

[57] Except for the claims which did not share the same fundamental basis as the contractual claims pursued before domestic courts.

[58] *Pantechniki* v. *Albania*, para. 61. [59] *Ibid.*, paras. 62–8.

forward. An interesting example is NAFTA Article 1121, which focuses on the identity of the *measure* in dispute rather than on the identity of *dispute* and avoids the difficult question of identity of dispute discussed above.[60] Moreover, the provision's inclusion of both the investors and the parties controlled by them emphasizes the economic unity over and above formal identity of parties.[61]

7.3.3 *Fork-in-the-road clauses in the human rights context*

Other areas of the law such as human rights also encounter the recurrent question about the application of standards of identity for assessing parallel and serial litigation. A number of human rights instruments include fork-in-the-road provisions.[62] As the right of individual application provided for by various human rights instruments frequently covers substantially similar protective norms on both the multilateral and regional levels, the potential for forum shopping across international bodies is significant. Serial litigation at the UN Human Rights Committee (HRC) after litigation before the European Court of Human Rights (ECtHR) offers interesting examples. Article 35(2)(b) of the European Convention on Human Rights (ECHR) provides a restriction on the admissibility of individual applications that are "substantially the same as a matter that has already been submitted to another procedure of international investigation or settlement and contains no relevant new information."[63] On the other hand, Article 5(2)(a) of the Optional Protocol to the International Covenant on Civil and Political

[60] Article 1121, NAFTA, reads in relevant part: "A disputing investor may submit a claim under Article 1116 to arbitration only if: (a) the investor consents ...; and (b) the *investor and, where the claim is for loss or damage to an interest in an enterprise of another Party that is a juridical person that the investor owns or controls directly or indirectly, the enterprise*, waive their right to initiate or continue before any administrative tribunal or court under the law of any Party, or other dispute settlement procedures, any proceedings with respect to *the measure of the disputing Party that is alleged to be a breach* ..." (emphasis added).

[61] See also Campbell McLachlan, Lis Pendens *in International Litigation* (The Hague: Martinus Nijhoff, 2009), at 267–8.

[62] See, for example, Article 22(5)(a), Convention against Torture and Other Cruel, Inhuman or Degrading Treatment or Punishment, 1465 *UNTS* 113; Article 4(2)(a), Optional Protocol to the Convention on the Elimination of All Forms of Discrimination against Women, 2131 *UNTS* 83; Article 77(3)(a), International Convention on the Protection of the Rights of All Migrant Workers and Members of Their Families, 2220 *UNTS* 3; Article 3(2)(c), Optional Protocol to the International Covenant on Economic, Social and Cultural Rights, adopted 10 December 2008, UN doc. A/63/435.

[63] Article 35(2)(b), ECHR.

Rights (ICCPR) states that the Committee shall not consider communication from individuals unless it has ascertained that "the same matter is not being examined under another procedure of international investigation or settlement."[64]

The textual difference between Article 5(2)(a) of the Optional Protocol to the ICCPR and Article 35(2)(b) of the ECHR can be relevant in two ways. First, the admissibility bar in Article 5(2)(a) of the Optional Protocol to the ICCPR applies only to matters *being examined* under another procedure. Put simply, Article 5(2)(a) is not strictly speaking a fork-in-the-road clause. Rather, it is akin to a rule of *lis pendens*.[65] Accordingly, individuals may petition the ECtHR under the European Convention and, after the matter has been examined there, resubmit their claims under the ICCPR to the HRC.[66] For example, in views made public on 7 January 2011, the HRC confirmed the rejection of a plea of inadmissibility by Greece because the same communication had already been examined by the ECtHR and the ECJ.[67] This is clear recognition that Article 5(2)(a) applies only to parallel litigation and is no bar to serial litigation. The recognition is no novelty, to be sure. In 1968, a Committee of Experts mandated by the Council of Europe to study problems arising from the existence of the ECtHR and the HRC as two independent control systems spotted the possibility of serial litigation before the HRC of claims previously decided by the ECtHR.[68] The Committee of Experts then

[64] Article 5(2)(a), Optional Protocol to the ICCPR, 999 *UNTS* 171.

[65] See discussion on *lis pendens* in Section 7.7 below.

[66] But see the discussion on *res judicata* in Section 7.6 below. The lack of discussion on the application of *res judicata* as a complementary objection to the admissibility of human rights-based petitions may be due to a perceived lack of judicial nature on the part of monitoring bodies by states, and to the reservations appended to the Optional Protocol to the ICCPR expanding the scope of preclusion to cases of serial litigation. It should also be noted that other, more recent human rights instruments have covered both parallel and serial litigation, correcting the (apparent) slip in the Optional Protocol to the ICCPR. See, for instance, Article 22(5)(a), Convention against Torture and Other Cruel, Inhuman or Degrading Treatment or Punishment; Article 4(2)(a), Optional Protocol to the Convention on the Elimination of All Forms of Discrimination against Women; Article 77(3)(a), International Convention on the Protection of the Rights of All Migrant Workers and Members of Their Families; Article 3(2)(c), Optional Protocol to the International Covenant on Economic, Social and Cultural Rights.

[67] *Panagiotis A. Sechremelis, Loukas G. Sechremelis and Angeliki widow of Ioannis Balagouras* v. *Greece*, Communication No 1507/2006, UN doc. CCPR/C/100/D/1507/2006/Rev.1, 7 January 2011, para. 6.2. See also *Frantisek Brychta* v. *Czech Republic*, Communication No 1618/2007, UN doc. CCPR/C/91/D/1618/2007, 26 November 2009, para. 6.2.

[68] Report of the Committee of Experts to the Committee of Ministers of the Council of Europe, Problems Arising from the Co-existence of the United Nations Covenants

recommended that member states of the Council of Europe append a declaration when ratifying the Optional Protocol to the ICCPR. The declaration was meant to make clear that matters previously litigated in Strasbourg could not be relitigated under the Optional Protocol.[69] Many European states have resorted to this type of reservation (Greece did not),[70] which the Committee has considered compatible with the objective of securing independent third-party review of human rights under the ICCPR.[71]

Second, the requisite degree of identity of matters in Articles 5(2)(a) of the Optional Protocol (i.e., "same matter") and Article 35(2)(b) of the ECHR (i.e., "substantially the same matter") is not textually the same. Questions then arise about what the identity threshold is and whether the threshold under the Optional Protocol is stricter than the one set forth in Article 35(2)(b) of the European Convention. Writing in 1999, Laurence Helfer argued that human rights bodies had inconsistently assessed dispute identity in cases of forum shopping.[72] This book agrees with Helfer that this was highly unfortunate, for it created confusion for petitioners and defending states about the disciplines on forum shopping. After Helfer, Yuval Shany has reviewed the practice of the HRC. Shany has referred, with support, to a "gradual erosion of the *electa una via* defence" with the progressive narrowing of the scope of preclusion by the application of stricter degrees of identity.[73] For instance, in approving the fork-in-the-road-like reservations to Article 5(2)(a) of the Optional Protocol to the ICCPR just discussed, the HRC in General

on Human Rights and the European Convention on Human Rights, doc. CM(68)39E / 29 February 1968.

69 The suggested draft of the declaration, which several states used as a model for reservations to the Optional Protocol to the ICCPR, reads as follows: "The Government of … ratifies the Optional Protocol … on the understanding that the provisions of Article 5(2) of the Protocol mean that the Committee provided for in Article 28 of that Covenant shall not consider any communication from an individual unless the Committee has ascertained that the same matter is not being examined or has not been examined under another procedure of international investigation or settlement" (*ibid.*, at 11).

70 Therefore, it was not necessary for the HRC to decide whether *Panagiotis A. Sechremelis* v. *Greece* had already been examined by the ECtHR.

71 See Human Rights Committee, 'Issues relating to reservations made upon ratification or accession to the Covenant or the Optional Protocols thereto, or in relation to declarations under article 41 of the Covenant,' General Comment 24, UN doc. CCPR/C/21/Rev.1/Add.6.

72 Laurence Helfer, 'Forum Shopping for Human Rights,' 148 *U Penn L Rev* (1999) 285.

73 Yuval Shany, *The Competing Jurisdictions of International Courts and Tribunals* (Oxford University Press, 2003) at 216.

Comment 24 reasoned that the reservations applied only "where the legal right and the subject matter are *identical* under the Covenant and under another international instrument."[74] This "erosion" of the defense, to use Shany's words, reduces the possibility of coordination across human rights bodies and increases the potential for parallel and serial litigation.

Strongly upholding the enabling function of procedural rules (i.e., eroding the *electa una via* objection) would be generally in line with the objective of securing maximum protection of human rights. Moreover, the human rights system is peculiar for various reasons: the likely overwhelming unbalance between the parties (i.e., individuals, who may not be fully aware of the hurdles to petition; versus states, repeated and more equipped players), the different remedial powers available (i.e., bodies with binding or recommendatory powers), and the different stages of development of the monitoring bodies. These peculiarities may be reasons for a narrower approach to preclusion than in other areas of the law. Still, two cases more recently decided suggest that the HRC is ready to uphold objections to serial litigation through an assessment based on *substantive* and *substantial* identity of matters rather than on *formal* and *strict* identity, notwithstanding the textual difference of Article 5(2)(a) of the Optional Protocol and Article 35(2)(b) of the European Convention. Generally, the HRC uses a triple standard to assess the degree of identity of matters: (i) same authors, (ii) same facts, and (iii) same substantive rights.[75] In applying the third prong of the standard in recent cases (same substantive rights), the Committee has taken for granted that the normative source of the rights will be different, thus assessing substantive as opposed to formal identity. Moreover, the Committee has focused on the substance of the prior examination by another body (in this case, the ECtHR), even though there may not be mathematical identity between the cases, thus assessing substantial as opposed to strict identity.

[74] Human Rights Committee, 'Issues relating to reservations,' General Comment 24.

[75] This standard was articulated and applied in *Ruppert Althamer* v. *Austria*, Communication No 998/2001, UN doc. CCPR/C/78/D/998/2001, 22 September 2003, para. 8.4, where the HRC considered the application admissible in light of the different matters at stake in the subsequent proceedings. The two other cases discussed below started from basically the same standard but concluded, in the circumstances, that the application was inadmissible because the matters were the same.

Consider, first, *Béatrice Marin* v. *France*.[76] Ms Marin failed an examination for recruitment of administrative judges in France. She contested the result and considered that the procedure to fight the examination was tainted. She did not succeed in obtaining relief domestically and resorted to the ECtHR, claiming that her right to a fair trial under Article 6(1) of the European Convention had been violated. Nevertheless, in the view of the ECtHR the procedure she was contesting did not concern either an appeal of her civil rights and obligations or the determination of any criminal charges against her within the meaning of Article 6 of the ECHR. This led the ECtHR to dismiss the suit for lack of a colorable case. Ms Marin subsequently turned to the HRC under the Optional Protocol to the ICCPR, claiming a violation of her right to a fair trial under Article 14(1) of the ICCPR. France then objected to the communication based on its reservation to Article 5(2)(a), arguing that the HRC should not have competence to consider a communication from an individual if the same matter is being examined or has been considered under another procedure. The HRC sided with France. It emphasized that the two cases "related to the principle of equality before the courts and tribunals on the same grounds."[77] Therefore, the Committee did not find it relevant that the sources of the rights and obligations before it and the ECtHR were formally different.

With regard to the degree of identity, although the detailed reasoning is hard to pierce, strict identity would also not be required. A case in point is *Edith Loth – and her heirs* v. *Germany*.[78] That communication dealt more directly (albeit succinctly) with the required degree of identity of matters. It involved Ms Loth's obligatory surrender to German tax authorities of land she had inherited, without compensation. Ms Loth unsuccessfully argued before the ECtHR that the obligation to reassign the land to German authorities infringed her rights (i) to the peaceful enjoyment of possessions under Article 1 of the ECHR and (ii) to not be discriminated against under Article 14 of the same Convention.[79] After

[76] *Béatrice Marin* v. *France*, Communication No 1793/2008, UN doc. CCPR/C/99/D/1793/2008, 14 September 2010.

[77] *Ibid.*, para. 6.3.

[78] *Edith Loth – and her heirs* v. *Germany*, Communication No 1754/2008, UN doc. CCPR/C/98/D/1755/2008, 21 May 2010.

[79] See *Case of Jahn and others* v. *Germany*, Applications Nos 46720/99, 72203/01 and 72552/01 Judgment of the Grand Chamber, 30 June 2005. Article 14, ECHR states: "The enjoyment of the rights and freedoms set forth in this Convention shall be secured without discrimination on any ground…"

the ECtHR's negative decision, she turned to the HRC. Her claim was based on Article 26 of the ICCPR which, as Ms Loth (and subsequently her heirs)[80] argued and the Committee agreed, offers greater protection than Article 14 of the European Convention.[81] Moreover, the authors emphasized that one aspect of the discrimination claim before the Committee had not been examined by the ECtHR. The HRC also appeared to agree with that. However, Germany objected to the admissibility of the communication based on its reservation to Article 5(2)(a) of the Optional Protocol – a reservation equivalent to the French one just referred to. The HRC affirmed the preclusive force of Germany's reservation with the following reasoning:

> [T]he independent right to equality and nondiscrimination in article 26 of the Covenant provides greater protection than the accessory right to non-discrimination contained in article 14 of the European Convention ... However the Committee notes that the authors are claiming to *have been broadly discriminated against on the basis of the deceased's property title*. It also notes that the European Court has examined whether the deceased *was discriminated against in connection with the enjoyment of her property*. To do so, the Court examined and assessed the treatment made by the legislator with respect to her property title and compared it with treatment of other categories of "new settlers' inheritors". The fact that the Court did not consider whether the deceased was discriminated against in comparison to an entirely separate category of property owners, "the Modrow purchasers", who bore no relationship to the deceased, does not detract from the fact that *the same substantive issue was considered* by the Court. Consequently, the Committee concludes that the "same matter" has been considered by the European Court...[82]

The HRC thus considered both cases to "relate to the same right of non-discrimination on the same grounds"[83] after a substantial evaluation of identity of matters. Before the ECtHR, a claim of discrimination was assessed relative to an alleged violation of the right to property. Before the HRC, a claim of discrimination was being pursued in connection

[80] Ms Loth passed away during the examination of her communication to Committee. Her heirs continued the claims.

[81] Article 26, ICCPR, 999 *UNTS* 171: "All persons are equal before the law and are entitled without any discrimination to the equal protection of the law. In this respect, the law shall prohibit any discrimination and guarantee to all persons equal and effective protection against discrimination on any ground..." Thus, while Article 14, ECHR is limited to "rights and freedoms set forth" in the ECHR, Article 26, ICCPR extends to "equality before the law" generally and guarantees "to all persons equal and effective protection against discrimination on any ground."

[82] *Edith Loth* v. *Germany*, para. 6.4 (footnotes omitted, emphasis added).

[83] *Ibid.*, para. 6.3.

with the property expropriated. The fact that the right to equality was formulated differently in the two instruments, in the circumstances, did not cause the matters to be different because the question facing both bodies was effectively the same. Moreover, the HRC did not find it relevant that the nuances of the claim on discrimination before the ECtHR and the Committee were different, since the same "substantive issue" had been considered in Strasbourg. According to the HRC, the lack of consideration of one aspect of the discrimination claim did not "detract from the fact that the same substantive issue was considered." Taking *Béatrice Marin* and *Edith Loth* together as a result, one can question whether the "gradual erosion of the *electa una via* defense" found by Shany is yet an identifiable trend. In the cases reviewed, the HRC has instead favored a case-by-case, substantive, and substantial assessment of identity.

7.3.4 Fork-in-the-road clauses in the international trade context

The outburst of preferential trade agreements has prompted not only a spaghetti bowl of regional and multilateral substantive trade rules, but also a complex web of dispute-settlement forums for claims that may be substantially similar. For instance, multilateral and myriad preferential trade agreements discipline national treatment and the technical barriers to trade, or resort to trade remedies. Amid several similar rights and obligations across the preferential and multilateral trade levels, preferential agreements have increasingly included fork-in-the-road clauses. Thus, NAFTA Article 2005(1) allows the complaining party to opt for the forum (i.e., NAFTA or the WTO) in disputes regarding matters arising under both the NAFTA and the GATT.[84] However, Article 2005(6) provides that, once dispute-settlement proceedings have been initiated, the forum selected shall be used to the exclusion of the other.[85] Many other preferential trade agreements are equipped with analogous fork-in-the-road clauses.[86]

[84] Article 2005(1), NAFTA: "Subject to paragraphs 2, 3 and 4, disputes regarding any matter arising under both this Agreement and the *General Agreement on Tariffs and Trade*, any agreement negotiated thereunder, or any successor agreement (GATT), may be settled in either forum at the discretion of the complaining Party."

[85] Article 2005(6), NAFTA: "Once dispute settlement procedures have been initiated under Article 2007 or dispute settlement proceedings have been initiated under the GATT, the forum selected shall be used to the exclusion of the other, unless a Party makes a request pursuant to paragraph 3 or 4."

[86] See, for example, Article 1.2, Olivos Protocol; Article 139, Agreement between Japan and the Republic of Singapore for a New-Age Economic Partnership

The preclusive effect of fork-in-the-road clauses such as NAFTA Article 2005(6) in WTO dispute settlement remains open, as discussed in Chapter 5. One explanation for this occurrence is that such provisions have not been expressly raised by respondents in previous cases. It should be noted that potential cases to date where preclusion clauses could have been at stake at the WTO essentially involved disputes between NAFTA parties.[87] In the one case that did not involve NAFTA parties, Argentina expressly objected to Brazil's alleged serial litigation of anti-dumping measures on poultry before MERCOSUR and then the WTO. In the circumstances, the MERCOSUR fork-in-the-road clause was not in force and was thus not available to Argentina. Nevertheless, this episode does indicate that the NAFTA parties' approach to preclusion clauses is by no means the only possible approach.[88] In *Poultry Anti-Dumping Duties*, pitting Brazil versus Argentina, the reason expressed by the panel as to why a preclusion clause did not change its assessment was clear enough. Essentially, the MERCOSUR preclusion clause was not in force then and did not apply to disputes already decided under the Protocol of Brasilia:

> There is no evidence on the record that Brazil made an express statement that it would not bring WTO dispute settlement proceedings in respect of measures previously challenged through MERCOSUR. Nor does the record indicate exceptional circumstances requiring us to imply any such statement... We note that Brazil signed the Protocol of Olivos in February 2002. Article 1 of the Protocol of Olivos provides that once a party decides to bring a case under either the MERCOSUR or WTO dispute settlement forums, that party may not

(Japan–Singapore New-Age Economic Partnership). See Kwak and Marceau, 'Overlaps and Conflicts of Jurisdiction' for an illustrative table containing several other examples of preferential trade agreements with fork-in-the-road provisions.

87 See Appellate Body Report, *United States – Measures Concerning the Importation, Marketing and Sale of Tuna and Tuna Products*, WT/DS381/AB/R, adopted 13 June 2012; Appellate Body Report, *Mexico – Tax Measures on Soft Drinks and Other Beverages*, WT/DS308/AB/R, adopted 24 March 2006; Panel Report, WT/DS308/R, adopted 24 March 2006, as modified by Appellate Body Report WT/DS308/AB/R; Appellate Body Report, *Canada – Certain Measures Concerning Periodicals*, WT/DS31/AB/R, adopted 30 July 1997, DSR 1997:I, 449; Panel Report, WT/DS31/R and Corr.1, adopted 30 July 1997, as modified by Appellate Body Report WT/DS31/AB/R.

88 The EU's readiness to invoke estoppel-based arguments and defenses from other agreements in WTO dispute settlement indicates that its posture may also be different than that of NAFTA parties. See, for example, Appellate Body Report, *European Communities – Export Subsidies on Sugar*, WT/DS265/AB/R, WT/DS266/AB/R, WT/DS283/AB/R, adopted 19 May 2005; Panel Report, *European Communities and Certain Member States – Measures Affecting Trade in Large Civil Aircraft*, WT/DS316/R, adopted 1 June 2011, as modified by Appellate Body Report WT/DS316/AB/R.

bring a subsequent case regarding the same subject-matter in the other forum. The Protocol of Olivos, however, does not change our assessment, since that Protocol has not yet entered into force, and in any event it does not apply in respect of disputes already decided in accordance with the MERCOSUR Protocol of Brasilia. Indeed, the fact that parties to MERCOSUR saw the need to introduce the Protocol of Olivos suggests to us that they recognised that (in the absence of such Protocol) a MERCOSUR dispute settlement proceeding could be followed by a WTO dispute settlement proceeding in respect of the same measure.[89]

Should a fork-in-the-road clause ever apply in WTO dispute settlement, then the same questions addressed in the context of investment arbitration and human rights would arise, namely (i) the relevance of the formal source of law in the assessment of identity and (ii) the degree of identity required. Regarding the former question, as discussed in the investment and human rights contexts, it is submitted that the formal source of the claims should normally have no bearing on the assessment of identity, since that source is likely to be different in all events. Naturally, the formal source of claims before WTO panels and in proceedings before a preferential trade tribunal will be different as a matter of principle. It need not invariably follow, however, that WTO and preferential agreements cases are always "different." A fork-in-the-road provision's very starting point is the recognition that a given matter may arise under two different agreements. Because this raises concerns, trade partners use preclusion clauses to preclude parallel or serial litigation of such (formally) "different" matters. Accordingly, an assessment of identity should be based on the substantive equivalence of the rights and obligations at stake rather than on their formal source. Concerning the degree of identity required for the preclusion to operate, adjudicators should not seek to find a mathematical equivalence between the disputes or matters. As a matter of treaty-text, Article 139(3) of Japan–Singapore's New-Age Economic Partnership Agreement provides an interesting approach. Pursuant to that provision, the fork-in-the-road clause does not apply when "substantially separate and distinct rights or obligations under different international agreements are in dispute."[90] To be sure, Article 139(3) does not define "substantially separate and distinct rights." However, the inclusion of Article

[89] See Panel Report, *Argentina – Definitive Anti-Dumping Duties on Poultry from Brazil*, WT/DS241/R, adopted 19 May 2003, para. 7.38 (footnotes omitted).

[90] Article 139(3), Japan–Singapore New-Age Economic Partnership.

139(3) and its emphasis on "substantially separate and distinct" makes it clear that strict identity is not required for the clause to apply.

7.4 Subsidiary jurisdiction clauses

Subsidiary jurisdiction clauses establish that a tribunal's jurisdiction or the admissibility of the complaint before that tribunal is subject to the lack or unavailability of another forum to try the issue. For instance, the Organization for Security and Co-operation in Europe (OSCE) Convention on Conciliation and Arbitration provides in Article 19(1)(a) that an arbitral tribunal under the convention shall take no further action if the dispute has already been submitted to a court or tribunal with automatic jurisdiction or if such body has already given a decision on the merits of the dispute,[91] thus targeting both parallel and serial litigation. Further, Article 19(1)(b) addresses choice of forum and states that there should be no further action if the parties have accepted in advance the exclusive jurisdiction of another tribunal or agreed to settle the dispute exclusively by other means.[92] Another peculiarly subsidiary jurisdiction is the International Criminal Court (ICC), under the principle of complementarity in relation to domestic courts.[93]

Perhaps the most notable example of a subsidiary jurisdiction regime is the UNCLOS, whose Articles 280–2 establish a preference for other

[91] Article 19(1)(a), The Convention on Conciliation and Arbitration within the OSCE, OSCE doc SEC/GAL/121/08, 20 June 2008, 71 (OSCE Convention on Conciliation and Arbitration): "1. A Conciliation Commission or an Arbitral Tribunal constituted for a dispute shall take no further action in the case: (a) If, prior to being submitted ..., the dispute has been submitted to a court or tribunal whose jurisdiction in respect of the dispute the parties thereto are under a legal obligation to accept, or if such a body has already given a decision on the merits of the dispute..."

[92] Article 19(1)(b), OSCE Convention on Conciliation and Arbitration: "(b) If the parties to the dispute have accepted in advance the exclusive jurisdiction of a jurisdictional body other than a Tribunal in accordance with this Convention which has jurisdiction to decide, with binding force, on the dispute submitted to it, or if the parties thereto have agreed to seek to settle the dispute exclusively by other means."

[93] Note that the ICC's "subsidiary-jurisdiction" gives rise to a question of admissibility under the ICC Statute. Article 17, ICC Statute reads, in part: "the Court shall determine that a case is inadmissible where: (a) The case is being investigated or prosecuted by a State which has jurisdiction over it, unless the State is unwilling or unable genuinely to carry out the investigation or prosecution; (b) The case has been investigated by a State which has jurisdiction over it and the State has decided not to prosecute the person concerned, unless the decision resulted from the unwillingness or inability of the State genuinely to prosecute."

options for settling disputes, under a direct and vertical model of jurisdictional organization, as discussed in Chapter 5. The subsidiary character of UNCLOS jurisdiction was first proclaimed in *Southern Bluefin Tuna*, which focused on Article 281 of the UNCLOS,[94] and then in *MOX Plant*, with respect to Article 282 of the UNCLOS.[95] In *Southern Bluefin Tuna*, Japan raised an objection to the jurisdiction of the UNCLOS mechanisms on the grounds that the dispute concerned the interpretation and implementation of the 1993 Convention for the Conservation of Southern Bluefin Tuna (CCSBT). According to Japan, the UNCLOS provisions on which the applicants relied were fully covered by the more specific provisions of the CCSBT, including the provisions on the settlement of disputes.[96] For their part, Australia and New Zealand asserted that the dispute also arose under UNCLOS and that, therefore, they had the right to a ruling based on UNCLOS provisions.[97] In the request for provisional measures before the International Tribunal on the Law of the Sea (ITLOS), the ITLOS had found that UNCLOS provisions appeared to afford a basis for jurisdiction[98] and asserted *prima facie* jurisdiction over the dispute. The ITLOS considered that the CCSBT did not "exclude" the applicants' right to invoke UNCLOS dispute settlement with regard to the conservation and management of southern bluefin tuna.[99]

For the arbitral tribunal under Annex VII of the UNCLOS, while the dispute arose under both the CCSBT and UNCLOS, it would be "artificial" to separate the two disputes for the purposes of asserting jurisdiction.[100] But instead of asserting its jurisdiction under the UNCLOS, the tribunal declined jurisdiction based on Article 281(1) of the UNCLOS, which it considered to be covered by Article 16 of the CCSBT.[101] More generally, in the view of the arbitral tribunal, the UNCLOS fell "significantly short of establishing a truly comprehensive regime of compulsory jurisdiction entailing binding decisions." This overall perspective influenced the tribunal's specific interpretation of the combined effect

[94] Article 281(1), UNCLOS is reproduced in Chapter 2 at note 72.
[95] Article 282, UNCLOS is reproduced in Chapter 5 at note 93.
[96] *Southern Bluefin Tuna Case (Australia and New Zealand* v. *Japan)*, Award on Jurisdiction and Admissibility, 4 August 2000, para. 38.
[97] *Ibid.*, para. 41.
[98] *Southern Bluefin Tuna Case (Australia and New Zealand* v. *Japan)*, ITLOS Cases No 3 & 4, Order on Provisional Measures, 27 August 1999, paras. 52 and 62.
[99] *Ibid.*, para. 51.
[100] *Southern Bluefin Tuna*, Jurisdiction and Admissibility, paras. 52, 54.
[101] *Ibid.*, paras. 54–65. Article 16, CCSBT is reproduced in Chapter 2 at note 68.

of Article 281(1) of the UNCLOS and Article 16 of the CCSBT. According to the tribunal, even though Article 16 of the CCSBT was more of a "menu of options" to settle disputes than *a* peaceful means to settle disputes, and despite the fact that Article 16 did not expressly exclude any further procedure as the text of Article 281(1) requires, the combined effect of Article 281(1), UNCLOS and Article 16, CCSBT was that the parties had agreed to attempt to settle their grievance under the CCSBT, and without recourse to UNCLOS. *Southern Bluefin Tuna* therefore illustrates the potential effect of a subsidiary jurisdiction clause: to prevent a judgment of merit where the alternative to the subsidiary jurisdiction should be used.

The decision of the arbitral tribunal in *Southern Bluefin Tuna* has been harshly criticized as detracting from the intention to provide for compulsory settlement of disputes under the UNCLOS.[102] By determining that a single dispute arises under two instruments and then stating that the absence of automatic jurisdiction in one instrument amounts to a derogation of the automatic jurisdiction of the other, the tribunal implies that a framework convention equipped with automatic dispute settlement may lose its teeth whenever an implementation agreement does not provide for automatic jurisdiction. That result arguably undermines dispute-settlement systems in framework conventions such as the UNCLOS. In my view, the critique is well placed: even though the disputes under the UNCLOS and the CCSBT were difficult to slice, the effect of Article 281(1) of the UNCLOS and Article 16 of the CCSBT would not be what the tribunal held. Article 281(1), like other subsidiary jurisdiction clauses, has enabling, protective, and allocative features that ought to be taken into account based on the specific interaction at stake. Its protective feature is to avoid multiplicative litigation while guaranteeing party autonomy. The enabling feature is to offer a subsidiary forum where another means of settlement has not been established. The allocative feature hierarchizes the options of the parties, and places UNCLOS on a subsidiary level in relation to another means of settlement. Considering the vertical, direct model of jurisdictional organization of UNCLOS, there is no allocative concern with respect to the subsidiary jurisdiction if no other jurisdiction is identifiable. In this scenario, the enabling features of a default jurisdiction should clearly dominate.

[102] See, for example, Alan Boyle, 'Some Problems of Compulsory Jurisdiction before Specialised Tribunals. The Law of the Sea,' in Patrick Capps *et al.* (eds.), *Asserting Jurisdiction: International and European Perspectives* (Oxford: Hart, 2003) 243.

Thus, the arbitral tribunal in *Southern Bluefin Tuna* overemphasized the protective function of Article 281(1) in contradiction with its text and overshadowed other important functions of the provision. Article 281(1) precludes dispute settlement under the UNCLOS only to the extent that the parties "have agreed to seek settlement of the dispute by a peaceful means of their own choice." Even then, UNCLOS procedures may apply if no settlement is reached "by recourse to those means" and the agreement of the parties "does not exclude any further procedure." Article 16 of the CCSBT, which sets forth a "menu of options" when it comes to dispute settlement under the CCSBT, is not an agreement to seek settlement by *a* means of choice as stipulated in Article 281(1), UNCLOS. Moreover, Australia, New Zealand, and Japan had not achieved a settlement under the CCSBT. Finally, Article 16 of the CCSBT does not exclude any further procedure. Rather, it leaves open the possibility that any other procedure may be used. In those circumstances, where alternative automatic jurisdiction mechanisms were not available to Australia and New Zealand (alleviating allocative concerns), the enabling features of Article 281(1) should have deserved more consideration.

The subsidiary nature of UNCLOS dispute settlement has also been made clear under Article 282 of the UNCLOS, at the center of the *MOX Plant* stay. In that case, the tribunal found that questions which would be subject to the exclusive jurisdiction of the ECJ were at play in the dispute between Ireland and the United Kingdom.[103] Having been informed that the European Commission was examining whether to institute proceedings against Ireland for violation of Article 292 of the EC Treaty, the UNCLOS arbitral tribunal reasoned that its jurisdiction could be precluded depending on the ECJ's decision.[104] The arbitral tribunal recognized the risk of delay and the possibility that certain UNCLOS provisions might not fall under the exclusive jurisdiction of the ECJ, but considered it inappropriate to proceed with the merits, and decided for a stay.[105] There were four main bases for the tribunal's conclusion that it would be inappropriate to move to the merits. First, the tribunal considered that the ECJ could be seized of the question whether for European Union members' UNCLOS provisions were within the Community competence, thus precluding the

[103] *MOX Plant Case (Ireland* v. *United Kingdom)*, Arbitral Tribunal under ITLOS Annex VII, Order No 3, 24 June 2003, para. 20.

[104] *Ibid.*, paras. 21–3. [105] *Ibid.*, paras. 25–30.

UNCLOS tribunal's jurisdiction entirely.[106] This would give effect to the protective function underlying Article 282 of the UNCLOS, which provides that the UNCLOS dispute settlement is a default mechanism applicable where parties have not agreed to another mechanism entailing binding decisions.[107] Second, the tribunal reasoned that the parties could not themselves clearly identify the provisions outside the competence of the ECJ and within the jurisdiction of the UNCLOS tribunal. Neither did it find it clear whether any such provisions would give rise to a distinct dispute.[108] Thus, the tribunal found itself unable to split up the dispute under UNCLOS from a possible dispute under Community law. This question raised an allocative concern. On the other hand, regarding the enabling function of Article 282 of the UNCLOS, underscored by that provision's insistence on binding decisions, the case did not raise a substantial concern: the parties could not themselves identify the provisions that would be outside the ECJ's exclusive jurisdiction. This both illustrates the complexity of the case and indicates the possibility that the ECJ's exclusivity could be triggered for the whole of the dispute. In sum, a potential denial of justice was not really at stake. Moreover, the UNCLOS tribunal opted for a stay, which is a softer and reversible measure of case management that raises less enabling concerns, as discussed in Chapter 6. Third, the allocative concern was also expressed by the tribunal's keeping in mind considerations of "mutual respect and comity which should prevail between judicial institutions."[109] As a follow-up to inseparability, the tribunal stayed its hand to avoid the risk of conflicting decisions. This "judicial courtesy" aspect of the order has been emphasized in the literature.[110] Curiously, none of the parties had expressly asked for a stay, and agents for both Ireland and the United Kingdom have expressed that they were surprised by the suspension.[111] The tribunal's

[106] *Ibid.*, paras. 20–5.

[107] See also *The MOX Plant Case (Ireland* v. *United Kingdom)*, ITLOS Case No 10, Order on Provisional Measures, 3 December 2001, Dissenting Opinion of Judge Treves.

[108] *MOX Plant*, Arbitral Tribunal, Order No 3, para. 26.

[109] *Ibid.*, para. 28.

[110] See, for example, Tullio Treves, 'Le Tribunal International du Droit de le Mer dans la Pléiade des Juridictions Internationales,' in Olivier Delas *et al.* (eds.), *Les Juridictions Internationales: Complémentarité ou Concurrence?* (Brussels: Bruylant, 2005) 9.

[111] Oral intervention by Philippe Sands and Michael Wood at PICT, *Conference on International Courts and Tribunals in the 21st Century: The Future of International Justice* (2007), The Hague, 30 November 2007.

approach, however, minimized the odds of conflicting decisions and at the same time allowed continuous judicial supervision of the dispute. Fourth, the arbitral tribunal was aware of the likelihood of conflicting decisions, "which would not be helpful to the resolution of the dispute between the parties."[112] In highlighting the risk of conflicting decisions as the reason for a stay in the proceedings, the tribunal gave substance to the notion that the function of international judicial bodies as dispute settlers may imply a need of coordination, recognizing that the higher the risk of conflicting decisions, the more reasons for coordination.

7.5 Preferential jurisdiction clauses

Preferential jurisdiction clauses restrict forum selection by either pointing both parties to a principal forum of choice or leaving the choice of forum to the respondent once the dispute is made known to it. An example of the first type of clause is found in Article 189(4)(c) of the EU–Chile Free Trade Agreement (FTA), which establishes:

> Unless the Parties otherwise agree, when a Party seeks redress of a violation of an obligation under this Part of the Agreement which is *equivalent in substance* to an obligation under the WTO, it shall have recourse to the relevant rules and procedures of the WTO Agreement, which apply notwithstanding the provisions of this Agreement.[113]

Based on the text of Article 189(4)(c), both the WTO's exclusive jurisdiction and applicable law for adjudication of obligations which are equivalent in substance to WTO obligations are to prevail. This is an interesting approach: while it expressly defines the forum of election and takes into account the comparative advantages of WTO dispute settlement, it also avoids potential multiplicity of proceedings. Moreover, the election of the WTO as the forum of preference for obligations equivalent in substance implies that preclusion under Article 189(4)(c) will normally be litigated exclusively before the preferential agreements' dispute-settlement machinery. This mitigates the uncertainties that yet exist over how the WTO is to deal with preclusion clauses from preferential agreements. Thus, if Chile brought a claim that the European Community is violating national treatment on

[112] *MOX Plant*, Arbitral Tribunal, Order No 3, para. 28.
[113] Article 189(4)(c), EU–Chile FTA (emphasis added).

internal regulations under Article 77.2 of the FTA, a provision arguably equivalent in substance to Article III.4 of the GATT, and the European Union disagreed, it is argued that adjudicators under the FTA should decline to hear the case.[114]

NAFTA Article 2005(3) and (4) provides an illustration of a preferential jurisdiction clause that gives the respondent the final say on the forum of election:

> 3. In any dispute referred to in paragraph 1 where the responding Party claims that its action is subject to Article 104 (Relation to Environmental and Conservation Agreements) and requests in writing that the matter be considered under this Agreement, the complaining Party may, in respect of that matter, thereafter have recourse to dispute settlement procedures solely under this Agreement.
>
> 4. In any dispute referred to in paragraph 1 that arises under Section B of Chapter Seven (Sanitary and Phytosanitary Measures) or Chapter Nine (Standards-Related Measures):
>
> (a) concerning a measure adopted or maintained by a Party to protect its human, animal or plant life or health, or to protect its environment, and
>
> (b) that raises factual issues concerning the environment, health, safety or conservation, including directly related scientific matters,
>
> where the responding Party requests in writing that the matter be considered under this Agreement, the complaining Party may, in respect of that matter, thereafter have recourse to dispute settlement procedures solely under this Agreement.[115]

As discussed before, NAFTA Article 2005(4) could have been at the center of the WTO *Tuna and Tuna Products* dispute brought by Mexico to the WTO. However, since the United States never objected to the admissibility of Mexico's WTO case, the preclusive effect of Article 2005(4) at the WTO remains untested. Interestingly, the United States requested a NAFTA panel claiming that Mexico's taking the case to the WTO violated the NAFTA preferential jurisdiction in Article 2005(4).[116] Nonetheless, since the NAFTA procedure for establishing panels is

[114] Also interestingly, Article 189(4)(d), EU–Chile FTA is a fork-in-the-road clause and establishes that any question of jurisdiction shall be raised within ten days of the establishment of the panel, and shall be settled by a preliminary ruling of the panel within thirty days of its establishment.

[115] Article 2005(3) and (4), NAFTA.

[116] See United States Trade Representative, 'United States Requests Dispute Settlement Panel in NAFTA Choice of Forum Dispute.' (Press Release, September 2010).

defective, it is also unlikely that the substantive effect of Article 2005(4) will be decided on or clarified in the short term.

7.6 The protection of *res judicata* and collateral estoppel

If there is no written preclusion clause to which respondents may refer and based on which adjudicators should decline from ruling, the question arises as to whether the protection of *res judicata* or collateral estoppel, in the event of serial litigation, or *lis pendens*, in the event of parallel litigation, can be resorted to as preclusive principles applicable to international adjudication.[117] There is little doubt that the protection of *res judicata* is a general principle of law applicable before international tribunals.[118] Indeed, it is suggested that it reflects "*une conviction juridique générale*"[119] and is a principle of law as such,[120] regardless of whether one speaks of a national or international legal system. In addition to being an established general principle of law, the protection of *res judicata* might also be considered a customary rule of international law, as states have traditionally complied with decisions by international tribunals and consistently recognized their finality, even when disagreeing with the substance of the decision.[121] Most international instruments

117 For the view that express provisions regulating an overlap dispense recourse to general principles such as the protection of *lis pendens*, see, for example, *International Company for Railway Systems (ICRS)* v. *Jordan*, ICSID Case No ARB/09/13, Procedural Order No 2, 9 July 2010, paras. 26–31.

118 See, for example, *Application of the Convention on the Prevention and Punishment of the Crime of Genocide (Bosnia and Herzegovina* v. *Serbia and Montenegro)*, Judgment of 26 February 2007, paras. 115–20; *Waste Management, Inc.* v. *Mexico*, ICSID Case No ARB (AF)/00/03, Preliminary Objection, Decision of 30 April 2004, para. 39; *Petrobart Ltd.* v. *The Kyrgyz Republic*, Arb. No 126/2003 SCC, 29 March 2005, para. 55; *Effect of Awards of Compensation Made by the United Nations Administrative Tribunal*, Advisory Opinion of 13 July 1954, at 53; *The Pious Fund (United States* v. *Mexico)*, 14 October 1902, 2 *AJIL* (1908) 900. See generally Leonardo Brant, *L'autorité de la chose jugée en droit international public* (Paris: LGDJ, 2003); Vaughan Lowe, '*Res Judicata* and the Rule of Law in International Arbitration,' 8 *Afr YBIL* (1996). See also Bin Cheng, *General Principles of Law as Applied by International Courts and Tribunals* (Cambridge University Press, 1953, 2006) 336–72; Hersch Lauterpacht, *The Development of International Law by the International Court* (London: Stevens & Sons, 1958), at 325–6.

119 Alfred Verdross, 'Les principes généraux de droit dans le système de sources du droit international public,' in *Recueil d'études de droit international en hommage à Paul Guggenheim* (Geneva: IUHEI, 1968) 524.

120 See Brant, *L'autorité de la chose jugée*.

121 See also Shany, *Competing Jurisdictions*, at 245; William Dodge, 'National Courts and International Arbitration: Exhaustion of Remedies and Res Judicata under Chapter XI of NAFTA,' 23 *Hastings Int'l Comp LR* (2000) 357, at 365.

declare the finality and binding force of awards proclaimed by the adjudicatory bodies they establish.[122]

The protection of *res judicata* can be considered to have three principal purposes. First, it preserves the stability of individual legal relationships by ensuring that disputes will come to an end. Second, it preserves the stability of legal systems, guaranteeing that identical cases will not be decided differently. Third, it protects the respondent in the second proceeding, avoiding relitigation. The protection of *res judicata* aims to achieve these purposes through a positive and a negative front, both deriving from the notion of finality. On the one hand, finality translates as a positive obligation on the defeated party to implement the award in good faith. Implementation closes the dispute from a juridical standpoint, thus accomplishing the primary purpose of adjudication. On the other hand, finality translates as a negative obligation not to relitigate, which preserves the court-based settlement: the party defeated in the first judgment must refrain from reopening the first decision against it – an aspect which operates as a protection to the winning party – whereas the party that won in the first judgment must not seek double recovery – an aspect which operates as a protection to the defeated party. The negative obligation on the first-in-time winning party is also expressed in the maxim of *ne bis in idem*.[123] The negative aspect of the protection of *res judicata* against relitigation means that the principle functions as a procedural shield against serial litigation. To that effect, a preliminary objection based on the protection of *res judicata* generally refers to the inadmissibility of the resubmitted issue and must be actively pleaded by the party seeking to avail itself of the objection.

Whereas the protection of *res judicata* is ostensibly a candidate for preventing serial litigation, its practical effectiveness is contingent on how the tribunal construes the conditions for the preclusion to operate. And while it is certain that the protection of *res judicata* is a general principle of law, the precise requirements for the application of the principle are difficult to pinpoint. The following three questions determine the faith of an objection based on *res judicata*: First, what actually

[122] See, for example, Articles 59, 60, ICJ Statute; Article 256, UNCLOS; Articles 44, 46(1), ECHR; Article 67, ACHR; Article 65, ECJ Rules of Procedure; Article 10, Olivos Protocol; Articles 1136(1), 1904(3), NAFTA; Article 52(1), ICSID Convention.

[123] See also William Dodge, '*Res Judicata*,' in *Max Planck Encyclopedia of Public International Law*, (Oxford University Press, 2007, electronic version) para. 1; Cheng, *General Principles of Law*, at 336–9.

is the *res judicata* in the first judgment? Second, what are the elements of identification between the *res judicata* and the issues allegedly being relitigated? Third, what type and degree of identity does the judge require for each element so as to recognize the preclusive force of the principle? To be sure, these questions overlap one another considerably. However, presenting them as separate questions is still useful because the answer to each may individually affect the outcome of an objection based on *res judicata*.

First, there is the threshold question about whether a given issue has the quality of *res judicata* at all, and whether it is therefore protected as such. This question relates to the judgment that has already been given. It refers to what the *res judicata* that should be protected is (as opposed to what that *res judicata* is protected from). Generally, the protection of the *res judicata* starts from a minimalist perspective, according to which only those issues expressly determined in the dispositive part of a judgment carry such quality.[124] Nevertheless, that minimalist perspective gives way to a subtler approach concerning essential parts of the adjudicator's determination not mentioned in the *dispositif*. As the ICJ confirmed in the *Bosnia Genocide* case, *res judicata* covers the issues expressly determined in the dispositive part of a judgment and those necessarily entailed therein.[125] Hence, the protection of *res judicata* certainly attaches to the issues expressly determined in the dispositive part of a judgment, but the scope of the protection also extends to the issues necessarily entailed in the judgment's dispositive part. As a result, one may have to read a general finding in the *dispositif* in context in order to ascertain if a particular matter is actually protected. On the other hand, peripheral or subsidiary matters and *obiter dicta* are certainly not *res judicata*.[126]

124 See, for example, *Case Concerning the Delimitation of the Continental Shelf between the United Kingdom of Great Britain and Northern Ireland and the French Republic*, Decision of 14 March 1978, 18 *UNRIAA* (2006) 271, at para. 28, considering "it to be well settled that in international proceedings the authority of *res judicata* … attaches in principle only to the provisions of [the] *dispositive* and not to [the] reasoning." See also *Interpretation of Judgments No 7 and 8 (Factory at Chorzów)*, Judgment of 16 December 1927, PCIJ Ser A No 13 (1927) 2, Dissenting Opinion of Judge Anzilotti, at 24–5.

125 *Genocide (Bosnia v. Serbia)*, Judgment of 26 February 2007, para. 126. See also *Continental Shelf between the United Kingdom and France*, at para. 28 ("If findings in the reasoning constitute a condition essential to the decision given in the *dispositif*, these findings are to be considered as included amongst the points settled with binding force"); *Polish Postal Service in Danzig*, Advisory Opinion of 16 May 1925, PCIJ Ser B No 11 (1925) 2, at 30; *Interpretation of Judgments No 7 and 8*, at 14–15; *Pious Fund*, at 900.

126 See, for example, *Genocide (Bosnia v. Serbia)*, para. 126.

A more expansive approach may include, besides matters that have been distinctively included in the dispositive part of a judgment or are necessarily entailed therein, issues which a party could have legitimately raised in the first proceeding, but did not. There is some early support for the application of this broader view. An example can be found in the *Delgado* case. In that case, a claimant before a United States–Spain Claims Commission sought indemnification and compensation for rents, issues, profits, and income of land, on account of the seizure and detention of a certain estate by Spanish authorities. After that claim was decided, he submitted a new claim based on the same seizure and detention for the value of the land. In this case, it was held that:

> Even if the claimant did not at the time of the former case ask for indemnity of the Commission for the value of the lands, the claimant had the same power to do so as other claimants in other cases where it has been done, and he cannot have the relief by a new claim before a new Umpire.[127]

More recently, in the *Bosnia Genocide* judgment, while the ICJ confirmed that something that has not been decided upon cannot fall under the scope of the protection of *res judicata*, the Court did consider a question which was never even discussed in the proceedings, let alone decided upon, as being necessarily entailed in the decision that the ICJ had jurisdiction in the case: the fact that Serbia was not a UN member and, in turn, a party to the ICJ Statute at the time of Bosnia's application. By doing so, the Court maintained the traditional view that questions of jurisdiction are to be decided by the Court *ex officio*: even though the situation of Serbia's membership in the UN after the dissolution of Yugoslavia was not free of legal difficulties, and the specific question of whether the ICJ was "open" to Serbia at the time of the application was never discussed, the Court was satisfied at the stage of its decision on preliminary objections that it had jurisdiction in all respects to entertain the case.

But a critic may still argue that the Court has suggested one standard for the definition of the *res judicata* and effectively applied another. It seems as though the Court implies that the complexities related to jurisdiction *ratione personae* in that case (i.e., whether Serbia was a party to the statute and, as a result, whether the Court was open to Serbia)

[127] *Delgado Case*, 27 May 1881, in John Bassett Moore, *History and Digest of the Arbitrations to which the United States has been a Party*, vol. III (New York: William S. Hein, 1995), at 2193, 2199.

were due to the previous conduct of the respondent, not to a previous decision by the Court (i.e., because Serbia always claimed to be continuing the personality of the former Yugoslavia, the question of membership to the UN was never at issue). If this reading is accepted, then the reasoning of the Court comes closer to a more expansionist view on *res judicata*. The result is that the reasoning in *Bosnia Genocide* might be referred to in support of the more expansive view on the scope of *res judicata*, which includes issues that could have been raised, but have not been raised.

Once the scope of the *res judicata* has been decided upon, one needs to define what the *res judicata* is protected from. That requires, initially, distilling the elements of identity between the claim, claims, or parts thereof that are *res judicata*, and the claim, claims, or parts thereof that would allegedly upset the previous decision. The view that appears to prevail was famously espoused and synthesized by Judge Anzilotti in a dissenting opinion in *Chorzów Factory*. According to Judge Anzilotti:

> Article 59 [of the ICJ Statute] ... determines the material limits of *res judicata* when stating that 'the decision of the Court has no binding force except between the Parties and in respect of that particular case': we have here the three traditional elements for identification, *persona*, *petitum*, *causa petendi*, for it is clear that 'that particular case' (*le cas qui a été décidé*) covers both the object and the grounds of the claim.[128]

Reference to the three elements of identification (i) the parties (*persona*), (ii) the request (*petitum*), and (iii) the cause of action or grounds (*causa petendi*) can be found in a series of other judicial decisions and in scholarly works.[129] By contrast, other decisions and scholars have considered not three but two elements of identification, namely (i) the parties and (ii) the "question at issue," "matter in dispute," or "subject-matter of the dispute."[130] The difference is that the latter view, by not expressly subdividing the question at issue into request and grounds,[131]

[128] *Interpretation of Judgments No 7 and 8*, Dissenting Opinion of Judge Anzilotti, at 23.

[129] See, for example, Panel Report, *India – Measures Affecting the Automotive Sector*, WT/DS146/R, WT/DS175/R and Corr.1, adopted 5 April 2002 at para. 7.65; *CME Czech Republic B.V. (The Netherlands)* v. *Czech Republic*, Arbitral Tribunal under UNCITRAL Rules, Final Award, 14 March 2003, at 432–6; and Shany, *Competing Jurisdictions*, at 22–3.

[130] See Cheng, *General Principles of Law*, at 339–48. See also *The Newchwang*, British American Claims Arbitral Tribunal, Case No 263, 9 December 1921, in 1 *ILR* (1932) 373, at 373–74; *Pious Fund*, at 900.

[131] According to Cheng, a similar divergence of views seemed to exist already in Roman law. Cheng, *General Principles of Law*, at 346, footnote 34.

may provide more flexibility to the application of the principle. To be sure, in the specific context of international law, the request (*petitum*) is frequently that the tribunal finds a violation of the grounds (*causa petendi*). Put differently, the request and the grounds often overlap in international law, especially where no specific compensation for the alleged harm is requested. For instance, a WTO panel examines a quantitative restriction under GATT Article XI(1) (the grounds) and finds a violation of GATT Article XI(1) (pursuant to the request); and the ICJ adjudicates and declares, in light of the alleged conduct of the respondent and the rules on the use of force (the grounds), that the respondent has breached the rules on the use of force (pursuant to the request). In such examples, the result is likely to be the same regardless of whether the three-pronged (identity of parties, grounds, and request) or the two-pronged (identity of parties and issues) approach is used. But in other contexts, such as in investment arbitration, where requests for damages are normally made, the second approach does offer more flexibility. For instance, it is conceivable that an investor might request monetary compensation for an expropriation, and after an unfavorable award, that investor might seek restitution in kind through a different request for arbitration based on the same cause of action. In such cases, the broader definition of "question at issue" instead of the more precise criteria of "request" and "grounds" may offer additional protection for respondents and restricts the scope of piecemeal litigation. In turn, using the three-pronged approach, the tribunal would be able to emphasize a distinction in the request between the first proceeding (compensation) and the second (restitution) that, alone, could lead to a rejection of the preliminary objection based on the protection of *res judicata*.

The broader definition of the question at issue evokes the notion of collateral estoppel and has echoes in international adjudication. Thus, the arbitral tribunal in *Grynberg and RSM* v. *Grenada* denied the claimants the right to a ruling on certain treaty-based claims because those claims were grounded on the essential predicate that conclusions of fact or law concerning the claimants' contractual rights by a previous arbitral tribunal could be relitigated.[132] The tribunal considered that reopening a previous tribunal's findings on contractual matters in order to decide on allegedly treaty-based matters would

[132] *Rachel S. Grynberg, Stephen M. Grynberg, Myriam Z. Grynberg, and RSM Production Corporation* v. *Grenada*, ICSID Case No ARB/10/6, Award of 30 November 2010.

be impermissible.[133] According to the tribunal, with support on other arbitral decisions, the doctrine of collateral estoppel determines that a finding concerning a right, question, or fact may not be relitigated if, in a prior proceeding: (a) it was distinctly put in issue, (b) the court or tribunal actually decided it, and (c) the resolution of the question was necessary to resolve the claims before that court or tribunal.[134] Noticeably, referring to the agreement of the parties and with support in other precedents, the tribunal framed the doctrine of collateral estoppel as a well-established general principle of law applicable before international tribunals such as that one.[135] From this perspective, even if *res judicata* were to be defined narrowly as requiring identity of request and grounds, collateral estoppel could be used to cover relitigation of questions more broadly.

Finally, but chiefly, there is the question of the type and degree of identity in each of the requirements (parties, grounds, request) for the preclusive force of *res judicata* to be recognized. If tribunals require absolute identity of form and substance, then *res judicata* will almost invariably not be an obstacle for the second tribunal to go ahead and decide the case anyway. In this sense, a more substantial analysis of identity as opposed to a formal approach would be necessary in order for *res judicata* to be of use as a procedure-coordinating tool across different international tribunals.[136] To begin with the grounds or cause of action, requiring strict identity most often means that an earlier ruling by one international tribunal will not preclude relitigation of even an identical factual background, against the backdrop of similar norms, before a different tribunal. This is because, as explained before, the formal source of the norms invoked as the grounds for relief before each tribunal will most likely differ. In this context, a tribunal may highlight the autonomy of the norms grounded on their different sources, and building simply on lack of formal identity quickly

133 The previous award was *RSM Production Corporation* v. *Grenada*, ICSID Case No ARB/05/14, Award of 13 March 2009, where all of RSM's substantive claims had been denied.

134 *Grynberg and RSM* v. *Grenada*, para. 7.1.1.

135 *Ibid.*, para. 7.1.2. The Tribunal referred to *Amco Asia Corporation* v. *Republic of Indonesia*, ICSID Case No ARB/81/1, Decision on Jurisdiction (Re-submitted Case), 10 May 1988, para. 30 and *Company General of the Orinoco Case*, which itself quoted the United States Supreme Court's Decision in *Southern Pacific Railroad Co.* v. *U.S.*

136 See August Reinisch, 'The Use and Limits of *Res Judicata* and *Lis Pendens* as Procedural Tools to Avoid Conflicting Dispute Settlement Outcomes,' 3 *LPICT* (2004) 37.

dismiss an objection based on the protection of *res judicata* with respect to a judgment by a different tribunal.[137] For instance, even if a NAFTA panel decided earlier that a given tax violates national treatment, this decision would not trigger the preclusive effects of *res judicata* for a subsequent WTO panel even between the same parties, on the same tax, since before the WTO the *causa petendi* is the WTO obligation to provide national treatment and before the NAFTA panel, it was the NAFTA obligation.

Now, if this approach is adopted, *res judicata* would hardly prevent a second ruling before a different tribunal. The potential reach of the protection for overlaps would be restricted to situations of overlap between specialized tribunals, on the one hand, and tribunals of more general jurisdiction that are entitled to consider exactly the same grounds for relief based on the same formal sources of the law of the specialized tribunal, on the other hand. Even then, reliance on different formal sources would suffice to evade the protection. By contrast, if the tribunal is ready to recognize as sufficient something less than absolute formal identity of cause of action, it could then recognize the effect of the first judgment on the outcome of the second one. To be sure, this may require a previous assessment of facts and arguments related to the merits in both the first and the second proceedings, in order to verify the substantial identity of cause of action. Hence, the protection of *res judicata* may not guarantee the objective of altogether avoiding further proceedings. But one must not lose sight of the fact that the protection of *res judicata* aims at more than simply avoiding any further proceedings. Its foremost aim is to have a previous settlement stand, avoiding conflicting outcomes. The protection of *res judicata* may still contribute to this effect even after extensive relitigation. For that matter, different tribunals would need to be ready to accept a type and degree of identity that is lower than formal and strict identity of cause of action.

The two other elements of identification (identity of relief sought and identity of parties) can also have an impact on the application of

[137] See also *Czech Republic* v. *CME*, Challenge of Arbitration Award, Judgment of the Court of Appeal, Case No T 8735-01 (2003, Sweden), where the SVEA Court of Appeal observed: "The mere fact that the arbitrations were initiated under different investment treaties which were entered into between different states, the Czech Republic and the United States in the one treaty and the Czech Republic and the Netherlands in the other, militates against these legal principles being applicable at all" (at 95).

the protection of *res judicata* as a preliminary objection. With regard to the identity of the relief, the issue is analogous to the discussion on the identity of cause of action just made: the formal source of the relief and minor differences between them can also be used as a differentiating factor between two claims or actions. Moreover, if the remedies that two given tribunals offer differ (say, prospective trade liberalization versus retrospective compensation or restitution), there may be no identity of request.

Last, the criterion of identity of parties seems to be of secondary importance in interstate disputes. On the other hand, where private parties are entitled to bring claims, there may be further complicating factors. Witness the complex situation in the series of *Softwood Lumber* cases under the NAFTA and before the WTO.[138] More acutely in the context of investment arbitration, actions by an aggrieved parent company, controlling or controlled entities, or shareholders may take place under one or more BITs regarding the same or substantially similar alleged violations by the same host state.[139] In such case, tribunals may choose to focus on the different claimants in the related disputes as a sufficient reason to dismiss any objection based on the protection of *res judicata*. Thus, in its challenge against the *Lauder* award before the SVEA Court of Appeal in Stockholm, the Czech Republic argued that the previous *CME* award constituted *res judicata* for the *Lauder* proceedings. However, the SVEA Court of Appeal quickly pointed to the lack of identity between Mr Lauder, a minority (albeit the controlling) shareholder of CME, and CME itself.[140] Previously, the London Arbitral Tribunal in *Lauder* had already distinguished between the London and the Stockholm arbitrations also, in part, because the parallel arbitration proceeding was between CME and the Czech Republic.[141] In order to prevent the type of contradictory result that took place in *Lauder/CME*, August Reinisch has argued that tribunals should adopt a "realistic attitude" for determining party identity in investment disputes before different tribunals. In particular, he suggested that parent and related companies may be regarded as the

[138] See Chi Carmody, 'Softwood Lumber Dispute (2001–2006),' 100 *AJIL* (2006) 664; Joost Pauwelyn, 'Adding Sweeteners to Softwood Lumber: The WTO-NAFTA Spaghetti Bowl is Cooking,' 9 *JIEL* (2006) 197.

[139] See, for example, Dolores Bentolila, 'Shareholders' Action to Claim for Indirect Damages in ICSID Arbitration,' 2 *Trade L&Dev* (2010) 87.

[140] *Czech Republic* v. *CME*, Court of Appeal.

[141] *Lauder* v. *Czech Republic* Arbitral Tribunal under UNCITRAL Rules, 3 September 2001 para. 165.

same party for the purposes of preventing relitigation of issues that have already been decided.[142]

As discussed in Chapter 5, in the *Lauder/CME* cases there was no need for the arbitral tribunals to entertain this issue because the Czech Republic refused to rely on the protection of *res judicata* to object to a ruling by either tribunal. But Reinisch has a point to emphasize that strict reliance on the formal structure of corporate investments and investors as a means to deny party identity would reduce the scope of the protection of *res judicata* in the investment arbitration context. Interestingly, in the more recent *Grynberg and RSM* v. *Grenada* decision, the tribunal took the "realistic attitude" called for by Reinisch. In that case, the tribunal reasoned that three individual shareholders who had not been claimants in the earlier contract-based arbitration, were "privies" of RSM and therefore also bound by the earlier tribunal's factual and legal determinations.[143] According to the tribunal, the fact that the company had a distinct legal personality did not alter the analysis because their only investment was a contract to which RSM was a party and the shareholders were not.[144] More generally, the tribunal warned that claimants who claim on the basis of their indirect interest in corporate assets "must be subject to defenses that would be available against the corporation."[145] In conclusion, the preclusive force of *res judicata* is limited by the adjudicator's approach to the requirements

[142] Reinisch, 'Use and Limits,' 57–77. Reinisch explains that arbitral tribunals have adopted a "realistic," "economic" approach to asserting jurisdiction over claims by related companies. The argument, however, should work both ways, and tribunals could adopt similar approaches to, this time, decline from ruling on the merits of re-submitted investment disputes by using different vehicles for the investment. See, for example, *Dow Chemical France* v. *Isover Saint Gobain*, ICC Case No 4131, Interim Award of 23 September 1982, 9 *YB Comm Arb* (1984) 131, at 136 ("[I]rrespective of the distinct juridical identity of each of its members, a group of companies constitutes one and the same economic reality … of which the tribunal should take account"); *Amco* v. *Indonesia*, Decision on Jurisdiction, 25 September 1983, 1 *ICSID Rep* (1983) 389, at 400 ("PT Amco was but an instrumentality through which Amco Asia was to realize the investment. Now, the goal of the arbitration clause was to protect the investor … : would it not be fully illogical to grant this protection to the controlled entity, but not to the controlling one?"); *Klöckner* v. *Cameroon*, 21 October 1983, 2 *ICSID Rep* (1983) 9, at 17 ("This Agreement, although formally signed by the Government and SOCAME, was in fact negotiated between the Government and Klöckner.… [I]t is undeniable that it was manifestly concluded in the interest of Klöckner.")

[143] *Grynberg and RSM* v. *Grenada*, para. 7.1.5.

[144] *Ibid.*, para. 7.1.6. The individual shareholders collectively owned 100 percent of RSM's stocks.

[145] *Ibid.*, para. 7.1.7.

underlying the principle. But the contours of the protection of *res judicata* are not yet entirely clear and remain subject to construction in the specific cases.[146]

7.7 A protection of *lis pendens*?

Questions similar to those relating to the scope of protection and elements of identification discussed in the context of *res judicata* would come into play in the context of an objection to the admissibility of a claim, claims, or parts thereof based on the protection of *lis pendens*. The protection of *lis pendens* is normally considered to require the same elements of identification embedded in the protection of *res judicata*. However, in contrast to *res judicata*, it is important to recognize that the status of the rule of *lis pendens* as a general principle of law is not wholly uncontroversial.[147] For instance, Reinisch argues that *lis pendens* applies in the international context,[148] Giles Cuniberti submits that it does not,[149] and Shany says that the answer is unclear.[150] One's answer to that question must be given even before one reaches the questions of the scope of the pending suit and the identity with the parallel suit.

Cuniberti supports the view that *lis pendens* is not and should not be a principle of international law on two grounds. First, he argues that *lis pendens* is not a general principle of law, but rather, it is essentially a civil law doctrine.[151] In his view, other legal traditions approach the same problem with very different procedural tools (e.g., the common law principle of *forum non conveniens* or the United States courts' abstention doctrines). Moreover, to consider *lis pendens* as a general principle of law applicable to international adjudication without the ancillary doctrines that come with it, such as the civil law rules on "related actions" would in Cuniberti's opinion offer an incomplete picture.[152] Second,

[146] One commentator puts it more dramatically in the context of commercial arbitration: "[R]*es judicata* in the context of international arbitration is presently in a no man's land, with considerable uncertainty as to its appropriate application." Audley Sheppard, 'The Scope and *Res Judicata* Effect of Arbitral Awards,' in CEPANI, *Arbitral Procedure at the Dawn of the New Millennium* (Brussels: Bruylant, 2005) 265, at 265.

[147] See Joost Pauwelyn and Luiz Eduardo Salles, 'Forum Shopping Before International Tribunals: (Real) Concerns, (Im)Possible Solutions,' 42 *Cornell ILJ* (2009) 77, at 106–10.

[148] Reinisch, 'Use and Limits.'

[149] Giles Cuniberti, 'Parallel Litigation and Foreign Investment Dispute Settlement,' 21 *ICSID Rev* (2006) 381, at 406.

[150] Shany, *Competing Jurisdictions*, at 241.

[151] Cuniberti, 'Parallel Litigation,' at 383.

[152] *Ibid.*, at 412.

and more importantly, the time factor of *lis pendens* – the court first seized decides the case – makes sense between hierarchically equal and similarly expert and legitimate domestic courts. It does not make sense between international courts that are not necessarily comparable, be it for reasons of hierarchy, procedural efficiency, legitimacy, or expertise. To apply in those circumstances the guillotine approach of "the first court seized decides" is, according to Cuniberti, not appropriate:

> [T]he fundamental goal of the institution [of *lis pendens*] has been to discriminate between adjudicators who were comparable in most respects. As it would not have been acceptable to find that one given first instance court was superior to or more legitimate than another first instance court of the same country, it was only natural that the institution would ultimately rely on a test that would be as neutral as possible [i.e. a simple time factor] to distinguish between them ... In an international setting, however, neither the equality nor the legitimacy of all adjudicators should be assumed. The issue of parallel litigation can therefore be addressed by discriminating between the competing adjudicators on very substantive grounds ... the policy decisions behind the *lis pendens* doctrine have no legitimacy to regulate parallel litigation in an international setting.[153]

With regard to the question of hierarchy between tribunals, Cuniberti does not seem to give enough consideration to the fact that, much like between two courts of first instance within the same country or across countries, no inherent legal hierarchy exists between international tribunals.[154] Nevertheless, he raises an interesting point as to whether in the current context of international law the presumption underlying *lis pendens* that two international suits before different tribunals are comparable but for the time of seizing can really hold water. For those that start from the opposite perspective – that is, two international suits before different tribunals will never be comparable – *lis pendens* would hardly be applicable before different tribunals.

While this book does not share this extreme latter view, the question raised by Cuniberti highlights the need for a critical approach to the application of *lis pendens*. Consider, for example, whether WTO panels should apply *lis pendens* automatically in the face of a substantially

[153] *Ibid.*, at 383–4.

[154] It must be noted that in Cuniberti's prime example there is the hierarchical superiority of an international tribunal over a domestic court. Note the PCIJ's early remark in *Case Concerning Certain German Interests in Polish Upper Silesia*, Preliminary Objections, Judgment of 25 August 1925, PCIJ Ser A No 6 (1925) 1, at 20, to which Cuniberti also refers, that international tribunals and domestic tribunals are "not courts of the same character."

identical request submitted to NAFTA dispute settlement by the same party. What if, after the request before the NAFTA, the respondent does not appoint panelists and the NAFTA proceedings are left in limbo, much like what happened in the broader sugar dispute that, according to Mexico, gave rise to the WTO *Taxes on Soft Drinks* case? In those circumstances, it could be argued that, at least in procedural terms, the WTO and NAFTA Chapter 20 panels are not comparable, and it would be unreasonable to enforce a protection of *lis pendens* against the respondent in both proceedings.[155]

By contrast to Cuniberti, Reinisch argues that *lis pendens* is a general principle of law in the sense of Article 38(1) of the ICJ Statute. In support of his arguments, he points to "[t]he widespread use and similarity of the concept of *lis pendens* in the national procedural laws of States of all legal traditions," its "inclusion in a number of bi- and multiparty agreements," and its appearance in a number of international court cases.[156] Second, and more interestingly, Reinisch argues that if international courts and tribunals were to accept the principle of *res judicata*, they would be logically compelled to also accept the principle of *lis pendens*:

> As a matter of legal logic it would be inconsistent to permit parallel proceedings between the same parties in the same dispute [i.e. not to apply *lis pendens*] before different dispute settlement organs up to the point where one of them has decided the case and then prevent the other ("slower") one from proceeding as a result of *res judicata*.[157]

155 In the case of *res judicata*, this concern does not necessarily arise, because the first judgment has already been issued. But one may suggest a related example: imagine that a party does not comply with a NAFTA panel ruling and the winning party before the NAFTA requests a WTO panel to examine the same measures, in light of substantially similar rules. Should the WTO respondent be protected in that case? In other words, should the NAFTA winning party be deprived of the opportunity to rely on the WTO enforcement machinery just because the NAFTA has already decided the case in its favor? It is suggested that the answer to this question does not depend on one's view on whether the adjudicators are comparable. Instead, the internal logic of *res judicata* affords the following response: to rely on the negative aspect of *res judicata* (no relitigation) in order to protect the respondent would simply not be appropriate, because the respondent did not respect the positive aspect of *res judicata* (its obligation to comply) in the first place. In other words, one could not claim the negative protection of *res judicata* if one does not respect the positive character of *res judicata*.

156 Reinisch, 'Use and Limits,' at 48–50.

157 *Ibid.*, at 50. See also Gabrielle Salvioli, 'Problèmes de Procédure dans la Jurisprudence Internationale,' in 91 *Recueil des Cours* I (1957) 533, 609 (deriving the protection of *lis pendens* from the applicability of a rule of *res judicata*).

However, one may question whether this is necessarily the case. While there are cost-related concerns both for the second-in-time adjudicatory body seized and for the "victim" of parallel litigation, there may be additional reasons to protect *res judicata* which do not apply with the same force for *lis pendens*. Two basic reasons are these. First, *res judicata* directly preserves the finality of rulings and the stability and security of the legal system, whereas allowing parallel proceedings does not upset any past ruling by another court.[158] Therefore, the concern over finality does not attach to parallel litigation as it does to serial litigation. Second, as the discussion above on the comparability of tribunals demonstrates, declining to rule on the ground that another proceeding is pending does not necessarily guarantee that the other proceeding will ultimately resolve the dispute. The PCIJ expressed an analogous preoccupation long ago in *Factory at Chorzów* and reasoned:

> [T]he Court, when it has to define its jurisdiction in relation to that of another tribunal, cannot allow its own competency to give way unless confronted with a clause which it considers sufficiently clear to prevent the possibility of a negative conflict of jurisdiction involving the danger of a denial of justice.[159]

In the *res judicata* context, by definition, the other proceeding has already been completed and the possibility of a "denial of justice" can be easily ruled out. But when it comes to *lis pendens*, one may not simply assume that the parallel proceedings will go on as expected, at least in the current stage of asymmetrical judicialization of international law. On the other hand, it may be appropriate to apply the underlying logic of *lis pendens* to justify a temporary stay, followed by the second-in-time seized tribunal's monitoring the first-in-time proceedings. Then, provided that the second-in-time seized tribunal is satisfied that there is no risk of a denial of justice, that tribunal could rule on the admissibility of the relevant claim, claims, or parts thereof that have been dealt with or are being dealt with by the first-in-time seized tribunal.

The above discussion in support of protecting *res judicata* but not *lis pendens* leads to the conclusion that tribunals should not automatically apply the protection of *lis pendens* as a preclusion doctrine that leads to dismissals so as to resolve overlaps between international proceedings

[158] Note that the Appellate Body in *Mexico – Taxes on Soft Drinks* highlighted that it was "undisputed that no NAFTA panel as yet has decided the 'broader dispute' to which Mexico has alluded." Appellate Body Report, *Mexico – Taxes on Soft Drinks*, para. 54.

[159] *Case Concerning the Factory at Chorzów*, Claim for Indemnity, Jurisdiction, Judgment of 16 July 1927, PCIJ Ser A No 9 (1927) 1, at 30.

in the context of contemporary international law. The preclusive force of *lis pendens* and its underlying time-based rationale should be resorted to on a case-by-case basis, on condition that the duplicative proceedings are before the same or comparable dispute-settlement mechanisms. Other than as a strict preclusion doctrine, however, the rationale underlying the protection of *lis pendens* also remains useful. As discussed previously, *lis pendens* considerations may sometimes justify a temporary stay in the proceedings of the second seized court. In fact, the above discussion reinforces the point made in Chapter 5: that using discretion when it comes to case management may lead to better solutions than strictly precluding the right to a ruling by one party.[160] Seen in this light, as one of the several factors that can be taken into account in an order of stay, the protection *lis pendens* can be a building block to the development of abstention doctrines in international law based on tribunals' power to manage the proceedings before them. Moreover, as is the case with the protection of *res judicata*, the underlying rationale in the protection of *lis pendens* should be stressed as a starting point for the drafting of treaty clauses on parallel litigation, especially in the context where treaty negotiators consider two tribunals to be comparable. In that case, it would also be interesting to emphasize substantive and substantial identity as opposed to formal and strict identity in the text of the clause, or to consider focusing on the measure at issue as the basis for preclusion, rather than on identity of object and cause. An ongoing procedure should then stop a later one in the event that explicit treaty clauses exist to this effect (such as a fork-in-the-road provision that, after all, has *lis pendens* features, or an explicit *lis pendens* rule).[161]

7.8 Aggregation doctrines

In parallel proceedings with related parties and issues, consideration can also be given to their potential aggregation. Aggregation is used herein as a general term expressing a variety of techniques of procedure integration, running from the complete integration of two or more proceedings into one proceeding that leads to a single judgment, to partial integration of proceedings which are decided under more

[160] See also McLachlan, Lis Pendens *in International Litigation*, at 346–62.

[161] Of course, in this case, the effect of the first proceeding would normally flow directly from the treaty clause, not from the principle of *lis pendens* as such.

than one judgment. In this sense, aggregation is conceivable in many different configurations, depending on the type of link between the proceedings or the issues they deal with. For instance, claims and counterclaims involving the same parties and related issues of fact can be joined, or proceedings involving multiple parties and similar issues of fact or law can be reunited. Depending on the link established between the proceedings, the type of consolidation envisaged can vary also; for example, harmonizing procedural timetables and organizing joint or sequential hearings for specific issues, establishing tribunals composed of the same members, and issuing a single decision or judgment for part of the issues or all of the issues at stake.

Partly as a result of the variety of potential configurations where aggregation may play a role and the diversity of methods to implement it, it is difficult to discuss aggregation techniques in the abstract. Aggregation tends to require that the dispute-settlement mechanism or the parties explicitly authorize it, in which case the corresponding provision would provide for the conditions and effects of aggregating proceedings. Indeed, when it comes to parallel litigation before a single permanent tribunal, rules of procedure often expressly contemplate consolidation. For instance, Article 47 of the ICJ Rules of Court authorizes the ICJ at any time to direct that the proceedings in two or more cases be joined; that written and oral proceedings, including the calling of witnesses, be in common; or that the Court order another common action in proceedings in more than one case.[162] Article 47 is therefore broad enough to include both formal joinder leading to one single judgment, and other types of consolidation for handling proceedings efficiently. For instance, in the *Use of Force* cases, where eight respondent-states filed different preliminary objections, the Court opted not to join the proceedings. Nevertheless, in organizing the oral proceedings of the preliminary objections stage, President Oda highlighted the ICJ's desire to "avoid unnecessary duplication of arguments." Therefore, each of the respondents presented its individual argument and Serbia responded to their arguments all at once.

By contrast, aggregation provisions are often not available when it comes to parallel litigation before different tribunals. This is a consequence of international tribunals' limited jurisdiction and a factor of the current state of asymmetrical judicialization. Take, for example, the *Swordfish* cases in their different elements before the dispute

[162] Article 47, ICJ Rules of Court. Article 47, ITLOS Rules of the Tribunal is identically worded.

settlement systems at the WTO and UNCLOS.[163] The ITLOS chamber could never decide the European Communities' claim that the alleged restrictions on the transit of swordfish through Chile's ports were WTO-inconsistent. Likewise, a WTO panel was not entitled to hear Chile's claim based on the UNCLOS. Indeed, since WTO and UNCLOS dispute-settlement rules establish the specific jurisdiction of their corresponding adjudicators, covering a different set of possible claims, it is hard to conceive of either the WTO or the ITLOS chamber taking up the whole of the claims at stake, even with the consent of both parties.

In other cases, nonetheless, the agreement of the parties to the dispute may be a sufficient condition for consolidation. Return to the *CME/Lauder* cases,[164] where both the *CME* and the *Lauder* tribunals were aware of the possibility that the awards could be mutually inconsistent. The *Lauder* tribunal, to which the claims were first submitted, noted the Czech Republic's disagreement with what the tribunal called "a de facto consolidation of the two proceedings by insisting on a different arbitral tribunal to hear CME's case."[165] The *CME* tribunal, for its part, recalled that the Czech Republic did not agree to consolidate the proceedings, a request that the claimant had made. Instead, the Czech Republic insisted on having each action determined independently and promptly.[166] In its final award, the *CME* tribunal returned to the question of procedural coordination, and explained that the respondent expressly rejected five specific proposals for coordination between the *Lauder* and the *CME* proceedings which, interestingly, the claimant had made: (i) to have the two arbitrations consolidated in a single proceeding, (ii) to have the same arbitrators appointed for both proceedings, (iii) to accept the CME's nomination in the *CME* proceedings of the same arbitrator Mr Lauder nominated in the *Lauder* proceedings, (iv) to agree that the parties in the *CME* case were bound by the *Lauder* tribunal's decision as to whether there had been treaty breaches, and (v) that the hearing in the *CME* case be postponed until after the issuance of the award in the *Lauder* case.[167] Indeed, had one of the techniques

[163] See *Chile – Measures Affecting the Importation and Transit of Swordfish*, WT/DS/193 (last joint communication by the parties to the DSB dated 3 June 2010); *Case Concerning the Conservation and Sustainable Exploitation of Swordfish Stocks in the South-Eastern Pacific Ocean* (Chile/European Community), ITLOS Case No 7, discontinued 16 December 2009.

[164] *Lauder* v. *Czech Republic*; *CME* v. *Czech Republic*, Partial Award, 13 September 2001, Final Award, 14 March 2003.

[165] *CME* v. *Czech Republic*, Final Award, para. 173.

[166] *Ibid.*, para. 412. [167] *Ibid.*, para. 427.

of coordination that the claimants proposed been used – techniques which were expressly suggested by one of the parties but rejected by another – we might have been discussing the *Lauder/CME* cases today as an example of the effective use of aggregation as a means to address the possibility of conflicting rulings inherent in parallel litigation.

A recent set of cases where aggregation has been implemented by party agreement is *ICRS* v. *Jordan*.[168] On 27 May 2009, Jordan instituted proceedings before an International Chamber of Commerce-based arbitral tribunal against ICRS. On 12 June, ICRS filed a request for arbitration before the ICSID. Before the ICSID tribunal, Jordan argued that priority should be given to the first-in-time proceedings and asked for a stay of the proceedings. Based on Article 26 of the ICSID Convention and on an implementation agreement between the parties in dispute, the ICSID tribunal rejected Jordan's request and continued the proceedings. Later, ICRS opted to withdraw its previous jurisdictional objections and submit a counterclaim in the proceedings before the International Chamber of Commerce tribunal. ICRS abstained from further pursuing the ICSID proceedings, "without conceding that ICSID is the tribunal of first resort," "in the interest of an expeditious resolution of the dispute and not having to be put through the financial strain of pursuing two arbitrations in the very same matter."[169] Subsequently, the ICSID arbitral tribunal discontinued the proceedings before it by agreement of the parties.[170]

An interesting example of a consolidation provision where different tribunals are in place is NAFTA Article 1126, which provides for the possibility of consolidating claims that have a question of law or fact in common, in the interests of fair and efficient resolution of the claims. Both the United States and Canada have concluded bilateral trade and investment agreements which include similar consolidation provisions with respect to investor-state arbitration.[171] NAFTA's experience with Article 1126 and the result of the *CME/Lauder* cases discussed previously have bolstered a discussion about whether the ICSID arbitration scheme could be revised so as to include a consolidation

[168] *ICRS* v. *Jordan*, Procedural Order No 2.

[169] *ICRS* v. *Jordan*, Procedural Order No 3, 26 November 2010, para. 3.

[170] *ICRS* v. *Jordan*, Order of the Tribunal Taking Note of the Discontinuance of the Proceedings, 22 February 2011.

[171] See, for example, Article G-27(2), Canada–Chile Free Trade Agreement, 36 *ILM* 1079; Article 10(24), United States–Chile Free Trade Agreement, 42 *ILM* 1026.

provision.[172] In light of the difficulties surrounding amendments to the ICSID Convention, it seems that the alternative of establishing an optional, additional ICSID consolidation facility would be a more feasible alternative.

In two sets of cases, respondents attempted to trigger Article 1126 of the NAFTA with different results. The *Corn Products* cases arose in the context of Mexico's imposition of a tax on soft drinks containing high fructose corn syrup.[173] Corn Products International, Inc., in 2003, and Archer Daniels Midland Company, Inc. and Tate & Lyle Ingredients Americas, Inc., in 2004, filed requests for arbitration against Mexico under NAFTA Chapter 11. Mexico then requested the establishment of an arbitral tribunal to decide on the consolidation of the claims pursuant to Article 1126 of the NAFTA. The tribunal first recalled the two steps of the test for the consolidation of claims. Under Article 1126(2) of the NAFTA, the tribunal "must be satisfied" that the claims have a "question of law or fact in common." If that requirement is met, the tribunal may, "in the interests of fair and efficient resolution of the claims," issue a consolidation order.[174] The tribunal quickly accepted that the first part of the test was met, and concentrated on the issue of whether it should consolidate the claims in the interest of their fair and efficient resolution. However, the tribunal rejected Mexico's request, emphasizing that the complainants were "global competitors." It considered this to be an impediment to consolidation, as the complainants would suffer unfairness from the procedural inefficiencies that would arise from consolidation. The basic thrust of the order is that "the direct and major competition between the claimants, and the consequent need for complex confidentiality measures … would render consolidation …, in whole or in part, extremely difficult."[175] As an ancillary reason for its decision, the tribunal also mentioned the problem of delays in the proceedings, since the cases were not close to procedural alignment.[176]

The decision in *Corn Products* can be contrasted to that in the *Softwood* cases, which are part of the storm of litigation related to trade in

[172] See, for example, Gabrielle Kaufmann-Kohler *et al.*, 'Consolidation of Proceedings in Investment Arbitration: How Can Multiple Proceedings Arising from the Same or Related Situations be Handled Efficiently?' 21 *ICSID Rev* (2006) 59.

[173] *Corn Products International, Inc.* v. *Mexico*, ICSID case No ABR(AF)/04/1, and *Archer Daniels Midland Company and Tate & Lyle Ingredients Americas, Inc.* v. *Mexico*, ICSID case No ARB(AF)/04/5, Order of the Consolidation Tribunal, 20 May 2005.

[174] *Ibid.*, para. 5 [175] *Ibid.*, para. 8. [176] *Ibid.*, para. 19.

softwood lumber between the United States and Canada.[177] Between 2002 and 2003, three Canadian producers submitted separate requests to arbitration under NAFTA Chapter 11 concerning the imposition of countervailing duties and anti-dumping measures by the United States. The United States sought to consolidate the proceedings under Article 1126 of the NAFTA. The consolidation tribunal granted consolidation, according heavy weight to the intended purpose and object of consolidation, that is, "procedural economy" in the sense of an "effective administration of justice." The tribunal clarified that the goal of Article 1126 is to alleviate the resources of the state parties in defending against multiple claims, and noted that consolidation is well known in many domestic court procedures, in particular in Canada, Mexico, and the United States.[178] It found questions of law and fact in common that warranted consolidation as to jurisdiction, liability, and possibly damages. The tribunal extensively discussed the question of efficiency in the resolution of claims as a condition to consolidate. According to the tribunal, fairness is analyzed by balancing the procedural interests and rights of all parties involved.[179] Efficiency, in turn, would be "an objective, fact-driven standard which an Article 1126 tribunal can apply as it deems appropriate under the circumstances."[180] The tribunal offered as a guiding efficiency test "a comparison with the situation as it exists, and would continue to exist, if no consolidation were ordered."[181] Such comparison should take into account: (i) time issues, which would include a consideration of the status of the Chapter 11 arbitration and of the delay that could result in the resolution of claims (thus, as the separate proceedings are more advanced, consolidation would less likely be ordered); (ii) cost issues, which would involve an assessment of the costs for all parties involved; and (iii) the need to avoid conflicting decisions. The tribunal recognized that the effective administration of justice "requires the avoidance of conflicting results." According to the tribunal, this included cases with different parties which may present the same legal issues arising out of the same event or related to the

[177] *Canfor Co.* v. *United States, and Tembec et al.* v. *United States, and Terminal Forest Products* v. *United States*, Order of the Consolidation Tribunal, 7 September 2005.

[178] *Ibid.*, paras. 75–7. [179] *Ibid.*, para. 125. [180] *Ibid.*, para. 124.

[181] *Ibid.*, para. 126. The tribunal develops its guiding test at paras. 126–33, and points to other factors less relevant or not relevant for the purposes of applying the term "in the interest of fair and efficient resolution of the claims," at paras. 134–8.

same measure: "[c]onflicting results then may take place if the findings with respect to those issues differ in two or more cases."[182]

The *Softwood* cases' approach to consolidation significantly departs from the *Corn Products* approach. Specifically, the different approaches can be deemed a result of the weight attributed to problems of confidentiality. The *Softwood* tribunal explicitly took issue with the *Corn Products* order proposition that "[t]wo tribunals can handle two separate cases more fairly and efficiently than one tribunal where the two claimants are direct and major competitors, and the claims raise issues of competitive and commercial sensitivity," and that "confidential information among competitors is more easily protected in separate proceedings."[183] More broadly, however, the veiled rationales for the orders are different. The *Corn Products* tribunal, on the one hand, focused on the unfairness to investors of a consolidation they did not agree to, and which would negatively affect their procedural interests. The *Softwood* tribunal, on the other hand, focused on the efficiency of resolving the claims in terms of procedural economy. Whereas the former order restricts the scope for consolidation under Article 1126, the latter expands it by focusing on the protective function of the consolidation rule.

7.9 Concluding remarks

This chapter provided an overview of procedure-regulating norms and discussed their application in cases where strategic forum selection and parallel and serial litigation were at stake. International law is populated with preclusion clauses that enable procedural coordination by means of preliminary objections. In some cases, preclusion norms have been successfully used as the basis for preliminary objections before international courts and tribunals. In other cases, it has been seen that the respondent's litigation strategy actually did not require the application of preclusion clauses, given the lack of an objection to admissibility based on the preclusive norm. It is hard to judge whether the litigation strategies employed by respondents – such as Mexico and the United States before WTO adjudicators and the Czech Republic before investor-state arbitrators – were just unfortunate strategies or deliberate

182 *Ibid.*, para. 131.

183 *Ibid.*, para. 222 (quoting *Corn Products* v. *Mexico*, and *ADM and Tate & Lyle* v. *Mexico*, 20 May 2005, paras. 9–10).

attempts to keep a hermetic separation between tribunals and treaty regimes. But an important consideration is that past cases where objections to admissibility were not raised should not restrict the future development of the law on forum shopping. This note is especially important for future cases where preclusion clauses are actively pleaded. Take WTO adjudication, where particular reluctance to refer to preclusion norms from other treaties and general international law may be identified. Such reluctance may be circumstantial, given that the issue has been restricted to litigation involving NAFTA parties. To conclude, on the basis of the limited past experience to date, that preclusion clauses cannot apply in WTO adjudication would leave dozens of explicit preclusion clauses negotiated by a large spectrum of the WTO membership in limbo and disregard the interdependence of the WTO and preferential trade agreements. There are many reasons to overcome this reluctance.

Regarding the assessment of a preliminary objection properly raised based on a preclusion clause, a key area of focus regarding the future application of such clauses is the definition of the claims or subject matter of the dispute for the preclusion to operate – in other words, the type and degree of identity required for preclusion. In order to permit coordination, preliminary objectors and adjudicators should focus on *substantive* and *substantial* identity of actions as opposed to *formal* and *strict* identity. Since a substantive and substantial assessment may be complex, it follows that parties may sometimes be required, in practice, to put forward arguments on issues that have already been decided or are pending before other tribunals. To prevent the complexity of the assessment from limiting the effect of preliminary objections and thereby hampering the administration of justice, especially in cases of parallel litigation before different international tribunals, consideration may be given for stays by the tribunal where the preclusive effect is sought (i.e., the tribunal receiving the objection). This again emphasizes the important, albeit limited, role of abstention doctrines discussed in Chapter 6. A discretionary and temporary stay should be carefully weighed relative to the likelihood of a quick and satisfactory decision by the other tribunal, and based on the specific circumstances at stake. The stay could be lifted as soon as the parties are ready to inform the tribunal where the preclusive effect is sought about the actual identity of the cases; and a more informed decision could then be made.

Regarding the decision of whether to grant the stay or recognize the preclusion to terminate the proceedings, the enabling and protective functions of jurisdictional and procedural rules are important signposts: (i) to what extent can the adjudicator receiving the objection be sure that there will be no denial of justice, guaranteeing the enabling function? (ii) to what extent does the preclusive norm in which the objection grounds cover the situation at hand, in light of the protective function? The allocative function is also critical: the easier to identify a systemic relationship between the tribunals, the more coordination is warranted. In deciding on the extent of the systemic relationship, adjudicators should consider whether the preclusion across international tribunals is grounded on a written norm or on a general principle such as *res judicata*, *lis pendens*, or collateral estoppel. Arguably, the lack of explicit regulation of forum shopping (that is, the lack of a written preclusion clause) indicates that the parties did not wish to limit resort to dispute settlement. In this event, a default preference for the complainant's autonomy would be on point. *A contrario sensu*, the existence of preclusion clauses should be a sign, for tribunals, that the parties have attempted to regulate the matter and to limit their options. The extent to which they have achieved their objective, of course, remains a question of interpretation.

For treaty negotiators, concerns regarding the potential application of principles of law as preclusion clauses only reinforce the need for including explicit procedure-regulating rules in the governing instruments to come. More generally, to avoid the shortcomings in the application and interpretation of the elements of identification of actions, explicit procedure-regulating rules should establish whether they aim to protect only strictly formal identity of claim, claims, or parts thereof, or rather, whether they aim to protect substantive and substantial identity. Additionally, consideration could be given for granting preclusive effect to prior or parallel litigation based on the measure in dispute (a fact-based standard) rather than on the more difficult standard focused on the identity of the dispute (which mixes fact- and law-based criteria that are harder to grasp).

Conclusion

A procedural tack on forum shopping

This book asked how parties and adjudicators may react to strategic forum selection, parallel litigation, and serial litigation in international adjudication. It sought to answer that question by providing a procedural framework within which the phenomenon of forum shopping can be grappled. To that effect, the book made an incursion into the technique of preliminary objections, which is a major channel through which respondents fight and adjudicators address forum shopping strategies, and an excursion into procedure-regulating norms applicable to the jurisdictional overlaps of international tribunals. Taken individually, neither the "problem" (i.e., forum shopping) nor the means to a "solution" (i.e., preliminary objections and procedure-regulating norms) addressed in this book could be claimed a novelty. But a specific articulation of the stories of forum shopping and preliminary objections had not been attempted before, at least certainly not from the broad perspective adopted here. The present articulation arguably makes clearer the legal bases and justifications for procedural coordination by autonomous international tribunals, and the means for implementing it, from a general perspective. An overlooked, quiescent role of preliminary objections thereby becomes visible: that of transmission belts of procedure-regulating norms on a new landscape of international adjudication.

A summary of the book

In Chapter 1, this book contextualized the upsurge in forum shopping by pointing to three structural changes in international adjudication:

(i) the multiplication of international tribunals, (ii) the intensification of inbuilt consent as the expression of pre-commitments to adjudication going forward indeterminately for disputes in pockets of the law, and (iii) the emergence of non-state actors in international adjudication. These significant changes open the door to forum shopping in international law. Such changes are superimposed on international adjudication's consensual structure and therefore pose challenging questions about the delegated nature of international adjudicatory jurisdiction. Moreover, complainants' ability to unilaterally resort to adjudication and pick a forum in the asymmetrical context of international adjudication raises concerns over fairness, systemic integrity, and consistency that may upset the balance underlying the enabling, protective, and allocative functions of procedural norms. Given that the above-mentioned concerns arise within the adjudicatory process, Chapter 1 set the stage for articulating a conceptual framework to address forum shopping from a procedural perspective.

Chapter 2 turned to the concept of procedure for the purposes of the analysis. The notion of procedure comprises the basic institutions of jurisdiction, action, and procedure in a narrow sense as the essential elements implicated in a procedural relationship. Procedure is the filter for forum shopping activity, and preliminary questions referring to jurisdiction, action, and procedure in a narrow sense are the filtering elements. Approaching forum shopping from a procedural perspective sheds light on the so-far latent role of preliminary objections as transmission belts of procedure-regulating rules, in addition to their traditional role as procedural shields.

Chapter 3 moved from the concept of procedure offered in Chapter 2 to the delineation of the central concepts of preliminary questions and objections. *Preliminary questions* were conceived as questions referring to the existence and development of the adjudicatory process as such (i.e., procedural requirements, which refer to jurisdiction, action, and procedure in a narrow sense). *Preliminary objections* are the most common subset of preliminary questions and certainly the most important one when it comes to forum shopping. While the former consist of the whole universe of questions about the requirements for the existence and development of the adjudicatory process, the latter consist of preliminary questions expressly raised by parties. Chapter 3 suggested that a general concept of preliminary questions and objections should focus on the fact that they are logically antecedent to questions of merit and potentially affect the outcome of litigation. It also recognized the timeline-related character (to be raised *in limine litis*) and effect (to interrupt the proceedings and lead to a new, "preliminary" stage) of preliminary objections, which are specific to certain tribunals and cases. The conceptualization of preliminary questions as procedural questions in Chapter 3 implies a separability of such questions from questions of merit. It was argued that separability lies in a functional and contextual distinction between the adjudicatory process and the object of that process. If, in deciding a question, the adjudicator provides a response to the request, this question is not preliminary in the sense discussed here.

Chapter 4 discussed the source, justification, and scope of adjudicators' power to rule on preliminary objections, as well as the effect of the exercise of such power. It argued that international tribunals have an inherent power to rule on preliminary questions. The adjudicatory function cannot be properly conceived without reference to the idea of process, and consequentially, without reference to the notion that the tribunal is a third party who is responsible for guarding the integrity of the process. A tribunal cannot permit the process to be abused, and it is accordingly entitled to rule on the fulfillment of any applicable procedural requirements. Thus, Chapter 4 argued that the justification for the power to rule on preliminary objections is its inevitability for the proper discharge of jurisdiction. As to the scope of this power, it extends beyond the governing instruments of a tribunal, since it flows from the location of the power to rule on preliminary objections in the incidental jurisdiction of international tribunals. Incidental jurisdiction – which extends more broadly than principal jurisdiction – is implicated depending on the need to answer an intervening question so as to discharge principal jurisdiction. Hence, disputed preliminary objections concerning a procedural relationship may demand a decision as a matter of incidental jurisdiction regardless of the legal source of the ground for the objection. On the other hand, the source of the ground for the objection and the ambit of jurisdiction in which the assessment is undertaken may be relevant for determining the effect of the exercise of a power to rule on the objection. Basically, procedural questions decided within principal jurisdiction may possess the quality of *res judicata*, whereas questions decided outside principal jurisdiction have a preclusive effect that is internal, restricted to the proceedings at stake.

Chapter 5 focused on the twofold categorization of preliminary questions into questions of jurisdiction and questions of admissibility, and on the application of that categorization to forum shopping strategies. It began by identifying traditional reasons to recognize the distinction. Among those, it highlighted an aggravated burden to raise matters of admissibility, whereas tribunals should normally assess jurisdictional issues on their own motion. This doctrinal distinction explains past cases before the WTO and investment tribunals and provides a lesson for forum-shopped respondents: they must actively plead preliminary objections to admissibility, lest they waive the ability to challenge the alleged procedural breach. That chapter also discussed the impact of recognizing the category of admissibility for the debate on jurisdictional coordination. In this regard, admissibility is the channel for preliminary objections based on the broader set of norms governing the procedural relationship of the parties. It is the means for indirect procedural coordination between otherwise unrelated tribunals. A tribunal may be required to uphold an objection to admissibility based on the need to maintain the integrity of the process itself, in the exercise of its incidental jurisdiction. This perspective adds to the debate over "conflicts of jurisdiction" between international tribunals, since it is not necessarily premised upon the systemic problems that are often of concern to international lawyers. It enables the debate to move forward from a good-faith, fairness-to-the-defendant perspective, regardless of whether a jurisdictional system, strictly speaking, is in place.

As for distinguishing between jurisdiction and admissibility, Chapter 5 labeled the predominant approach to this exercise as "conventionalism-residualism." This approach categorizes as jurisdictional those questions which refer to adjudicators' authority to adjudicate, a question of consent. Admissibility questions, in turn, are a residual category of procedural requirements, linked to the action and procedure in a narrow sense. Considering the consensual basis for jurisdiction in international law, the categorization of a question as pertaining to jurisdiction or admissibility depends upon the structure of the jurisdictional clauses or instruments at stake. Applying the "conventionalist–residualist" approach to questions arising from forum shopping strategies, jurisdictional questions would take place where there is an immediate link between tribunals in the governing instruments of the tribunal handling the question. This suggests a direct model of jurisdictional organization and procedural coordination. On the other hand, admissibility objections would take place where there are intermediate, indirect conventional links between tribunals, or where coordination takes place under general principles of law. These signposts to categorization roughly approximate jurisdictional issues to the delegation function of procedural norms; and matters of admissibility to their enabling and protective function.

Chapter 6 then centered on the question of how international tribunals conceive the nature of their adjudicatory power, in order to verify the extent to which abstention techniques can be used to address forum shopping. It looked at tribunals' discretion to react to preliminary questions under two dimensions. First, it argued that tribunals have at best very little discretion to dismiss, and that this is a weak potential brake on forum shopping. It then surveyed discretion to stay, and argued that this dimension offers some leeway for procedural coordination. Stays can be used especially in situations of parallel litigation, where the stay may be employed to convert parallel into sequential proceedings, with numerous potential applications. Stays have been resorted to in the contexts of concurrent pursuit of remedies, of claims that were considered premature before a previous determination elsewhere, and of difficult preliminary questions of jurisdiction – where a clearly more appropriate forum to decide on those questions was about to be seized and the risk of conflicting decisions was important. Another potential application is the determination of admissibility issues where a preclusion clause within the principal jurisdiction of a different tribunal is raised. Because of the uncertainties that surround the ability of international tribunals to effectively deliver justice, stays may permit striking a compromise between the enabling and protective functions of jurisdictional rules, pending the resolution of an issue. Finally, stays permit potential systemic concerns to be taken into account, while being far less threatening than dismissals.

From Chapter 1 to Chapter 6, therefore, this book articulated a procedural framework that contemplates the concept and operation of preliminary objections in international adjudication, and the powers of adjudicators in tackling them, particularly in the context of the rise in forum shopping strategies. These chapters and the examples given therein indicated that preliminary objections have an ability to become transmission belts of procedure-regulating norms across international tribunals. However, if preliminary objections are transmission belts, this book could not complete the task it set for itself without also examining in more detail what can be transmitted by these belts. In short, it was also necessary to specifically discuss the operation of procedure-coordinating norms. After all, these are the norms that set limits on forum shopping and that can be invoked by means of the technique of preliminary objections.

Procedure-regulating norms were specifically explored in Chapter 7, which presented them and discussed their application. That chapter grouped procedure-regulating norms as preclusion norms and aggregation norms. While aggregation rules are currently of secondary importance, preclusion norms appear in many international treaties and are crystallized in general principles of law. Preclusion norms were divided into six headings: (i) exclusive jurisdiction clauses, (ii) fork-in-the-road clauses, (iii) subsidiary jurisdiction clauses, (iv) preferential jurisdiction clauses, (v) *res judicata* and collateral estoppel, and (vi) *lis pendens*. Chapter 7 called for a substantive and substantial threshold for preclusion clauses to be given effect, as opposed to a formal and strict threshold. A requirement of formal identity and strict identity of claims would nullify most written preclusion norms. If written preclusion clauses are to be given effect, in their application adjudicators should pinpoint the substance of the request.

Forum shoppers, preliminary objectors, and the case-by-case management of jurisdictional overlaps

Should holders of security entitlements in sovereign-issued bonds receive compensation for expropriation in the context of sovereign-state-debt renegotiation and recovery? Does the International Covenant on Civil and Political Rights afford more protection against discrimination than the European Convention on Human Rights? Do plain-packaging tobacco regulations violate WTO-TRIPS' commitments allegedly incorporated into investment treaties? Does an internal regulation on a "dolphin-friendly" label to be affixed on tuna cans amount to a prohibited trade restriction according to NAFTA and/or WTO rules? Does the application of anti-dumping duties to curb injurious price-discrimination violate rules under the WTO Anti-Dumping Agreement and MERCOSUR? These may be hotly debatable questions that raise very substantive concerns, all of which have arisen or been implied in the context of recent international disputes.

Yet, within the international adjudicatory process, each of these questions embeds logically antecedent, preliminary questions. As these lines are being written, forum selectors, parallel and serial litigators before international tribunals are fighting fiercely over threshold, procedural questions before they reach the questions suggested in the above paragraph: may investor-state tribunals adjudicate mass-claims by holders of security entitlements related to sovereign-debt instruments at all? Does the fact that such instruments provide for a different forum selection matter? May an aggrieved European citizen have a second try on a discrimination-based claim before the United Nations Human Rights Committee, after she has litigated a discrimination-based claim before the European Court of Human Rights? May an investor-state tribunal rule on a country's regulations on tobacco packaging, on the grounds that these regulations violate that country's WTO commitments? Where must two NAFTA parties litigate a dispute over internal technical regulations allegedly based on environmental concerns: before the NAFTA or the WTO? May a MERCOSUR member that is not satisfied with a MERCOSUR ruling ask for a subsequent ruling on the same anti-dumping measures at the WTO? These are not fanciful questions. For the foreseeable future, questions of this type will be asked in different forms before different forums, and the major technique of international law that will be used to deal with them will be the technique of preliminary objections.

The potential contribution of the technique of preliminary objections to procedural coordination stems from its ability to carry preclusion and abstention doctrines over given proceedings, across normative and institutional spaces. In a nutshell, when forum shopping takes place, preclusion and discretionary abstention operate as coordination techniques in the following way. First, a procedure-regulating norm (i.e., the ground for the preliminary objection) or a concern with the development of given proceedings (in the case of abstention doctrines) is required. Second, the given procedure-regulating norm (or concern, in the case of abstention doctrines) is carried over to the specific proceedings at stake. Normally, this will take place in the context of preliminary questions, essentially by means of a preliminary objection. Third, if the preliminary objection is upheld, the tribunal that accepts the objection stays or terminates the proceedings. Ideally, but not necessarily, this will occur at an early stage in the proceedings. Fourth, the tribunal where the action should continue proceeds with the analysis, reaching a decision on the point on which the other tribunal was prevented (or temporarily abstained) from ruling. And possibly fifth, the tribunal that had stayed the proceedings resumes the proceedings and proceeds to its own decision, possibly taking into account the previous decision.

Coherence, deference, and respect may not ultimately ensue from this exercise, but preliminary objections make concrete the possibility of a dialogue, with procedure serving as an arena for the potential mediation – and thereby compatibilization – of jurisdictional overlaps. Preliminary objections may then be approached from a systemic perspective. Amid fears about the fragmentation of international law, they may help to buffer fragmentation to the extent that they enable tribunals to avoid an idiosyncratic vicious circle in which specialized law under the principal jurisdiction of one tribunal is interpreted by a different specialized tribunal, which may lead to a modified type of specialization anew, or conflicting interpretations of the same law. Or preliminary objections may enable cross-fertilization by turning synchronic into diachronic proceedings, which allow a "hindsight effect" for subsequent proceedings that can more easily take previous judgments into account than simultaneous proceedings. If adjudicators assume a jurisdictional system in assessing preliminary questions arising from forum shopping, they can decide in a way that retro-feeds the systemic contours of the international judiciary. In this regard, the technique of preliminary objections permits "comity-inspired" tribunals to enhance their coordination.

Nonetheless, a core argument throughout this work was that adjudicators need not necessarily assume a previously existing international jurisdictional system to decide on questions such as the ones mentioned above. They may approach those questions with a primary concern over the integrity of process before them, based on the notion of party autonomy – regardless of their position on the broader systemic question. Interestingly, the end result of this party-focused concern over the integrity of proceedings may also lead, indirectly and progressively, to the forging of something akin to a judicial structure. States often regulate their reciprocal entitlements to sue from the rearview mirror when they establish a new tribunal. Treaty negotiators should not miss their opportunity to do that every time they debate over the creation of a new adjudicative body. If adjudicators value such regulation and seize the opportunities to engage each other in the application of preliminary objections from a party-autonomy perspective, a structure of international tribunals may progressively emerge based on a combination of the direct and the indirect model of jurisdictional organization. While in this case the prime reason for upholding a preliminary objection against forum shopping will not be a prior systemic concern, a party focus will help to put into effect an organization that is latent in the procedure-regulating rules at play. In sum, preliminary objections offer a focal point for managing or forging the international judiciary, case-by-case.

References

ARTICLES, CONTRIBUTIONS TO COLLECTIVE WORKS, COURSE COLLECTIONS AND SPEECHES

Abi-Saab, Georges, 'Fragmentation or Unification: Some Concluding Remarks,' 31 *NYUJILP* (1999) 919.

'La coutume dans tous ses états, ou le dilemme du développement du droit international dans un monde éclaté,' in Ronald S. J. Macdonald (ed.), *International Law at the Time of its Codification: Essays in Honour of Roberto Ago* (Milano: Giuffrè, 1987) 53.

'On Discretion: Reflections on the Nature of the Consultative Function of the International Court of Justice,' in Laurence Boisson de Chazournes and Philippe Sands (eds.), *International Law, the International Court of Justice and Nuclear Weapons* (Cambridge University Press, 1999) 36.

'Whither the Judicial Function? Concluding Remarks,' in Laurence Boisson de Chazournes, Cesare Romano, and Ruth Mackenzie (eds.), *International Organizations and International Dispute Settlement: Trends and Prospects* (New York: Transnational Publishers, 2002) 241.

Alvarez, Jose, 'The New Dispute Settlers: (Half) Truths and Consequences,' 38 *Texas ILJ* (2003) 441.

Alvarez-Jiménez, Alberto, 'The WTO Appellate Body's Exercise of Judicial Economy,' 12 *JIEL* (2009) 393.

Andersson, Torbjörn, 'Parallel and Conflicting Enforcement of Law,' in Torbjörn Andersson (ed.), *Parallel and Conflicting Enforcement of Law* (The Hague: Martinus Nijhoff, 2005) 18.

Antonietti, Aurelia, 'The 2006 Amendments to the ICSID Rules and Regulations and the Additional Facilities Rules,' 21 *ICSID Rev* (2006) 427.

'Apartheid Foes Lose Suit In World Court over South-West Africa; an 8–7 Verdict; South Africa is Victor on a Technicality in UN Mandate Case,' *New York Times*, 19 July 1966.

Bartels, Lorand, 'Applicable Law in WTO Dispute Settlement Proceedings,' 35 *JWT* (2001) 499.

Bentolila, Dolores, 'Shareholders' Action to Claim for Indirect Damages in ICSID Arbitration,' 2 *Trade L&Dev* (2010) 87.

Bodansky, Daniel, 'The Legitimacy of International Governance: A Coming Challenge for International Environmental Law?' 93 *AJIL* (1999) 596.

'*Non Liquet*,' in *Max Planck Encyclopedia of Public International Law* (Oxford University Press, 2007, electronic version).

'*Non Liquet* and the Incompleteness of International Law,' in Laurence Boisson de Chazournes and Philippe Sands (eds.), *International Law, the International Court of Justice and Nuclear Weapons* (Cambridge University Press, 1999) 153.

Bohanes, Jan and Sennekamp, Andreas, 'Reflections on the Concept of "Judicial Economy" in WTO Dispute Settlement,' in Giorgio Sacerdoti, Alan Yanovich, and Jan Bohanes (eds.), *The WTO at Ten: The Contribution of the Dispute Settlement System* (Cambridge University Press, 2006) 424.

Bowett, David, 'Estoppel Before International Courts and Tribunals and its Relation to Acquiescence,' 33 *BYBIL* (1957) 176.

Boyle, Alan, 'Some Problems of Compulsory Jurisdiction Before Specialised Tribunals. The Law of the Sea,' in Patrick Capps, Malcom Evans, and Stratos Konstadinidis (eds.), *Asserting Jurisdiction: International and European Perspectives* (Oxford: Hart, 2003) 243.

Briggs, Herbert, 'The Incidental Jurisdiction of the International Court of Justice as Compulsory Jurisdiction,' in K. Zemanek, F. A. v. d. Heydle, I. Seidl-Hohenveldern, and St. Verosta (eds.), *Völkerrecht und Rechtliches Weltbild Festschrift für Alfred Verdross* (Berlin: Springer, 1960) 87.

Broude, Tomer, 'Fragmentation(s) of International Law: On Normative Integration as Authority Allocation,' in Tomer Broude and Yuval Shany (eds.), *The Shifting Allocation of Authority in international Law: Considering Sovereignty, Supremacy and Subsidiarity* (Portland OR: Hart, 2008) 99.

Brown, Chester, 'The Inherent Powers of International Courts and Tribunals,' 76 *BYIL* (2005) 195.

Buchanan, Allen and Keohane, Robert, 'The Legitimacy of Global Governance Institutions,' in Rüdiger Wolfrum and Volker Röben (eds.), *Legitimacy in International Law* (Berlin: Springer, 2008) 25.

Buergenthal, Thomas, 'Proliferation of International Courts and Tribunals: Is it Good or Bad?' 14 *LJIL* (2001) 267.

Burbank, Stephen, 'Jurisdictional Equilibration, the Proposed Hague Convention and Progress in National Law,' 49 *AJCL* (2001) 203.

Busch, Marc, 'Overlapping Institutions, Forum Shopping, and Dispute Settlement in International Trade,' 61 *IO* (2007) 735.

Busch, Marc and Krzysztof, Peter, 'The Politics of Judicial Economy at the World Trade Organization,' 64 *IO* (2010) 257.

Buteau, Michèle and Oosthuizen, Gabriel, 'When the Rules Are Silent: The Inherent Powers of the Tribunal,' in R. May and G. Kirk McDonald (eds.), *Essays on ICTY Procedure and Evidence in Honour of Gabrielle Kirk McDonald* (London: Kluwer, 2001) 65.

Byers, Michael, 'Abuse of Rights: An Old Principle, a New Age,' 47 *McGill LJ* (2002) 389.

Cappelletti, Mauro and Garth, Briant, 'Introduction: Policies, Trends and Ideas in Civil Procedure,' in Mauro Cappelletti (ed.), *International Encyclopaedia of Comparative Law: Civil Procedure* (Leiden: Mohr Siebeck/ Martinus Nijhoff, 1988, inst. 24).

Carmody, Chi, 'Softwood Lumber Dispute (2001–2006),' 100 *AJIL* (2006) 664.

'When "Cultural Identity Was Not at Issue": Thinking About *Canada – Certain Measures Concerning Periodicals*,' 30 *L Policy Int'l Bus* (1999) 231.

Caron, David, 'Towards a Political Theory of International Courts and Tribunals,' 24 *Berkeley JIL* (2006) 401.

Charney, Jonathan, 'Is International Law Threatened by Multiple International Tribunals?' 271 *Recueil des cours* (1998) 101.

Cogan, Jacob, 'Competition and Control in International Adjudication,' 48 *Vand JIL* (2008) 411.

Combacau, Jean, 'Le droit international: bric-à-brac ou système?' 31 *Arch Phil D* (1986) 85.

Cook, Walter, '"Substance" and "Procedure" in the Conflict of Laws,' 42 *Yale L J* (1932) 333.

Cover, Robert, 'The Uses of Jurisdictional Redundancy: Interest, Ideology, and Innovation,' 22 *W&M L Rev* (1981) 639.

Cuniberti, Giles, 'Parallel Litigation and Foreign Investment Dispute Settlement,' 21 *ICSID Rev* (2006) 381.

Davey, William, 'Dispute Settlement in the WTO and RTAs: A Comment,' in Lorand Bartels and Federico Ortino, *Regional Trade Agreements and the WTO Legal System* (Oxford University Press, 2006) 343.

'Has the WTO Dispute Settlement System Exceeded its Authority? A Consideration of Deference Shown by the System to Member Government Decisions and its Use of Issue-Avoidance Techniques,' 4 *JIEL* (2001) 79.

Davey, William and Sapir, Andre, 'The *Soft Drinks* Case: The WTO and Regional Trade Agreements,' 8 *WTR* (2009) 5.

Davis, Christina, 'Forum Choice in Trade Disputes: WTO Adjudication, Negotiation, and US Trade Policy,' Paper prepared for presentation to the International Political Economy Society Annual Meeting 2007, 9–10 November 2007, Stanford University.

Dodge, William, 'National Courts and International Arbitration: Exhaustion of Remedies and *Res Judicata* under Chapter XI of NAFTA,' 23 *Hastings Int'l Comp LR* (2000) 357.

'*Res Judicata*,' in *Max Planck Encyclopedia of Public International Law* (Oxford University Press, 2007, electronic version).

Drahos, Peter, 'Weaving Webs of Influence: The United States, Free Trade Agreements and Dispute Resolution,' 41 *JWT* (2007) 191.

Dupuy, Pierre-Marie, 'L'unité de l'ordre juridique international: cours générale de droit international public,' 297 *Recueil des cours* (2000) 1.

Dworkin, Ronald, 'Is Law a System of Rules?' in Ronald Dworkin (ed.), *The Philosophy of Law* (Oxford University Press, 1977) 38.

Fischer-Lescano, Andreas and Teubner, Gunther, 'Regime Collisions: The Vain Search for Legal Unity in the Fragmentation of Global Law,' 25 *MJIL* (2004) 999.

Fitzmaurice, Gerald, 'The Problem of *Non-Liquet*: Prolegomena to a Restatement,' in Charles Rousseau and Suzanne Bastid (eds.), *Mélanges Offerts à Charles Rousseau* (Paris: Pedone, 1974) 92.

Ford, Christopher, 'Judicial Discretion in International Jurisprudence: Article 38(1)(c) and "General Principles of Law",' 5 *Duke J Comp&Int'l L* (1994) 35.

Friendly, Henry, 'Indiscretion about Discretion,' 31 *Emory LJ* (1980) 747.

Gaeta, Paola, 'Inherent Powers of International Courts and Tribunals,' in Lal Vohrah, Fausto Pocar, Yuonne Featherstone, Olivier Fourmy, Christine Graham, John Hocking, and Nicholas Robson (eds.), *Man's Inhumanity to Man: Essays on International Law in Honour of Antonio Cassese* (The Hague: Kluwer, 2003) 353.

Gattini, Andrea, 'Un regard procédural sur la fragmentation du droit international,' 110 *RGDIP* (2006) 303.

Grossman, Nienke, 'Legitimacy and International Adjudicative Bodies,' 41 *Geo Wash ILR* (2010) 107.

Guillaume, Gilbert, 'Préface,' in Olivier Delas, René Côté, François Crépeau, and Peter Leuprecht (eds.), *Les juridictions internationales: complémentarité ou concurrence?* (Brussels : Bruylant, 2005) vii.

'Proliferation of International Courts: A Blueprint for Action,' 2 *JI Crim Just* (2004) 300.

Heisnaken, Veijo, 'Dealing with Pandora: The Concept of "Merits" in International Commercial Arbitration,' 22 *Arb Int'l* (2006) 597.

Helfer, Laurence, 'Forum Shopping for Human Rights,' 148 *U Penn L Rev* (1999) 285.

Higgins, Rosalyn, 'A Babel of Judicial Voices? Ruminations from the Bench,' 55 *ICLQ* (2006) 804.

'Policy Considerations and the International Judicial Process,' 17 *ICLQ* (1968) 58.

Hudec, Robert, 'Transcending the Ostensible: Some Reflections on the Nature of Litigation between Governments,' 72 *Minn L Rev* (1988) 211.

Jacob, I. H., 'The Inherent Jurisdiction of the Court,' 23 *Curr Leg Probs* (1970) 23.

Karagiannis, Syméon, 'La multiplication des juridictions internationales: un système anarchique?' in SFDI, *La juridictionnalisation du droit international* (Paris: Pedone, 2003) 7.

Kaufmann-Kohler, Gabrielle, Boisson de Chazournes, Laurence, Bonnin, Victor, and Mbengue, Makane Moïse, 'Consolidation of Proceedings in Investment Arbitration: How Can Multiple Proceedings Arising from the Same or Related Situations be Handled Efficiently?' 21 *ICSID Rev* (2006) 59.

Kelsen, Hans, 'Compulsory Adjudication of International Disputes,' 37 *AJIL* (1943) 397.
Keohane, Robert, Moravcsik, Andrew, and Slaughter, Anne-Marie, 'Legalized Dispute Resolution: Interstate and Transnational,' 54 *IO* (2000) 457.
Kingsbury, Benedict, 'Is the Proliferation of International Courts and Tribunals a Systemic Problem?' 31 *NYUJILP* (1999) 679.
Koch, Charles Jr, 'Judicial Dialogue for Legal Multiculturalism,' 25 *MJIL* (2004) 879.
Kohen, Marcelo, 'L'avis consultatif de la CIJ sur la licéité de la menace ou de l'emploi d'armes nucléaires et la fonction judiciaire,' 8 *EJIL* (1997) 336.
'Manifeste pour le droit international du XXIe siècle,' in Laurence Boisson de Chazournes and Vera Gowlland (eds.), *The International Legal System in Quest of Equity and Universality:* Liber Amicorum *Georges Abi-Saab* (The Hague: Kluwer, 2001) 123.
Kolb, Robert, 'Aperçus sur la bonne foi en droit international public,' 54 *RHDI* (2001) 1.
'General Principles of Procedural Law,' in Andreas Zimmermann, Christian Tomuschat, and Karin Oellers-Frahm (eds.), *The Statute of the International Court of Justice: A Commentary* (Oxford University Press, 2006) 793.
Korowicz, Marek, 'The Problem of the International Personality of Individuals,' 50 *AJIL* (1956) 546.
Koskenniemi, Martti and Leïno, Paivi, 'Fragmentation of International Law? Postmodern Anxieties,' 15 *LJIL* (2002) 553.
Kress, Ken, 'Legal Indeterminacy,' 77 *U Cal L Rev* (1989) 283.
Kumm, Mattias, 'The Legitimacy of International Law: A Framework of Analysis,' 15 *EJIL* (2004) 907.
Kwak, Kyung and Marceau, Gabrielle, 'Overlaps and Conflicts of Jurisdiction between the World Trade Organization and Regional Trade Agreements,' in Lorand Bartels and Federico Ortino (eds.), *Regional Trade Agreements and the WTO Legal System* (Oxford University Press, 2006) 465.
Laborde, Gustavo, 'The Case for Host State Claims in Investment Arbitration,' 1 *JIDS* (2010) 97.
Laird, Ian, 'A Difference Without a Distinction? An Examination of the Concepts of Admissibility and Jurisdiction in *Salini v. Jordan* and *Methanex v. USA*,' in Todd Weiler (ed.), *International Investment Law and Arbitration: Leading Cases from the ICSID, NAFTA, Bilateral Treaties and Customary International Law* (New York: Cameron May, 2005) 200.
Lauterpacht, Elihu, 'Partial Judgments and the Inherent Jurisdiction of the International Court of Justice,' in Vaughan Lowe and Malgosia Fitzmaurice (eds.), *Fifty Years of the International Court of Justice* (Cambridge University Press, 1996) 465.
Lauterpacht, Hersch, 'Some Observations on the Prohibition of "*Non Liquet*" and the Completeness of the Law,' in Elihu Lauterpacht (ed.), *International Law: Collected Papers of Sir Hersch Lauterpacht*, vol. II (Cambridge University Press, 1975) 216.

Lavranos, Nicolaos, 'The MOX Plant and IJzeren Rijn Disputes: Which Court is the Supreme Arbiter?' 19 *LJIL* (2006) 223.
Lister, Matthew, 'The Legitimating Role of Consent in International Law,' 11 *Chi J Int'l L* (2011) 1.
Little, Scott, 'Preliminary Objections to Panel Requests and Terms of Reference: Panel and Appellate Body Rulings on the First Line of Defence in WTO Dispute Settlement,' 35 *JWT* (2001) 517.
Lowe, Vaughan, 'Overlapping Jurisdictions in International Courts and Tribunals,' 20 *Australian YBIL* (1999) 191.
'*Res Judicata* and the Rule of Law in International Arbitration,' 8 *Afr YBIL* (1996) 38.
Main, Thomas, 'The Procedural Foundation of Substantive Law,' 87 *U Wash L R* (2010) 801.
Marceau, Gabrielle, 'A Call for Coherence in International Law: Praises for the Prohibition Against "Clinical Isolation" in WTO Dispute Settlement,' 33 *JWT* (1999) 87.
'Conflicts of Norms and Conflicts of Jurisdictions: The Relationship between the WTO Agreement and MEAs and other Treaties,' 35 *JWT* (2001) 1081.
Martinez, Jenny, 'Towards an International Judicial System,' 56 *Stanf L Rev* (2004) 429.
McLachlan, Campbell, 'The Principle of Systemic Integration and Article 31(3)(c) of the Vienna Convention,' 54 *ICLQ* (2005) 279.
Mehren, Arthur von, 'Theory and Practice of Adjudicatory Authority in Private International Law: A Comparative Study of the Doctrine, Policies and Practices of Common and Civil-Law Systems,' 295 *Recueil des cours* (2002) 1.
Mestral, Armand de, 'NAFTA Dispute Settlement: Creative Experiment or Confusion?' in Lorand Bartels and Federico Ortino (eds.), *Regional Trade Agreements and the WTO Legal System* (Oxford University Press, 2006) 359.
Michaels, Ralf, 'US Courts as World Courts,' Project, Manuscript (on file with the author).
Michaels, Ralf and Pauwelyn, Joost, 'Conflicts of Norms or Conflicts of Law? Different Techniques in the Fragmentation of International Law,' 22 *Duke J Comp&Int'l L* (2012) 349.
Mitchell, Andrew, 'Good Faith in WTO Dispute Settlement,' 7 *Mel JIL* (2006) 340.
Mitchell, Andrew and Heaton, David, 'The Inherent Jurisdiction of WTO Tribunals: The Selective Application of Public International Law Required by the Judicial Function,' 31 *MJIL* (2010) 558.
Morelli, Gaetano, 'La théorie générale du procès international,' 61 *Recueil des Cours* III (1937) 253.
Nollkaemper, Andre, 'International Adjudication of Global Public Goods: The Intersection of Substance and Procedure,' 9 Shares Research Paper (2012), ACIL 2012-08.

Note, 'Forum Shopping Reconsidered,' 103 *Harv L Rev* (1990) 1677.

Oda, Shigeru, 'Dispute Settlement Prospects in the Law of the Sea,' 44 *ICLQ* (1995) 863.

Orakhelashvili, Alexander, 'The Concept of International Judicial Jurisdiction: A Reappraisal,' 3 *LPICT* (2003) 501.

Oxman, Bernard, 'Complementary Agreements and Compulsory Jurisdiction,' 95 *AJIL* (2001) 277.

Parra, Antonio, 'The Development of Regulations and Rules of the International Centre for Settlement of Investment Disputes,' 41 *Int'l Lawyer* (2007) 47.

Pasqualucci, Jo, 'Preliminary Objections Before the Inter-American Court of Human Rights: Legitimate Issues and Illegitimate Tactics,' 40 *Va JIL* (1999) 2.

Paulsson, Jan, 'Jurisdiction and Admissibility,' in Gerald Aksen, Karl Bockstiegel, Paolo Patocchi, and Anne Whitesell (eds.), *Global Reflections on International Law, Commerce and Dispute Resolution* (Paris: ICC Publishing, 2005) 601.

Pauwelyn, Joost, 'Adding Sweeteners to Softwood Lumber: The WTO-NAFTA Spaghetti Bowl is Cooking,' 9 *JIEL* (2006) 197.

'How to Win a World Trade Organization Dispute Based on Non-World Trade Organization Law? Questions of Jurisdiction and Merits,' 37 *JWT* (2003) 997.

'Legal Avenues to "Multilateralizing Regionalism": Beyond Article XXIV,' in Richard Baldwin and Patrick Low, *Multilateralizing Regionalism: Challenges for the World Trading System* (Cambridge University Press, 2008) 368.

'A Typology of Multilateral Treaty Obligations: Are WTO Obligations Bilateral or Collective in Nature?' 14 *EJIL* (2003) 907.

Pauwelyn, Joost and Salles, Luiz Eduardo, 'Forum Shopping Before International Tribunals: (Real) Concerns, (Im)Possible Solutions,' 42 *Cornell ILJ* (2009) 77.

Piérola, Fernando, 'The Issuance of Preliminary Rulings Before the Issuance of the Panel Report: A Development in the Management of Panel Proceedings?' 6 *GTCJ* (2011) 35.

Piérola, Fernando and Horlick, Gary, 'WTO Dispute Settlement and Dispute Settlement in the "North-South" Agreements of the Americas: Considerations for Choice of Forum,' 41 *JWT* (2007) 885.

Posner, Eric and de Figueiredo, Miguel, 'Is the International Court of Justice Biased?' University of Chicago Law & Economics, Olin Working Paper 234 (2004).

Rao, Pemmaraju, 'Multiple International Judicial Forums: A Reflection of the Growing Strength of International Law or its Fragmentation?' 25 *MJIL* (2004) 929.

Reinisch, August, 'The Proliferation of International Dispute Settlement Mechanisms: The Threat of Fragmentation vs. the Promise of a More Effective System? Some Reflections from the Perspective of Investment

Arbitration,' in I. Buffard, J. Crawford, A. Pellet, and S. Wittich (eds.), *International Law between Universalism and Fragmentation:* Festschrift *in Honour of Gerhard Hafner* (The Hague: Brill, 2008) 107.

'The Use and Limits of *Res Judicata* and *Lis Pendens* as Procedural Tools to Avoid Conflicting Dispute Settlement Outcomes,' 3 *LPICT* (2004) 37.

Reisman, Michael, 'Introduction,' in Michael Reisman (ed.), *Jurisdiction in International Law* (Aldershot: Ashgate 1999), xi.

Reuter, Paul, 'Quelques réflexions sur l'équité en droit international,' 15 *RBDI* (1980) 165.

Romano, Cesare, 'The Proliferation of International Judicial Bodies: The Pieces of the Puzzle,' 31 *NYUJILP* (1999) 709.

'The Shift from the Consensual to the Compulsory Paradigm in International Adjudication: Elements for a Theory of Consent,' 39 *NYUJILP* (2007) 791.

'A Taxonomy of International Rule of Law Institutions,' 2 *JIDS* (2011) 241.

Rosenberg, Maurice, 'Judicial Discretion of the Trial Court, Viewed from Above,' 22 *Syracuse LR* (1971) 635.

Rosenne, Shabtai, 'International Courts and Tribunals, Jurisdiction and Admissibility of Inter-State Applications,' *Max Planck Encyclopedia of Public International Law* (Oxford University Press, 2008, electronic version).

Salles, Luiz Eduardo, '"Conflitos de Competência" entre tribunais internacionais,' in Barbara Oliveira and Roberto Luiz Silva, *Manual de Direito Processual Internacional* (São Paulo: Saraiva, 2012) 75.

Salvioli, Gabrielle, 'Problèmes de procédure dans la jurisprudence internationale,' in 91 *Recueil des Cours I* (1957) 533.

Sarooshi, Danesh, 'The Powers of the United Nations International Criminal Tribunals,' 2 *Max Planck YB UN L* (1998) 141.

Schachter, Oscar, 'The Invisible College of International Lawyers,' 72 *Nw ULR* (1977) 217.

Schneiderman, David, 'Judicial Politics and International Investment Arbitration: Seeking an Explanation for Conflicting Outcomes,' 30 *Nw J Int'l L Bus* (2010) 383.

Schreuer, Christoph, 'Travelling the BIT Route: Of Waiting Periods, Umbrella Clauses and Forks in the Road' 5 *JWIT* (2004) 231.

Scow, Aaron, 'The Sports Illustrated Canada Controversy: Canada Strikes Out in its Bid to Protect its Periodical Industry from U.S. Split Run Periodicals,' 7 *Minn JGT* (1998) 245.

Shapiro, David, 'Jurisdiction and Discretion,' 60 *NYULR* (1985) 543.

Sheppard, Audley, 'The Scope and *Res Judicata* Effect of Arbitral Awards,' in CEPANI, *Arbitral Procedure at the Dawn of the New Millennium* (Brussels: Bruylant, 2005) 265.

Shetreet, Shimon, 'Judicial Independence: New Conceptual Dimensions and Contemporary Challenges,' in Shimon Shetreet and Jules Deschenes, *Judicial Independence: The Contemporary Debate* (Boston: Martinus Nijhoff, 1985) 590.

Shihata, Ibrahim and Parra, Antonio, 'The Experience of the International Centre for the Settlement of Investment Disputes,' 14 *ICSID Rev* (1999) 299.

Simma, Bruno, 'Bilateralism and Community Interest in the Law of State Responsibility,' in Yoram Dinstein and Mala Tabory (eds.), *International Law at a Time of Perplexity: Essays in Honour of Shabtai Rosenne* (The Hague: Kluwer, 1989) 825.

Skubiszewski, Krzysztof, 'Implied Power of International Organizations,' in Yoram Dinstein and Mala Tabory (eds.), *International Law at a Time of Perplexity: Essays in Honour of Shabtai Rosenne* (The Hague: Kluwer, 1989) 855.

Slaughter, Anne-Marie, 'A Global Community of Courts,' 44 *HILJ* (2003) 191.

Solum, Lawrence, 'On the Indeterminacy Crisis: Critiquing the Critical Dogma,' 54 *U Chi L Rev* (1987) 462.

'Procedural Justice,' 78 *S Cal L R* (2004) 181.

Speech by H. E. Gilbert Guillaume, President of the ICJ, to the Plenary Session of the United Nations General Assembly, 26 October 2000.

Speech by H. E. Gilbert Guillaume, President of the ICJ, to the Plenary Session of the United Nations General Assembly, 26 October 2001.

Speech by H. E. Rosalyn Higgins, President of the ICJ, to the Sixth Committee of the General Assembly, 31 October 2008.

Spelliscy, Shane, 'The Proliferation of International Tribunals: A Chink in the Armor,' 40 *Colum J Transnat'l L* (2001) 143.

Steiger, Heinhard, 'Plaidoyer pour une juridiction internationale obligatoire,' in Jerzy Makarczyk (ed.), *Theory of International Law at the Threshold of the 21st Century: Essays In Honour of Krzystof Skubiszweski* (The Hague: Kluwer, 1996) 817.

Stone, Julius, '*Non Liquet* and the Function of Law in the International Community,' 35 *BYBIL* (1959) 124.

Tardu, M. E., 'Protocol to the UN Covenant on Civil and Political Rights and the Inter-American System: A Study of Coexisting Procedures,' 70 *AJIL* (1976) 778.

Teubner, Gunther, '"And God Laughed ..." Indeterminacy, Self-Reference and Paradox in Law,' 12 *German L J* (2011) 376.

Thirlway, Hugh, 'Dilemma or Chimera? Admissibility of Illegally Obtained Evidence in International Adjudication,' 78 *AJIL* (1984) 622.

'The Law and Procedure of the International Court of Justice 1960–89: Part Nine,' 68 *BYBIL* (1998) 1.

'Preliminary Objections,' in *Max Planck Encyclopedia of Public International Law* (Oxford University Press, 2007, electronic version).

'Procedural Law and the International Court of Justice,' in Vaughan Lowe and M. Fitzmaurice (eds.), *Fifty Years of the International Court of Justice: Essays in Honour of Robert Jennings* (Cambridge University Press, 1996) 394.

Joel Trachtman, 'The Domain of WTO Dispute Resolution,' 40 *HILJ* (1999) 333.

'Jurisdiction in WTO Dispute Settlement,' in Rufus Yerxa and Bruce Wilson (eds.), *Key Issues in WTO Dispute Settlement: the First Ten Years* (Cambridge University Press, 2005) 136.

Treves, Tullio, 'Le Tribunal International du Droit de la Mer dans la Pléiade des Juridictions Internationales,' in Olivier Delas, René Côté, François Crépeau, and Peter Leuprecht (eds.), *Les Juridictions Internationales: Complémentarité ou Concurrence?* (Brussels: Bruylant, 2005) 9.

United States Trade Representative, 'United States Requests Dispute Settlement Panel in NAFTA Choice of Forum Dispute,' (Press Release, September 2010), available at www.ustr.gov/about-us/press-office/press-releases/2010/september/united-states-requests-dispute-settlement-panel, last accessed 10 June 2013.

Van Damme, Isabelle, 'Inherent Powers of and for the WTO Appellate Body,' CTEI Working Paper (2008).

Verdross, Alfred, 'Les principes généraux de droit dans le système de sources du droit international public,' in IUHEI, *Recueil d'études de droit international en hommage à Paul Guggenheim* (Geneva: IUHEI, 1968) 524.

Verzijl, J. H. W., 'Problems of Jurisdiction in the Ambatielos Case,' 1 *NILR* (1953) 58.

Weil, Prosper, 'The Court Cannot Conclude Definitively ...: *Non-Liquet* Revisited,' 36 *Colum J Transnat'l L* (1998) 119.

Weiss, Friedl, 'Inherent Powers of National and International Courts,' in Federico Ortino and Ernst-Ulrich Petersmann (eds.), *The WTO Dispute Settlement System 1995–2003* (The Hague: Kluwer, 2004) 177.

Wessel, Jared, 'Judicial Policy-Making at the International Criminal Court: An Institutional Guide to Analyzing International Adjudication,' 44 *Colum J Transnat'l L* (2005) 377.

Witenberg, J., 'La recevabilité des réclamations devant les juridictions internationales,' 41 *Recueil des Cours* III (1932) 1.

Wohl, Isaac, 'The Antigua-United States Online Gambling Dispute,' web version, July 2009, available at www.usitc.gov/publications/332/journals/online_gambling_dispute.pdf, last accessed 10 June 2013.

Wolfrum, Rüdiger, 'Legitimacy of International Law from a Legal Perspective: Some Introductory Considerations,' in Rüdiger Wolfrum and Volker Röben (eds.), *Legitimacy in International Law* (Berlin: Springer, 2008) 1.

Wyatt, Julian and Marceau, Gabrielle, 'Dispute Settlement Regimes Intermingled: Regional Trade Agreements and the WTO,' 1 *JIDS* (2010) 67.

Young, Ernest, 'Institutional Settlement in a Globalizing Judicial System,' 54 *Duke LJ* (2005) 1143.

BOOKS

Abi-Saab, Georges, *Les exceptions préliminaires dans la procédure de la Cour Internationale* (Paris: Pedone, 1967).

Amerasinghe, Chittharanjan, *Jurisdiction of International Tribunals* (The Hague: Kluwer, 2003).

Austin, John, *The Province of Jurisprudence Determined* (London: John Murray, Prometheus Books: 1832, 2000).

Bedaque, José Roberto, *Efetividade do Processo e Técnica Processual* (São Paulo: Malheiros, 2006).

Bell, Andrew, *Forum Shopping and Venue in Transnational Litigation* (Oxford University Press, 2003).

Black's Law Dictionary, 9th deluxe edn (2009).

Bos, Maarten, *Les conditions du procès en droit international public* (Leiden: Brill, 1957).

Bower, George S., *The Doctrine of* Res Judicata (London: Butterworth 1924).

Brand, Ronald and Jablonski, Scott, Forum Non Conveniens: *History, Practice and Future under the Hague Convention on Choice of Court Agreements* (Oxford University Press, 2007).

Brant, Leonardo, *L'autorité de la chose jugée en droit international public* (Paris: LGDJ, 2003).

Broude, Tomer and Shany, Yuval, *The Shifting Allocation of Authority in International Law: Considering Sovereignty, Supremacy and Subsidiarity* (Oxford: Hart Publishing, 2008).

Brown, Chester, *A Common Law of International Adjudication* (Oxford University Press, 2007).

Brownlie, Ian, *Principles of Public International Law*, 5th edn (Oxford University Press, 1998).

Cançado Trindade, Antonio, *International Law for Humankind: Towards a New* Jus Gentium (Leiden: Martinus Nijhoff, 2010).

Carlston, Kenneth, *The Process of International Arbitration* (Westport: Greenwood Press, 1946).

Cheng, Bin, *General Principles of Law as Applied by International Courts and Tribunals* (Cambridge University Press, 1953, 2006).

Cintra, Antonio Carlos, Pellegrini Grinover, Ada, and Dinamarco, Cândido Rangel (eds.), *Teoria Geral do Processo*, 28th edn (São Paulo: Malheiros, 2012).

Collier, John and Lowe, Vaughan, *The Settlement of Disputes in International Law* (Oxford University Press, 1999).

Dictionnaire de l'academie française dédié au roi (Paris: Jean Baptiste Coignard, 1694).

Dinamarco, Cândido Rangel, *Instituições de Direito Processual Civil*, 4th edn (São Paulo: Malheiros, 2004).

Douglas, Zachary, *The International Law of Investment Claims* (Cambridge University Press, 2009).

Dworkin, Ronald, *Law's Empire* (Cambridge, MA: Harvard University Press, 1986).

Feller, Abraham, *The Mexican Claims Commissions, 1923–1934: A Study in the Law and Procedure of International Tribunals* (New York: Macmillan, 1935).

Fitzmaurice, Gerald, *The Law and Procedure of the International Court of Justice*, vol. II (Cambridge: Grotius, 1986).
Franck, Thomas, *The Power of Legitimacy Among Nations* (Oxford University Press, 1990).
Gadamer, Hans-Georg, *Truth and Method*, 2nd edn (London: Sheed and Ward, 1989).
Gaillard, Emmanuel, *Anti-suit Injunctions in International Arbitration* (Huntington, NY: Juris Publishing, 2005).
Gardiner, Richard, *Treaty Interpretation* (Oxford University Press, 2008).
Grant, John and Barker, J. Craig, *Parry and Grant Encyclopaedic Dictionary of International Law*, 2nd edn (Oxford University Press, 2003).
Guinchard, Serge, Ferrand, Frédérique, and Chainais, Cécile (eds.), *Procédure Civile: Droit interne et droit communautaire*, 29th edn (Paris: Dalloz, 2008).
Institut de Droit Comparé Edouard Lambert, *L'étendue de l'autorité de chose jugée en droit comparé* (manuscript, available at www.courdecassation.fr/IMG/File/Plen-06-07-07-0410672-rapport-definitif-anonymise-annexe-2.pdf, last accessed 10 June 2013).
International Commission of Jurists, *International Principles on the Independence and Accountability of Judges, Lawyers and Prosecutors: A Practitioners Guide* (Geneva: International Commission of Jurists, 2004).
Jackson, John, *Sovereignty, the WTO and Changing Fundamentals of International Law* (Cambridge University Press, 2006).
Jenks, Wilfred, *The Prospects of International Adjudication* (London: Stevens & Sons, 1964).
Kazazi, Mojtaba, *Burden of Proof and Related Issues: A Study on Evidence Before International Tribunals* (The Hague: Kluwer, 1996).
Lauterpacht, Elihu, *Aspects of the Administration of International Justice* (Cambridge: Grotius, 1991).
Lauterpacht, Hersch, *The Development of International Law by the International Court* (London: Stevens & Sons, 1958).
Lavranos, Nicolaos, *Jurisdictional Competition: Selected Cases in International and European Law* (Groningen: Europa Law, 2009).
Linderfalk, Ulf, *On the Interpretation of Treaties: The Modern International Law as Expressed in the 1969 Vienna Convention on the Law of Treaties* (Dordrecht: Springer, 2007).
Luhmann, Niklas, *Law as a Social System* (Cambridge University Press, 2004).
Mabrouk, Mohieddine, *Les exceptions de procédure devant les juridictions internationales* (Paris: LGDJ, 1966).
Mani, V. S., *International Adjudication: Procedural Aspects* (Leiden: Martinus Nijhoff, 1980).
McLachlan, Campbell, Lis Pendens *in International Litigation* (Leiden: Martinus Nijhoff, 2009).
Mehren, Arthur von, *Adjudicatory Authority in Private International Law: A Comparative Study* (Leiden: Martinus Nijhoff, 2007).

Merrils, John, *International Dispute Settlement*, 3rd edn (Cambridge University Press, 1999).

Moore, John Bassett, *History and Digest of the Arbitrations to which the United States has been a Party*, vol. III (New York: William S. Hein, 1995).

International Adjudications: Ancient and Modern, History and Documents, vol. II (Oxford University Press, 1929).

Nuyts, Arnaud, *L'exception de* forum non conveniens*: étude de droit international privé comparé* (Brussels: Bruylant, 2003).

Pauwelyn, Joost, *Conflict of Norms in Public International Law: How WTO Law Relates to Other Rules of International Law* (Cambridge University Press, 2003).

Podetti, José Ramiro, *Teoría y Técnica del Proceso Civil y Trilogía Estructural de la Ciencia del Proceso Civil* (Buenos Aires: Ediar, 1963).

Rawls, John, *A Theory of Justice* (Cambridge, MA: Harvard University Press, 1971).

Riquelme Cortado, Rosa, *Derecho Internacional: Entre un Orden Global y Fragmentado* (Madrid: Ortega y Gasset, 2005).

Rosenne, Shabtai, *The Law and Practice of the International Court, 1920–2005*, vols. II and III, 4th edn (Leiden: Martinus Nijhoff, 2006).

Procedure in the International Court: A Commentary of the 1978 Rules of the International Court of Justice (The Hague, Martinus Nijhoff, 1983).

Sands, Philippe, Mackenzie, Ruth, and Shany, Yuval, *Manual on International Courts and Tribunals* (London: Butterworths, 1999).

Schreuer, Christoph, *The ICSID Convention: A Commentary* (Cambridge University Press, 2001).

SFDI, *La juridictionnalisation du droit international* (Paris: Pedone, 2003).

Shaffer, Gregory, *Defending Interests: Public-Private Partnerships in WTO Litigation* (Washington D.C.: Brookings Institution, 2003).

Shany, Yuval, *The Competing Jurisdictions of International Courts and Tribunals* (Oxford University Press, 2003).

Regulating Jurisdictional Relations Between National and International Courts (Oxford University Press, 2007).

Shihata, Ibrahim, *The Power of the International Court to Determine its Own Jurisdiction* (The Hague: Martinus Nijhoff, 1965).

Terris, Daniel, Romano, Cesare, and Swigart, Leigh, *The International Judge: An Introduction to the Men and Women Who Decide the World's Cases* (Oxford University Press, 2007).

Van Damme, Isabelle, *Treaty Interpretation by the WTO Appellate Body* (Oxford University Press, 2009).

Witenberg, J., *L'organisation judiciaire, la procédure et la sentence internationales: Traité pratique* (Paris: Pedone, 1937).

Index

CAMBRIDGE STUDIES IN INTERNATIONAL AND COMPARATIVE LAW

Books in the series

Forum Shopping in International Adjudication: The Role of Preliminary Objections
Luiz Eduardo Salles

International Law and the Arctic
Michael Byers

Cooperation in the Law of Transboundary Water Resources
Christina Leb

Underwater Cultural Heritage and International Law
Sarah Dromgoole

State Responsibility: The General Part
James Crawford

The Origins of International Investment Law
Kate Miles

The Crime of Aggression under the Rome Statute of the International Criminal Court
Carrie McDougall

Crimes against Peace and International Law
Kirsten Sellars

The Non-Legal in International Law
Fleur Johns

Armed Conflict and Displacement: The Protection of Refugees and Displaced Persons under International Humanitarian Law
Mélanie Jacques

Foreign Investment and the Environment in International Law
Jorge Viñuales

The Human Rights Treaty Obligations of Peacekeepers
Kjetil Larsen

Cyberwarfare and the Laws of War
Heather Harrison Dinniss

The Right to Reparation in International Law for Victims of Armed Conflict
Christine Evans

Global Public Interest in International Investment Law
Andreas Kulick

State Immunity in International Law
Xiaodong Yang

Reparations and Victim Support in the International Criminal Court
Conor McCarthy

Reducing Genocide to Law: Definition, Meaning, and the Ultimate Crime
Payam Akhavan

Decolonizing International Law: Development, Economic Growth and the Politics of Universality
Sundhya Pahuja

Complicity and the Law of State Responsibility
Helmut Philipp Aust

State Control over Private Military and Security Companies in Armed Conflict
Hannah Tonkin

'Fair and Equitable Treatment' in International Investment Law
Roland Kläger

The UN and Human Rights: Who Guards the Guardians?
Guglielmo Verdirame

Sovereign Defaults before International Courts and Tribunals
Michael Waibel

Making the Law of the Sea: A Study in the Development of International Law
James Harrison

Science and the Precautionary Principle in International Courts and Tribunals: Expert Evidence, Burden of Proof and Finality
Caroline E. Foster

Transition from Illegal Regimes in International Law
Yaël Ronen

Access to Asylum: International Refugee Law and the Globalisation of Migration Control
Thomas Gammeltoft-Hansen

Trading Fish, Saving Fish: The Interaction between Regimes in International Law
Margaret Young

The Individual in the International Legal System: Continuity and Change in International Law
Kate Parlett

The Participation of States in International Organisations: The Role of Human Rights and Democracy
Alison Duxbury

'Armed Attack' and Article 51 of the UN Charter: Evolutions in Customary Law and Practice
Tom Ruys

Science and Risk Regulation in International Law
Jacqueline Peel

Theatre of the Rule of Law: Transnational Legal Intervention in Theory and Practice
Stephen Humphreys

The Public International Law Theory of Hans Kelsen: Believing in Universal Law
Jochen von Bernstorff

Vicarious Liability in Tort: A Comparative Perspective
Paula Giliker

Legal Personality in International Law
Roland Portmann

Legitimacy and Legality in International Law: An Interactional Account
Jutta Brunnée and Stephen J. Toope

The Concept of Non-International Armed Conflict in International Humanitarian Law
Anthony Cullen

The Challenge of Child Labour in International Law
Franziska Humbert

Shipping Interdiction and the Law of the Sea
Douglas Guilfoyle

International Courts and Environmental Protection
Tim Stephens

Legal Principles in WTO Disputes
Andrew D. Mitchell

War Crimes in Internal Armed Conflicts
Eve La Haye

Humanitarian Occupation
Gregory H. Fox

The International Law of Environmental Impact Assessment: Process, Substance and Integration
Neil Craik

The Law and Practice of International Territorial Administration: Versailles to Iraq and Beyond
Carsten Stahn

Cultural Products and the World Trade Organization
Tania Voon

United Nations Sanctions and the Rule of Law
Jeremy Farrall

National Law in WTO Law: Effectiveness and Good Governance in the World Trading System
Sharif Bhuiyan

The Threat of Force in International Law
Nikolas Stürchler

Indigenous Rights and United Nations Standards
Alexandra Xanthaki

International Refugee Law and Socio-Economic Rights
Michelle Foster

The Protection of Cultural Property in Armed Conflict
Roger O'Keefe

Interpretation and Revision of International Boundary Decisions
Kaiyan Homi Kaikobad

Multinationals and Corporate Social Responsibility: Limitations and Opportunities in International Law
Jennifer A. Zerk

Judiciaries within Europe: A Comparative Review
John Bell

Law in Times of Crisis: Emergency Powers in Theory and Practice
Oren Gross and Fionnuala Ní Aoláin

Vessel-Source Marine Pollution:The Law and Politics of International Regulation
Alan Tan

Enforcing Obligations Erga Omnes *in International Law*
Christian J. Tams

Non-Governmental Organisations in International Law
Anna-Karin Lindblom

Democracy, Minorities and International Law
Steven Wheatley

Prosecuting International Crimes: Selectivity and the International Law Regime
Robert Cryer

Compensation for Personal Injury in English, German and Italian Law: A Comparative Outline
Basil Markesinis, Michael Coester, Guido Alpa, Augustus Ullstein

Dispute Settlement in the UN Convention on the Law of the Sea
Natalie Klein

The International Protection of Internally Displaced Persons
Catherine Phuong

Imperialism, Sovereignty and the Making of International Law
Antony Anghie

Necessity, Proportionality and the Use of Force by States
Judith Gardam

International Legal Argument in the Permanent Court of International Justice: The Rise of the International Judiciary
Ole Spiermann

Great Powers and Outlaw States: Unequal Sovereigns in the International Legal Order
Gerry Simpson

Local Remedies in International Law
C. F. Amerasinghe

Reading Humanitarian Intervention:Human Rights and the Use of Force in International Law
Anne Orford

Conflict of Norms in Public International Law: How WTO Law Relates to Other Rules of International Law
Joost Pauwelyn

Transboundary Damage in International Law
Hanqin Xue

European Criminal Procedures
Edited by Mireille Delmas-Marty and John Spencer

The Accountability of Armed Opposition Groups in International Law
Liesbeth Zegveld

Sharing Transboundary Resources: International Law and Optimal Resource Use
Eyal Benvenisti

International Human Rights and Humanitarian Law
René Provost

Remedies Against International Organisations
Karel Wellens

Diversity and Self-Determination in International Law
Karen Knop

The Law of Internal Armed Conflict
Lindsay Moir

International Commercial Arbitration and African States: Practice, Participation and Institutional Development
Amazu A. Asouzu

The Enforceability of Promises in European Contract Law
James Gordley

International Law in Antiquity
David J. Bederman

Money Laundering: A New International Law Enforcement Model
Guy Stessens

Good Faith in European Contract Law
Reinhard Zimmermann and Simon Whittaker

On Civil Procedure
J. A. Jolowicz

Trusts: A Comparative Study
Maurizio Lupoi

The Right to Property in Commonwealth Constitutions
Tom Allen

International Organizations Before National Courts
August Reinisch

The Changing International Law of High Seas Fisheries
Francisco Orrego Vicuña

Trade and the Environment: A Comparative Study of EC and US Law
Damien Geradin

Unjust Enrichment: A Study of Private Law and Public Values
Hanoch Dagan

Religious Liberty and International Law in Europe
Malcolm D. Evans

Ethics and Authority in International Law
Alfred P. Rubin

Sovereignty Over Natural Resources: Balancing Rights and Duties
Nico Schrijver

The Polar Regions and the Development of International Law
Donald R. Rothwell

Fragmentation and the International Relations of Micro-States: Self-determination and Statehood
Jorri Duursma

Principles of the Institutional Law of International Organizations
C. F. Amerasinghe

For EU product safety concerns, contact us at Calle de José Abascal, 56–1°,
28003 Madrid, Spain or eugpsr@cambridge.org.

www.ingramcontent.com/pod-product-compliance
Lightning Source LLC
LaVergne TN
LVHW011529200926
848484LV00001B/199
9781107035966